Bullying and Racist Bullying in Schools

Bullying and Racist Bullying in Schools

What ARE we missing?

Dr. Sairah Qureshi

Copyright © 2013 by Dr. Sairah Qureshi.

ISBN:	Softcover	978-1-4836-2797-7
	Ebook	978-1-4836-2798-4

All rights reserved. No part of this book may be reproduced or transmitted in any form or by any means, electronic or mechanical, including photocopying, recording, or by any information storage and retrieval system, without permission in writing from the copyright owner.

This book was printed in the United States of America.

Rev. date: 04/22/2013

To order additional copies of this book, contact:
Xlibris Corporation
1-888-795-4274
www.Xlibris.com
Orders@Xlibris.com
130057

CONTENTS

Introduction 15
Overview.. 15
Aims, Objectives and Methodology...................................... 20
Key Findings and Structure of Book..................................... 22

Chapter 1: An Examination of School Bullying and its Dynamics ... 29
Introduction... 29
Definition and Nature of Bullying.. 30
The Extent of Bullying 36
Victims, Offenders and Place 42
Victims Impact, Risk and Fear.. 42
Coping Strategies 47
Explaining Bullying... 50
Psychological/Educational Studies 50
Power-based Perspectives.. 50
Social Learning Perspectives... 52
Mind Skills Perspectives... 55
Sociological Studies 57
Social Control Perspectives... 57
Social Disorganisation Perspectives.................................... 60
Social Ecological Perspectives... 61
Masculinity Perspectives 64
Peer Relations and Bystanders 68
Summary and Discussion 73

Chapter 2: Racism, Bullying and the School Response 76
Introduction... 76
Racist Bullying and Victimization 77
Racist Harassment and Victimization.................................. 86
Racist Bullying and Offending 92

Bullying, Racism and School Response...101
   UK Legislation 101
   Developing a Holistic and Restorative Approach to Preventing
     and Responding to Bullying...106
   Preventative Measures for Racist Bullying...........................113
Summary and Discussion 120

Chapter 3: Research Site 123
Introduction...123
Local Regional Context of the North East of England.................124
Education in Newcastle-upon-Tyne...130
Anti-Bullying and Equality for All...134
Schools Sampled in this Study...137
   Old East End Community College 137
   Modern Eastern Suburban School......................................141
   School for the Excluded 145
Summary and Discussion 149

Chapter 4: Methodology 151
Introduction...151
Research Aims, Objectives and Approach 152
Gaining Access 159
Data Collection..161
   Focus Groups...161
   Old East End Community College 165
   Modern Eastern Suburban School......................................166
   School for the Excluded 167
   Delivering Focus Groups..168
   Semi-Structured Interviews..176
   Semi-Structured Interviews with Teachers, Parents and Youth
     Workers...181
Data Handling and Analysis...185
Political and Ethical Issues...188
   Respect for Children's Rights..188
   Safety of Participants and Researcher..................................189
   Child Confidentiality and Informed Consent.......................191
   Data Handling...193
   Gate Keeping and Consent 194
Summary and Discussion 196

Chapter 5: The Nature of Bullying and Racist Bullying............198
Introduction..198
Pupils Perceptions of School Bullying and Racism.....................199
The Nature of Racist Bullying..206
Perceptions in Context: Socio-Economic and Demographic
    Consideration..213
Adults Perceptions of Bullying and Racist Bullying....................221
Bullying, Victimization and Place..230
Summary and Discussion 242

Chapter 6: Explaining Bullying and Racist Bullying.................245
Introduction..245
Explanations for Bullying 246
    Status, Power and Reputation...246
    Family Experiences and Childhood Victimization 250
    Relative Deprivation..254
    Negative Influence of the Media and Social Context.............255
Explanations for Racist Bullying...256
    Individual and Cultural Differences......................................257
    Unfair Advantage..263
Adults' Explanations for Bullying and Racist Bullying 268
Explaining Bullying and Racist Bullying from Socio-Economic
    and Geographic Perspective...276
Racist Bullying 278
Summary and Discussion 281

Chapter 7: Bullying and the School Response 284
Introduction..284
The Reporting and Under Reporting of Bullying 285
Punishment, Retribution and Deterrence 297
Prevention and Intervention...303
    Mentoring..310
    Arguments For and Against the Use of Prevention and
    Intervention Measures 314
School Response and the Socio-Economic and Geographical
    Perspective...320
Summary and Discussion 323

Chapter 8: School Bullying, Racism and the School Response .. 326
Summary of Thesis 326
Methodology 327
    Key Findings 330
Key Themes 332
    Using Qualitative Methodology to Study Bullying and Racist
        Bullying 332
    Differences in Perceptions of Bullying and Racist Bullying 334
    Impact of Socio-Economic Factors 338
Increase in a Holistic Restorative/Whole School Approach 341
Summary 347

List of Tables
Table 1: Old East End Community College 139
Table 2: Modern Eastern Suburban School 142
Table 3: School for the Excluded 146
Table 4: Focus Groups in Old East End Community College 166
Table 5: Focus Groups in Modern Eastern Suburban School 167
Table 6: Focus Groups in the School for the Excluded 168
Table 7: Individual Interviews with Pupils in Old East End
    Community College 180
Table 8: Individual Interviews with Pupils in Modern Eastern
    Suburban School 180
Table 9: Individual Interviews with Pupils in the School for the
    Excluded 180
Table 10: Interviews with Teachers in Old East End Community
    College 184
Table 11: Interviews with Teachers in Modern Eastern Suburban
    School 185
Table 12: Interviews with Teachers and a Parent in the School
    for the Excluded 185
Table 13: Interviews with Detached Youth Workers 185

List of Figures
Figure 1: Model for Locating Racist Name-Calling 80
Figure 2: Prespecified versus Unfolding: the timing of structure 157

List of Maps

Map 1: Map of 26 Wards in Newcastle-upon-Tyne 126

List of Appendices

Appendix 1: Spider Diagram, Focus Group, Year 8.
Modern Eastern Suburban School 348

Appendix 2: Spider Diagram, Focus Group, Year 7.
Modern Eastern Suburban School 349

Appendix 3: Spider Diagram, Focus Group, Year 7.
Old East End Community College..350

Appendix 4: Spider Diagram, Focus Group, Year 9.
Old East End Community College..351

Appendix 5: Module: Using Social and Emotional Learning to
Promote Confidence and Pride in Ethnic Difference and
Diversity..352

Appendix 6: Module: The Role of Bystanders as Upstanders in
Bullying 381

Appendix 7: Bullying Prevention Lesson Plan: The Courage to
be an Upstander 392

Appendix 8: Class-based Activity: Christina's Poem—Anti-Bullying
Week 2008..397

Appendix 9: Class-based Activity: Is this Bullying or not? What
would you do?...400

List of References..403

ABSTRACT

ACADEMIC RESEARCH ON school bullying has revealed that it is a significant and growing issue in contemporary society. Nevertheless, a problem remains in accurately measuring the extent of school bullying, in addition much less still is known about racist bullying. Current government legislation requires that all schools implement various procedures in order to handle bullying both in and out of the school vicinity. All schools employ numerous intervention mechanisms to record incidents, support victims and raise awareness about the impact of bullying, with the intention of encouraging victims to speak out.

Much academic research is informed by quantitative research methodologies and undertaken from a broadly psycho-educational perspective. However, this approach fails to not only explore pupils' perceptions and experiences in depth; it fails to encompass the ongoing and cumulative nature of bullying in the lives of students. The aim of this study is to critically explore the perceptions and experiences of bullying and racist bullying in three schools in a Northern city using data collected from pupils and adults, through focus groups and semi-structured individual interviews with pupils in years 7 to 9. The field work was carried out between November 2005 and June 2006 and a total of fifty one interviews were conducted.

Three themes constitute the findings of this study. Firstly, pupils identify the nature and characteristics of bullying and racist bullying to be the same, yet explanations for both acts differ markedly. Bullies are held responsible for their actions; however, victims of racist bullying are seen to be responsible for their own victimisation, due to the common conviction that they hold an unfair advantage over the indigenous white working class community. Secondly, tolerance towards victims of racist bullying differed substantially between schools, suggesting that various socio-economic factors play a substantial role, implying that the understanding of such actions is a consequence of the subject's own life experiences. Thirdly, despite the implementation of anti-bullying procedures, victims largely prefer to remain silent and peers prefer not to intervene. Most pupils prefer a combination of sanctions and preventative measures implemented over the long term, yet desire immediate and often harsh punishment. This book has been amended from a PhD thesis awarded in November 2011 and recommends a need for an increase in school response that is informed by restorative whole school and emotional literacy approach.

ACKNOWLEDGEMENTS

TO MY FAMILY and all my closest and dearest friends, for your love and endless support!

My darling husband Shoaib, my beautiful Mother . . . . . and to ALL the victims of bullying, including the bullied perpetrators, this book is dedicated to you!

INTRODUCTION

Overview

S CHOOL BULLYING AND racism are one of the most contentious social issues that society faces (Ma *et al.,* 2001). Bullying has been recognized in academic research as a major social problem that affects the lives not only of young people but families, peers and often communities (Olweus, 1993). Similarly, racism is a major social problem across England and Wales and beyond (Richardson, 2008). Yet accurately measuring the extent and prevalence of school bullying and racism remains problematic. Not least because of differing levels of understanding, but also reporting and recording. The Department for Schools and Education, (now Department for Education, DfE 2010) first introduced an anti-bullying resource pack 'Don't suffer in silence' for schools in September 1994 with the intention of improving the programmes for combating school bullying. This was followed in 1999 by a legal requirement for schools to have some form of anti-bullying policy and race equality policy. The Department for Education's latest research publication (Green *et al.,* 2010), suggests that a range of approaches are required in order to identify and deal with bullying in different situations and contexts. The research also indicates that identifying victims proves difficult due to young people's perceived differences in socio-economic backgrounds and different cultures (Green *et al.,* 2010: 89). With the latest Equality Act 2010, which came into full force in April 2011 in England and Scotland and spring/summer 2011 for Wales, this will replace all previous existing equality legislation such as the Race Relations Act (2000), Disability Discrimination Act (2005) and Sex Discrimination Act (1995) (DfE 2010) and will provide a single legislation consolidating and covering all forms of discrimination that is unlawful, in order to provide a simple law for schools to follow.

Schools presently implement a variety of anti-bullying and anti-racist initiatives and activities in the classroom. They employ numerous intervention mechanisms in order to support victims, as well as raise awareness of the problem of bullying and its impact. This support is with the intention to encourage victims and/or encourage peers to speak out on the victims behalf. To deter bullies and bullying from taking place and to create a safe and harmonious environment for all pupils. Despite such mechanisms, a major concern that schools face is the problem of underreporting. The general view from research is that young people prefer not to intervene and most victims would rather remain silent (Oliver and Candappa 2007). In order to try to alleviate this problem, as of March 2006, all schools in the UK have had a duty to record incidents of bullying placed upon them, however in 2009 under the Labour government, the then Department for Children, School and Families (2009-2010) published a specialist guidance advising schools to report all incidents of racist bullying to their local authority, (DCSF, 2009:29/30). To strengthen this guide, in 2009, the DCSF proposed to make it a statutory requirement for all schools to record and report all serious incidents of verbal and physical abuse, whether racist or not, to their local authority. A twelve week consultation had also been undertaken by the DCSF about this anticipated new duty (DCSF press notice, 2009). However, a decision was unable to be arrived under the previous Labour government. Even with the current Department for Education under the Conservative/ Liberal Democrat coalition, this proposed duty has yet to be addressed and a decision reached. To agree with consultants working in school anti-bullying and racist bullying, this duty appears to be of little priority with the current DfE, as they have opted to allow schools more control with less interference from the local authorities. Furthermore, the DfE declared explicitly that all schools should leave 'local authority control' (Insted, 2010), yet still maintain that schools should continue to record all reported incidents of bullying and racist bullying. This legislation was implemented by the Department for Children, Schools and Families (DCSF) under the previous government.

Much of the research carried out on bullying in schools is informed by quantitative research methodology and delivered from a broadly psycho-educational perspective (Rigby, 2004; Frisen *et al.,* 2007; Gianluca, *et al.,* 2008). Studies that have examined school bullying have largely explored the subject using questionnaire or surveys. Whilst statistically quantitative research can provide a useful insight into the prevalence of bullying, this methodological approach fails to go into any real detail. Whilst quantitative research fails to document in depth. For instance, individual bullying experiences and repeat victimization. In addition, there is no substantial discussion from young peoples' or adults' opinion to the nature and explanations for bullying. Furthermore, studies written from the psycho-educational perspective fail to examine the socio-economic structural factors which make an important contribution towards the explanation of why bullying occurs.

Research usually begins by providing a definition of what bullying is (Rigby 2002) before discussing its nature, characteristics and prevalence, the victim and the dynamics between the two (Olweus 1993; Rigby and Slee 1994; Boulton and Underwood 1992). The academic literature has disclosed that bullying is a contested concept as there is no universal agreement to its definition. In particular, international research offers a different definition for bullying. Unlike the research conducted in the UK, the international definition is associated with feelings of hurt, anger and physical harm. More emphasis is given to aggression, and less upon power relations (Smith, *et al.,* 2002). As well as inconsistencies in its definition, Smith *et al.,* (2002) argue, young people construct bullying according to their experiences. Bullying behaviour is part of many young people's experiences as perpetrators and as victims. This fits into a broader spectrum of behaviours that also include delinquency and disorder, anti-social behaviour and violence. Research has also focused on peers and the role of bystanders and their relationship to the bullying environment as well as their role as peer supporters (Cowie *et al.,* 2008; Salmivalli *et al.,* 2005; Rigby, 2006). More recently, academic research has examined bullying through technology, known as Cyberbullying, as the perceived problem of it has rapidly increased and it has become more prevalent and complex as the perpetrator can easily remain anonymous (Shrock and Boyd 2008; Coloroso, 2008).

The literature has also recommended further research into school anti-bullying prevention and intervention measures, with an emphasis on developing understanding of the impact of more restorative and holistic approaches in educating pupils. It has been suggested that a process of restorative justice and holistic approach helps to curb bullying (Littlechild, 2009; Samara and Smith, 2008; Ahmed and

Braithwaite, 2006; Rigby, 2004; Smith 2004; Bishop 2003; Salmivalli 1999). The Department for Education (2011) and broader academic research (Littlechild, 2009; Morris, 2002) has encouraged schools to use a whole school approach. This involves teachers, parents and pupils developing the schools own anti-bullying policies which best suit the environment of the school and addresses the core problem of bullying that exists in the school. This also includes using a restorative approach to dealing with the problem. This literature increasingly suggests that this would best be delivered through an emotional literacy style. Reaching out to pupils' emotions has been considered to be more effective by raising awareness and relating to experiences. This has been considered key to allowing pupils to understand the problem of bullying (Goleman 1995 in Sharp, 2000). The use of emotional literacy has also been suggested by academic research (Woolfson *et al.*, 2004) to be used to reduce racism in schools. Whilst schools implement anti-racist education and multicultural education, much of the delivery style has been criticized by the academic research, who argue that the teaching styles are underdeveloped and strategies could be developed upon by using proactive strategies (Cole and Stuart, 2005). Further incorporation of the emotional literacy style of teaching is one positive way to improve such techniques (Richardson, 2009). This recommendation comes as a more positive suggestion compared to critics (Hart, 2009) who believe that anti-racist education and multicultural education should be eradicated altogether. They believe divisions are created amongst pupils due to poor teacher training who lack a real understanding of other races. There is a dearth in the literature that supports one of the findings from this thesis; a combination of preventative, intervention and sanctioning approach should be implemented in schools and delivered on long term basis. From the findings in chapter 7, pupils desire such an approach and considered this to be the most effective way to eradicate bullying and racist bullying. This argument could be developed upon through further research that explores young people's perceptions of bullying and racist bullying and comparing and contrasting the findings with this thesis.

There is less evidence of in-depth research into young people's perceptions of the dynamics of bullying and the motivations for racist bullying as well as the perceived experiences of victims. What research that has been conducted has identified that for many victims, racism occurs almost on a daily basis and that there is much under reporting and under recording (Barter, 1999; Connolly and Keenan, 2002). Academics that have conducted studies on school racism include: Troyna and Hatcher, (1992); Kailin, (1999); Smith and Tomlinson (1989) and Kelly and Cohen, (1988). The academic research on racism and racist violence has developed in numerous ways. One perspective that racist perpetration is motivated by unacknowledged shame of the perpetrators' own life and lifestyle, when they contrast what immigrants, in particular the South Asian community have accomplished in their lives. They feel they have accomplished very little in their lives compared to them (Ray *et al.*, 2004). It is suggested that these feelings are deep rooted in the numerous disadvantages in the lives of the white working class community; in witnessing the success of the South Asian community, they believe it upsets the natural hierarchy of races, and therefore motivates racist perpetration. Another perspective that has developed is where racist perpetration is driven by the notion of unfair advantage over the local majority white working class community. They perceive minority ethnic groups, and particularly asylum seekers and refugees to be receiving many benefits by the local government and schools, (Cockburn 2007). Thus racist perpetration can be explained by these perceptions of preferential treatment amongst the non-white community as this is deemed to be unfair. This research offers not only an interesting insight into hate and racist crimes and victimization, but also assists in understanding the literature on school racism, which fail to adequately explain to the motivations behind racist bullying.

With the changing makeup of Britain today and the growth of its multicultural society, the impact of racism in schools is important. It is evident a gap that exists within the broader literature on bullying and racism which strongly requires attention. This thesis examines the perceptions of pupils and adults along with their experiences of school bullying and racism in a northern city of England. In particular the thesis demonstrates how pupils' perceptions differ according to the different socio-economic background of their home, community neighbourhood and of their school.

Aims, Objectives and Methodology

The aim of the research is to examine the pupils' and adults' perceptions of bullying and racist bullying and how they are manifested in a school environment in a City in the North East of England.

Within this aim, a number of research questions have arisen, which the thesis is interested in exploring. These include: how do young people explain bullying and racist bullying? What factors impact upon their thinking? What role do socio-economic factors, if any, play on young people's perceptions, both of bullying, and of school responses? What are young people's perceptions of the responses of victims to experiences of bullying? What do adults perceive to be the main issues relating to bullying and racist bullying and how do these compare with that of young people? These broad questions have helped to narrow and focus the overall PhD aim, as well as inform the literature findings, as discussed below. As a result, two of the original objectives, that are discussed below have been refined:

Originally one objective was to explore the perceptions of pupils aged 11 to 18, however, the age range was reduced from 11-18 to 11-15 years, (Years 7-9) as this aptly mapped onto the findings from the broader review of research that suggests that school bullying primarily begins during the latter part at Primary School and is much more apparent during the early years at Secondary/Middle school. There is also a tendency to be an age decline in bullying after it peaks in early adolescence, which then tails off throughout secondary school (Sullivan *et al.,* 2005:8). Another original objective included the use of questionnaires, in addition to interviews. However, during the literature search, it was noted that survey/questionnaires was a traditional choice of method amongst many researchers of bullying, thus it was decided to adopt a pure qualitative approach.

The study has been carried out in two secondary schools and a Pupil Referral Unit in the east end of Newcastle-upon-Tyne, using qualitative research methodology undertaken with pupils and adults. Focus groups and semi-structured individual interviews have been conducted amongst pupils whilst adults are interviewed individually. The field work was carried out between November 2005 and June

2006 and a total of fifty one interviews were conducted. Various activities have been used during the focus groups in order to stimulate and engage pupils' discussions. These include an anti-bullying video 'Kick-It Bullying'; spider diagrams; post-it notes; an anti-bullying and anti-racist scenario quiz and a large sketch-pad containing anti-bullying and anti-racist statements. With regards to pupils (both focus groups and individual), the sample comprise of victims, perpetrators and bystanders (although this information arose from the research rather than formed part of the sampling). A basic list of questions was drawn up that focused upon obtaining in depth response from all participants which targets all areas in identifying the nature, characteristics of bullying and racist bullying. Also what, how and why they occurred. For the focus groups, the questions are structured around four main areas, (i) What was bullying and racist bullying and how did it occur? (ii) Why does bullying and racist bullying occur? (iii) What did the pupils do? Tell a teacher, intervene or do nothing? (iv) How do schools respond to preventing and intervening when incidents were reported and in pupils opinion, were they effective? The rationale behind these four key areas is to allow respondents to reveal individual as well as shared perspectives in their responses. Particularly so, this occurs when discussing issues such as why bullying and racist bullying occurred, why victims largely preferred to remain silent and why fewer pupils prefer to inform the teachers.

When conducting the individual interviews amongst young people, there is only one prompt used in these interviews. These were a series of images/pictures downloaded from Google Images, targeted to all year pupils during the interviews, and pupils have been questioned and gave their immediate opinion when viewing the pictures. The images served as an icebreaker to lead into the questions; however their primary use was to assist in generating pupils' understanding and interest in the subject. The questions drawn up for the semi-structured individual interviews are intended to ask pupils about their perceptions on the occurrence and manifestation of bullying and racist bullying and to sufficiently allow pupils to develop their views. The questions are structured around four key areas, (i) pupils identification of bullying and racist bullying (ii) any lived experiences of victimization or witnessed; (iii) pupils actions, either informing an adult or remaining silent; (iv) effectiveness of adult (parent or teacher) intervention. The purpose behind the questions in each key area is primarily to allow for any shared or individual perceptions. Any narrative purposes and to explore pupils' perceptions and where necessary, lived experiences.

The adult interviews included speaking with Head Teachers, Assistant Head Teacher, pastoral teachers; learning mentors; form teachers and house tutors. In addition, two youth workers and a parent have been interviewed.

Key Findings and Structure of Book

There are three themes that underpin the findings of this study.

Firstly, pupils identify the nature and characteristics of bullying and racist bullying to be the same. However, pupils' perception of school bullying differs to the way they make sense of racist bullying. In pupils' estimations, school bullies are perceived to be responsible for their actions. However, in relation to racist bullying, it is the victims themselves who are held responsible. Furthermore, pupil's tolerance towards victims of racist bullying differs across each school and much of this has been determined by the socio-economic climate of the school and neighbourhood.

Secondly, this research identifies that across the board pupils hold the perpetrator responsible for their bullying actions. However, there are notable differences between both Old East End Community College and Modern Eastern Suburban School when talking about bullying and maintaining a reputation of the school. The socio-economic environment reflects upon pupils' decisions.

Thirdly, this research identifies that despite all anti-bullying mechanisms put into place, victims largely prefer to remain silent. There is a universal desire by pupils for a combination of sanctioning, preventative and intervention measures to be implemented for all pupils and delivered over the long term.

This book is divided into eight chapters. Each chapter commences with a brief discussion of its main aims and purposes and concludes with a summary and discussion, highlighting key themes.

Chapter one examines the literature on school bullying. Specifically it discusses the literature relating to the nature and complexity of the definition of bullying. The various traditional social psychological and more contemporary sociological theoretical explanations for bullying are discussed. An interdisciplinary approach is argued, which allows for a broader and deeper understanding of the characteristics of the bully, the victim, and an explanation into why bullying occurs. The chapter examines the relationships between victims, offenders and place. It recognises that place/location is an important medium for bullying to come together. It also acknowledges the importance of the role of peers, as supporters, mentors and as positive bystanders. Bullying by and large, occurs in the presence and acquiescence of peers, (Sullivan *et al.*, 2005). Peers have been depicted in many ways, whether bullying occurs to impress them and they cajole the event, or silently witness bullying, or actually intervene to discontinue the bullying (Ma *et al.*, 2001; Salmivalli, 1999). Thus, peers can also have a positive or negative impact upon the victims physical and psychological well-being, (Smith and Shu, 2000; Coloroso, 2008; Oliver and Candappa, 2007). The chapter also notes that serious aggression is also found in girls, yet least expected by society (Goodey, 2006; 1997). The role and presence of peers whether as peer supporters and mentors, positive bystanders or in the negative role of bystanders has been associated with each section.

One key theme raised in this chapter is that, although the individual social psychological perspectives provide an insight into the bully and the bully's individual characteristics. There is a need for a more holistic approach in order to draw upon the victim, offender and place. Therefore, it is suggested that a sociological perspective assists to broaden an understanding of why bullying occurs by discussing the social and economic background to the bullying environment. A second theme raised is that by combining the psychological, sociological and criminology disciplines, a deeper understanding of the multiple relationships peers have with the perpetrator and also, with the victim, can be developed.

Chapter two examines the literature as it relates to school racism and the school response. Drawing upon the nature and extent of racism in schools, the chapter also examines the impact bullying has on victims (Troyna and Hatcher, 1992; Connolly and Keenan, 2002; Verkuyten and Thijs 2002). Key to this chapter is the suggestion that a review of the literature on racist perpetration and racist victimization is required in order to allow for a rich theoretical framework within which, racist bullying can be understood. The chapter therefore reviews the broader sociological literature on victims and victimization, and in particular how incidents are under reported (Chahal and Julienne, 1999; Bowling 1993; Sampson and Phillips 1992 and Rai and Hesse 2008 in Spalek; 2008). Chapter two also critically explores the broader sociological literature on racist bullying and offending helping to provide an understanding for the motivations behind racist perpetration (Sibbit, 1997; Webster, 1994, 2007; Hewitt, 2005; Ray and Smith, 2002; Nayak, 2003 and Cockburn, 2007). Finally the chapter examines the UK government policy and legislation on bullying and racism and how schools respond to them.

Two key themes are drawn from this section of the chapter. First that the sociological research on racist perpetration offers a broader understanding to the factors that contribute towards racist perpetration. Second, school racism can be understood by academic research that acknowledges the socio-economic environment. In areas of socio-economic deprivation, high unemployment and crime, there is most likely to be inequality. Therefore the presence of minority ethnic groups fuels anger and are used as scape goats to blame for all of the social and economic problems in the white working class people's lives.

The chapter also explores attempts to develop wider and more inclusive approaches to preventing and restoring harm done by general bullying as well as racist bullying. Focusing on responses categorized as (1) pre-empting or preventing bullying and (2) responding to/punishing the bully. The chapter promotes a more holistic/emotional literacy and restorative approach (Goleman, 1995 in Sharp, 2000; Smith *et al.,* 2008; Wolke, 2003; Samara and Smith, 2008; Pitts, 1999, Littlechild, 2009; Morris, 2002; Morrison, 2002 and Ahmed and Braithwaite, 2006). Key to this argument is that using a holistic and restorative approach, the greater the potential is for an effective prevention and response to bullying. Thus creating a safe and happy environment for all pupils (Ahmed and Braithwaite, 2007; Morrison, 2007). Also, to encourage pupils to act as peer supporters; mentors and positive bystanders.

Chapter three describes the research site. The aim of the chapter is to outline and contextualise the educational system in the areas studied together with an overview of the schools sampled. In addition the chapter explores the characteristics of each school according to the socio-economic and demographic context within the city of Newcastle-upon-Tyne. The chapter begins with an overview of the socio-economic and demographic characters of Newcastle-upon-Tyne; it discusses the education system and the role and duty of the Local Education Authority. Within this, a discussion on anti-bullying policies and race and equality policies is founded. Finally, the chapter describes the schools involved in the research, detailing their social make-up and linking each school environment with the wider regional context, general performance, educational and anti-bullying policies.

Chapter four details the methodology used in the research. The aim of the chapter is to detail the research methodology selected and the process of the fieldwork and data analysis. The purpose of the chapter is to show that qualitative research methodology is used. This chapter identifies a gap in the wider academic research that examines school bullying and racist bullying in those schools mostly using quantitative research, largely through questionnaires and survey based methods. This PhD study provides a more qualitative approach to other studies in this area by giving authority to the use of qualitative research. Starting with a discussion of the original aim and objectives of the research. The chapter reveals the manner in which they have been modified as a consequence of entering the field. This section includes detail about the methods chosen, namely focus groups and semi structured individual interviews. It presents an explanation as to why this methodological approach is best suited to the research programme. In addition, this section details a variety of methodological approaches in quantitative and qualitative, and presents a nuanced discussion of both the advantages and limitations to each approach. One major reason why qualitative research has been selected is the aim to explain in-depth pupils and adults perceptions of school bullying and racist bullying. The chapter also explores the ways in which access has been secured and samples decided upon. The chapter includes a discussion of the ways in which the data has been recorded, handled and analysed, followed by an examination of the political and ethical issues that has been involved when working with children.

BULLYING AND RACIST BULLYING IN SCHOOLS

Chapter's five to seven are the three data findings chapters.

Chapter five presents pupils' and adults' perceptions of school bullying and racist bullying. It begins with a background to the socio-economic and demographic character and profile to each school in order to allow for an understanding of differences in opinions and perceptions. The chapter then reveals pupils' perceptions of the nature of bullying and racist bullying followed by an analysis of teachers' perceptions of bullying and racist bullying. The chapter then examines the relationship between the bully and victim, followed by an exploration of the location of bullying and the significance of the relationship between peers as bystanders and perpetrators.

Two main arguments emerge. Firstly, there are fundamental differences into how pupils talk about the nature and characteristics of bullying and racist bullying. It can be suggested that the socio-economic environment determined how pupils perceive bullying and racist bullying. Pupils from Modern Eastern Suburban School discus bullying in greater depth and are able to establish that accumulated incidents amount to bullying and not one off incidents. They are also empathetic towards victims of racist bullying. This empathetic attitude could be attributed by the positive ethos of the school, which provides numerous support mechanisms, not only as part of the curriculum, but also support to victims through peer support, mentoring and counselling. Whereas pupils from Old East End Community College reveal prejudices by being hostile towards the presence of victims of racist bullying. These contrasting opinions suggest that the more socio-economically deprived a school and neighbourhood is, the stronger the resentment would be towards minority groups. In contrast, pupils from the School for the Excluded also recognize that bullying is an accumulative process. Yet whilst the school is also located in a socially and economically deprived area in Newcastle-upon-Tyne, anti-bullying support and preventative education was strong and the school ethos towards eradicating bullying was positive. Secondly, peers are identified as a driving force for bullying by their presence and influence towards the perpetrator, whether as an enabler or detractor of the bullying act. Pupils establish that peers have the power to control the bullying or to prevent the bullying from continuing.

Chapter six presents findings relating to pupils' and adults' insight into what motivates the bully, bullying and racist bullying in schools. The aim of the chapter is to explain bullying and racist bullying as discussed by the pupils. The purpose of this chapter is to disclose both individual as well as shared perspectives on why bullying and racist bullying occurs and how the socio-economic and geographic environment contributes particularly towards pupils' responses. Two main arguments emerge from the chapter. Firstly, pupils explained bullying by placing the blame on the perpetrator for their actions. That is, their upbringing, socialization, individual characteristics and socio-economic background are key factors they believe for their perpetrating behaviour. Secondly, when explaining racist bullying, pupils largely from Old East End Community College and indirectly from the School for the Excluded identify and suggest that it is the presence and cultural lifestyles of victims which provoke racist behaviour. This perception is further linked to a belief that minority ethnic groups are at an unfair advantage over the indigenous white working class community. Much of the pupils' rationale from both Old East End Community College and School for the Excluded can be associated to the deprived neighbourhood/community from which they derive from. In comparison, pupils from Modern Eastern Suburban School reveal more empathy towards victims of racist bullying; the affluent and middle class environment could assist in their contrasting opinions.

Chapter seven, the final data findings chapter, explores pupils' and adults' perceptions of the key issues relating to under reporting and the various ways in which schools respond to bullying and racist bullying. The aim of the chapter is to explore the inadequate reporting of incidents and the conduct of the schools in response to bullying and racist bullying. The purpose of this chapter is to reveal shared and multiple responses to the effectiveness of the school's preventative education was towards anti-bullying as well the schools' response. Two main arguments unfold from this chapter. Firstly, despite the development of school responses to reported cases of bullying and racist bullying, victims largely prefer to remain silent. This also indicates that there remains a high degree of under-reporting in schools. However, the importance of informing a teacher is an option that has been considered by some pupils. Second, pupils have clear views on the importance of school sanctions and favour immediate punishment as well as the idea that corporal punishment should make a return to school. Pupils, particularly at Modern Eastern Suburban School however believe that the referral unit is over used and perceive this to be futile, placing more emphasis upon preventative education as well as finding peer support highly beneficial. Across the board at each school, pupils also suggest that schools need a more combined approach with sanctioning preventative and intervention measures for the long term.

The final chapter in the thesis summarizes the key purpose of the study and draws out the core themes. Four themes emerge from this chapter. First, the thesis demonstrates that a qualitative research methodology allows for an examination of both of the individual as well as the sociological perspectives of school bullying and racist bullying, offering a broader perspective when explaining the nature, causes and motivations for each. By using a qualitative methodology the thesis, it is suggested allows for a forum where pupils' voices can be heard. Due to the extent of quantitative research, this is one area of the research that is limited.

The second theme is that differences in perceptions of bullying and racist bullying reflect pupils' broader beliefs which often are drawn from family and the socio-economic environment. When pupils discuss bullying, the sole focus is often upon the individual perpetrator and their characteristics and motivations, whilst the discussion on racist bullying focuses entirely upon the victim personal and social characteristics. Third, it is argued that socio-economic structural factors contribute towards the ways in which pupils perceive and understand bullying and racist bullying. The final theme reveals that there is a need for schools to increase in their holistic restorative/whole school approach to bullying. In particular, this theme strongly asserts that this form of preventative education has greater benefits when delivered through the style of emotional literacy.

CHAPTER 1

An Examination of School Bullying and its Dynamics

Introduction

BULLYING IN SCHOOLS has remained a contested and complex problem. Whilst understanding of bullying has developed over the last 30 years, for the most part, the social psychological and educational psychology literature remains focused on the physical and psychological characteristics of the perpetrator and their individual bullying behaviour. The sociological literature however, considers the social environment in which the individual resides in and is socialized into, although much of it focuses upon young people, delinquency and victimization, rather than bullying. An interdisciplinary approach enables a broader and deeper understanding of the characteristics of the bully, the victim, and an explanation into why bullying occurs. Furthermore, an examination into school bullying utilizing qualitative research methodology will enable young people to voice their opinion. This is particularly important as much of the literature on school bullying predominately uses quantitative methodologies. Finally, by combining the psychological, sociological and criminology disciplines that examine both the individual features as well as the social environment, a deeper understanding of the multiple relationships peers have with the perpetrator and also with the victim is developed.

This chapter is structured as follows. First, it discusses the definition of bullying and the nature and extent of bullying. This section puts into context, themes which allow the reader to be clear of the ways in which the definition of bullying is multi-faceted. That it is a contested concept and raises a significant point that bullying has been difficult to measure accurately. Second, the chapter examines the relationships between victims, offenders and place and acknowledges that the place/location is an important medium for those to come together. Third, the chapter explores the explanations for bullying. In doing so, it reviews the traditional and contemporary theories of bullying that focus upon the explanations of the bully, their mind and learning processes. It further draws upon a wider set of literature from the sociological discipline in order to demonstrate the weaknesses from traditional theories. Finally, the chapter acknowledges the importance of peers and peer/bystanders relationships and argues that bystanders have a significant role to the offender/victim dynamic.

Definition and Nature of Bullying

Although there is no universally agreed definition of bullying, in England and Wales, the current Department for Education guidance report (2011:3), now considers bullying as:

> "Bullying can be physical or emotional and it can take many forms (for example, cyber-bullying). Immediate physical safety and stopping violence come first but bullying can also be because of prejudice against particular groups (for example, because of Special Educational Needs, on grounds of race, religion, gender, sexual orientation or transgender status, or because of caring duties)" (DfE, 2011:3)

Whilst the guidance report has now included all forms of discrimination, it fails to effectively discuss the frequency of the act and therefore leaves an open interpretation as to what can be considered to be bullying. There is also no mention of intention to harm. Instead, more emphasis has been given to the characteristics of bullying when providing schools with a uniform definition of bullying.

Some academics (Smith and Monks, 2006, Tattum, 1993 in Rigby *et al.,* 2004: 5), view bullying as essentially the intent to 'hurt' or put someone under pressure, particularly so to Rigby (2002: 51), "bullying is now widely defined as a systematic abuse of power, . . . and more specifically as intentional aggressive behaviour that is repeated against a victim who could not readily defend him or herself". Academics, such as Griffin *et al.* (2004: 381) suggest that the classification of bullying includes any and all intentionally aggressive behaviour towards others, whereas other researchers specify that such behaviour must be carried out repeatedly in order to be classified as bullying. It therefore, can be argued that an issue about inconsistency and validity of data results in a vague definition of bullying, used by some researchers may lead to the over classification of children as bullies or victims. As Rigby (2002; 30 in Griffin *et al.*, 2004: 382), comments ". . . a formulation of bullying that equates it with aggressive behaviour has been seen as over inclusive and attention has been paid to what it is not". Yet to Lines (2008:20), the concept of bullying exudes the notion of power and control and intense manipulation over the victim. Lines therefore concentrates more on power and control and less on aggression. He, however, confirms Rigby's view that the more developed forms of definitions of bullying attempt to reveal internal processes between the injurer and the injured such as the intent to hurt as opposed to accidentally bringing pain to another person.

Internationally, there are variations given to the definition of bullying. For example, in Japan, the discussion of what bullying is has been demonstrated to be largely associated with the feeling of hurt, anger and physical harm, with less emphasis upon power relations and therefore reveals that the definition of bullying can be a contested concept (Smith, *et al.,* 2002:1120). Arora (1996 in Smith *et al.,* 2002) drew attention to the various terms associated with bullying in English and in several other languages and agrees that the study of bullying in a number of different countries indicates that the word bully is not easy to translate, (Genta *et al.,* 1996; Morita, 1996; O'Connell *et al.,* 1999; Rigby and Slee, 1991 in Smith *et al.,* 2002:1121). For instance, the terms 'bully' and the aggressive action of 'mobbing' are widely associated in Scandinavian and Germanic languages, but they fail to include indirect actions which are also bullying. The word 'bully' is also familiar in the United States (USA), however, the terms 'victimization' and 'peer rejection' are often used to denote negative actions of peers toward another young person and not necessarily linked to the term 'bullying' (Asher and Coie in Smith, 2002). Another example where the definition of bullying is seen to be contested is provided by Masden (1997 in Smith *et al.,* 2002:1121), where in Scandinavian countries, there is also gender differences in perceptions of bullying and related terms. Masden argues that this is an issue, given the evidence of gender differences found in the use of direct and indirect or physical and psychological forms of aggression including bullying (Bjorkvist *et al.,* 1992; Crick and Grotpeter; 1995; 1996; Rivers and Smith, 1994). Smith *et al.,* (2002: 1132) further argue that there is a lack of gender differences in understanding what bullying is and the use of the term 'bullying' despite the gender differences in bullying behaviour. Thus this also contributes towards the argument that defining bullying is a contested concept. In addition, and to agree with Smith *et al.,* (2002) who argue that young people construct bullying according to their experiences, bullying behaviour is part of many young people's experiences as perpetrators and as victims which can also fit into a broader spectrum of behaviours which also include delinquency and disorder. Therefore, whilst this PhD is focused on bullying and racist bullying, it must be acknowledged that bullying is also part of a broader aspect of young people's delinquent behaviours including, anti-social behaviour and violence.

Therefore, for this PhD, the definition used will be that as provided by the Department for Education as it is more comprehensive. As bullying is carried out in numerous forms and for a variety of purposes, the type of social skills a young person has, the school and home and community environment shapes an individual's personality. Where one young person has sufficient social skills to adequately understand their perpetrating behaviour, for another young person, behavioural attitudes could largely depend upon their own victimized experiences. Therefore to the latter individual, certain behaviour may be perceived as being normal and how they have been socialized into behaving as a result of their home and community surroundings and attitude.

Bullying is associated with verbal name calling, indirect actions such as staring and physical bullying. Verbal name calling, which is the most common use of bullying in schools, often involves reference to specific visible differences of the victim, such as their weight, wearing glasses or wearing different styles of clothes. Verbal abuse is also identified as the most common form of racist bullying in schools (see chapter two)

(Barter, 1999; Connolly and Keenan, 2002), and is serious due to the psychological and emotional impacts sustained on victims (Rigby, 2004). With physical bullying however, this involves a range of repeated physical acts against the victim that include, hitting, kicking, pushing, shoving, holding as well as hostile gesturing and stealing personal items or money (Ma *et al.*, 2001: 249). Similar to verbal bullying, the nature of physical bullying can vary from minor to more extreme. Indirect forms of bullying include physical bullying which range from threatening and intimidation to spitting on the victim. Other indirect forms of bullying include verbal bullying which involves subtle actions such as staring, ostracizing the victim and rumour spreading (Sullivan *et al.* 2006: 6). Dixon (2007:8) asserts that this is a process which is defined in stages and occurs if an individual is perceived to have broken a group norm. Therefore, where a norm has been broken, aversive behaviours are targeted at coercing the individual to conform through physical attack as well as rejection from the social group, although the behaviour varies between verbal, physical and then threats to exclude, whether it is temporary or actual exclusion (Dixon, 2007:8). Failure to conform to subcultural norms often results in permanent exclusion (Dixon, 2007).

In recent years bullying has also been affected by technology, which has become a viable and popular tool used to violate the victim. Often this form of bullying is termed Cyberbullying (Schrock and Boyd 2008). Cyberbullying appears where abusive messages can be posted in chat rooms by instant messaging, or isolating the victim in chat rooms. Bullies further use the internet to develop offensive web pages against the victim (*http://www.bullying.co.uk/advice/anti-bullying-advice*, 2011). Cyberbullying can also appear through the abuse of mobile phones such as silent or abusive phone calls and offensive texts. Furthermore, during physical fights, bystanders can record the incident on their mobile phones and subsequently forward the bullying event to all their friends. This also was previously known as 'Happy Slapping' (Coloroso 2008:10). This form of bullying has become increasingly popular in secondary schools as it involves the sophisticated use of technology and the victim can be abused 24 hours a day. Cyberbullying has therefore become increasingly problematic. A key difference between Cyberbullying and the traditional face-to-face bullying is that the abuse follows the victim, whereby the home no longer provides protection and the abuser is able to remain anonymous. Coloroso (2008) identifies that this has changed the fundamental nature of bullying as young people are increasingly venturing into the global neighbourhood via the Internet, mobile phone and the BlackBerry. She further argues that where bullies have long tormented their victims with low-tech verbal, physical bullying, they now also use high-technology tools to intimidate, threaten, stalk and spread rumours about their targets and this has often resulted in teenage suicide (Coloroso, 2008: 206).

In addition to these studies discussed so far, which have provided a constructive review of the nature of bullying, academic research has also investigated gender differences in bullying. The nature of bullying and in particular physical bullying, is such, that boys are more likely to be involved than girls (Branwhite 1994 in Charach *et al.,* 1995); boys are also more likely than girls to target the same victim repeatedly (Craig, 1993). Boys bully both boys and girls; however, girls tend mostly to bully girls only (Griffin *et al.,* 2004:383). Others, (Siann *et al.,* in Noaks and Noaks, 2000:72) challenge this, and suggest that females are involved in bullying just as much as males are considering the variety of forms of bullying that take place, for example social isolation are very frequent acts engaged in by females. Reid *et al.* (2004), and particularly Deakin's (2006: 380) findings based upon the Children and Young People's Safety Survey 1988, revealed that whilst boys were more susceptible to experiencing physical bullying, which included assault as well as theft, girls were more likely to be bullied verbally and more seriously, to experience sexual victimization. Deakin's (2006) findings are significant as they also show it is possible to correlate age with victimization; especially the more serious physical assaults. However, Deakin's research falls short as she does not discuss physical bullying amongst girls or indirect bullying in any depth. Yet, most recently, a study by the Cambridge Educational Psychology Service identified that girls were more likely to resort to cyberbullying, while male pupils tend to use physical and verbal intimidation (http://www.ncb.org.uk, 2011).

An earlier, yet widely referenced study on the nature of bullying was by Boulton and Underwood (1992:84), whose research examine problems amongst pupils aged 8 and 9 and six classes of 11 to 12 year-old-children, attending middle schools in England, using the 'Olweus Self-report Bullying Inventory' (1992: 74). Reports of both bullying and being bullied are more prevalent amongst boys than girls, and among the younger group than the older group. Similarly, Milligan *et al.*, (1992, in Mills, 2001:2) argues that a significant amount of research into school violence suggests that "by far the majority of bullying incidents into schools are perpetrated by boys"). Goodey's (1997:402) research explains that boys largely perpetrate by physical bullying that is built upon a foundation where boys are expected to be tough and fearless. This is particularly because boys' experience stems from every day social interactions and social expectations. Boys largely perpetrate physically and are expected to be fearless (Goodey, 1997:403). Interestingly, for the most part, previous research associates masculinity with aggression and claim that it is largely perpetrated by boys (Rigby 2004; Cranham and Caroll 2003; Olweus, 1994). A flaw remains in these studies as there are limited studies that acknowledge aggressive bullying behaviour amongst girls (Gini and Pozzoli 2006). Gini and Pozzoli (2006) argue that aggressive bullying behaviour is gender stereotyped, i.e. least accepted by society, whereas aggressive behaviour amongst boys is more accepted.

The location of bullying largely contributes towards its nature and extent. Although limited in academic research, it is significant as it provides a visual understanding of how bullying occurs (Boxford 2006). Open spaces allow bullies the freedom to attack their victims both verbally and physically and more frequently, however compared to classroom bullying, where space is more confined, or the teacher rarely leaves pupils alone, victims are more likely to be targeted through verbal bullying. Nevertheless, Sullivan *et al.*, (2005:11), claim that bullying is random and can occur to anyone at anytime. Pupils in undefined public spaces such as hallways, cafeterias, playgrounds, bathrooms and routes to and from school that are unmanned by school community members, such as students and staff, are more prone to bullying. (Sullivan *et al.*, 2005).

Key to this discussion of the nature of bullying is the difference in bullying between gender and age. Whilst the studies suggest that boys are more likely to bully, particularly physical bullying and at a younger age, girls have been identified to carry out all forms of bullying, including direct, indirect and increasingly cyberbullying. However, physical aggression amongst girls is present (Griffin *et al.*, 2004), but least considered normal or tolerated by society, unlike social tolerance towards physical aggression amongst boys. Another key issue is the indication that bullying amongst boys decreases with age (Oliver and Candappa, 2003); however, there is no evidence to suggest that this is the same with girls. There is the possibility that the nature varies, largely amongst girls, with the increasing practice of indirect bullying also largely amongst girls.

The Extent of Bullying

On examining the nature and extent of bullying, research has been conducted both on a national and international basis. The systematic examination of the nature and prevalence of school bullying began with the work of Olweus in the 1970s in Scandinavia (Smith 2001: 1). Much academic research has been informed by Olweus. His original large-scale project conducted in 1983/84 involved survey research across forty two schools in Bergen, Norway, (1978; 1991a). Olweus reveals that 15% of Norwegian school age children have experienced bullying either as victims or offenders. Based upon his nationwide survey in 1983/84, Olweus (1993:13) estimates that approximately 84,000 or 15% of the total number of pupils in primary and junior high schools, (568,000 in 1983-84) are involved in bully/victim problems 'now and then' or more frequently as offenders or as victims. Bullying was thus to be a significant problem in Scandinavian countries (Olweus, 1993: 14).

Further to this, research into the extent of school bullying in the USA has recently been investigated and from those few studies, there is an emphasis upon extreme violence (Worrall, 1997:76). A research review carried out by Dake *et al.* (2003: 173) focuses upon the prevalence of school bullying particularly in the USA. Referring to the work undertaken by Pelligrini *et al.* (2002 in Dake *et al.,* 2003), who compares the extent of bullying and the prevalence of victimization in US middle schools, Dake *et al.* argue that between 9% and 11% of middle school children are bullied either occasionally or more persistently. However, unusually, they also discover that the prevalence for victimization is 19% and therefore much higher than for bullying (in Dake *et al.,* 2003:173). Whilst this suggests that extreme physical bullying is much more prevalent in American schools, these figures could also possibly be a consequence of the frequent use in quantitative research methodology. Therefore, this indicates further research using qualitative methodology is required as it is lacking in the literature on school bullying. It should be noted that these quantitative studies fail to consider the socio-economic and geographic factors of the schools and neighbourhood. The significance of Chaux *et al.*'s (2009) research into schools in Columbia is one of the few studies to recognize the significance of these structural factors. Their work is significant as not only do they acknowledge the sparsely related research into examining socio-economic and geographical factors, they also acknowledge that there is still much to understand about contextual factors relating to school bullying (Chaux *et al.*, 2009: 521). Furthermore, their study identifies differences in bullying at school level and at classroom level than at municipality level and are unable to identify much difference between extreme poverty and inequality. Yet bullying is found to be higher at private schools compared with public schools. A larger diversity in income found in these schools and such differences must be taken into account (Chaux *et al.*, 2009). As Graham (1996:185) argues, relative deprivation is more a cause for bullying than absolute poverty. Yet within public schools, differences in bullying relates to those in urban and rural settings where the dropout rate, particularly amongst aggressive students is higher in schools that are more prone to violence (Chaux *et al.*, 2009: 521). This indicates that anti-bullying programs must be designed to cater for the type of school, rather than one design to fit all as Chaux *et al.* (2009) have identified that whilst most programs develop awareness, newer programs which place more emphasis upon competent development for all students, especially bystanders are more beneficial.

Furthermore, Rigby and Slee (1994) conducted survey research in Australia and have found that 14% of primary and secondary school students are bullied at least 'once a week' or 'more often' (1994: 8). Particularly, they show that 26% of children in grades three to seven are bullied at least 'once a week' or 'more often'. Slee (1995:57) claims that such findings highlight the need for early identification of, and intervention with children at risk from peer relation problems. Upon reflection, whilst this recommendation is linked to their discovery of early depression amongst victims which also can trigger them to bully other pupils, they do not consider social structural factors.

Furthermore, studies that consider the socio-economic factors and school ethos are very limited.

Studies discuss a decline in self-reported victimization as pupils grow older, (Olweus, 1991; Whitney and Smith, 1993; Rigby, 1996; O'Moore, Kirkham and Smith, 1997). However, Salmivalli (2002:275), findings reports that neither peers nor teachers confirm this finding. Further analysis was carried out based on classifying children into groups of self-identified victims, peer-identified victims, self-peer identified victims and non-victims (Perry *et al.* 1988; Crick and Rigby, 1998; Graham and Juvonen, 1998; Schuster, 1999 and Juvonen, Nishna and Graham, 2001; in Salmivalli 2002). This analysis reveals that what actually decreases with age is the frequency of self-identified victims. That is, a child who self reports being bullied does not have the reputational status of being a victim amongst their peers. On the other hand, the number of self-peer-identified victims was steady through grades four-six (Graham and Juvonen, 1998 in Salmivalli 2002). Missing from the above mentioned studies is the lack of qualitative approaches to determine whether bullying does actually decrease with age, or whether it simply changes in nature, as indicated by Rivers and Smith, (1994).

Research suggests that victims of bullying are most likely to be a particular target for a sustained period of time. In England and Wales, Perry *et al.,* (1988) assert that once becoming a victim, the student is likely to be consistently bullied for a period of about 3 months, and that "a stable propensity to be victimized is established by the time children reach middle school" (1988: 182 in Ma *et al.,* 2001: 255). Whilst Perry's analysis seems quite plausible as other academic researchers have affirmed similar views and indicate a larger period of victimization (Olweus, 1991, Whitney and Smith, 1993), he does not acknowledge that schools, in particular primary schools, support victims and that peer support is much stronger than it is in middle and secondary schools (Perry *et al.,* 1988 in Ma *et al.,* 2001). Boulton and Underwood (1992) find that many victims are bullied for two consecutive school terms whilst Slee's (1994) research reports that 28% of victims are bullied for a period varying from a few months to more than half a year. From these studies, findings suggest that since schools have begun to raise anti-bullying awareness, pupils have begun to reveal the extent of the frequency of bullying. Findings further suggest that pupils reveal that bullying declines with age, yet, indirect methods of bullying increases with age (Rivers and Smith, 1994). Pitts and Smith's (1995:33) study of prevention programmes in schools in two deprived inner-city areas of Liverpool and London identifies the incidence of anti-social behaviour is so high that students lack the confidence to report bullying incidents (Pitts and Smith, 1995). This also indicates that with indirect bullying, victims are less likely to report the incident as often many believe the bullying is less detrimental because there is no physical harm involved (Oliver and Candappa, 2003).

Findings from the 1998/1999 Youth Lifestyle Survey reveal that 33% of 12 to 16 year-olds report being bullied at school in the past year and 9% report bullying others over the same period (Flood-Page *et al.*, HORS 1999: 39). Furthermore, the MORI Youth Survey (2002) reveal that of 5,000 school children, 35% have been physically attacked, 45% threatened, 34% racially abused and 34% suffered from theft in school alone (Muncie, 2004: 22). As part of the national evaluation of the 'On Track' multiple intervention programmes, youth lifestyle surveys were conducted in 2003. This was amongst 30,000 young people in 29 secondary schools, 6 middle and 95 primary schools in England and Wales amongst 7 to 11 year olds in primary schools and 10-16 in secondary schools (Armstrong *et al.*, 2005). Exploring pupils' experiences as victims of crime and as victims of bullying over the previous twelve months, Armstrong *et al.* (2005) identifies firstly, that 13% of secondary school pupils report to being bullied over the previous week, secondly that bullying decreases with age, and thirdly that bullying is experienced more frequently by boys than girls. Furthermore, there is a strong correlation between experiencing bullying and variables of race, ethnicity, exclusion and educational learning (Armstrong *et al.*, 2005: ix). For instance, Black, 'looked after' children, who have been excluded and victims of crime are all far more likely to report being bullied than other groups (Armstrong *et al.*, 2005: 29). Findings from the Crime and Justice Survey 2003 (Wood, 2005:3), reveal that among 10 to 17 year olds, 19% admit to being bullied and those aged 10 to 11 were significantly more likely to be victims of bullying within this age group with 27% compared to 9% of those aged 16 to 17 year old (2005).

The MORI Youth Survey (2008) also reveals that the proportion of young people concerned about being bullied decline as they grow older and over a period of time with 22% in 2008 (2008:37). This can be compared to the results found in previous MORI surveys, with 34% in 2005 and 35% in 2004. The level of concern exists more amongst pupils aged 11 to 14 where 25% report to being moderately to very worried about being bullied, compared to 13% of pupils aged 15 to 16 (2008:37). With the findings from the MORI Youth Survey (Anderson *et al.,* 2009:13), it reveals that overall the majority of young people in mainstream education and attending Pupil Referral Units, are not worried about being a victim of bullying and there has been a decrease in the number of young people in mainstream education who are worried about being a victim of theft (33%) and of racism (19%) which is lower than in 2008 (Anderson *et al.,* 2009). Yet the survey also reveals that the actual experience of being a victim of bullying in the last 12 months remain the same as in 2008 for young people in mainstream education (51% in 2008 and 52% in 2009). However, for those attending the Pupil Referral Unit, there has been a significant increase with 66% in 2009 compared with 61% in 2008 (Anderson *et al.,* 2009:13). Questions can be further raised on these perceptions of age decline in bullying and how much underreporting actually occurs.

The key conclusion that can be drawn from the above studies, is that there are clear discrepancies with accurately measuring the extent of bullying in schools. The majority of studies involve quantitative survey research and the use of qualitative methodology barely exists. As pupils grow older, they are less likely to report their experiences of bullying (Rivers and Smith, 1994), under reporting therefore, increases and whilst it is suggested that bullying may decline with age (Oliver and Candappa, 2003), the nature of how bullying changes must be explored in greater detail. It can be agreed that there are strong possibilities that bullying does not decline, however the nature changes and it becomes more indirect, subsequently, it can be speculated that indirect bullying is not considered as detrimental as direct bullying and therefore, less important to report. Furthermore, with the lack of qualitative research that has examined school bullying; this also suggests that young people's voices are not being brought to the forefront in academic research.

Further to this, academic research into school bullying largely derive from the psychological and educational psychology disciplines concentrating on physical and psychological issues, yet minimizing socio-economic and geographical factors.

Whilst quantitative studies are valuable in detailing the nature and extent of bullying owed to their large sample sizes, they remain problematic as they are limited to providing statistical data and fail to document repeat victimization. The research using qualitative methodologies however provides more in-depth information of, for instance, individual experiences, and repeat victimization, for where young peoples' voice can be heard. Despite their limited generalisability due to their small sample size, qualitative studies however attest to two key themes. Firstly, they reveal that bullying is widespread and persistent in nature, (Smith, 1991; Smith and Shu 2000; Sweeting and West, 2001). Secondly, rather than periodic they identify that bullying has many characteristics, such as being physical, verbal, direct and indirect as is demonstrated in the previous section.

The purpose of this section is to identify three key issues. First it recognizes that the term bullying is a contested concept and that there is no universal agreement to the definition. Based largely upon the Department for Education (2010) present definition of bullying, this PhD identifies bullying as harmful behaviour ranging from both physical and psychological, yet also socially learned behaviour against an individual that is repetitive and persistent, and "intentionally harmful, involving an imbalance of power and causing feelings of distress, fear, loneliness and lack of confidence in those who are at the receiving end" (DFE: 2010:16).

Second, there are a range of studies that examine bullying through quantitative research methodology and particularly explore the nature and extent of bullying, yet there are limitations to quantitative research and therefore inaccurately measure the extent and nature of bullying. Due to these limitations in measuring the extent, it indicates that fewer victims report their experiences; therefore highlighting the gross amount of underreporting that exists in schools. While few studies are conducted using qualitative research, they explore the experiences of bullying in greater detail, though are limited as their sample sizes are much smaller than quantitative research. There is the need to exert more authority to qualitative research when examining bullying and racist bullying in schools. This would allow for a stronger platform in which young people can air their voices and third, to establish the existence of under reporting and that a more qualitative approach would assist to determine that bullying does not in fact decrease with age, but varies in nature and gender.

Victims, Offenders and Place

In general, the wider academic research identifies that victims are primarily targeted for being different, (Rigby, 1999; Whitney & Smith, 1993; Sullivan *et al.,* 2005). However, this notion of 'being different', can be based on a number of physical, cultural and social elements and acts as a main instigator for the perpetrator to commit the bullying. For example, victims are targeted due to individual physical differences such as being perceived as overweight, wearing glasses, having a different hairstyle. Yet victims have also been targeted due to their individual cultural and religious differences. Furthermore, from the findings of a Department for Education's (Green *et al.,* 2010:89), report, due to young people's different socio-economic backgrounds and different cultures, identifying victims prove to be difficult. This section explores the literature on victimization in two main areas, victims and the impact upon them, their risk and fear and secondly, the numerous coping strategies in which victims employ in order to deal with their bullying experiences.

Victims Impact, Risk and Fear

Victim's statuses have been constructed into two groups (Olweus, 1978 in Olweus 2000: 43), the passive victim and the proactive victim. Olweus's study is significant as his research is one of the earliest to examine victim's characteristics. Firstly, the 'passive group' are victims who tend to be anxious, insecure, cautious, sensitive and defenceless, whereas the second group, the 'proactive group', tends to contain victims who are quick-tempered, hyperactive, anxious and defensive (Bernstein and Watson, 1997; Olweus, 1991a; 1991b in Ma *et al.,* 2001). Perry *et al.* (1988) present a similar idea, though using different terms; the low and high, which refer to the low aggressive victims and the high aggressive victims (Perry *et al.,* 1988).

Victim's are often identified as having "low self-esteem, difficulty asserting themselves, but are generally not aggressive or violent" (Stephenson and Smith, 1989). This identification of low self-esteem and high social anxiety are considered to be major characteristics of victims (Hoover and Juul, 1993 in Ma *et al.,* 2001), who tend to perceive themselves as stupid and unattractive (Lane 1989; Slee, 1995) and whilst appealing for social approval, victims rarely initiate prosocial behaviours when interacting with peers (Troy and Sroufe, 1987 in Ma *et al.,* 2001). Rigby's results generally indicate that low self-esteem is associated with repeat victimization (Rigby, 2003: 586). This indicates that low self-esteem may derive from feelings of anxiety and/or depression (Perry *et al.,* 1988: 76; Salmon *et al.,* 1998:925). Yet Sullivan *et al.,* (2005:16) identify another victim type, the 'bully-victim', those who victimize younger or smaller than themselves as personally they have often been victimized by their peers or pupils who are older. They claim that many bullies fall into this category (2005: 16). Lacking in these studies is a discussion of victimization in relation to the structural factors of the school and victims perceptions on risk and space. Ma *et al.* (2001:253), further argue that research studies are inconsistent regarding the distribution of victims (2001). For instance, Olweus (2000: 58) discovers that less than one in five victims are proactive, whereas Perry *et al.* (1988) report that there are roughly equal numbers of low and high aggressive victims. They therefore present an issue where accurately identifying who the victims are becomes problematic.

Findings from cross sectional surveys and longitudinal studies reveal that a child experiencing bullying at school, in particular repeat bullying, can be considered at high risk of developing strong psychological problems, especially where they lack adequate social support (Rigby, 2003:583). Through this, victims can develop both psychological and physical disorders. Rigby considers psychological distress to be the more serious of the two and includes high levels of anxiety, depression and suicidal thinking. With victim's physical unwellness disorders, this illness has been medically diagnosed (Rigby, 2003: 584). However, to critique Olweus (1993) and Perry (1988), the major limitation that arises with Rigby's sample is an uncertainty over how far to generalize. Further to this, numerous investigations (Olweus, 1993; Smith *et al.,* 1994; Sharp, 1995; Rigby, 2002) have with a high degree of consistency, supported the case for an association between being victimized and the manifestation of symptoms of poor psychological and/or physical health. Overall, results from cross-sectional surveys suggest that being victimized by peers is significantly related to comparatively low levels of psychological well-being and social adjustment and to high levels of psychological distress and adverse physical health symptoms. Stronger support for the view that repeat victimization is a possible contributory factor in the development of negative health conditions has been provided by longitudinal studies involving children (Rigby 2000:443). For instance, Joscelyne and Holttum (2006:105), suggest that bullying gradually allows the victim to self-blame. Victims blame their character or personality, and subsequently feel that they have no control of the situation and are helpless (Joscelyne and Holttum, 2006). Research also suggests that victims' low self-esteem at school very often remains with them as they grow older (Cranham and Caroll, 2003; Oliver and Candappa, 2007).

There is also an association between hierarchy and the victim's bullying status. Where there is a tendency for a hierarchical structure to exist in class, this is prone to sustain bullying (Sutton *et al.*, 1999). For victims this increases the likelihood of perceiving their situation as consistently running out of control, while also interacting with peers can be experienced as being unpredictable and unreliable. From an outsider's perspective, it leaves the victim further stigmatized (Olweus and Endresen, 1998; Rigby, 1997). However, a victim may become traumatized, as confidence in both their own value and in the reliability of peer relationships is shattered. Further evidence that suggests victims experience poor relationships between pupils and teachers in school due to bullying is examined by Glover *et al.* (2000:153) who suggest that victims feel insecure at school. In partnership with a research team at Keele University, Glover e*t al.,* (2000) carried out their questionnaire research in 25 secondary schools. Their main findings demonstrate that 40% of those who felt less secure within school found it difficult to talk in front of the class. Indeed a breakdown in relationships between other pupils and teachers only enhances victim's feelings of insecurity.

Examining the research on repeat victimization from the broader social context is important in order to develop some understanding of the social and psychological impact of repeat bullying upon victims. From a sociological perspective, it appears that for many victims, repeat victimization is something that is considered to be normal (Menard, 2000). Wolke *et al.* (2009:836) asserts that generally it is agreed that the prevalence of victims decreases but the stability of victimization increases, in particularly amongst adolescents. Similarly Goodey's study (2005), considers the only real form of understanding victims experiences is through their daily routine activities. This is with particular regards to repeat victimization and how this experience has become normal to them.

It seems therefore, that there is a greater risk of bullying in schools for victims than in the community. Peer pressure and their influence over the bully play a large role in the victims' risk of fear (Melde, 2009) and therefore, this suggests that bullying in the school environment is more unique because of the high fear for further victimization. Multiple victimization is more common in schools than one off events and this occurs more frequently than in the community (Reid and Sullivan, 2009). This is an area that is omitted in the field of psychology and educational psychology and under researched from the sociological perspective. One notable study by Deakin (2006:377) examines victim's risk of fear from the perspective of those who have already been victimized. Deakin argues that victims fear further risk of being victimized to a greater extent to those who have not been victimized. Yet, Deakin's study is unclear about how much fear of risk occurs inside or outside of the school. This discrepancy is further exacerbated by the complex nature of the relationship between victimization and fear and depends upon both the type of victimization experienced and the type of fear expressed (Deakin, 2006:378). For example, experiences of bullying differ per gender, age and location. In respect of gender, whilst not specifying a particular age group, Deakin's (2006) study finds a significant amount of fear in girls who have experienced sexual and verbal harassment. For young people fear tends to be directed towards strangers; the perpetrators are most likely known, however, Deakin's study does not specify if perpetrators were located in the school or in the community. Deakin (2006) acknowledges that a considerable amount also occurs in schools as a result of peer influence. She does not however, specify which characteristics of peer influence causes bullying in schools and therefore her study proves weak on measuring risk. Furthermore, this limited knowledge on victim's experiences, especially young people proves that measuring victimization is problematic. However, Deakin does identify that children from rural areas are less at risk of physical assault or theft from other children than those in suburban areas (Deakin 2006:387), whilst children living in inner city areas and peripheral council estates are more vulnerable. This indicates that most victimization occurs outside of the schools and in public spaces and on the streets, perhaps occurring on the way to and from school. Had any qualitative research been conducted in this study, greater detail of the nature and extent of young people's victimization might have been secured, especially more narrative accounts of what young people experience and how often, in addition to how they felt at the time of victimization.

One review which sought to measure victimization was Goodey's (2005:51) research review of other studies, notably Sparks *et al.,* (1977 in Goodey, 2005) and examines victims' fear through geography and space. Drawing upon Sparks *et al.,* data findings from victims' surveys, Goodey (ibid) identifies that a victim's fear is demonstrated through the types of crimes reported, where they occur and how these crimes are counted. For example, young men are reported to be at more risk of public place violence, but display low levels of 'fear' of crime. Whilst the elderly who are at low risk of public place violence, reveal high levels of 'fear' (Goodey, 2005:51). From her review of Sparks *et al.* survey findings, particular patterns emerge through replications of these findings (Goodey, 2005:61). She however, argues that due to such replications of findings, these surveys are weak and poorly represent the data. However, there are limitations to this review, namely there is no link to young people's repeat victimization with schools and no detail of the socio-economic factors of the school and neighbourhood. Further to this, Green (2006:91) acknowledges that minimal research has been carried out that examines the individual's vulnerability of victimization according to economic status, that according to Green (ibid), this is most likely to affect risk of victimization and repeat victimization. In Green's study, the self-reported studies appear to demonstrate a much less clear relationship between offending and economic status. Therefore, it becomes more complicated to make inferences or adequate remarks about the general level of victimization among low economic groups by examining offender rates (Green, 2006). A further limitation, as within Goodey's research review, is a failure to examine victimization in schools on bullying that does not engage with the socio-economic status, school ethos and vulnerability. This has been argued to be directed by a governmental agenda.

Thus to agree with Menard (2000:544), to victims, repeat victimization has become somewhat the norm, yet as he argues, no study explains why this is the case. Davies *et al.,* (2007:220) acknowledge this dearth in the literature and contribute by suggesting that poor reporting of victimization, particularly secondary/repeat victimization in crime surveys, a lack of research that considers young people's voice, and the lack of association with their socio-economic position, can be linked to young people's fear of risk and vulnerability. This is because of the home and neighbourhood environment (Davies *et al.,* 2007:220). Their study is limited with the depth of evidence regarding how repeat victimization is linked to impoverished backgrounds and pupils offending in school. However, they also acknowledge the difficulties of gaining information and access to victims who will reveal their experiences in order to make young people's voices count (Davies *et al.,* 2007).

Coping Strategies

Studies offer evidence of a variety of coping mechanisms used by victims. Victims largely remain silent as a prime coping strategy (Roberts and Coursel 1996, in Ma, *et al.,* 2001:254) for two reasons: firstly, fear of retaliation and secondly, because of experience of inadequate support from adults when they do ask for help. Yet Naylor *et al.* (2001:118) use a questionnaire survey in 51 secondary schools in the UK, and offer some insight into this and reveal that in addition to not telling, victims often cope through either ignoring, enduring the bullying or retaliating. Similarly, Hunter *et al.,* (2004:378) conduct their research in primary schools in Scotland using self-reported questionnaires and propose that coping strategies should be judged according to how well they prevent problems to avoid emotional stress. They suggest that younger students are more likely to tell someone (Hunter *et al.,* 2004:378). However, Hunter *et al's.* study fails to articulate gender differences or differences in the nature of bullying with regards to asking for help. Bijtteber and Vertommen (1988 in Cowie, 2000) report that gender differences in the coping strategies adopted by victims result in boys tending to fight back more often than girls. Furthermore, it must be understood that younger students, particularly primary children are more likely to speak out due to the smaller numbers in the school and in the class, and the support received by teachers. In fact, Roberts and Coursel (1996 in Hunter *et al.,* 2004) find that the elementary school counsellor plays a significant role in the aftermath of peer victimization in the school setting. Counsellors are most effective when trained in crisis intervention, when working towards prevention in schools and when developing plans to address victims' needs when bullying occurs. Yet these studies fail to consider the socio and economic background of the school and community neighbourhood. With regards to secondary schools, it is also unclear how supportive the schools are towards promoting an environment where victims are encouraged to speak out, what preventative education is provided for them and whether provisions have been made for victims through counselling. As Rigby particularly notes:

> "Research has already reported prevalence of telling, who/where, when children tell and efficiency of telling. However, seeking help can be viewed as a coping behaviour and coping processes such as appraisal and emotion may be important predictions of whether pupils ask for help" (Rigby, 2002:176).

Hunter *et al.* (2004:375), reveal that telling someone seems to be an effective way of helping to stop bullying, but pupils' own views regarding the effectiveness of telling have been neglected (Borg, 1998 in Hunter *et al.,* 2004). Many trainee teachers report that telling someone is the number one coping strategy that they would recommend to students (Nicolaides, Toda and Smith, 2002 in Hunter *et al.,* 2004), but it is important to consider the factors such as young people's own code of behaviour, that is, not to tell tales as Oliver and Candappa, (2007:26) reveal. Other factors include a fear of retaliation by the bullies, or inadequate support by adults for instance not taking the victims incident seriously or overzealous intervention that results in escalating the problem. Such factors encourage or discourage pupils to 'tell'.

The characteristics of pupils affect whether bullying incidents are reported. Survey findings by Naylor *et al's.* (2001:119) indicate that older girls at school are more likely to tell someone about being bullied, whether a peer or adult, than older boys as they feel more comfortable about sharing personal issues than boys did (Naylor *at al.,* 2001). Furthermore, Hunter *et al.* (2004) claim that girls are more likely to inform a teacher/parent about their bullying as they perceive that this is the best strategy for both making them feel better and preventing the aggression from recurring (Hunter *et al.,* 2004: 388). In addition to age and gender, academic researchers have identified other variables such as type of victimization, which appear to influence whether or not students will ask for help when being bullied (Borg, 1998; Smith and Shu, 2000; Coloroso, 2008; Oliver and Candappa, 2007). This could be applied to those victims, who possess few friends, especially those who can be trusted as well as victims who are shy and possess poor coping strategies such as crying. Such variables along with the school context influence whether victims will seek help or not (Smith and Shu, 2000 in Smith, 2000:299).

In a study carried out in primary and secondary schools across England using focus groups and questionnaires, Oliver and Candappa (2007:72) explain that pupils' reluctance to tell teachers and their anxieties are not without foundation. Their research shows significance in its varied description for why pupils prefer not to approach an adult. A survey of 296 pupils aged between eight and eleven years from three middle schools, has found that only a third of respondents report that teachers 'almost always' try to stop bullying in school. This is a further factor likely to have an impact on young people's peer group cultures. In a study of children's attitudes to those who report incidents of bullying, comments in support of 'telling' outweighs negative comments, however, this differential reduces over time (Oliver and Candappa, 2007:76). A substantial proportion of children also demonstrate mixed feelings, with some showing strong condemnation of victims who complain to adults (Rigby and Slee, 1993). Thus pupils who inform others about their experience of being bullied might risk rejection by their peer group. This suggests that there is a collective environment, sustained by a more positive school ethos where peers are encouraged to prevent bullying in addition to victims being encouraged to speak out. As found in Craig and Pepler's (2001) research, after peers are encouraged to support victims, the majority of those who do intervene, are able to prevent the bullying. Furthermore, Naylor and Cowie (1999:476) discover that bullied pupils admit that having someone in whom they can confide who actually listens to them was helpful and gave them "the strength to overcome the problem". What needs further clarity from these studies is how frequently pupils share their problems with peers. From those peers who were willing to intervene it needs to be considered were they in the minority or majority? It is therefore important to understand why children and adolescents turn to others for help as well as who they ask, for this particular information may be helpful to those advising or helping victims to better understand what is expected or asked of them (Naylor and Cowie, 1999; Smith and Sharp, 1994). The reasons for reporting or not reporting an incident of bullying, including racist bullying, is one theme which is explored in the data chapters of this PhD.

Explaining Bullying

There are a variety of ways in which bullying has been explained within the scholarly research literature. There is a tendency for theories to differ due to subject discipline differences. In the psychological and educational psychology discipline, this section draws upon the structure drawn upon by Ma *et al.*, (2001) that discusses three perspectives of bullying: (a) Power-based theory; (b) Social learning theory and (c) Theory of mind skills. These three perspectives have been selected as they offer a broad critical insight into the individual characteristics that can help explain bullying. Primarily these models consider the individual factors in greater detail that contribute towards explaining bullying, offering limited discussion on structural factors.

Psychological/Educational Studies

Power-based Perspectives

Firstly, Ma *et al.* (2001) explain bullying through the power based model and discuss a number of studies that are associated with this model (Olweus, 1991; Hoover and Juul, 1993 and Eron and Husemann, 1984). Furthermore a number of studies not referenced by

Ma *et al.* (2001) have been used in this section as their work associates with the power-based model.

In general, the power based model is associated with the psychological wellbeing of the perpetrator and largely explains bullying as a desire for power and control (Ma *et al.*, 2001:261). The power-based theory is a social psychological concept. The key proponent of this theory is Olweus (1991a; 1991b), who explains the psychological characteristics and mannerisms of bullies as aggressive, dominating, non-empathetic and physically strong, with a "positive attitude towards an instrumental violence and a favourable self-image" and having little or no empathy towards victims (Hoover and Juul 1993 in Ma *et al* 2001). This extreme behaviour can be interpreted as the 'heartless' type of bully, (Lines 2008:62) who appears to have no form of remorse. Although the power based theory identifies bullying as "all about control", in addition to their aggressive, and domineering nature, bullies, as identified by Cranham and Carroll (2003:114), are also impulsive, physically stronger and much more violent than their peers. The above work is significant, argues Cranham and Carroll (2003) as bullies are not willing to accept any responsibility and instead attribute their behaviour to the actions of their victims (2003:129). Yet these studies are limited in their discussion relating to the varying forms of aggressive behaviour amongst the bully. These studies serve only to identify differing forms of aggressive behaviour and limited in discussing potential causes for such behaviour. Furthermore, they do not discuss the social environment and socio-economic environment in greater depth as to explain why pupils are aggressive, such as learned behaviour from the family/community and from a life of social deprivation.

Indeed, developing the discussion on aggression as a component to the power based theory; this is in the work of Price and Dodge (1989 in Griffin *et al.*, 2004: 456). Their research is significant as they develop a link when depicting proactive aggression as an "unprovoked aversive means of influencing or coercing another person and is more goal-directed than reactive aggression" (Griffin, *et al.*, 2004:456). Proactive aggression is more likely to be an effective means of accomplishing goals. Two subtypes of proactive aggression can be identified; instrumental and reactive aggression (Griffin, *et al.*, 2004:379). Firstly, instrumental aggression is characterized by an attempt to claim an object, such as a toy, and bullying, usually in the form of aggression directed towards another individual in an effort to dominate or intimidate. Secondly, reactive aggression is typically portrayed in the literature as being a fairly impetuous, immediate response to a perceived threat, without the component of cognitive evaluation of a situation.

Receiving approval by peers has also been identified as another key characteristic of the power based theory (Ma *et al.*, 2001:261) which is important as Sullivan *et al.* (2005:17) claim that teenagers are usually dependent upon peer approval and acceptance to the exclusion of all else. This therefore, explains that the perpetrators bully in order to maintain their reputation. As they grow older, their sense of individuality becomes stronger (Sullivan *et al.*, 2005).

A fundamental limitation to this model is the discussion on proactive aggression. Since this behaviour is extreme, it suggests that the bully is feared by peers in their group and is supported in order to avoid victimization (Pellegrini, 1998:167). Upon reflection, this therefore to a degree contradicts with the notion of bullying for peer group approval and acceptance. As Ma *et al.* (2001) and Sullivan *et al.* (2005) have identified the need for the bully to receive peer approval, yet where peers fear the bully; this support for the bullying is not done willingly. Therefore, the bullying behaviour is secretly not condoned.

Social Learning Perspectives

Theoretical perspectives have also explored the correlation between perpetrators of bullying and individual victimization of abuse. Studies suggest bullies who have been abused are more likely to be violent, aggressive and disruptive than non-abused bullies (Ma *et al.* 2001). This is identified as the social learned behaviour model. This can be contrasted with the power based behaviour as there is no desire to attain power and control; rather the bullying is a consequence of a behaviour that is socially learned. Yet there are elements of the social learning theory that can be linked to the power-based theory, for example that the bully may also have low social communication skills and that peer influence may encourage the bullying. The studies that Ma *et al.* (2001) references for this model are cited in Batsche and

Knoff (1994) and Oliver *et al.* (1994). Other studies not referenced by Ma *et al.* have also been used as their work associates with this model (Rigby, 2003; Haynie 2001 in Sullivan *et al.*, 2005; Galloway and Roland in Rigby 2004). All of these authors place substantial emphasis upon the aggressive nature of the individual; however, they also acknowledge social structural factors which are more sociological than individual.

It has been theorized that early on in the child's life; a child's character is centrally formed and shaped by family values and lifestyle. In addition studies such as those by Oliver *et al.*, (1994, in Ma *et al.*, 2001: 252) claim that other family characteristics such as financial and social problems; emotional environment; lack of family structure; social isolation; parental conflict and poor child management skills all contribute in shaping the bully. They further argue that such behaviour also serves to reinforce aggression. Failing to reward, and often punishing non-aggressive, pro social behaviours (Oliver *et al.*, 1994, in Ma *et al.*, 2001: 201). This study can be linked with that of Batsche and Knoff, (1994 in Ma *et al.*, 2001:261) in that many children with strict controlling and stringent parents, are more likely to be victims themselves. They release their emotions through aggressive behaviour towards other children, thus appropriating the personality of the parent. Furthermore, Rigby (2003:584) identifies that children coming from a dysfunctional family environment with over controlling parents often feel unloved and therefore have the tendency to act aggressively with other children. This behaviour is further enhanced where the school's attitude towards bullying is poor (Rigby, 2003). Yet, even though structural factors, emanating from a sociological perspective rather than a psychological, are indicated in the above research, particularly with Rigby (2003), there is very little depth to the discussion into the socio-economic background of the perpetrator and criminal activity in the neighbourhood in which the perpetrator resides. However, Rigby's research does acknowledge the significance of the social climate of the school in constructing the bully.

Where pupils have been identified as bullies and victims, they are also described as 'particularly high risk; having higher rates of problem behaviour, depressive symptoms, and lower self-control, social competence and poorer school functioning (Haynie, 2001: 44

in Sullivan *et al.,* 2005). In addition, bullies have been reported to be at greater risk of deviant peer group involvement. They are less able to form positive peer friendships, and have a greater likelihood of engaging in anti-social adult behaviour (Haynie, 2001:45 in Sullivan *et al.,* 2005). Furthermore, when trying to understand the psychological factors associated with bullying, in particular, persistent bullying, issues relating to the social skills, social information processing and the social perspective of the bully, should take into account the abilities of the child involved. Whilst Haynie (2001 in Sullivan *et al.,* 2005) also associates the social climate of the school with bullying, this discussion revolves around peer relations and gives an insight into how peers affect the bullying behaviour. Primarily peers, who cheer and rally around the bully and the bullying event, reveal strength to their influence and contributes towards the bullying to continue.

A major limitation with the social learned behaviour model is that it assumes that the individual is constantly surrounded by a negative environment (i.e. schools) that condones aggressive behaviour. Schools progressively offer more support to victims through implementing a variety of preventative and intervention measures and many, but not all, operate a zero tolerance policy towards violent bullying. A second limitation with this model is that there is overlap with the power based theory that also implies that the perpetrators suffer from low social and communication skills and peer influence that allows the bullying to continue. Also as demonstrated by Rigby's (2004:2) criticism of this model, evidence has been provided to suggest that bullies lack social skills and do not always come from particular kinds of families, nor do rates of reporting always support the interpretation that bullying is caused by the family pathology (Galloway and Roland 2004 in Rigby, 2004). Individuals, who are different in personality however, tend to belong to the same socio-cultural group and seek to bully those whom they consider as outsiders; outside this socio-cultural group. Therefore, bullying in this sense has no solid connection to the family background (Rigby 2004: 2), revealing a third limitation to this model.

Whilst the social learning theory acknowledges bullying is individually based, it also recognizes the importance of the social context. Whilst agencies are important (i.e. schools, family, neighbourhood), the ways they influence how bullying has been carried out however, is seen as psychological. In the above context, the driving factor that explains bullying is through society and peer influence.

Mind Skills Perspectives

A final way in which Ma *et al.* (2001) presents models of bullying is through the theory of mind skills. This model suggests that individuals skilfully exercise their minds to manipulate and control victims. Both Kaukainen *et al.* (1999) and Sutton *et al.* (1991), depict bullies as powerful but 'oafish' individuals who have little understanding of others, (Rigby, 1999; Rigby and Slee, 1991). Other academics (Kaukainen *et al.*, 1999, Ma *et al.*, 2001: 262; Sutton *et al.*, 1999: 120) reject this view and believe that bullies possess sharp social cognition and mind skills who are able to control the bullying situation and foresee how the victim will react. Indeed this theoretical model has been further developed to include bullies gaining satisfaction by inflicting maximum suffering on the victims. Albeit in a subtle way, whilst not being caught, this tends to add excitement for the perpetrators and further challenges them to apply this mental manipulation in a variety of situations (Kaukainen *et al.*, 1999; Sutton *et al.*, 1991 in Ma *et al.*, 2001: 262; Train 1995: 88). This model has been particularly challenged by Sutton *et al.* (1999: 120) who advocate that bullies become part of a highly structured social group, carefully deliberating and choosing who to recruit into their group and strongly assert that

> "Although bullying is an aggressive act, this by no means implies that bullies and aggressive or conduct disordered children are a homogenous group demanding one explanation".

Sutton *et al.* (1999) further assert that if bullying could be considered to be part of this conceptual framework, then it can be assumed that the perpetrator would possess strong social skills. They therefore believe that:

> "many bullies may in fact be skilled manipulators, not social inadequate" (Sutton, *et al.*, 1999:120). In this regard then:

> "The context and skills of bullying are largely based on an ability to understand or manipulate the minds of others a 'theory of

mind', or social cognition. Consequently, there are reasons for assuming that a successful bully will in fact have a superior theory of mind" (Sutton *et al.*, 1999).

Where Sutton *et al.* fall short in their research is within their methodology. Their research in this area explore the theory of mind skills, to compare with the social skills deficit model and test the theory of mind skills. Their findings fail to support this social skills deficit model. Furthermore, it does not consider the varied behaviour of young people who bully. Not all perpetrators fit within the traditional framework of mind skills. For example, an aggressive and hot headed proactive bully/victim may fall under this model (Sutton *et al.*, 1999:123). The study fails to associate the theory of mind skills with peer acceptance/rejection in bullying as the influence of peers is a crucial element when explaining bullying and also indicates that hegemonic masculinity is played out. The above limitations result in implications for further research.

Three main limitations can be applied to the theory of mind skills model. Firstly, the model is consistent with the Social Information Processing (SIP) theory and therefore overlaps with the social learned theory as not all children are able to predict how the victim will react. Secondly, the model focuses only upon one social cognitive mechanism and does not acknowledge any other perspectives of bullying, such as direct verbal and physical bullying and therefore there is less discussion on this theory. Thirdly, and concurring with Crick and Dodge (1999:131), the idea that social cognitions associated with hostile, harmful behaviour can be labeled as 'superior', as Sutton *et al.* (1999) advocates, is problematic in that it implies that aggression is a characteristic that other pupils who are less 'skillful' should emulate. However, since this model overlaps with the social learned theory, it also implies that social cognitions can result in incompetent behaviour and therefore is contradictory, imprecise and can be easily misconstrued (Crick and Dodge, 1999). In the field of psychology, bullying behaviour therefore needs to be understood by incorporating a variety of models, such as those mentioned, including the group process theory model.

A major contribution in which all three theories make is that they explain bullying through discussing the individual social psychological characteristics of the perpetrator. Furthermore, the focus of these theories is more inclined towards the offender as an individual and that the bullying behaviour is in some ways individually motivated and individually constructed, rather than considering social structural factors. The three theories invariably fail however, to emphasize and examine in detail the social factors that can influence bullying.

Not all theories of bullying however can be agreed upon; there are aspects that make relevant contributions to reveal the individual and social explanations for why bullying occurs. This section has considered the theoretical perspectives on bullying as a social psychological concept, also including educational psychology as well as from the sociological concept. The sociological research that does examine these social and structural factors, and are much more focused and explanatory variables are discussed below.

Sociological Studies

Theories located within the sociological discipline that have relevance to the study of bullying point toward the structural and socio-economic factors of the perpetrator's home, neighbourhood, community environment and school. Yet many of the studies use delinquent behaviour as opposed to 'bullying' directly. However, it must be acknowledged that 'bullying' behaviour is part of a continuum that involves delinquency and delinquent behaviour. Four theories that apply to these are (i) social control theory; (ii) social disorganization theory; (iii) social ecological theory and (iv) masculinity. Whilst these theories are more structural than individual (although the social ecological theory acknowledges psychological elements) they assist in explaining why bullying occurs and is allowed to continue.

Social Control Perspectives

Social control theory argues that bullying behaviour is a function of the breakdown of societal bonds. Hirschi, (1969 in Greenberg, 1999:66), who was one of the first to develop and apply social control theory to delinquency, poses that youth who are strongly bonded to society are less likely to engage in delinquency. His work displays four principal elements of the social control theory (Espelage and Swearer 2009; Stewart, 2003; Greenberg, 1999). (i) Positive interactions, particularly amongst teachers as Hirschi theorizes that classroom practices and teachers attitudes are strong components to the school climate which can contribute towards the prevalence of bullying. (ii) Commitment to conventional activities, here Hirschi believes that as commitment particular to attending school and engaging in community activities involves a large amount of time and energy in conventional activities. Young people therefore, will be able to foster more positive attitudes and behaviour, which are inconsistent with delinquent behaviour (Espelage and Swearer, 2009:153). (iii) Actual involvment to conventional activities, particularly with extra curricular actvities. Hirschi theorises that young people who are involved with such extra curricular activities are less likely to display problematic behaviours in high school (Mahoney, 2000 in Espelage and Swearer, 2009). (iv) Belief in conventional values. To Hirschi, if a young person fails to acquire a positive sense of community/existence of a commmon value system within the society, (Hirschi, 1969), the young person would be less apt to follow conventional rules of good behaviour. Thus having a strong sense of community involvement has shown to be effective in preventing delinquency (Kadzin, 1987 in Espelage and Swearer, 2009:154). The type of relationship a young person has with adults and in society is important and the social control perspective emphasises the need for a positive and healthy relationship with adults, such as parents, teachers and the schools (Espelage and Swearer 2009:152). Therefore, the social control theory acts as a preventative theory. Where social control theories assist to explain bullying in schools, Stewart (2003:583) research is significant, as his research acknowledges that the social control theory assists to understand why bullying occurs and is allowed to continue. His study drew data collected from a comprehensive national probability study of students, teachers, schools and families and from this, it addresses a number of hypotheses that link individual and school-level influences to explain school misbehaviour, especially bullying.

The hypothesis concerning actual involvement to conventional activities is not supported in his research which is one element to Hirschi's theory of social control. Although this relationship had been observed at the zero-order level, the multivariate results failed to yield a significant relationship. It can be explained that this is possibly because the conventional activities are limited to activities during the day therefore providing possible opportunities for deviance and bullying behaviour after school (Stewart, 2003: 596). Stewart's research also acknowledges where schools contain a poor ethos, the greater the behavioural problem. Therefore, a positive interaction between pupils and teachers as linked back to Hirschi's first social control model is crucial to improving such behaviour. Indeed Stephenson (2007: 6) further asserts that in the absence of effective supervision by the school, bullying and crime will therefore tend to increase, thereby explaining how bullying behaviour can continue. As Stewarts (2003) study used cross sectional data, it thereby proves to be weak and limited. The use of qualitative and longitudinal data may prove to provide a balanced set of results.

Three main limitations can be applied to Hirschi's theory of social control. First and to concur with Greenberg, (1999:74), the social control theory is unfeasible to be the only theory found to explain for bullying. Greenberg's findings of a cross sectional analysis of self-reported delinquency data from the Richmond Youth Survey (1999) are consistent with Hirschi's theory of social control as his analysis is based upon using Hirschi's formulation for the social control theory. Second, this reanalysis of the self-reported delinquency data from the survey indicates that social control theory has limited power (Greenberg, 1999:66). Where social control theory states that weak bonding or relationships increases levels of involvement in delinquency, to test this suggestion, weak bonding should be measured at an earlier time than at which delinquency is measured. Greenberg's cross-sectional design however, does not provide for sequencing of measurements. As a result, Hirschi's theory would have used a low bonding at the time of the data collection to predict earlier, not later, involvement in delinquency (Greenberg, 1999:75). Third, the results from the youth survey imply that although social control has some effect on involvement in delinquency, it has only a modest effect in explaining variation in delinquency involvement across individuals. Therefore, it can be argued that Greenberg's results should be taken at face value (Greenberg, 1999). From a differential association perspective, low social control increases the likelihood that young people will associate with peers who engage in similar levels of non-normative behaviour (Sutherland, 1947). This association can also include bullying behaviour. Thus, combining social control, strain and differential association theories provides an explanation for how bullying perpetration might emerge during and late adolescence (Espelage and Swearer, 2009:154).

Social Disorganisation Perspectives

The second theory attributes deviant behaviour to socially disorganised cities that are characterised by impoverished economic and social conditions that limit a community's ability to control or supervise adolescent behaviour (Espelage and Swearer, 2009:155). To Stewart, (2003), low economic status; ethnic heterogeneity and high residential mobility are the three major structural factors that contribute towards the disruption of the family home and the extent of community cohesion and organisation. Furthermore, young people from socially disadvantaged inner city neighbourhoods are at greater risk with victimization than those from an affluent home and community environment (Bradshaw, 2009). This can be linked back to the social learning theory where the perpetrator is also a victim of bullying. Whilst Espelage and Swearer (2009) acknowledge that little is known about the potential application of social disorganisation theory to bullying perpetration and/or victimization, it is plausible that positive peer support, collective efficacy within communities, including neighbourhoods and schools, is related to lower levels of perpetration and victimization.

Academic research further reveals that the school climate and organisation also makes a major contribution towards the construction of a bullying environment (Bradshaw *et al.,* 2009:2004). As noted by Barnes *et al.* (2006 in Bradshaw *et al.,* 2009), a disordered school environment has been revealed to not only negatively impact children's ability to learn, but also serves to undermine the teacher's ability to efficiently manage the classroom and student behaviour. This suggests that implications for bullying behaviour can be explicit. Thus explaining bullying can be viewed as an institutional as well as social behaviour (Asao, 2003). Similarly, Stephenson (2007:6) argues that social disorganisation theorists perceive schools as reflecting a wider process of community disintegration which diminishes their capacity for effective socialisation. From this perspective, it can be speculated that if the school system fails to promote bullying behaviour, neither does it restrain it (Stephenson, 2007). Bradshaw *et al.* (2009:206) use a multi-level analysis to examine bullying-related attitudes and experiences among 22,178 students in 95 elementary and middle schools in Maryland USA. They also examine if school-level predictors of disorder are related to bullying-related outcomes that were over and above the influence of individual-level risk factors. School-level predictors including a high student-teacher ratio; a high concentration of student poverty, the location of the school (for e.g. urban vs. Suburban) and a high number of student suspensions are found to be associated with a diminished school climate and an increased risk of school violence including bullying (Bradshaw *et al.*, 2009: 206). Bradshaw *et al.* (2009) have concluded that the school-level indicators of disorder are associated with bullying-related attitudes and experiences among both elementary and middle school students and are largely consistent with the social disorganisation theory.

Social Ecological Perspectives

The third social ecological theory explains bullying through environmental factors. Such factors are organised in a contextual representation where the level of framework consist of the immediate social environment or social environment impacting development indirectly and as well as the macro systems focusing upon the broader societal factors, such as the socio-economic status, culture (Andrews, 1985 in Espelage and Swearer, 2009: 155). Focusing upon the broader societal factors, examining young people's bullying behaviour in relation to their neighbourhood and community environment is rather limited. Neighbourhood disadvantage is built upon a number of issues for example, the extent of adult criminality which might play a significant role in influencing young people's behaviour (Elliott *et al.*, 1996). Their study is significant in being one of the earliest studies to highlight the dearth of research on home and neighbourhood environment, and acknowledging the process in which neighbourhood disadvantage influences individual behaviour and social development. This process can be characterised through the various cluster of traits that make up the disadvantaged neighbourhood.

Although poverty is a central feature of the cluster, it also includes high rates of unemployment (Pitts, 2001:78); cultural diversity; population turnover; changes in the structure of the job market and family composition, particularly the prevalence of single-parent families with children and the impact of urban renewal and other housing policies (Elliott *et al.*, 1996:382). Elliot *et al.* (1996:389) use a path analysis to test the hypothesis that organisational and cultural features of disadvantaged neighbourhoods in Denver and Chicago, mediate the effects of ecological disadvantage on adolescent development and behaviour. Through their hypothesis of the neighbourhood organization, they develop three measures, (i) informal control; (ii) social integration and (iii) informal networks. In relation to disadvantaged neighbourhood effects on adolescent development and behaviour, their findings reveal that this is largely mediated by informal control in both locations. The authors agree that the higher the level of informal control, the higher the neighbourhood rates of prosocial competence and involvement with conventional friends, and the lower the neighbourhood rates of problem behaviour (Elliott *et al.*, 1996:414). This can be linked back to the social disorganisation theory. Yet the hierarchical linear model (HLM) used to test the theory is weak. As working class neighbourhoods have a tendency to rely on each other in all social aspects, whereas affluent neighbourhoods do not, therefore, the sample used is too small and without the use of qualitative methodology, the interpretations are weak (Elliott *et al.*, 1996). Furthermore, this study does not explore this relationship between ecology pupils' behaviour in schools.

Evidence suggests there is still a strong correlation between the neighbourhood environment and young people's behaviour, particularly, their behaviour in schools (Chaux *et al.*, 2009: 521). Research has now begun to consider the differences in bullying between private and public schools, and between rural and urban schools indicating that more violence exists in urban schools than rural, despite the higher dropout rates in rural schools (Chaux *et al.*, 2009: 523). Chaux *et al.* (2009:523) use a multilevel analysis in middle and high schools in Columbia, USA to explore the relationships between bullying and socio-economic and socio-political contextual variables. This study makes a valuable contribution towards understanding the influential factors upon bullying in schools by considering the larger contexts in which it is embedded (Chaux *et al.,* 2009). Their results reveal that inequality leads to higher levels of bullying than poverty. Yet, discrepancies lie with the multilevel analysis infused, in Chaux *et al's.* (2009) study. The sample is too small and questions tend to be too leading, thereby limiting the validity of the study. The results were further limited to addressing only direct forms of bullying, thereby omitting indirect forms as well as Cyberbullying. Furthermore, in their discussion on poverty, population density or homicide rates, they are unable to explain for why bullying occurs. David (2010:262) acknowledges that there is limited research which examines the extent of behavioural issues in various schools and how this affects them due to socio-economic disadvantage and geographical areas. Yet in his study, he claims that disruptive pupils, especially those with behavioural and mental disorders have a long lasting negative impact on other pupils, especially in primary schools in the worst socially and economically affected areas (David, 2010). However the results from his survey lack depth and detail, due to the low response rate. This reveals a growing need for more research in this area and utilizing qualitative research.

Thus, whilst the social ecological theory affirms developmental determinism, and does not reject the importance of childhood psychological risk factors, it seeks to address the relative neglect of neighbourhood/community-based and socio-structural risk factors and their potential influence on psychosocial risk factors and behaviour (Case and Haines, 2009:83). This therefore reveals an overlap between the individual psychological approaches and sociological approaches to explaining bullying. Yet a major limitation with the social ecological theory is that it is under-developed and inconclusive. For instance in Wikstrom and Loeber's study (2000) that follows factorisation and analysis of data from the Pittsburg Youth Study, they identify that neighbourhood/community risk factors exert little independent effect on offending and that most of their influence is mediated by individual risk factors. Other research has discovered only an indirect effect of neighbourhood risk factors on offending through their influence on other risk factors, such as family functioning (Sampson and Laub, 1993; Espelage and Swearer, 2009; Elliott *et al.,* 1996). It can be agreed with Sampson *et al.* (1997) who conclude that neighbourhood characteristic can significantly influence offending/bullying behaviour, although not to the extent of influencing individual characteristics, yet to agree with Case and Haines (2009:85), this is a claim without any strong empirical foundation.

Masculinity Perspectives

Relevant to this section is hegemonic masculinity as it can be theorized as being the dominant form of masculinity that achieves the highest status, strongest influence and rewards, thereby potentially exerting an influence upon bullying behaviour. Theorizing masculinity has many components to it, however, they can be grouped into four main types that reflect the overall 'gender order' and its related 'configuration of practice' (i) hegemonic; (ii) subordinate; (iii) marginalized and (iv) complicit masculinities (Connell, 1995 in Connolly, 2005:59). Hegemonic masculinity is not static or fixed however; it continually evolves and reinvents itself through time, taking different forms in different contexts (Connolly, 2005). As Kenway and Fitzclarence (1997:121) summarize:

> "At this stage of Western history, hegemonic masculinity mobilizes around physical strength, adventurousness, emotional neutrality, certainty, control, assertiveness, self-reliance, individuality, competitiveness, instrumental skills, public knowledge, discipline, reason, objectivity and rationality" (in Skelton, 2001:50).

The socialization of males and females and what society expects and regarding behaviour what is acceptable from society is an important feature of hegemonic masculinity. The display of verbal and physical aggressive behaviour amongst males has been accepted by society as a particular norm and is considered a form of masculine bravado. However, this behaviour is considered abnormal and atypical amongst females. A central feature of Goodey's (1997:401) research is identifying the socialization of adolescent's gendered fear of crime. She theorizes that

> "While various theories from anomie, subcultural studies and psychoanalysis have offered explanations from criminal and anti-social behaviour, the processes by which boys can become criminal men demand contextualization within what it is to become and be male in its various guises; that is, in the context

of the individual's class, race, age and sexuality. Examination of 'growing up male' through research on childhood, adolescence and masculinities can present criminology with a solid base from which well-established and reworked 'facts' can be readdressed and reinterpreted" (Goodey, 1997:401).

Whilst Goodey refers to the 'criminal man', this is relevant to explaining bullying as her theory suggests that male adolescents who bully and engage in anti-social behaviour are likely to offend later on in life (Goodey 1997). Goody (ibid) argues that the image of the 'fearless' male from childhood onwards, is not a helpful one and relates the benefits to the male sex from taking on a 'fearless' persona, alongside its negative social implications and links this to hegemonic masculinity (1997: 401). Goodey's belief is that hegemonic masculinity presents such a hierarchy of oppression in reference to how western, 'white, middle-class, heterosexual and 'thirty-something' masculinity is placed at the top of this hierarchy of privileged masculinities (Goodey, 1997). Where society stereotypes gender and expects boys to be tough, Goodey suggests that fear amongst boys should not tarnish their masculine identity. Upon reflection, this can assist to understand why boys under-report their victimization despite their fear, supporting the need for more research into male victimization.

Class and race are also considered as significant variables in the development of hegemonic masculinity's emotionally inarticulate persona (Goodey, 1997). Her research highlights class and race as the most unattractive expressions of exaggerated masculinity (Goodey, 1997). For example, a middle class white male may be in a favourable position to support a black colleague or and especially in the sports world, the non-white footballer. Furthermore, Goodey argues that, black or Asian boys would adopt the norms of the dominant, white culture, in order to avoid racist tension and/or verbal abuse, yet tend to practice their racial and ethnic culture if it was currently favoured by the dominant culture's normative masculinity, for instance, black rap music. As Goody (1997:405) asserts, "To step outside the realms of acceptable masculinity is to endanger oneself as an atypical male". Thus, males are socialized into being tough. This aggressive behaviour also indicates that bullying is instigated because of what society considers normal, it also indicates a desire for power and control,

(Sullivan *et al.,* 2005; Eron and Husemann, 1984 in Ma *et al.,* 2001; Oliver *et al.,* 1994; Amber, 1994), and reflects upon the power based theory as well as overlapping with the social psychological concept of the power-based theory. Whilst Goodey's research strongly indicates and advocates multicultural education, her work reveals a limitation in particular with boy's fear and fearlessness in and around the school environment and the existence of aggressive behaviour amongst girls.

One study that may open up the forum to this debate is by Phillips' (2003), research review in the early 1990's that focuses upon the aggression and violence experienced by young people in local schools and neighbourhoods. Phillips (ibid) argues that aggression is as much present in girls as it is for boys, however, such aggression decreases with age largely because society deems such behaviour as less favourable for girls (Phillips, 2003: 720). Drawing upon the work by Campbell (1986 in Phillips, 2003), who had conducted semi-structured interviews with 31 young women attending a further education college in South London, Phillips notes that within female involvement in physically aggressive and violent behaviour, it is more common that previous research suggests (Phillips, 2003:713). Moreover, such behaviour has been exhibited by a relatively small minority of participants. She thus acknowledges that there is a dearth of literature that examines aggressive behaviour amongst girls.

By applying sociological perspectives to bullying, these four theories have made a fundamental contribution in explaining how the social environment impacts upon bullying behaviour and how it is allowed to continue. Yet it must also be acknowledged that whilst these studies have been used in the context of explaining bullying behaviour, for the most, they focus on delinquent behaviour. Bullying however, is part of a continuum that involves delinquent behaviour and these studies draw upon the broader form of delinquent and disorderly behaviour, including bullying behaviour. Thus the above theories cmanating from the sociological perspective have one notable factor; they all emphasize the negativity in all social aspects, such as in social relations, socio-economic climate, culture and gender stereotyping and how this can explain for bullying behaviour. Furthermore, examining bullying from these sociological perspectives is important, particularly the social control theory, as they combine both the social psychological approach with the sociological approach in order to explain bullying.

The main purpose of the social control theory is that it allows an understanding of negative relationships young people have with adults and society, for example, parents and teachers, and how these relationships are more likely to cause young people to perpetrate in bullying behaviour. Therefore, acting as a preventative theoretical form, the social learning theory allows for an understanding that a positive relationship with adults and a willingness to participate in legitimate activities in schools can reduce the likelihood of individuals engaging in bullying behaviour.

The social disorganization theory makes a relevant contribution by explaining the role of poor social and economic environment and deprivation and subsequent low levels of community efficacy and informal social control in producing bullying, which hinders the community from monitoring bullying behaviour. This coupled with an unenthusiastic school, produces a negative impact upon young people therefore that allows bullying to thrive. A further significant contribution made by the social ecological theorists is that it reveals how the negative social and cultural environment has a negative impact on young people or their development. This is depicted mainly through the factors that constitute a disadvantaged neighbourhood. The neighbourhood also has been discovered to influence young people's bullying behaviour in schools. The social ecological theory also acknowledges the individual psychological factors; therefore, combining individual and social structures, presents a fuller theory. Through exploring gender stereotyping, hegemonic masculinity explains that societal attitudes are revealed to be the driving force for bullying and the continuation for bullying.

The above studies have attempted to explain bullying by addressing both the social psychological individual factors and the sociological social structural factors. However, rarely have studies combined the two, other than the social ecological theory. This enables for a deeper and fuller understanding of bullying behaviour. Furthermore, peer influence is a key factor throughout all theories. In the power-based model, peers influence the bullying by approving such behaviour;

yet, under this model, more emphasis is given to the perpetrator who largely bullies in order to impress peers. With the social learning theory, peers who witness and encourage the bullying influence such behaviour as they allow the bullying to continue. With the theory of mind skills, peers influence the bullying behaviour by either doing nothing and silently accepting such behaviour or by walking away. From the social control perspective, peers can influence the bullying by developing an atmosphere and culture whereby anti-social behaviour is part of the norm. The social disorganization theory however, reveals thatpeer influence can be demonstrated in a positive way through peer support and therefore prevent the bullying or by being unsupportive towards victims, therefore, allowing bullying to occur. This is not so dissimilar to the mind skills model. Within the social ecological model, areas of social deprivation both in the community and in schools, academic research has shown that disruptive pupils can negatively impact upon peers, therefore examining peer influence from a different perspective. Finally, theories of hegemonic masculinity suggest that aggressive bullying behaviour is acceptable amongst peers, particularly boys, which is similar to the power-based and social learning theoretical models. To concur with Hamarus and Kaikkonen (2008), when explaining bullying, considering the social psychological as well as sociological perspectives, this also better informs anti-bullying prevention and intervention measures.

Peer Relations and Bystanders

There has been much interest in peer relationships and mainly their roles as bystanders, particularly with regards to the impact they have on school bullying and victimization (Salmivalli, 1999; Atlas and Pepler, 1988; Rigby 2003). For the purpose of this section, bystanders will be examined in the context where negative actions, that is, the will to do nothing, occur at secondary level education and bare no connection to the socio-economic climate of the school or neighbourhood environment. Thus, it can be suggested that since the socio and economic environment does not adversely affect negative bystander behaviour manifested in the school environment, a poor school ethos therefore, can determine how peers interact with each other (Gini *et al.*, 2008).

A number of studies have previously examined the bully and victim relationship; however, it was not until the mid to late 1990s when researchers began to take the presence of bystanders as an important factor. Atlas and Pepler (1988 in Reid *et al.*, 2004:243) discover that in 85% of cases peers were drawn in to the bullying process to varying degrees either through active participation or as passive bystanders. Atlas and Pepler (ibid) acknowledge that various roles were developed by individual pupils, including: (i) the assistants of the bully, who are direct supporters and actually assist by joining in (Sullivan *et al,* 2005:19; McLaughlin *et al.,* 2005: 19); (ii) the reinforcer of the bully, where peers support the bully by passively watching, laughing and jeering and thereby encouraging the bullying to continue (Rigby, 2004: 99); (iii) the outsider type of bystanders, where peers do nothing but watch the bullying and in their silence and neutrality, appear to condone and approve of the behaviour, as well as appearing immune to it (Sullivan et al 2005: 20) and (iv) the defender of the victim, where peers directly confront the bullies with an intention to stop the act (McLaughlin *et al.,* 2005:19). Yet by and large, categories (ii) and (iii) appear most common in schools (Cranham and Carroll, 2003).

Indeed, it is possible that bystanders, in witnessing the bullying may also become distressed by their inability or failure to take any action against the perpetrator, potentially leading to learned helplessness (Cranham and Carroll 2003:114). Although their behaviour could be seen as external to the bully/victim paradigm, their presence contributes to the event (Cowie, 1998). Similarly, those who witness the bullying and do nothing fall within the power-based, social learning and hegemonic masculinity theories (Olweus, 1991; Cranham and Carroll, 2003; Rigby, 2004; Goodey, 1997; Phillips, 2003). In witnessing bullying behaviour (outsiders), bystanders have considerable power as this reinforces the bullying behaviour and indirectly encourages the perpetrator, which negatively impacts the victim. Allowing the perpetrator to bully not only indicates to the bully that this behaviour is acceptable, this also condones bullying. Furthermore, this can be linked back to the theory of hegemonic masculinity where society tolerates aggressive bullying behaviour, especially physical aggression amongst boys (Goodey, 1997). If peers join in, yet do nothing, they are still maintaining this power balance. This characteristic is identified in the power-based, social learning and mind skills theories, particularly, the power-based theory.

The passive action of a bystander allows for bullying to carry on uninterrupted, regardless of whether bystanders are greater in number than perpetrators, as is often the case (Cowie, 1998 in Crantham and Carroll 2003: 113). Evidence of the frightened passive bystanders has also been reported in various studies. For example, Rigby and Johnson (2006: 437) claim that it seems most likely that in a real bully/victim situation in the presence of bystanders, unanticipated contingencies might dissuade children with good intentions from actually intervening (2006). Similarly, Baldry (2005:31) refers to this type of bystander as 'outsiders' who do nothing, remaining outside the situation. Roldider and Ochayon (2005), discuss that a somewhat larger proportion of bystanders are prepared to ignore what is going on. In contrast, Hazler, (1996 in Ma *et al.,* 2001), identifies younger and older females more likely than older males to intervene on behalf of victims (defender of the victim by intervening by directly confronting the perpetrator to stop the bullying, a positive bystander role, associated with social control theory). Halzer (1996 in Ma *et al.,* 2001) asserts that passive bystanders may actually find enjoyment in witnessing others' distress (reinforcer of the bully). Reinforcing bullying by encouraging the behaviour can be associated with the power-based and social learning theory as indications of bullying to be accepted as well as social tolerance of the behaviour. Whilst these studies contribute in their explanation of why many bystanders remain passive, what is absent from these studies are examinations of the aggressive behaviour types that occur in the schools, and the subsequent lack of intervention by peers.

One study that examines aggressive behaviour types is a review of the importance of indirect aggression by Garandeau and Cillessen (2006). Supporting the work of Sutton and Smith's (1999) study of bullying and the theory of mind skills, they argue that the discrepancy between anti-bullying attitudes and pro-bullying behaviours lies in most students feeling pressurized by peers not to thwart the aggression (2006: 616). Whilst the aggression is positively correlated with perceived popularity, it is negatively correlated with social preference (Vaillancourt *et al.,* 2003). The fact that aggressive children are not well-liked, may mean that their peers are unlikely to believe the rumours they are told and that instead, fear of ridicule and exclusion may be the main motive to acquiescence (Garandeau and Cilessen, 2006: 616). However, aggressive pupils who are less well liked are prone to be bullied. Yet what has not been examined in the above studies is the role of the school and how far the school attempts to foster a positive environment for all pupils. This is particularly relevant as fostering a positive atmosphere would include schools encouraging pupils to act in positive roles as bystanders to intervene in the bullying act and report the bullying incident whenever it may occur.

One way that schools can foster a safe environment suggests Salmivalli (1999: 454), is by studying bullying in school in the social context of the peer group, thereby, viewing bullying as a group phenomenon which is largely enabled and sustained by peers. Yet Salmivalli does not consider the social climate and ethos of the school contained in her sample. Whilst her suggestion is relevant, this theory remains incomplete without gaining an understanding of attitudes of the school towards promoting and implementing anti-bullying preventative and intervention measures. Rigby and Johnson (2006:425) assert that promoting an intervention action on the part of student bystanders witnessing peer victimization is currently seen as a promising way of reducing bullying in schools (2006) (Please also see Appendix 6-9 for modules and classroom based activities on the positive role of bystanders). This can be linked back to the social control and social disorganization theories which both promote preventative actions in order to reduce bullying behaviour. Rigby and Johnson's (2006) research, conducted in Australia, show a considerable variability in the reported readiness of students to intervene to assist victims of bullying. However, pupils from primary schools express more willingness to intervene than those from secondary schools (2006: 437). Many academics (Reid *et al.,* 2004; Naylor and Cowie, 1999; Gini *et al.,* 2008; Craig *et al.,* 2000) explain that whilst most bystanders at secondary level education feel extremely uncomfortable for not intervening, and feel sympathetic towards the victim, their fears of becoming the next target of bullying overshadow their feelings of guilt in failing to support the victim. Charach *et al.* (1995 in Reid *et al.,* 2004) suggest that the low rate of peer intervention may not reflect apathy, but rather a lack of effective strategies. This indicates a weakness in the schools' attitude towards promoting a safe and happy environment. It is crucial that students need to feel confident in their own skills to intervene and know that they will have the support of teachers (Craig *et al.,* 2000b).

It is without a doubt that bystanders hold much power in preventing a bullying incident from occurring, or effectively intervening when it is happening (Sullivan *et al.,* 2005). This realization of the full extent in the power held by bystanders is acknowledged by Salmivalli. In one of her earlier studies conducted in 1996, she asserts that "children are reasonably aware of their participant roles in bullying, although they tend to underestimate the results of their participant roles in active bullying" (Salmivalli *et al.,* 1996: 5). Sullivan *et al.* (2005) claim that bullying is usually a group activity that flourishes with an audience. If the peer group rejects bullying, then it will be directionless, without direction or a leader, there will be no bully. Sullivan *et al.* (2005) however argue that attitudes are difficult to change unless it is strongly encouraged and supported by the school. As set out in the social control and social disorganization theory that promotes effective intervention by peers and the community. However, Salmivalli and Sullivan *et al.* (2005) are limited as they fail to examine the attitude of the teachers in schools. Gini *et al.,* (2008) are one of the few studies to attempt to establish a connection between peer relations, bystanders and the school environment. This study contributes as it acknowledges that social factors such as adherence to peer group norms, homophily and social identity concerns might also contribute to inter-group conflicts and aggressive conduct among peers (Gini *et al.,* 2008: 618). Unfortunately, this is only briefly discussed and without sufficient differentiation between the roles of the bystanders. Despite this limitation in the right direction since it demonstrates that students' perceptions of bullying and their sense of safety differed according to school type thereby acknowledge the relevance of social contextual factors (Gini *et al.,* 2008).

To sum up, this section identifies the various roles that peers perform as bystanders in bullying. The academic research clearly shows that bullying is by and large unable to take place without their presence. Nevertheless, despite bystanders having such a strong influence over bullying with the power to prevent it, many lack the courage and motivation to intervene or support the victim, due to their fear of becoming the next target. Academic research that provides recommendations for prevention and intervention programs reveal fundamental flaws and prove to be ineffective unless they also consider the social climate of the school as well as the neighbourhood. Each program must be designed to suit the needs of the particular school. An examination of individual characteristics of bullying, victims, peer relations as well as the social structural factors of the school and neighbourhood will effectively inform appropriate preventative and intervention measures as well as encourage schools to foster a positive ethos. This can be linked back to the social ecological theory (Espelage and Swearer, 2009; Elliott *et al.,* 1996; Chaux *et al.,* 2009) which argues that the cultural characteristics of disadvantaged neighbourhoods contribute towards peer interactions and particularly bullying behaviour.

Summary and Discussion

From the review of the research on school bullying, three key findings emerge. First bullying has been demonstrated to be a contested concept that involves a variety of behavioural acts that include verbal and physical acts of aggression, violence, harm, disorder and delinquency. Whilst negative behaviour from young people can be placed within a broader spectrum of delinquency and disorder, bullying behaviour is also part of this behaviour which occurs not only within the school, but also outside of the school. Whilst national based literature assist to suggest that the concept of bullying includes the traditional direct as well as indirect, academic literature that examines the international perspectives allow for bullying to be perceived as a contested concept. Much of this depends upon how young people experience bullying and through these experiences they construct bullying as it means to them. Thus there is more emphasis from the international perspective to view aggressive behaviour as bullying rather than also considering indirect forms of behaviour as is considered in the UK. The complexity in the concept of bullying therefore exists as aggressive behaviour can also be perceived as delinquent behaviour rather than bullying.

Second, although the individual social psychological perspectives offer an insight into the bully and the bully's individual characteristics, there is a need for a more holistic approach in order to draw upon the victim, offender and place. Thus, the sociological perspectives assist to broaden an understanding of why bullying occurs by discussing the social and economic background to the bullying environment and of peer and neighbourhood links. Particularly the sociological perspective (social control theory; social disorganization theory; social ecological theory and masculinity); reveal how the socio-economic deprivation in the home and community can contribute towards explaining bullying by focusing largely on delinquent behaviour that exists in such environment. However, through a broader spectrum, this delinquent behaviour includes bullying behaviour and discussing the social deprivation, high unemployment and crime rate, this allows for an understanding to the bullying problem that occurs in the school. They also emphasize the negativity in all social aspects, such as social relations, socio-economic climate, culture and gender stereotyping and that this can explain for bullying behaviour. Furthermore, the sociological studies disclose that in such negative and disorderly home and community environments, the school ethos are less likely to be as positive than those that are located in a more affluent and middle class environment. By considering both the psychological and sociological perspectives, this can also inform for an efficient anti-bullying preventative education as it needs to focus on the particular environment of the school and community and what is most appropriate to the school.

Third, there is an important need to understand the multi-faceted roles which peers play in relation to bullying. They can have a negative or positive impact on victim's psychological and physical wellbeing. Yet crucial to this examination of peers is to consider the socio-economic and structural factors which argue that disadvantaged neighbourhoods contribute towards bullying behaviour and academic research in this area is limited. Examining schools with a poor ethos is largely determined to have a negative effect upon how pupils interact with each other and studies that consider the socio-economic and structural factors of the school and community environment assist in an understanding of negative behaviour amongst peers and particularly bystanders. Furthermore, additional research into this area assists to open up a forum, in which young people views and perceptions on bullying; appropriate measures to prevent bullying can be given greater attention, which the social psychological literature omits.

Whilst the sociological perspectives have assisted in providing a broader understanding of bullying and its causes, crucial to this literature search is an exploration of how the broader sociological studies on racism provides an understanding to the nature and motivation of racist bullying in schools. This is discussed in the next chapter.

CHAPTER 2

Racism, Bullying and the School Response

Introduction

RACIST BULLYING IN schools is a somewhat contested as well as a complex problem. Where the existence of bullying has been more widely recognized by schools, the manifestation of racism has been downplayed. Unlike the previous chapter which drew upon and was greatly critical of the individual nature of research into bullying, this chapter explores in much greater depth the importance of the wider sociological literature in order to develop an understanding of racist bullying. This is achieved in two ways. First, the chapter begins by examining the research carried out on racist bullying in schools (Troyna and Hatcher, 1992, Connolly and Keenan, 2002, Kailin 1999). Yet from studies such as these there is a strong indication that a broader review of racist victimization is required in order to allow for a rich theoretical framework within which racist bullying can be understood. Much academic research on racist bullying in schools, fails to address issues relating to the historical context of racist bullying. Such a failing is a particular shortcoming in the literature and a leaves a gap in our understanding of why racist bullying occurs. It provides a deeper understanding into white people's attitude and hostility towards the presence of minority ethnic groups occurring from the late 19th and early 20th centuries, to the present day. Furthermore, an examination of the historical context allows for an understanding of how such racist prejudice and hostility has evolved as Britain, in particular has rapidly become multicultural.

An examination of the broader literature on racist victimization allows this research to draw upon the historical analysis, contextual and structural issues as most studies on racist bullying in schools acknowledge racism, but existing outside the of context of history. For example, white people's perceptions of why 'other' people are here. Moreover, it is important to examine the context in which the socio-economic and demographic locations of which racism exists in the literature as the findings from this study are located by exploring the social-political and demographic characteristics in which each school sampled are situated within. In doing so, a set of explanations for racist violence in the broader sense are provided by exploring the literature of racist violence and harassment. The chapter examines a variety of ways in which schools have responded to bullying and racist bullying. In doing so, the literature acknowledges the vast contribution research has made to supporting schools and developing systems and policies. The research acknowledges that for the most part, responses can be assembled into two categories aimed at (1) pre-empting or preventing bullying and (2) responding to/punishing the bully. It develops an argument that the more holistic approach given, the greater the potential is for an effective prevention and response to bullying in order to create a safe and happy environment for all pupils.

The chapter is structured as follows. Firstly there is a critical review of the academic research on racist bullying which begins with an official definition on racism. This section continues with a discussion of the nature and extent of racism in schools and the impact upon victims. This is followed by a review of the broader sociological literature on victims, in particular how incidents are under reported. Secondly the chapter critically explores the literature on racist bullying, racist offending and offers a historical analysis to provide an understanding for the motivations for racist perpetration. Finally the chapter looks at government policy and legislation on bullying and racism and how schools respond to them.

Racist Bullying and Victimization

Much of the academic literature on school racism concentrates upon the self-reported evidence of bullying and the incidence of victimization. Few studies however, discuss pupils' perception of bullying and racism. Furthermore, in comparison to the academic research on the wider issues of race, including the historical context on racism (see introduction); the academic research undertaken and written about racist bullying in schools is limited. The main purpose of the studies used here is to provide a review of work carried out in schools, indicating three main issues. First that measuring the extent and prevalence of school racism is problematic due to the extent of survey research, second, for the most, schools downplay the existence of racist bullying and there are signs of condoning racist behaviour, which subsequently indicates a third issue, that much underreporting exists.

The official definition for racist bullying is:

"The term racist bullying refers to a range of hurtful behaviour, both physical and psychological, that makes a person feel unwelcome, marginalized, excluded, powerless or worthless because of their colour, ethnicity, culture, faith community, national origin or national status." (DfE 2010: 18).

Updated in April 2011 (Department for Education, 2011; 384) the DfE has enforced that under the Race Relations (Amendment) Act 2000 (RRAA), which amended the Race Relations Act 1976, schools and LAs and other public bodies are now required to:

- eliminate unlawful racial discrimination;
- promote equality of opportunity;
- promote good relations between persons of different racial groups.

Academic research confirms racist bullying as involving both verbal and physical abuse. Verma *et al.* (1994:20), state that Racism and Racist Bullying, ". . . can take a variety of forms. It can be personal and direct, as in the case of racist name-calling. It can be social and discriminatory against whole groups. It can be institutional, hampering in perhaps the most insidious way . . ." Existing research repeatedly asserts that name-calling is the most common form of racist bullying or peer victimization and that being excluded from social groups is also a common form (Kelly and Cohen, 1988; Smith and Shu, 2000;

Whitney and Smith, 1993; Veland *et al.,* 2009). Barter (1999:20) indicates that all ethnic minority pupils who complain about experiencing bullying in school describe it as racist bullying which, primarily include name-calling, teasing and harassment.

Identifying and examining the nature of racist harassment and bullying in schools has primarily been established in the work by Barry Troyna and Richard Hatcher, (1992:49). Particularly, their research has given much authority to qualitative research methodology. They clearly demonstrate that there is a range of very different factors that tend to precipitate racist harassment and that such harassment cannot be understood without being located within the context of a range of wider social processes, practices and events (Tryona and Hatcher, 1992:49). By developing a model to demonstrate a particular way to locate racist name-calling (See Figure 1, pp 55), this enables the authors to develop a distinction between ideologies based on theory and ideologies based on interaction. In addition, the model has enabled them to locate racist name-calling and racist name-calling incidents through the use of two axes. One, which represents the user's racist beliefs and racist attitudes, and the other, that represents the user's interactional repertoire ranging from racist to non-racist. Where the interactional racist goal is not to persuade, Troyna and Hatcher suggest that pupils are not racist, although pupils' use of racist terms, has resulted in offence and hurt.

THEMATIC RACIST

Use of racist name-calling which expresses racist attitudes	Non-use of racist name-calling by children who have racist attitudes
INTERACTIONAL RACIST	**NON-RACIST**
Use of racist name-calling by children who hold racially egalitarian beliefs	Non-use of racist name-calling by children who hold racially egalitarian beliefs

ANTI-RACIST

(Tryona and Hatcher, 1992: 76. Figure 1: Model for Locating Racist Name-Calling)

Developing critical thinking, it is found that racist name-calling most commonly exists in schools, but the racist beliefs caused racist name calling by young people emanate from the home and in the community. A further argument made by Troyna and Hatcher is that where schools lack in anti-racist policies, with young people developing their own anti-racist strategies. However, Troyna and Hatcher have not been able to qualify this. Interestingly, Troyna and Hatcher refer to another study Hartman and Husband (1974 in Troyna and Hatcher, 1992), whose work examines racism and racist attitudes by investigating it in the neighbourhood, locality and community and has found much social exclusion (1974 in Troyna and Hatcher, 1992: 142). The very fact that Troyna and Hatcher acknowledge that much of young people's racist belief emanates from the attitudes in the home and community, but decide to only focus on incidents occurring in local Asian shops limits their data findings. They do not consider the socio-economic factors of the home and issues' relating to another form of racist bullying that is, social exclusion as a result of social background disadvantages. Whilst this comparison adds to an understanding of where racist tension derives from, it is not a complete perspective.

One study that may open up a forum to this discussion, is that by Veland *et al.* (2009) whose research is based upon a study of 7,372 students in grades 5-10 (aged 11-16) in a representative sample of Norweigan compulsory schools. The study has aimed to examine the relationship between students' reported socio-economic status (SES) and their perceived social inclusion (SI), particularly refugee pupils from various minority ethnic groups, forming 2.3% (Veland *et al.*, 2009: 515). Where the SES and SI affect how pupils perform academically, their study reveals that lack of material wealth and in particular with MEG's the language barrier ultimately increases the existence of racist perpetration, namely through social exclusion. From their result findings, it suggests that additional social background disadvantages intensifies the effects of SES on a perceived social inclusion in school (Veland *et al.*, 2009: 525). Two main limitations can be applied to this study however; first there are obvious methodological limitations as this study is carried out using quantitative research only. More so, it does not take into account teacher's attitudes towards racist bullying and this could provide a possible explanation to the under-reporting and poor relationship the working class pupils from minority ethnic groups had with the teachers. Second, repeat victimization is not measured accurately as the sample size that could inflate correlations is too small.

Further to the nature of racist bullying found in schools, Whitney and Smith (1993:3) have sampled over 6,000 pupils from 17 junior, middle and 7 secondary schools in Sheffield. They report that 15% of non-white primary school children and 91% of non-white secondary school children in their sample claim to have been called racist names (1993). Yet in Smith and Tomlinson's survey (1989: 62) of 18 multi-ethnic secondary schools in different parts of England, they have found that just 1% of parents mentioned 'racial attacks', leading them to conclude that "there was little indication of overt racism in relation to pupils or between pupils and staff" (1989). Their study reveals that physical attacks were rare. These figures from their 1989 survey refer to participating students from primarily Afro-Caribbean and Asian and South Asian ethnic minority groups who have been targeted by white pupils. In contrast, name-calling has been found to be common in Kelly and Cohen's study (1988:21). Their study indicates that racist name calling and harassment permeate everyday relationships in a Manchester school, suggesting that the frequency of racist bullying through name-calling is very high. Current academic research strongly indicates that this is an increasing problem and that incidents are very much under reported.

One such study that substantiates this argument is that conducted by Woods (2007:7) where racist bullying appear on a continuum from racist name-calling, through to social exclusion (2007:7). Her research is conducted at a primary school in West London, 'Woodhull Green', and she incorporates interviews with children, questionnaires with adults and participant observation in the classrooms, playgrounds and afterschool club. Woods' main argument is that whilst conducting the fieldwork, she had witnessed 13 incidents of racist behaviour, which were both direct and indirect. Ten involve one child insulting or swearing at another. Whilst the wider academic research reports less on the impact that racist bullying has on victims than it does for regular bullying, studies, such as Woods (2007) are important as they clearly articulate that the creation and maintenance of an environment of harassment can take place through a range of differing forms of behaviour. Yet Woods considers that language and accent difference does not resonate with larger tensions in the same ways that religion in the 21st Century does, however, this is debatable. Language and accent amount to as much tension as religion as this research and previous studies suggest (see Veland *et al.,* 2009). Despite this, religious discrimination is rapidly growing and much of the anger targeted towards such groups, in particular Muslims, has been reinforced by the media's distorted view of recent world events. Oka (2005:29) reveals that the media portrayal has had profound effects upon how Muslims are viewed by many of the British public and as such, are more vulnerable to racist bullying than other ethnic minority groups. During the coverage of 9/11, the U.S. media has demonstrated how it could suddenly reshape people's knowledge about 'others' and people's notions of citizenship in public and private spheres. This ability to reinforce old or hidden suspicions has had a profound effect on society's consciousness and conceptions of 'normality', and therefore, suggests that for many of the British white society, Muslims being terrorists is now perceived as normal (Oka, 2005: 29).

Studies that have attempted to measure the extent of racist bullying in schools have been critical in that they do not accurately represent victims experiences, particularly those subjected to repeated victimization (Connolly and Keenan, 2002, Verkuyten and Thijs, 2002). A gap in the data also indicates a gross amount of under reporting in schools. In the UK Smith and Tomlinson (1989:3), have followed a group of 3,000 children in 18 multi-racial comprehensive schools, for five years up to the age of 16. This was conducted using surveys with them and their parents (Smith and Tomlinson, 1989). Their findings reveal that school effectiveness found little evidence of racist bullying and hostility in particular amongst pupils aged 12 and 13 (1989:305). Yet Gillborn and Gipps (1996 in Gillborn 1997:355) are critical of Smith and Tomlinson's study. They argue that there are limitations to survey-based methods that explore harassment (See also Connolly and Keenan 2002). They do however, support Troyna (1991), as their work suggests that racist bullying is not only under reported in schools, but also in surveys. Gillborn's (1995:133) study, which combines surveys, interviews and observational approaches in two secondary schools has been carried out at approximately the same time as Smith and Tomlinson's (1989) study. His study explores the effectiveness of quantitative research on racist harassment and the academic achievement of ethnic minority pupils. In contrast to Smith and Tomlinson's findings, Gillborn suggests that "racist attacks (usually, but not always, verbal) were a regular fact of life for most Asian pupils" (1995:78). To concur with Verma *et al.* (1994:19), who point out, what is really lacking is hard evidence of the size and extent of any racial problems which might exist. Troyna, (1991), also argues that the failure to obtain such hard evidence is due at least in part to the very research methodologies that have been employed.

Another significant study that highlights the inaccuracy of measuring the extent of racist bullying in schools is that of Connolly and Keenan's (2002:341) research, which is carried out in Northern Ireland. Their study draws upon in-depth interviews with a total of 32 children and 43 parents, who have been chosen from the four largest minority ethnic groups in the region of Belfast including: Chinese, Irish Travellers, South Asians and Black Africans. Their study indentifies that racist harassment is a significant problem in schools and include varied forms of racist abuse from physical and verbal abuse to more covert and subtle forms of teasing and 'friendly' banter. Furthermore the teachers' overt racist attitude suggests that such behaviour is condoned by the schools (Connolly and Keenan, 2002). For example, 66% of those who interviewed attend mainstream schools and reveal that they have been called racist names with half reporting that this occurs on a daily basis or rather frequently (Connolly and Keenan, 2002).

The extent of school racist bullying is also examined by Verkuyten and Thijs research (2002:311) through questionnaires administered to pupils attending 182 classes and reported findings from research conducted in 82 primary schools across the Netherlands. A total of 3,806 children are involved in the study and the sample include 1,641 of an ethnic Dutch background, 612 who were Turkish; 463 who were Moroccan and 135 children who were Surinamese. 49% were girls and 51% were boys (Verkuyten and Thijs, 2002:316). Using a multilevel analysis, their main aim assesses the extent of racist victimization among different ethnic groups in relation to school (de)segregation and multicultural education. They focus upon the degree of experience of racist name-calling and social exclusion among 10 to 13 year olds (Verkuyten and Thijs, 2002:311). It is acknowledged that in many Western countries, there is a growing concern about racist attitudes and behaviour among children, aged 10 to 13, both at schools and in neighbourhoods. However, little is known about the extent of racism and whether it is a widespread phenomenon (Verkuyten and Thijs, 2002:310). There is a lack of large-scale studies on racist bullying in schools, furthermore, Verkuyten and Thijs (2002) report that ethnic minority children are more often victims of racist name-calling and social exclusion than Dutch children. They also suggest that, in all ethnic groups, fewer children report experiences of racist bullying as they believe that if they told their teacher about it the teacher would react.

Examples of the extent of school racism outside of the UK also emphasize methodological problems in accurately measuring the prevalence of school racism. Again, this refers to questionnaires and survey research. A few studies conducted in the US have argued that a major weakness with survey research is that they do not accurately represent victims of racist bullying similar to those in the community, and that questions need updating in order to probe more questions that allow for more detailed answers (Bonilla-Silva and Forman, 2000). Another US study by Kailin (1999:727) focuses upon the perception of white teachers attitudes towards the problem of racism at their school, Lakeview High School. Data is gathered from workshops and classes and also through the use of questionnaires. Kailin (1999) discover that nearly all of the respondents (i.e. teachers) answer the question or pose the problem in Black and White terms. This study shows relevance as Kailin acknowledges that very little research has been carried out that examines teachers' perceptions and understanding of the prevalence and manifestation of racist bullying at the school. A major criticism of the teachers is that they live in racially segregated areas, thus suggesting that teachers are far removed from students of different colour. However, as Kailin reveals, white teachers do little when they witness racist attitudes and when questioned, become defensive in their reply, believing they are powerless to intervene, thereby indicating that they feel victimized (Kailin, 1999:730). As there is no discussion of how racist prejudice manifests around the school, measuring the extent of racist bullying again proves to be a problem. This study therefore raises three important issues, first that there were narrow perceptions of racism as a Black/White issue; second a degree of racism exists amongst teachers and third and most importantly, according to Kailin (1999) there is an unwillingness for the schools to tackle racism. From this, there is a great need to improve upon teachers perceived and impaired consciousness, only then with a deeper understanding of culture, their perceptions would reflect upon an improved anti-racist education.

Whilst it is clear from these studies that racist bullying in schools most commonly exists through name calling and also through social exclusion, discrepancies lie within poor measurement of the extent. Most studies utilize quantitative research through survey research and questionnaires and this has been criticized for not documenting repeat victimization properly. Particularly, surveys are more likely to under-record incidents of racist bullying. Furthermore, beyond noting the tendency for name calling and social exclusion as forms of racist bullying, surveys say very little about the experiences of the victim. Not only does research acknowledge prejudice amongst teachers and/ or those who downplay the existence of racism in their school, there is a widespread acknowledgement of under reporting. Furthermore, these studies fail to explore in any real depth, young people's voices, victims' experiences and the impact that racist bullying has upon them. There is therefore, a fundamental need for more qualitative research into examining school racism as well as a need for deeper understanding amongst teachers and improved strategies when applying the school anti-racist policy into practice. As Troyna and Hatcher, (1992:200) conclude in their research, schools have little impact upon changing the attitudes of pupils and anti-racist education needs developing upon in order to offer pupils with real experiences assisting in addressing and interpreting such experiences. Furthermore, from Connolly and Keenan's (2002:341) research findings, this clearly emphasizes a need for more effective anti-racist measures and the lack of social cohesion and interaction with white pupils that were found at these schools, only enhances the problem of racist bullying. Finally, one argument which can be drawn from the work by Verkuyten and Thijs, (2002) is the suggestion that the extent of racist name-calling and ethnic exclusion is affected by actual practices more directly than through formal aspects of multicultural education (Verkuyten and Thijs, 2002).

There is a dearth of literature on school racism that explores young people's perspectives of racist bullying, therefore there is a need to focus on the broader sociological research on racist victimization in order to allow for a rich theoretical framework within which racist bullying can be understood. Even still, few qualitative studies explore the views, perspectives and attitudes towards racist bullying by young people. This includes issues that relate not only to the nature of racist bullying, but also the motivations for it. Missing from academic research is a broader perspective on young people's moral viewpoint as well as their understanding towards victims of racist bullying. Therefore, it is important to examine studies of racist victimization that are not merely confined to young people in order to indicate the impact that racist bullying is likely to have. There is also limited research that examines victims' experiences of racist bullying.

Racist Harassment and Victimization

Due to the inadequacy of research into racist bullying, the inclusion of these studies attempt to broaden our understanding on victim's experiences and impact and draw similarities with the literature on school racism in relation to repeat victimization. A similarity that can be drawn through these studies to the research on school racism is that as the frequency of racist victimization was high, it can be implied that this contributes to gross under reporting.

Victims are identified through four dimensions as to how they experience racist harassment and violence (Rai and Hesse 2008:218). These are; multiple, cyclical, secondary and spatial victimization. Multiple victimization is experienced through a variety of verbal and physical violations that are directed against victims personally as well as their property. Victims also experience various forms of racial harassment in different places. Thus, cyclical victimization can be even more distressing (2008: 219). Victims are subjected to racial harassment over a varying period of time including confronting different Asian and Black individuals and families at random periods. Secondary victimization however, is experienced after the crime/ incident itself. (Rai and Hesse, in Spalek 2008: 220). This, as Rai and Hesse suggest, occurs when victims report their incidents and receive negative and unhelpful responses. Spatial victimization, involves Asian and Black people who develop mental spaces of areas that they perceive to be racially acute, that is, areas perceived to be unsafe and those that are safe to move around in. (Rai and Hess, in Spalek, 2008: 221). Subsequently, they argue that despite Asian and Black individuals and/ or families experiencing different forms of racist harassment, the impact that these experiences have upon victims are extremely traumatic and psychologically damaging. In the literature on school racism, space and risk areas have not always been clearly distinguished, yet there have been much written on multiple victimization and namely that it occurs primarily through verbal racist name calling and exclusion (Woods, 2007; Verkuyten and Thijs, 2002; Veland *et al.,* 2009).

It is acknowledged in academic research (Bowling, 1993), that survey data and official statistics are limited in what they can say about the extent and nature of racist crime and a major criticism is that they inadequately measure racism, especially documenting repeat victimization. This is quite synonymous with the limitation in academic research on school racism. Hall's study (2005:60) analyzed racist hate crime incidents in England and Wales between 1996/97 and 2002/03 and shows particular relevance when discussing locality. He reports that there had been 48,525 recorded incidents and discovered that in England in particular, the higher rates of racist hate crimes exists in metropolitan areas, in particular, London, West Midlands, Greater Manchester and West Yorkshire; while fewer incidents occurred in rural areas (2005). Within the Metropolitan areas, recorded racist incidents between 1998/99 and 1999/2000 have risen from 11,050 to 23,346. One main explanation for this is that there is a greater concentration of minority groups in larger cities; however, Hall also attributes police practice as a contributing factor (Hall, 2005). Yet Ray and Reed's (2005:213) study show a comparison to these high rates of hate crime. They note that in semi-rural areas, such as Kent, where a high ethnic minority, refugees and asylum seekers population exists, the rates of racist violence are lower, however, they identify that ethnic minorities are more likely to encounter overt racism (Ray and Reed, 2005). Whilst statistics reveal very little about racist victimization other than providing recorded figures, Hall draws upon the work by Docking, Keilenger and Paterson to reveal that male victims of racist incidents report being victims of racist hate crime which involved violence, whereas female victims report being the recipients of racist threats and harassment. Docking Keilenger and Paterson (2003 cited in Hall: 60) also reveal that where the police record these incidents, the majority of victims did not know their attacker (2005: 61). Incidents would occur near the victims' home, their place of work or their school. Therefore, Hall's (2005) conclusion is not so dissimilar to Connolly and Keenan's (2002) argument that racist victimization generally occurs as victims go about their daily lives as discussed earlier. A further observation that can be made is that for those victims who did report incidents, this was most likely not the first racist event to have occurred.

As there is a tendency for most victims who experience racist violence and harassment to either not report their experiences, or not initially, surveys identify the issue of under reporting as well as for the broader need for qualitative research (Rai and Hesse 2008:205). Similarly, the literature on school racism also reveals that there is a lack of reporting by victims of racist bullying and highlights the weaknesses in survey research (Verma *et al.*, 1994; Tryona, 1991; Verkuyten and Thijs, 2002). Bowling's study (1993: 231) is particularly poignant as he suggests that surveys tend to reveal racial victimization as an incident, arguing that this is not the case as such victimization is more dynamic and complex. His 1998 study conducted in North Plaistow based on a sample size of 1,174 residents reveal that approximately 114 (70%) of the 163 respondents complete a victim questionnaire. However, three incidents are recorded in detail per victim, although not all subsequent incidents have been recorded (1998:192). Bowling therefore criticizes surveys as they can inaccurately measure data. Not only does he press for more qualitative research in order to capture victim's experiences, Bowling emphasizes that a combination of quantitative and qualitative research would effectively document repeat victimization, therefore providing a deeper understanding into victims' experiences.

Further advocates for qualitative research are Chahal and Julienne (1999:1-2), whose work examine the effects of racist harassment and the ways in which black and minority ethnic people develop strategies to manage and reduce the incidence of racist victimization where they lived. Part of their research cover the experiences of seventy four young people from primary to middle school level in Belfast, Cardiff, Glasgow and London, using focus groups and in-depth interviews. Being made to feel different in a variety of social situations and locations is largely seen as routine, and in some instances expected as this became a common form of everyday activity (Chahal and Julienne, 1999:1). Further evidence suggests that when speaking with victims, their reported incident is not the first racist incident to have occurred. Reporting is viewed as a strategy only when victims feel that they could not tolerate any more harassment and abuse, and that the problem is becoming more serious and even life-threatening, or that there had been serious property damage and physical attack (Chahal and Julienne, 1999: 4). In addition, Chahal's (2008: 22) recent research examines case work practitioners who work with victims to empower them to speak out about racist incidents that occurred in their home. Her study reveals that the levels of non-reporting of incidents remain high and victims eventually report their ordeals after a series of incidents, with victims fears continuing and developing (Chahal, 2008). Sampson and Phillips' (1992: 5) research is conducted on an East London estate where racial attacks and harassment incidents are high amongst the Bengali and Somali community. Their findings are similar to Chahal (2008) in that incidents are recurrent and grossly underreported to the police. What is particularly poignant about these studies, in addition to highlighting underreporting, are that they evidence to a degree, victims experiences and perceptions of racism and the impact it has upon them.

Further evidence of under-reporting derive from the key findings from the 1988 British Crime Survey (Maung and Mirrlees-Black, HORS, 1994:1), which reveal that racist harassment largely appears through verbal abuse and indicate that incidents went largely underreported. Afro-Caribbeans and Asians workers were significantly vulnerable to a variety of forms of racist victimization. Yet, the 1988 British Crime Survey indicates levels of verbal abuse by the public against workers to be most common and similar for both ethnic groups (1994). Of the ethnic minority workers who are verbally abused, about half the incidents involve racial insults (Maung and Mirrlees-Black, HORS, 1994). The findings also reveal that 29% of ethnic minorities report racially motivated crimes to the police compared with 55% of white victims (BCS 1998 in Knight and Chouhan 2002: 108). This reinforces the claim that the majority of victims of racist bullying are reluctant to report their ordeals thereby revealing a weakness in accurately measuring repeat victimization. This can be compared with the studies on school racism where victims' experiences were also more frequent and inaccurately documented. Further to this, findings from the 2000 British Crime Survey reveal that incidents of racially motivated crime take place over a period of time and largely appear as verbal abuse due to the use of racist language (Clancy *et al.,* 2001:31). Additionally, the findings from the 2004/2005 British Crime Survey reveal that reporting racist incidents to the police, particularly amongst the Asian community is low. 83% of BCS Asian respondents state that they do not report crimes to the police because they believe that the incident is considered to be "too trivial to report", or that the "police could do very little about it", followed by "the incident was thought to be a private matter and/or dealt with privately" (Jansson, 2005/6: 29).

On considering the impact that racist victimization has, it has been argued that fear and risk of being a victim shape how people interact with the wider environment (Chahal and Julienne, 1999:3). Chahal and Julienne (1999) indicate that there tends to be a reluctance to leave the home, allow children to play outside and reluctance to go out until later in the evening. Furthermore, they assert how Black and Ethnic Minority communities would become anxious about when the next racial attack/incident would occur. Further implications on health are another factor to consider as it has been suggested that being a direct victim of racist harassment/bullying has a profound impact on health and well-being (Chahal and Julienne, 1999). During their interviews, they discovered that although the majority of individuals were not physically attacked, the consequences of racist victimization had changed their lives. This added to the sense of isolation and lack of support the victim generally felt, particularly if they were living in predominately white estates (1999:3). Similarly, findings from the British Crime Survey 2000 (Clancy *et al.,* 2001:37), indicate that the impact on victims from minority ethnic groups from racially motivated incidents are generally more severe compared to those of non-racially motivated incidents. Victims are reported to be in either a state of shock, anger or feeling fearful. This is significant as it shows how quantitative and qualitative findings are able to support each other. This study shows further significance as it raises the issue of victims' personal revelation of the impact that racism has upon their lives, an area that is lacking in the research on school racism and racist bullying, one which this research attempts to accomplish.

The main purpose of exploring racist victimization in the broader sociological research is to enable a deeper understanding of racist bullying in schools. Whilst these studies draw parallels to the research carried out on school racism, namely similarities in the nature of racist bullying (verbal and exclusion), methodological problems with quantitative research limited findings and inaccurately measuring victimization, especially repeat victimization and finally the issue of under-reporting. However, where these studies have allowed for a subtle yet rich theoretical framework within which school racist bullying can be understood is through an understanding of young people's perspectives and the victims' experiences and through a discussion of the impact that racist victimization has. There is a dearth of literature on racist bullying in schools, however, existing literature emphasizes that racist bullying occurs and exists largely through the racist name calling. Much of the literature on school racism fails to document how the victim is feeling and what they experience during the racist incident. There is also little discussion on the impact this has upon victims which these studies provide, namely the fear and risk that repeat victimization has, such fear that has forced victims to make lifestyle changes, such as perceived risky locations, in order to avoid being victimized again. Moreover, our understanding can be developed further by drawing upon the research on racist victimization, often from a sociological perspective, as it allows us to understand further the socio-economic and geographical environment which racism occurs and how these factors contribute towards why racist perpetration occurs. Yet whilst the literature on racism touches upon victims' experiences, this is still limited. There is therefore, a greater need for more research to be conducted that utilizes a combination of quantitative and qualitative research methodologies to explore largely young people's perceptions as well as exploring victims' experiences of racist violence and harassment.

Racist Bullying and Offending

The previous section has reviewed the nature and extent of school racism, identifying methodological limitations, and a lack of research that explores victim's experiences of racist bullying and the impact. The section also provides a deeper understanding of the wider sociological contexts within which school racism exists by exploring broader studies that examines racist victimization in the community. This section however, looks to the broader sociological research that explores the motivation for racist perpetration through racist offending, as there is nothing specifically on racist bullying in schools that adequately examines why racist bullying occurs. Therefore, an examination of perpetrators rationale for racist violence and harassment informs racist bullying. Whilst there remains a weakness in accessing adequate interview samples, the data however, would be beneficial to undertake strategies for dealing with racial harassment and violence. Currently, victims of racist bullying are perceived as contributing towards their own victimization rather than there being a psychological problem with the perpetrator, as was the case in the previous chapter which explored bullying.

In general, there is limited range of literature that clearly explains the motives of racist perpetrators. There are various opinions that help explain why racist bullying occur. First racist perpetration is motivated by a fear of unknown cultures. Sibbit's (1997) work is one of the earliest research studies carried out on racist perpetrators, motivations and the context within which perpetration was carried out. Particularly so, Sibbit's work is important as her study suggests that racist bullying is a manifestation of, and reaction to, racism on a broader scale. Similarly, the academic research on school racism indicates that young people's racist behaviour and perceptions originates from a broader spectrum of racist ideas emanating from the home and wider community, and subsequently young people have been influenced by such racist prejudicial ideas (Tryona and Hatcher 1992; Connolly and Keenan, 2002). Furthermore, whilst Connolly and Keenan's research identify that verbal racist name calling was the most common form of abuse to occur at the school, they also found that the school failed to effectively challenge pupils' racist behaviour (Connolly and Keenan, 2002:353). They also found that schools fail to acknowledge that racist bullying was a real problem and did not respond to incidents in a sensitive manner and failed or teach against racist behaviour with positive messages, the schools instead remained neutral, which only encouraged racist perpetration to continue (Connolly and Keenan, 2002). Sibbit's study had been carried out in London using primarily qualitative research methodology and based upon a review of the existing literature and case studies in two areas. Out of 64 interviews, Sibbit interviewed three identified perpetrators comprising of one woman aged 57 and two men, aged 17 and 22. The other 61 interviews had been carried out amongst staff from various agencies including the police service; housing department, local education authority, youth service, probation service and Race Equality Council. The findings identify three ways in which racist attitudes are conveyed from generation to generation (Sibbit, 1997: ix). With young people in primary school to earlier years in middle/secondary school, racist bullying and attitudes are expressed mostly through racist name-calling, primarily with the desire to hurt. This suggests that this may be due to attitudes coming from home. From teenager to young adult (15-18 year olds), the manner of carrying out racist bullying/harassment is mainly through physical and other violent acts. The attitude conveyed again is with the desire to hurt, but also to entertain and be entertained (1997). The final group examined was that of pensioners who lived on council estates, where racial attitudes were embedded in racial prejudice for a variety of reasons. As many have witnessed changes to the country, there is a lack of acceptance of the influx of minority ethnic groups. There are also prejudicial attitudes derived from ignorance of minority ethnic culture and lifestyle. It can be suggested from Sibbit's (1997) findings that this lack of knowledge became apparent due to a certain fear of such groups. Furthermore, this particular age group hold racist attitudes towards minority ethnic groups, as scapegoats. In their perceptions, the presence of such groups was the prime cause for all the country's problems. The pensioners' role in racism therefore, was to pass on racist attitudes to the younger generations.

Sibbit's study is strong when examining this concept of fear of unknown cultures as the data is gathered from a wide variety of ages that reveal prejudicial attitudes based upon unknown cultures and identities. Furthermore and due to this, the white communities feel a loss of their British white identity. Missing from this research however, are adequate responses from self-confessed racist perpetrators. The study also fails to consider the broader foundations upon which race and racism is built in order to provide a historical understanding of why racist prejudice and perpetration occurs.

One broad foundation in which race and racism is built includes the socio-economic situation and geographical location of communities which contributes towards explaining for racist perpetration. Where there is socio-economic deprivation bordering on poverty, the greater the risk will be for racist perpetration. This historical assumption assists to explain why racist bullying and violence occurs as inequality breeds hatred, particularly where the hatred is directed towards individuals due to their difference in race, but also ethnicity, which can be linked back to Veland (2009), who associates racism in schools to socio-economic deprivation. Poverty allows for minority ethnic groups to be used as scapegoats for the working class people's lifestyle. It is also suggested that young people with criminal past are most likely to racially perpetrate. Webster's (1994) survey reports the experiences of crime and racial harassment amongst young people in the locality of Keighley, West Yorkshire (1994:7). Webster's (2007:86) review of racist violence and harassment suggests that past research has paid less attention towards the motives and characteristics of racist perpetrators and indicates that racist perpetration can be explained by examining the social and economic background of the perpetrators, in particular young offenders. Where extreme poverty, high unemployment and poor social transitions of the white lower working class youth into the employment sector is found in the North East of England, there is a stronger chance for racist prejudice (Webster 2004:34). His study reveals that even though young adults are motivated to work, some experienced high levels of social exclusion which resulted in poor future prospects, especially in relation to the employment sector (Webster, 2004:3). As young adults were hindered by de-industrialization there is a decline in any decent stable jobs thus, their poor economic plight assists in shaping their perpetrating behaviour (Webster 2004). This indicates that poverty, inequality and unemployment can lead some white people to look for scapegoats to explain for their position. There is an indication that geographical location strongly determines for racist perpetration amongst certain age groups as Webster asserts:

"The best evidence about racially motivated crime and harassment suggests that south Asians and Afro-Caribbeans are at considerably higher risk than white people of being victims of a number of kinds of crime. To some extent, this is because they fall into demographic groups (such as the young) which are at higher than average risk" (Webster, 1994: 36).

Thus in addition to the assumption of racial superiority, Webster has identified a new risk for racist perpetration linking age and geographical location, which is an important identification. Yet this is only one study which raises such issue.

Upon reflection, since young offenders are suggested to most likely racially perpetrate, is there an association to their aggressive behaviour towards minority ethnic groups and perpetrating behaviour? Hewitt (2005:19) agrees with Webster and further suggests that where those non-white communities are increasingly becoming socially and economically independent, the white community, in particular, the lower white working class increasingly felt like the 'underclass' (Hewitt, 2005:19). Yet since Webster acknowledges that survey methods reveal weaknesses, accurately measuring racist offending and repeat victimization remained problematic as the sampling size for self-reporting is weak. A further limitation to this research is the geographical location; Webster's study is confined only to the North of England. Is racist perpetration therefore higher in the northern part of England compared to the south of England? These studies whilst explaining the motivation behind the perpetrating acts, they do not deliver explanations beyond the act. Ratcliffe (2004:16) identifies that people of different races, i.e. white and non-white assume inequality and that this serves as a justification and legitimate grounds for differential treatment and argues that colonialism and 'racial' equality are incompatible because of 14th and 15th century historical race thinking. Where much significance is paid to skin colour and facial features, black therefore, is linked with dark, dirty and evil, whereas white is associated with purity and goodness, white communities were less interested in even wanting to know people from other races (Ratcliffe, 2004). Such deeply embedded thinking remains to the current day and this would explain for the racist perpetration especially in areas where poverty and inequality exists. Again and similar to Sibbit (1997), integration was essential in order to alleviate people's fear of the unknown culture.

Racist perpetration is also suggested to be borne out of the notion of unacknowledged shame. Based upon their findings from interviews that had been conducted amongst racist offenders from Greater Manchester, Ray *et al.* (2004:350) argue that offenders' shame is deep rooted in "multiple disadvantages and that rage is directed against south Asians who are perceived as more successful, but illegitimately so, within a cultural context in which violence and racism are taken for granted". Racist offenders, therefore, are more ashamed of themselves and their lifestyles when viewing what immigrants have accomplished in their lives and this subsequently acts as the main driving force to commit acts of racist violence (Ray *et al.*, 2004). In one research study conducted by Ray and Smith, (2002:6), they claim that such attacks are exceptions rather than the norm among acts of racist violence because the victim is not known by the perpetrators, however, the focal point is that the victim is chosen because of their membership of a social group.

They continue to suggest that perpetrators of racist violence believe that the success of the South Asian community upsets the natural hierarchy of races. However, the authors make clear that acts of racist violence are not solely motivated by racist attitudes; indeed they suggest that the perpetrators' feelings of shame need to be examined in more detail (Ray *et al.,* 2004:355). Where racist perpetration is part of a wider pattern of criminality and where unemployment or poorly paid jobs, casual or insecure work is high, it can be implied that an underlying idea exists where there is a thread of racism behind the racist perpetration (Ray *et al.* 2003a: 117). This takes form when some of the white communities believe that they are superior to the non-white community. This attitude includes the belief that they deserve a better lifestyle and should receive more state help than the non-white community, especially the minority ethnic groups, asylum seekers and refugees. Furthermore, for many of the white British community, there is a sense of the white culture losing their power to the overwhelming presence of BME and ethnic minority groups and the richness of their culture. Where a gap remains in their work, is to explore attitudes of unacknowledged shame in young people at schools. Considering the complexities when examining the concepts of 'race' and 'ethnicity', it allows for a deeper understanding of how individuals, especially racist perpetrators have developed their way of thinking in relation to other groups and in particular why they believe that they are better than others. This notion of hierarchy of races is the basis for stereotyping, as suggested in the work of Ray and Smith (2002). Ratcliffe (2004:27) argues that ethnicity is more to do with language, religion, identity, national origins and/or skin colour. Yet the problem remains where ethnicity is confused/mistaken for with culture, especially the culture in different localities. The point of ethnicity lies in who we are, how we identify ourselves, but also that identity in other people and how they perceive 'us' to be (Ratcliffe, 2004). Thus, where particular members of the white community perceive their race to be superior to the non-white, witnessing a better lifestyle for those who are not of the same race becomes a challenge to accept and consider unfair. This therefore, helps to explain as Ray *et al.* (2004) do so why racist perpetration is caused by unacknowledged shame.

Racist perpetration is also explained through perceptions of preferential treatment amongst the non-white community. This is a current and common perception towards minority ethnic groups being at an unfair advantage over the white working class community. For many of the white British community, they have witnessed vast changes not only in the country, but also in their local neighbourhood and community and such changes have been difficult for many to accept. For example, Cockburn (2007:547) explores issues of racial identities of young male supporters of the political far right in the North of England. Ethnographic and retrospective interviews demonstrate that the participants in his research felt that they were 'hard done by' and this notion can be strongly associated with this attitude due to their lower working social class background. Yet Cockburn (2007:550) also points out that the young men are capable of being empathetic and sympathetic towards ethnic minority people. They are also capable of forming positive relationships with others and therefore, his research is significant in that it shows that polarization is possible amongst the younger generation. However, participants also emphasize a feeling of being overwhelmed by minority ethnic communities and show resentment towards refugees and asylum seekers as they perceive that they are receiving preferential treatment and 'more than their fair share'. This suggests that these groups are seen as a threat to both their economic well-being and sense of identity. There is also a popular belief that prejudice and prejudicial attitudes derive from parents (Cockburn, 2007:551), as the young men had revealed that their parents did not challenge or change their prejudicial attitudes. This echoes the work by Sibbit (1997) who also emphasizes that racism is motivated by the influence of the family and white people's resentment towards the success of the non-white community. Thus, can this feeling of resentment amongst white working class young people be classed as racism as they are influenced by prejudicial attitudes derived from their community? Therefore poverty and inequality breeds feelings of social ills and a lack of integration. Young people are not born racist, yet develop an attitude of white defensiveness. Where this perception of white people feeling victimized in their community/country has developed, this thinking has been used as an implement in an attempt to restore a form of dominance. As Nayak (2003: 172) argues,

> ". . . it could be that it is whiteness and Englishness that is being called into question . . ." and Mercer (1994:259) also states ". . . identity only becomes an issue when it is in crisis, when something assumed to be fixed, coherent and stable is replaced by the experience of doubt and uncertainty".

This is particularly significant as 'whiteness' used to be associated with relative privilege and a higher status than that granted to the non-white community. As can be related to the work by Woods (2007) and Oka

(2005), much of the racist perpetration drew upon the foundations of fearing the 'unknown' culture of minority ethnic groups and particularly towards the Muslim community.

Another way in which racist perpetration can be explained is the through the lack of social cohesion amongst both the white and non-white communities. A fundamental complaint from white communities is the failure of minority ethnic groups to integrate positively and a lack of positive community development and social harmony (Gilroy 2002). Furthermore, a lack of acceptance of other cultures increases social disharmony. In this context, the concept of integration to the white community revolve around the idea where the minority ethnic communities are expected to integrate and assimilate, whilst accepting and celebrating cultural diversity has not been considered by the white communities. To agree with Gilroy (2002:42) this is a 'new racism'. He states that the novelty of this new racism falls within discourses of "patriotism, nationalism, xenophobia, Englishness, Britishness, militarism and gender differences into a complex system which gives 'race' its contemporary meaning" (2002: 42). Thus, the social and educational learning of British schools has now changed, with the influx of newly arrived immigrants, refugee and asylum seekers. Crucial to this is that schools now teach anti-racist and multicultural education with the intention of promoting inclusion of all pupils. Integration presently includes mixing and acceptance of all cultural diversity including the British culture. Whilst the concept is a new one, this has not been so far removed from ideas on integration as discussed in the earlier parts to this section. That is, whilst anti-racist education and multicultural education promote against prejudice, equality and inclusion of all, this does not necessarily imply that people's conception of superiority of race and hierarchy of race may necessarily change. As cultural diversity may be embraced by the white/ non-white communities, personal preferences as to which race is more superior may remain the same.

In order to better understand the history of racism and offending which in turn can help to understand the history of racist bullying, academics such as Epstein (1997:11) note that racist perpetration is largely caused by widespread reaction to the rapid demographic changes amongst the British population since the 1960s and many communities inability to come to terms with this. Furthermore, the report asserts a particular level of blame upon the politics of immigration control and media coverage when referring to racial prejudice and how it influences the public (Epstein, 1997). For example, the report suggests they enhance racist sentiment and violence among white people who subsequently view 'immigrants' as the source of their own problems. This reveals how people find scapegoats to blame for their situation, and focus on visible newcomers at the same time as seeing their scapegoating legitimized by the state. This can be concurred and related to the work by Smith (1989) and Hesse *et al.* (1992) who have argued that various white working class neighbourhoods have prevented ethnic minorities from settling within their community by intentionally excluding them. Such an action can be agreed by Gordon (1993:52) who perceives this social exclusion to be an expression of racism and such exclusion not only has manifested within families and the community, however also through institutional racism, for example through agencies such as the police (Gordon 1993). This historical assumption of racial superiority assists to understand why this causes racist bullying in schools. The lower white working class community similarly fail to understand the presence of large numbers of the minority ethnic community, and along with issues of socio-economic deprivation, this acts as a justification for racist prejudicial ideas. Therefore, young people are able to react to such ideas through racist perpetration. Where racial prejudicial ideas become deep rooted, racist perpetration therefore becomes more justified. A fundamental difference in the hierarchy of race is that in this context, racial superiority is developed/influenced by the socio-economic environment, where poverty is the underlying factor of racial prejudicial ideas.

Furthermore, Layton-Henry (1992) has described how the continuing campaigns against immigration to Britain in the 1970s and 1980s, along with the increased publicity and activity of the National Front; create a climate of hostility towards black immigration and immigrants. This in turn may have presented some groups as more 'legitimate' targets for those who were predisposed towards violence. In this context racism perpetrated through racist violence is primarily instigated through the notion of why are immigrants present in the country and the hostility is further deep rooted. Thus, a fundamental link exists between the motives of racist perpetration is the idea of using minority ethnic groups as scapegoats in order to account for the poor social and economic position of the white working class community. Where resentment against minority ethnic groups existed, this was further aggravated by unemployment and underachievement. Similar to Sibbit (1997), this study also fails to consider the broader foundations upon which race and racism is built. Therefore, to Mason (2000:7), the concept of race is characterized on human diversity and difference and this conception become deeply linked to the notion of hierarchy in which all differences both history and future potential were seen as a product of biological variation. Even as far back as the early 18th Century, such difference has been used in order to justify for slavery. Race was more than just about human differences; the relationships were characterized by an unequal distribution of power and resources (Mason 2000). Therefore, to refer to Sibbit and Epstein, witnessing an influx of 'non-white' population with difference in lifestyle and culture in a country that inherently was indigenous white, was a cause for prejudicial thinking and a justified cause to blame immigrants for all social and economic problems. The concept of integration in this context would less likely occur due to white people's hostile reaction to the sheer presence of minority ethnic groups and the lack of willingness to accept them into their community. Whilst ethnicity has overtaken the 'physical' connotation of race, racist thinking still remains. Yet the recognition of the term 'ethnicity' has indicated, as argued by Back (1996), that it is essential to acknowledge diversity and difference. This view can be also related to Sibbit's argument that much racist perpetration occurred due to the fear of unknown culture.

Bullying, Racism and School Response

UK Legislation

Prior to the 1990s there has been limited support around bullying in schools and no legal requirement by the government to implement any anti-bullying initiatives. The 1990s saw much progress (Department for Education, 1991-1994), and along with academic research (Olweus, 1993; Smith and Sharp 1994; Rigby, 2002; Cranham and Caroll, 2003 and Smith 2004) increased resources for schools followed. The then Department for Education (1991-1994), which became the Department for Schools and Education, (DfES) in 1994, developed an anti-bullying resource pack called 'Don't suffer in silence' for schools. This had been established in September 1994 and was designed to improve the programmes for containing school bullying. It was followed in 1999 by a legal requirement for schools to have some form of anti-bullying policy as there had been a great deal of publicity which led to increased public and political pressure on schools to be seen to be doing something about bullying (Samara and Smith 2008: 671).

In 2000, the DfES officially launched their new Don't Suffer in Silence 2000, anti-bullying pack, which was substantially updated from the 1994 version and contained new ideas and practical techniques for schools (DfES Summary, 2005: 1). Overall, it recommends that schools should work on a 'whole-school' policy. The 'whole-school policy' includes four main steps; awareness raising; consultation; implementation; and monitoring and evaluation. This approach had also been recommended in the 2007 Anti-Bullying Guidance for Schools—'Healthy Schools, Healthier Living and Learning' (2007), which combined reflections on research undertaken by academics from the University of York in 2006, commissioned by the Children's Commissioner, with practical advice on how schools can tackle bullying through different anti-bullying approaches. (DCSF, 2007:8). The Government's vision for children's services also led to the publication of the 'Every Child Matters' consultation paper, in September 2003. The aim of Every Child Matters is to reshape children's services to help achieve the outcomes which children and young people informed them were key issues to their well-being in childhood and in later life. These outcomes, which have appeared on each 'Every Child Matters' report, stipulate that every child, whatever their background or their circumstances, should have the support they need to be healthy; stay safe; enjoy and achieve; make a positive contribution; and achieve economic wellbeing (PSA 2008: 3).

In June 2007, the DfES officially changed its name to the Department for Children, Schools and Families (DCSF). The first ever 'Children's Plan', was published with a vision for change to make England the best place in the world for children and young people to grow up. As a result, in September 2007, the DCSF launched their latest anti-bullying guidance for schools entitled *"Safe to Learn: embedding anti-bullying work in schools"*. The DCSF clearly state in their guidelines that all children ought to be able to learn in a school environment free from bullying of any kind and in which they feel safe and supported (DCSF, 2007). Under this guidance, Children's Services Authorities are required to make provision to promote co-operation between the authority, its partners and others with a view to improving the well-being of children in their area (Sc 10 (1) and (2) Children Act 2004). This includes children's physical and mental health and emotional well-being, protection from harm and educational and social well-being (Sc 10 (2) CA 2004) in (DCSF, 2007: 14). Guidelines from the Department for Children, Schools and Families 2007, strongly recommend that schools adhere to and implement the principles in the 'Bullying—A Charter for Action' document, which provides a framework for self-evaluation, in order to develop their anti-bullying policies. The Charter recommends that schools discuss, monitor and review bullying, its definition, characteristics and what the school is doing to tackle the issue. They are required to support everyone in the school community by identifying and responding to bullying; the Charter also recommends that schools ensure that pupils are aware that all bullying concerns will be dealt with sensitively and effectively. Furthermore, it suggests that schools ensure that parents/guardians who express bullying anxieties are taken seriously. Finally, schools should learn from effective anti-bullying work that is carried out elsewhere, for instance, the voluntary sector (2007: 8). This charter shows how schools can develop a whole school policy in order to deal with bullying. The DCSF published a report from the original 2007 Children's Plan, (2009:5), in which it was suggested that school bullying should be tackled by a range of mechanisms that should (1) pre-empt or preventing bullying and (2) responding to the bully.

Most recently, the DCSF changed its name back to the Department for Education (DfE) in May 2010 under the new coalition government. In July 2010 the DfE published their latest research report in which they reveal that the range of characteristics relating to bullying is wide and complex (DfE, 2010:4). From their findings, they place a greater emphasis upon schools to follow policies and reduce bullying further and provide more support for young people, particularly asserting "A greater although somewhat more difficult ambition would be to increase understanding and tolerance of diversity in the classroom and reduce the victimization of those who are different" (DfE, 2010:4).

The government also considers that an understanding and tolerance by pupils is key to tackling racist bullying. This has also been supported by the research findings, particularly, Connolly and Keenan (2002); Troyna and Hatcher (1991); Verkuyten and Thijs, (2002); Woods (2007) and Kailin (1999). Furthermore, under their latest guidance report for schools (Department for Education, 2011:1), which now replaces previous advice under the 'Safe to Learn: embedding anti-bullying work in schools, head teachers now have specific statutory power to discipline pupils for poor behaviour, including bullying that occurs outside of the school premises. Where bullying outside of the school is reported to school staff, the schools have a duty to investigate and act upon such reported incidents (DfE, 2011:2).

Thus, with this in notion of understanding and tolerance in mind, the latest Equality Act 2010, came into full force from April 2011 in England and Scotland and spring/summer 2011 for Wales. This replaces all previous existing equality legislation such as Disability Discrimination Act and Sex Discrimination Act, (DfE 2010), but recently re-enforced the Race Relations (Amendment) Act 2000 (RRAA), which amended the Race Relations Act 1976. In April 2011, the Equality Act now provides a single legislation that consolidates and covers all forms of discrimination that is unlawful, in order to provide a simple law for schools to follow. Under this Equality Act, the duty relates to eight 'protected characteristics, which are: age; disability; gender; race; religion or belief; sexuality; gender reassignment; pregnancy and maternity. For schools however, age is exempt from the duty (Anti-Bullying Alliance, 2010). According to the recent brief from Anti-Bullying Alliance (Anti-Bullying Alliance 2010:3), it is claimed that currently equality and diversity are 'limiting judgment' and that if schools do not fulfil these measures, it can restrict their overall inspection grade. From the Equality Act, schools therefore have specific duties to ensure that equality and diversity are not met with any discrimination. Schools are therefore liable for the actions of its employees unless they are able to prove that 'reasonable steps' have been taken to prevent discrimination, both direct and indirect discrimination, harassment or victimization taking place, which includes issues to do with bullying, but especially so for racist bullying. The Equality Act further allows schools to tackle such issues by taking a positive action approach using resources and/or bespoke approach to actively promote equality and diversity as well as providing support for disadvantaged groups (Anti-Bullying Alliance, 2010).

In relation to schools and decisions for when to use sanctioning, the Department for Education (Anti-Bullying Alliance, 2011:16) has clearly stated that the case of exclusion should be used towards those who perpetrate only. In their guide to school governors, the DfE state that it is unlawful to exclude any victims of bullying or harassment, even if this exclusion is carried out unofficially in justification that it is for the well being of the victim. Furthermore, excluding a victim is deemed unlawful even if the bullying has been systematic and the school was unaware of the recurring incidents (Anti-Bullying Alliance, 2011).

Since 2006, schools across England have been able to apply for and if they have met all the criteria, they can be awarded an Anti-bullying award and be accredited the status for achieving good practice for anti-bullying. Two out of the three schools sampled in this study have already been awarded and accredited for good anti-bullying practice (for a full discussion of procedure and criteria, see chapter 3). Drawn directly from government initiatives in the Bullying—A Charter for Action, 2003, the award is based on the recognizing the schools efforts and positive results in its anti-bullying policy and practice development (Newcastle City Council, 2007:3). The main criteria which all schools must have before they can apply for the award are having a healthy school status and a minimum of grade two in their Ofsted report in the following areas: the extent to which pupils feel safe; the extent to which pupils contribute to the school and wider community; the effectiveness of care guide and support; the effectiveness with which the school promotes equal opportunity and tackles all forms of discrimination and the effectiveness with which the school promotes community cohesion (Newcastle City Council, 2007). The third criteria now are how the school deals with the policies under the new Equality Act and the new enforced Race Relations (Amendment) Act 2000 (RRAA).

Under the latest Education Act, the White Paper (Miles, 2011:42), further encourages head teachers to take a strong stand against all forms of bullying and therefore asserting more authority and responsibility to the schools. The latest Equality and Human Rights Commission report

(EHRC) launched a major research report on prejudice-related bullying in UK schools with an intention to establish what local authorities do to prevent and respond to different forms of identity-based bullying in schools and discovered that racist bullying was the most widely recognized and addressed of all forms of bullying as a result of statutory duties and government guidelines (Miles, 2011). Yet Miles argues that since the White Paper proposes to give more authority to schools, in practice, head teachers will encourage more sanctioning such as exclusions which is less satisfactory. Where the Equality Act promotes further positive preventative action, Miles further adds that such procedures should include recording and reporting incidents to the local authority to monitor what is happening at a school, local authority and national level. At present, schools only have a duty to report incidents of racist bullying (DCSF 2009). To agree with Miles (ibid), there needs also to be clear provisions with prevention measures and that exclusion should be a last resort, as Miles asserts: "The role of prevention links also to the provisions on curriculum, and in particular to the provisions on curriculum, and in particular to the proposals on Citizenship Education and PSHE" (Miles, 2011:43).

Developing a Holistic and Restorative Approach to Preventing and Responding to Bullying

The wider academic literature broadly discusses how schools have become increasingly aware of bullying, yet adopt a bureaucratic approach in order to ensure that they are protected against accusation of allowing bullying to intentionally occur, code of conduct and care of duty. As to agree with Smith *et al.* (2008:10) who concur with Woods and Wolke (2003), there is a need to know if schools are willing to engage with a process of policy review and improvement and whether anti-bullying policies are little more than false piety to legal requirements, or whether they do have some resonance to the entire school community and its practice. Smith *et al.*'s (2008:2) findings indicate that from an analysis of 142 school anti-bullying policies from 115 primary schools and 27 secondary schools, over all schools only had up to 40% of the anti-bullying items in their policies. This 40% were from an anti-bullying policy scheme with 31 categories and were divided into 4 sections; (a) 11 categories concerning the definition of bullying; (b) 11 categories concerning the reporting and responding to bullying; (c) four categories concerning recording bullying and evaluating the policy and (d) five categories on strategies for preventing bullying (Smith *et al.,* 2008: 6). Missing from the policy lists were coverage of responsibility beyond those of teaching staff, follow-up of incidents, management and use of records and specific preventative measures, such as peer support (Smith *et al.,* 2008:2). This therefore reiterates the above question about schools willingness to fully become involved in eradicating bullying. Developing within this, academic literature have attempted to offer a more holistic, that is relating to incidents and experiences of bullying and a much more restorative approach to the theory of bullying, yet not all schools undertake this, as indicated by Smith *et al.* (2008). Whilst there has been a shift to developing more holistic and restorative approach, for the most part it has been pre-emptive and post experience response to bullying. The wider academic literature argues that the more holistic teaching approach given by schools, the greater the potential for an effective prevention and response to bullying in order to create a safe and happy environment for pupils. On the other hand, the use of punishment and sanctioning as an immediate response to bullying is necessary also. Schools that often issue sanctions when pupils have broken school rules, include bullying (Rigby 2002). These often include depriving pupils of certain privileges, detention or in severe cases, being suspended or excluded from the school. Minor sanctions often include the bully being required to apologize to their victim and arranging appropriate compensation for example, if property has been damaged. From this literature it must be questioned where would the effectiveness in the use of holistic and restorative approach to bullying be found? Would this result in fewer incidents of bullying or racist bullying? Furthermore, to what extent is this all associated to what research is found and what young people say?

Prevention or pre-emptive education can be construed as action taken to prevent an incident from occurring. Schools therefore implement a variety of preventative methods to stop bullying. These have taken shape through developing an anti-bullying programme within the curriculum which include teaching pupils what constitutes bullying, harm caused to victims, exploring how pupils can support the victims and each other and identifying who victims can approach to get help. Activities have included role plays, team work, hands on activities such as drawings and videos followed by discussion with the class. Schools also distribute questionnaires to pupils which provide reliable data on bullying incidents while pupils remain anonymous (Samara and Smith, 2008). Preventative work has also included outside researchers/youth workers who work with pupils in small groups. In addition to this, some schools may implement preventative measures through providing individual support to pupils in the form of counsellors, mentors and nominating peers to support each other. There are some schools that place teachers on anti-bullying training courses and there are organizations such as the Anti-bullying Alliance that provide in-service training to teachers against all forms of bullying, Insted and local anti-bullying organizations, such as Newcastle Response team deal with schools in the Tyne and Wear area.

There is a universal belief that a positive school environment prevents bullying and harassment from flourishing (Hazler, 1994; Barone, 1997). Furthermore, effective schools encourage students to interact positively with teachers, and set up tougher sanctions against bullying (Barone, 1997). Such approach has also allowed schools to teach pupils through emotional literacy by encouraging pupils to act as positive role models via peer support and as bystanders to intervene or prevent a bullying incident. A variety of anti-bullying resources and strategies are identified and put together by Banks, (1997) and Batsch and Knoff (1994) in order to assist schools in combating the school bullying problem. Preventative mechanisms have included support from outside workers, such as youth workers and Fekkes *et al.'s* (2005:89) research discovered that such support assists in reducing bullying as their work with pupils positively enhances their emotional well being. It is also suggested that combating bullying in schools is a long-term endeavour, requiring at least two years for an intervention programme to be effective (Andreou *et al.,* 2007; Elsea and Smith 1998). In keeping with this, Slee and Mohyla's (2007: 104) research in Australian schools examined one preventative measure called the PEACE Pack programme. This provided a framework for schools to assess the status of their anti-bullying policy in relation to policy and grievance procedures, curriculum initiatives and student social support programmes and it also provided practical resources (Slee, 2002, 2003, in Slee and Mohyla, 2007: 104). Their study results in approximately one-fifth of pupils in the overall sample reporting that they were bullied 'less' as a result of the year-long programme (Slee and Mohyla, 2007). In addition, recent research has indicated that preventative education also assists bullies from offending later on in life (Farrington *et al.,* 2011; Farrington and Ttofi, 2011 and Ttofi *et al.,* 2011). This research on school bullying has been indicated to increase anti-social tendency or violent offending later on in the perpetrator's life and that effective preventative work can prevent this (Farrington and Ttofi, 2011:91).

Academic writers who have suggested that a whole school as a form of holistic approach is one of the most effective preventative measures include Samara and Smith (2008: 673) and Olweus, (2001:259). Pitts (1999) argues that bullying thrives in an atmosphere of secrecy, where victims and bystanders fear reprisals if they report a bullying incident. Without knowledge of the incident, the teaching staff are unable to intervene to protect the victim and accordingly, they are not viewed by many pupils as an effective source of help. Therefore, members of the school community can easily become trapped in this cycle and become resigned to their powerlessness (Pitts, 1999: 121). His 1995 research examined good practices which emerged from schools in deprived areas in inner-city Liverpool and London. Particularly at secondary schools, staff/student meetings were set up, initiatives were created, a half day conference was scheduled between the whole school to discuss bullying in order to keep the issue of bullying alive and local police became involved (Pitts, 1995:vi). From this, it had been discovered that all types of bullying had decreased, yet there had been no evidence of a reduction in racist bullying. Pitts (1999) therefore, argues that, it is imperative to institute consultative exercises which enable members at all levels of the school to participate in the analysis of the problem, and the construction of a collective response to it. By encouraging pupils to act in a positive manner via using emotional literacy techniques, as well as implementing restorative justice approach, this holistic approach enables for these to be possible.

Academic literature is strong in its benefits to the use of restorative justice using a whole school approach when aiming to achieve a positive school ethos. However, restorative justice can only work with a delivery using emotional literacy teaching strategy. To be effective, restorative principles normally require the victim feeling safe and comfortable about sharing their incident in a safe forum where they feel emotionally and physically protected in the preparation for the process and during the meeting where matters are discussed (Littlechild, 2009: 5). Restorative justice also focuses upon the relationship between the victim and offender with a key aim to facilitate the healing and restoring the effects of conflicts, arguments and rifts between those involved (Littlechild, 2009; Morris, 2002). Morrison's (2002:1) framework based on restorative justice, promotes the use of the emotional literacy approach, in relation to reintegrating those pupils affected by wrongdoing back into the community as resilient and responsible members. A curriculum had been developed for year 5 pupils in an Australian primary school. Over a period of five weeks, pupils met with facilitators twice weekly and participated in various activities through poster-making through to role plays and used the REPAIR (repair harm, expect the best, acknowledge feelings, care for others, take responsibility) keys to work out how to resolve harm (Morrison, 2002:4) the findings from the study reveal a positive benefit from the programme and data indicate that the programme was able to create a difference in how pupils felt and interacted with each other in terms of the core components of respect, consideration and participation (Morrison, 2002). Ahmed and Braithwaite (2006:350), similarly suggest that a process of restorative justice should curb bullying. They argue that restorative justice theory sets, as a premise, that there is someone somewhere who can provide the right kind of emotional support for the child who is having problems and assist them to adopt good behaviour for the future (Ahmed and Braithwaite, 2006: 365). It can be agreed that through this approach, it can encourage pupils to become positive peer supporters and bystanders to intervene and/or inform teachers about any bullying incident. Whilst Ahmed and Braithwaite ideas offer positive alternatives to zero tolerance, they can be limited in the sense that they need to be relevant to the school environment. Schools that are more prone to violence may not benefit from this technique, however, would do so using a zero tolerance approach to bullying as shaming may only incur further physical bullying amongst young people (Morrison, 2007).

Conversely, research into emotional literacy reveals that teaching young people to become emotionally literate is a positive preventative tool that can assist in giving students alternatives to violence and dysfunctional relationships (Bocchino, 1999; Elliot and Faupel, 1997; Miller, 2001).

As Goleman (1995 in Sharp, 2000:9) have suggested, a curriculum that addresses topics of self-awareness, decision-making, managing feelings, self-concept, handling stress, communication through 'I' messages, group dynamics, and conflict resolution may indeed empower young people to address a climate of violence in schools. Moreover, giving students the tools of self-confidence, clear thinking and knowledge of how to handle distressing feelings may empower victims to assert themselves and may encourage passive bystanders to intervene when witnessing bullying incidents (Sharp and Herrick, 2000 in Sharp 2000:9). Furthermore, Lewis (2006:175), had found that schools that promoted the use of emotional literacy it may be crucial to create a comprehensive anti-bullying prevention programme that include a component on moral values related to bullying and victimization (2006: 231). Roffey (2008:29) carried out qualitative research in six Australian schools; her research explores the processes and practices of the use of emotional literacy teaching in relation to young people's pro-social behaviour and learning outcomes. Her study reveals that according to young people, positive changes in the school culture were as a direct result of shared relational values, a belief in inclusive practices and by maximum ownership by the whole school community in the change process (Roffey, 2008). Students who feel respected and who had experienced a positive approach in the classroom are more cooperative, thus showing the benefits of teaching through the use of emotional literacy. (Roffey, 2008: 36). Whilst using emotional literacy as a teaching strategy may allow pupils to develop self awareness and become empowered, this is also beneficial as part of school preventative and intervention measures, however, care must be taken as pupils with low social skills competence, may not necessarily benefit from this delivery style (Roffey, 2008).

It has been suggested that bystanders are able to reveal important information about bullying to school personnel who can take action on it (Ahmed 2005:23). Ahmed's study investigates the importance of adaptive shame management in encouraging bystanders to prevent bullying. Using an emotional literacy style of delivery makes this more possible. School prevention schemes target bystanders by seeking to raise their awareness that they have a responsibility towards victims, improving their strategies and making them feel sufficiently confident to intervene in bullying situations, reassuring them that they will be supported by the teachers (Craig *et al.,* 2000b). Craig and Pepler's (2001:512) research reveals that peer intervention is effective and of significant importance as it is based on naturalistic observation. During this observation they discover that peers were present 58% of the time bullying occurred, and 57% of the time they had effectively intervened and prevented the bullying from continuing (Craig and Pepler, 2001). Carney (2000:82); Rigby, (2006) and Salmivalli, Huttunen and Lagerspetz (1996, cited in Sutton and Smith, 1999), emphasize that bystanders must be targeted if schools wish to be successful in reducing bullying behaviour and pupils should be enabled to stand up for what is right (Soutter and McKenzie, 2000). From a regulatory perspective therefore, bystanders can be considered the 'soft targets' as they possess enormous preventative capabilities. Furthermore, in a whole-school approach, the soft targets are more easily moved by a sense of shame and responsibility than the 'hard targets' (i.e. the bullies), (Ahmed 2005: 28). Ahmed concludes that by empowering the 'soft targets' through teacher support, much of the bullying can be prevented at an early stage, resulting in a healthy and safe school (2005: 28).

Evaluations suggest that peer counselling practices can foster social interaction skills (Garner *et al.,* 1989) and prevent and/or reduce bullying (Cartwright, 1995). Using a whole school approach through an emotional literacy form of teaching encourages peers to act as positive role models. Carey (1997: 101) argues that peers as agents can provide powerful sources of reinforcement for learning and maintaining behaviours. Peers can model, reinforce, extinguish, and monitor behaviours even at very young ages. Salmivalli (2005: 457) emphasizes that, when it comes to bullying, peer 'counselling' has mostly been used to provide support for the victimized children. In recognition that not all pupils wish to speak to teachers or parents or guardians about such an issue, peer support systems have also been developed in which students are used to tutor, reinforce positive behaviour and to counsel or advise other pupils (Naylor and Cowie, 1999; Smith and Sharp, 1994). Lines' (2005) case study research suggests that peer counselling could be effective for relatively little money. Research suggests that peer support has a positive impact on victims (Cowie *et al.* 2008: 63). Cowie *et al.* (2008) conducted a study in four secondary schools in the UK, using questionnaires that looked into the impact of peer support schemes on pupils' perceptions of bullying, aggression and safety at school. Pupils who are aware of the peer support schemes at the school feel much safer in lessons, perceived school as a friendlier place to be, and worried significantly less about being bullied in comparison with those who were unaware (Cowie *et al.*, 2008: 70). Therefore, anti-bullying schemes that focus on mobilizing peer responsibility and supporting victims may have a role in preventing bullying in schools (Field, 1999 in Cranham and Carroll, 2003:130). Furthermore, school administrators and teachers, according to Cranham and Carroll (2003), claim that this could assist in changing the behaviour of passive bystanders by fostering the development of self-efficacy. Implementing restorative justice approach, this may also be possible with a whole school approach. These studies identify that using a whole school approach particularly through an emotional literacy delivery style is the most effective. The studies also identify that through this preventative approach, this encourages peers to act and use their power to become positive role models, as through supporting the victim through peer support, as positive bystanders, by intervening in the bullying incident/walking away/informing an adult. Whilst these studies reveal the many strengths that peers have to support victims, whether in the positive role of bystanders or as peer support groups/counselling. Yet schools that maintain a poor ethos and possess inadequate training and delivery style, foster a negative attitude amongst young people. Thus, even peer support becomes ineffective. It can be questioned therefore why little research argues for a combination of preventative/pre-emptive and intervention/punishment measures to be implemented in schools and delivered on a longer term basis.

Preventative Measures for Racist Bullying

A school's culture may not only be exclusionary regarding children's individual differences of religion, race, ability, or sexual orientation, but often, it can be a hostile environment that fosters prejudice, harassment and precludes learning (Dessel, 2010:413). Supporters of greater equality of opportunity in education advocate for preventative measures for racist bullying in schools. As discussed in the previous section, the use of a whole school approach delivered through emotional literacy would be the most efficient approach in order to effectively deal with preventing racist bullying (please also see appendix 5 module). One measure that contributes to meeting these requirements is through multi-cultural education which addresses cultural diversity and encouraging assimilation, between both the white and non-white community. Multiculturalism as taught in UK schools has tended to de-politicize questions of race and racism (Raby, 2004: 379), therefore allowing schools to concentrate on teaching to solely embrace all cultures. Mason (2000:7) agrees that multiculturalism views ethnic difference as a cause for celebration and in this way contributes to fighting against racism and in this way; it trivializes the seriousness behind the concept of difference. Furthermore, multicultural education tends to foster a celebration of difference, tolerance and understanding, an acceptance of diversity and empathy for minorities. However, it has been criticized for perpetuating divisions amongst both white and none-white cultures (Dei and Calliste 2000). The main purposes of multicultural education in schools include; teaching English as a second language; removing ethnocentric bias from the curriculum and encouraging pupils to recognize differences within groups of people. It also includes judging people on the basis of internal rather than external qualities, accepting different ways of living as equally valid and providing information about other cultures including similarities, nature of everyday life and positive achievements (Keho and Mansfield 1993:3). Thus, teaching using emotional literacy would make multicultural education possible as well as encourage assimilation and acceptance from both white and non-white pupils, rather than as a one-sided expectation from the white community. Whereas, adopting the white culture is deemed necessary for the non-white community except for their skin colour. Ratcliffe (2004: 76) acknowledges that multicultural education would be successful if pupils of different heritages understood about other pupils' ethnic, religious and cultural backgrounds. This would result in a healthier and more productive learning environment. Furthermore, it would assist in developing long term benefits to society as a whole (2004:77). However, Ratcliffe (2004: 76) criticizes multicultural education for failing to recognize the persistent significance of 'race' and 'racism'. A further failing with MCE is that it predominantly occurs in schools which have a higher percentage of ethnic minority pupils (Verkuyten and Thijs, 2003: 258).

Billings (1998:22) argues that those consistent manifestations of multicultural education in the classroom were superficial and trivial "celebrations of diversity". She argues that adopting and adapting Critical Race Theory for educational equity would mean that researchers would have to expose racism in education and propose radical solutions for addressing it (1998:22). Furthermore, Billings (1998) is concerned that rather than engaging students in provocative thinking about the contradictions of U.S. ideals and lived realities, teachers often encouraged tokenism, that is, students to sing 'ethnic' songs, eat ethnic food and learn ethnic dances. However, Troyna and Williams (1986:24) and Carby (1982:194-5) argue that multiculturalism often amounts to little more than attempts at social control. A further difficulty is that multicultural initiatives have often been viewed as having relevance only for schools with significant minority ethnic populations. There is often the view that it is not necessary for white pupils living in other parts of the country to be exposed to other cultures (Gaine, 1995). Yet, despite these criticisms of multiculturalism in practice, Mason (2000:70) argues that it represents an advance over the old assimilations models which previously assumed that minority ethnic groups would have to, in all circumstances conform to the white culture, except for their skin colour, in order to have any recognition and acceptance amongst the white community. It problematizes the curriculum and recognizes that there is an onus on the school to respond to at least the cultural needs of minority ethnic pupils (Mason, 2000). It further is able to have an independent and positive effect on students' self-esteem (Verkuyten and Thijs, 2003: 258).

Furthermore, schools are the agencies for the production of racial identities via the multicultural curricula, beliefs, values and attitude propagated (Nayak, 2003:147). However, in Nayak's (2003) ethnographic research with young people, this reveals that the school's sensitivity to racist harassment appeared to bolster a sense of white injustice among respondents which led to a feeling that such forms of 'moral' anti-racism were 'not fair'. Whilst Nayak acknowledges from his interviews that racism exists, yet so does anti-white racism and argues that this leads to a defensive attitude as he asserts: "That teachers were said to ignore claims of name-calling made by black students, yet expel white students for using racist taunts, affirmed a sense of white defensiveness" (Nayak, 2003: 147). Alongside this there was also an overwhelming feeling amongst white youths that black students had an identifiable culture that they could draw on which was denied to English whites. For example, the youths complained about Pakistani pupils talking about others in their own language (Nayak, 2003). Therefore, resentment towards minority ethnic groups can be drawn upon by two factors, first for having distinctive cultures which the white community did not understand and second, for the perceived preferential treatment amongst these groups which the white community believed was unnecessary as well as unfair.

Anti-racist education is a more radical measure to tackle racism. It begins from the premise that racism exists and includes a focus on systemic racism. Furthermore, anti-racist education recognizes intersecting forms of inequality and assumes the role of power in the perpetuation of racism (Raby, 2004). Unlike multicultural education, anti-racist education requires a political standpoint which includes an examination of the role of the school in the perpetuation of inequalities. "Anti-racism shifts the talk away from tolerance of diversity to the pointed notion of difference and power" (Dei and Calliste, 2000: 21). It has been argued that schools need to shift their focus towards a basic understanding of racial inequalities and the ways that institutional discrimination works before embarking on anti-racist education (Lane, 2008:150). Anthias and Lloyd (2002:7) assert that the focus of anti-racist education is two-pronged. On the one hand the correct response is to be taken in relation to those who are seen to require differential treatment on the basis of their special needs. On the other hand, racist ideas in the school and the media are to be tackled by making white people aware of their own racism. Yet it is important that schools need to learn how to engage in anti-racism while raising all the complex issues to do with racism, such as identifying those who are intentionally racist and dealing with racist stereotyping (Karumanchery 2005:179). Like the previous section, developing a whole school approach delivery through emotional literacy is crucial in order to allow pupils to rid of any stereotyped prejudices and hatred. These could be delivered through various classroom curriculum exercises, as well as encourage peers to support victims of racist bullying.

Pedagogically, those working in anti-racist education also aim to work throughout the curriculum, rather than simply 'adding-on' a component of anti-racist education (McCaskell, 1995). They urge teachers to reflect on their own racialized locations and involve others, such as community and parents in their classrooms. This suggests that this could assist in dealing with the lack of space for anti-racist education in the national curriculum. The use of a whole school approach in educating pupils through emotional literacy delivery could assist here. Teachers could allow pupils to reflect on their own environmental surroundings as well as in the school and encourage them to voice their opinions on what they find problematic with both the minority ethnic community as well as the white community. In the UK, Gaine (2000) had examined the outcomes of anti-racist developments in education in largely white areas in the UK between the early 1980s and 1997. It is found that cultural practices and shared frames of reference which, in white areas, need to change within the limited contexts of institutions. Gaine asserts that the "task is to change minds, shared beliefs, schools, curricula, structures, representations and all at once with potential implementation gaps in all directions. This is a practical, strategic, intellectual, political and also moral task" (Gaine, 2000:79).

The importance of raising awareness of racist bullying amongst pupils has been highlighted in academic research. Woolfson *et al.* (2004: 16) had conducted a study in one primary school in the UK and argued that as pupils became more wary of racist incidents than parents/carers, teachers/support staff, victims of racist bullying became increasingly reluctant to report. Thus, despite the school possessing a very inclusive anti-racist ethos, pupils still experienced racist bullying, and failed to report it (Woolfson *et al.,* 2004). Therefore, anti-racist education as Woolfson *et al.* (2004) argue is ineffective if it takes place in a school with a 'no problem here' attitude. This strongly indicates that despite the school's anti-racist ethos, schools with a 'no problem here' attitude may well have been failing to adopt a whole school approach more than failing to develop emotional literacy. Cole and Stuart (2005: 363) argue that schools fail to develop proactive strategies to counter the issues that they found: racism, xenophobia and ignorance. They recommend an urgent need for schools to fully abide by the Race Relations (Amendment) Act (2000) and be proactive in the pursuit of 'race' equality (Cole and Stuart, 2005). Yet again, with reference to the previous section that had discussed a whole school approach and teaching delivery through emotional literacy, this would also be beneficial for proactive anti-racist education.

Even though anti-racism has been professed to be about "rupturing the dominant power structures that continually exclude people of colour and marginalize them in this society" (Walcott, 1990:110), Hart (2009:2) argues that anti-racism through anti-racist education has led to further segregation amongst, in particular, primary school children, as their 'race awareness' has led to defensive attitudes amongst children, believing that this formal education has caused this attitude. Assimilation in this context as Hart argues could provoke further resentment towards minority ethnic groups and therefore has led to further segregation. Hart argues that this education needs to be removed from the curriculum. However, to agree with Richardson (2009:4) by ridding the curriculum of all anti-racist education, this fails to resolve the problem and that assimilation from both communities are crucial to develop a deeper understanding and acceptance amongst each other. Furthermore, the sample which Hart used to formulate his argument is not sufficient evidence on which to base such a drastic claim. Richardson concludes that rather than removing anti-racist education and multicultural education, anti-racist techniques should be improved in order to develop relations between pupils. Further incorporation of the emotional literacy style of teaching is one positive way to improve such techniques (Richardson, 2009).

It can be noted that other than multi-cultural and anti-racist education, there are few initiatives that tackle racist bullying specifically. In the UK, the voluntary organization, Kidscape (2001:1) have recommendations for preventing racist bullying in schools. They recommend that pupils should refuse to tolerate racist bullying from day one and that schools should undertake an anonymous survey of pupils in order to fully ascertain the extent of the problem and then acting upon it. Acting upon this could be by informing parents. Schools are recommended to use materials and resources to teach against such behaviour and to cover such topics during PSHE modules. In addition, the written guidelines of schools should be intended to inform pupils about their safety rights and maintain an ethos that respects and values other cultural, ethnic and religious backgrounds. Kidscape (2001) further recommends training staff and governors in equality issues, working with parents, supporting victims and changing negative behaviour and school procedures in order to resolve racist bullying (Kidscape, 2001). A consultancy organization, 'In-service Training and Education Development', (INSTED) provide in service training to teachers primarily on anti-racist bullying in schools. However, there are few agencies in the UK that support schools in dealing with anti-racism, compared to the number of organizations that work directly with schools against bullying, for example, Anti-Bullying Alliance. Over all, measures to prevent racism can be effective, when delivered with the correct attitude and with improved strategies in that they will help to develop pupils' awareness of different cultures and emphasize to pupils the importance of inclusion and equality for all. A whole school approach and reaching out to educate pupils through the use of emotional literacy learning can enable for this to occur.

It must be noted that weaknesses remain in the research on anti-racist education that argue where there is poor teaching training, often due to a lack in understanding other races, this can lead to divisions amongst young people. Multicultural education therefore can assist to understand racial cultural heritage. Yet multicultural education is weak as it obstructs what life would be like to be British, yet anti-racist education can positively allow white pupils to include pupils from minority ethnic groups and asylum seekers/refugees background and encourage positive social cohesion amongst minority ethnic groups into white society. Thus, assimilation in this respect would work as it would involve a positive cohesion amongst both the white and non-white society. Upon further reflection, it can be agreed with the research which argues that there must be a positive integration of both improved anti-racist education and multicultural education, yet not emphasized in the research; this should be implemented full time in the curriculum at schools in order to foster a positive and safe environment for all pupils. Finally, multicultural education and anti-racist education both have importance for improving relations between all pupils. Whilst multicultural education should be specifically about promoting and embracing different cultures including the British culture, and taught via classroom activities as well as through events. Anti-racist education on the other hand needs to focus more academically, but also using emotional literacy by providing a historical analysis to the background of where racism emerged, teaching by questioning and relating to pupils experiences and attitudes and challenge prejudicial attitudes with the aim to eradicate prejudice.

Summary and Discussion

In summary, this chapter critically reviews the academic research on racist bullying which primarily focuses on the nature and extent of racism in schools and the impact upon victims. This is followed by a review of the broader sociological literature on victims and victimization, in particular how incidents are under reported. Secondly the chapter critically explores the literature on racist bullying and offending offering a historical analysis which helped to provide an understanding for the motivations behind racist perpetration. Finally the chapter examines UK government policy and legislation on bullying and racism and how schools respond to them.

From the review of research on racist bullying, three key findings emerge. Firstly, there is a gap in the literature on racist bullying, particularly from a sociological perspective, however, there is much that can be drawn and learned from some of the useful literature on racist victimization and racist perpetration, which in turn allows for an understanding of the motivations for racist bullying in schools. Whilst the academic research on racist victimization offers broader perspectives from the sociological research, the key findings are the same as the literature on school racism, in terms that surveys inaccurately measures victims' experiences. Furthermore, the prevalence of racist victimization is not so dissimilar to the research carried out on school racism in that there is gross under-reporting.

Whilst the literature on school racism and racist bullying acknowledges its nature and prevalence, very little is offered as to the motivations for racist perpetration. The sociological research on racist perpetration offers a broader understanding to these causes and there are a number of factors that contribute towards racist perpetration. The historical analysis allows for an understanding that there is a hierarchy amongst races and where the white race is always considered being pure and therefore above all other races. The academic research on school racism can also be understood through the sociological research that discusses a fear of unknown cultures. This lack of understanding towards other cultures breeds racist perpetration primarily as the white community feel and fear a loss of their own white British identity and witnessing an influx of minority ethnic groups where little is known about religious and cultural differences enhances the likelihood for racist perpetration. From this, lack of social cohesion amongst both the white and non-white communities and where the non-white are expected to conform to the British way of living, contributes towards the causes for racism.

Secondly, school racist bullying can also be understood by academic research that acknowledges the socio-economic environment. This plays a significant role in the causes of racist perpetration, particularly racist violence. Where there are areas of socio-economic deprivation where unemployment and crime rate is high, thus where inequality exists the presence of minority ethnic groups fuels anger and hate. They may used as scape goats to blame for all of the social and economic problems in the white working class people's lives. This particular cause of racist perpetration can be extended by a newer idea for the cause of racist perpetration and that is the notion and belief that the non-white communities, particularly asylum seekers and refugees receive preferential treatment over the white community. Witnessing an influx of these communities living amongst the white working class community fuels further hatred and therefore, a cause for racist perpetration as such treatment has been perceived to be unfair and unwarranted. This perception also can be found in schools and therefore a justified cause for racist bullying. Finally, witnessing the lifestyle particularly amongst minority ethnic groups who financially are in a better position has also been a cause for racist perpetration, due to the white working class unacknowledged shame of their own life. This particular motivation for racist perpetration can assist to understand why racist bullying occurs in schools. Those who live in a community where many are unemployed and rely on government help, there is an embedded sense of resentment towards minority ethnic groups who live amongst them, yet have managed to achieve a more prosperous life, especially those who have their own businesses and much can be perceived that they have been receiving financial gain from the local government. These factors from the literature on racist victimization and racist perpetration are significant as whatever little academic research on school racism has been found, this sits within the broader sociological context of racism.

Thirdly, there are attempts to develop wider and more inclusive approaches to preventing and restoring harm done by general bullying as well as racist bullying. They attempt to do so by using a whole school and more holistic approach that teaches young people through the use of emotional literacy. More specifically, this would enable to eradicate/ prevent bullying and racist bullying as such an approach enables for schools to reach pupils emotions. A number of ways that a whole school and holistic approach is explored would be through developing policies which pupils, staff and even parents agree upon. Another way is the use of classroom based activities to teach against all bullying and racist bullying, and finally encourage peers to act as peer supporters; mentors and as positive bystanders towards victims.

CHAPTER 3

Research Site

Introduction

THE AIM OF this chapter is to describe the research site including the educational system of Newcastle-upon-Tyne and the schools that were sampled in this research. The purpose to this chapter is to differentiate between the characteristics of each school according to the socio-economic and demographic differences in which each school is located within the city of Newcastle-upon-Tyne. In doing so, this provides a visual setting and basis for the following chapter, the methodology, where qualitative semi-structured focus groups and individual interviews are employed and from this, how perceived findings (discussed in findings chapters 5, 6 and 7) vary quite substantially amongst pupils as a result of pupils' locale and socio-economic surroundings.

The structure of this chapter is as follows. First the chapter provides a brief historical review of the North East region, particularly focusing upon the socio-economic factor, in order to set the context for the following discussion, which reviews the current demographic and socioeconomic profile of Newcastle-upon-Tyne. Key to this argument is the decline in the population of the North East, especially Newcastle-upon-Tyne. Second, the chapter offers an overview of education in Newcastle-upon-Tyne, detailing the Local Education Authority's structure, role and obligations to its schools. The chapter then provides a discussion on anti-bullying policies and race and equality policies. The final section in the chapter examines the schools that were sampled, including the geographical demographics of each, their performance as well as their educational and anti-bullying policies.

Local Regional Context of the North East of England

As processes of globalization have become powerfully inscribed alongside those of internationalization into the political economy of contemporary capitalism, many industrialized regions have experienced severe economic decline over the last two decades (Hudson, 1997:15). The North East of England is one example of an industrial region which experienced large scale social and economic change in the final decades of the 20th century. Its growth from the middle of the 18th century to the end of the 19th was linked to the industries of the coal mining and the steam age. By the end of the twentieth century scarcely anything was left of these industries leading to a dramatic growth of unemployment. The region's development has been affected by changes in technology and markets and its shifting role in the national and international division of labour and political and policy developments in the UK and the EU (Tomaney, 2006:3).

During the period between the First and Second World Wars, with global depression, collapsing markets for coal and ships in particular led to the emergence of mass unemployment and social conflict. The Miners' Lockout and General Strike of 1926, widely supported in the region, presented an uprising threat to the British state. Its defeat helped reshape Labourism in the region in the direction of more accommodative practices. Thus, the Jarrow Crusade, ten years after the General Strike, was more plaintive than revolutionary and helped mark this transition (Tomaney, 2006:5).

Thus, the North East became defined as a "problem region" during this inter-war period (Tomaney, 2006). National government eventually responded to the crisis by experimenting with regional policy involving the provision of new factory space and incentives for firms to locate in the region, while local industrial interests began to form regional organizations in order to represent their interests. At the same time a debate began concerning the appropriate forms of governance for the region, focusing on the need to move beyond a highly localized and fragmented form of local government towards a direction of stronger regional action (Tomaney, 2006). As a result, the wealth of the North East grew and, in 2005, its unemployment rate was substantially lower than it had been in the 1980s. Yet, the North East region had the lowest income per head, the largest proportion of communities characterized by multiple forms of deprivation, the lowest rates of employment, the lowest levels of educational attainment, the lowest rates of entrepreneurship and, yet still, the highest rate of unemployment. For the last thirty years of the twentieth century, the region lost population (HM Treasury, 2001). Although the region experienced strong employment growth at beginning of the 2000s, almost all of this growth occurred in the public sector. This rapidly resulted in an important trend becoming visible in the second half of the 20th century, a growth in dependency on the state, whilst hidden unemployment destroyed numerous localities across the region. Therefore, despite this recent growth, the relative position of the North East continued to deteriorate as well as continued to decrease in population (Tomaney, 2006: 21).

Today, Newcastle-upon-Tyne is the largest city between Leeds and Edinburgh and is the regional capital of the North East of England. After declining by around 15% between 1971 and 2002, the population of Newcastle-upon-Tyne turned a corner by increasing to 26,500 (ONS, 2004 in Newcastle City Council, 2006:2). Today, Newcastle-upon-Tyne is resident to a population of approximately 300,000. Partially this growth in population and occupancy has been associated in some neighbourhoods with high property values and developmental pressures, and in others with multiple occupation of older properties. In addition, the City Centre has experienced a new and buoyant housing market estimated around 5,000 residents which do not include students (Newcastle City Council, 2004:3). Furthermore, Newcastle has been described to be the most cultural out of the North eastern region with many theatres, particularly the Theatre Royal which hosts up to a variety of 50 or more productions a year ranging from opera, ballet; Royal Shakespeare Company, to contemporary productions to the Sage auditorium, now a pinnacle landmark in Newcastle-upon-Tyne and Gateshead. Newcastle-upon-Tyne has also been favoured as possessing the best student life out of all Europe (Newcastle City Council). Yet,

Newcastle has can also be described as having areas that are socially and economically deprived.

The City of Newcastle-upon-Tyne is comprised of up to 26 wards that are broken down into three areas, the north, east and west end of which the Newcastle City Council (see Map 1). Rowntree, (2010:1) recently produced socio-economic profiles relating to all households across Newcastle-upon-Tyne. This report approximately identifies and evidences where potentially the most vulnerable groups and most affluent groups are located within the city.

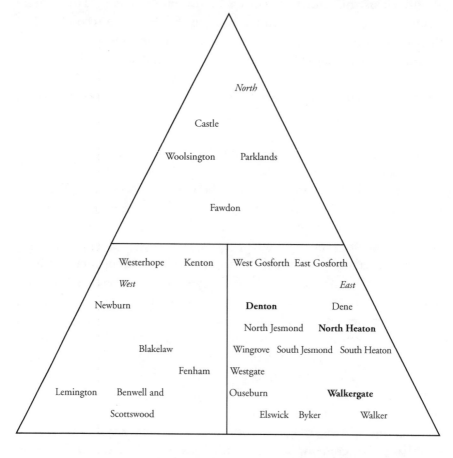

(Map 1) Map of 26 wards in Newcastle-upon-Tyne (Based upon Ordinance Survey, Newcastle Plan for Children, 2006:73). NB. The wards in italics are the wards in which the three schools sampled are located within.

North of Newcastle-upon-Tyne consists of the wards, Castle; Woolsington; Parklands and Fawdon. These wards are predominantly affluent and located in rural areas of Newcastle-upon-Tyne. Castle particularly is more rural than the other wards. Whilst the Newcastle City Council produced the socio-economic profiles to all 26 wards, there are two distinguishing characteristics to all four wards in the north of Newcastle. Primarily, there consists of younger families living in newer homes, with 30.7% in Castle, which is the largest out of the city. Secondly, there are a large percentage of older families living in the suburban parts to Newcastle, particularly a large percentage if this population reside in Parklands with 17.2% (Rowntree, 2010).

In the west end of Newcastle-upon-Tyne, are the wards, Westerhope; Kenton; Newburn; Blakelaw; Fenham; Lemington and Benwell and Scottswood. These wards are located in the more suburban part to Newcastle-upon-Tyne and relatively socially and economically deprived areas. This relative deprivation can be assessed according to one key feature to these wards. There is a high population of low income families living in estate based social housing with 28.7% in Kenton, which is quite significant as it is the highest percentage out of all 26 wards. In comparison, to Castle which has the highest population of younger families living in newer homes (30.7%), located in the north of Newcastle (Rowntree, 2010:2), there are more wards with such groups located in the west end of Newcastle-upon-Tyne than the north or the east. These are Westerhope, and Kenton.

The east end of Newcastle-upon-Tyne consists of up to 15 wards, which is significantly higher than the north or west end to the Newcastle. These wards are, West Gosforth; East Gosforth; Denton; Dene; North Jesmond; South Jesmond; Wingrove; Westgate; Elswick; Ouseburn; Byker; North Heaton; South Heaton; Walkergate and finally, Walker. Also located in suburban Newcastle-upon—Tyne, these wards differ from each other in that there are both middle class communities in affluent areas as well as the lower income working class families residing in some of the most socially and economically deprived areas of the city. For instance, West Gosforth has the highest population of career professionals living in the most sought after locations situated in relatively affluent wards at 41.4%, which is the highest in Newcastle-upon-Tyne, whilst Westgate possesses the largest community of people living in social housing in deprived areas of uncertain unemployment, standing at 55.9% in Newcastle-upon-Tyne (Rowntree, 2010:3). Another key characteristic amongst the socially economic deprived wards are that there is a high population of close knit inner city and manufacturing town communities with Elswick possessing the highest at 27.4% (Rowntree, 2010).

In relation to minority ethnic groups, in Newcastle, the inner city wards of Elswick (25.7%) and Wingrove (24.9%) are the only two wards to have a population of minority ethnic groups over 17.6%, which is a metropolitan county average. Additionally, a large proportion of the minority ethnic group population reside in Moorside (16.4%) and Fenham (10.2%) (Osiewacz *et al.,* 2004:48). The city's black and minority ethnic population however, is approximately 6.9% of the total which is a relatively low figure in comparison to many other major cities in the UK (Newcastle City Council). Thus, Christianity is the dominant religion in all the areas considered with Muslims (Pakistani and Bangladesh communities) being the next largest group. In Tyne and Wear, this represents 1.4% of the population. This is considerably lower than in England (3.1%) and the metropolitan counties (6.3%) as a whole. Whilst Newcastle has the largest proportion of Muslim population at 3.6%, Gateshead has the largest proportion of Jewish population (0.8%). Tyne and Wear has a smaller migrant population than England and the metropolitan counties. With Newcastle, it has the greatest proportion of migrants (16.6%) whilst Gateshead has the smallest (9.9%), (Osiewacz, *et al.,* 2004: 1).

The three schools sampled in this study were; Old East End Community College; Modern Eastern Suburban School; and the School for the Excluded. Old East End Community College is a community college in the east end of the city. Situated within the Walkergate ward, the area in which Old East End Community College is heavily socially and economically deprived, wherein the area is significantly run down, a rough neighbourhood, litter strewn on the roads and pathways and there is a general feeling of an unsafe environment after daylight. There exist a high ratio of council housing, most of which are old terraced houses or semi-detached houses, many of which are back to back houses and even the windows are bordered up with cardboard. The community that resides in the Walkergate ward are of lower working class, not only in dress, but mannerism also. During the daytime hours there are many young people loitering around, who either appear as truanting, or unemployed. There were a high percentage of young teenage mothers in the area also.

In comparison, Modern Eastern Suburban School located in the North Heaton ward, is a large comprehensive in the east end of the city and in contrast to Walkergate, is a clean, affluent neighbourhood surrounded by with modern looking buildings and very suburban. In general the appearance of North Heaton is decent and there is a sense of safety being in this area. The houses are semi-detached and detached and more refined in appearance and there are more of a middle class and affluent community which exists here, this is not only in how the community dress, but also in mannerism. Meanwhile the School for the Excluded is a community school for the excluded located in the border between the east and west end of the city and is situated within the Denton ward. Similar to Walkergate, Denton is heavily socially and economically deprived area, but in appearance, whilst it is also run down, the environment is very green and pasteurized, also suburban, there is lots of land in between the streets and estates, it therefore has a less vulnerable feel to the area, but is ridden with council housing, many houses are semi-detached and rural looking cottages. Similar to Walkergate, much of the community are lower working class and this shows through not only in how people are dressed, but also in mannerisms, yet there the area comes across as more civilized.

Both Old East End Community College and Modern Eastern Suburban School, regardless of gender, race, religion and colour, report that the prime objective is to provide an environment in which a student's rights and freedoms are respected, and to provide opportunities which stimulate and challenge the student's interests and abilities to his/her highest potential. This is demonstrated, according to each school by promoting good relations between different racial groups within the school and the wider community, ensuring that an inclusive ethos is established and maintained, while acknowledging the existence of racism and implementing measures to prevent it.

In addition, Modern Eastern Suburban School states that it opposes all forms of racism, adverse discrimination, racial prejudice and racial harassment and aims to tackle and eliminate any unlawful discrimination. Clear procedures are in place and staff are trained to deal with incidents of bullying, racist bullying and racial prejudice. Finally, both secondary schools' equal opportunity aims have been specifically designed to ensure that they meet the needs of everyone associated with them taking account of ethnicity, culture, religion, language, gender, age, ability, special educational needs and social circumstances.

With regards to the School for the Excluded: its aim is to create an appropriate environment that is a necessary prerequisite to implementing any policy concerned with racial harassment or abuse (School for the Excluded, Anti-Racist Policy, 2007:1). By implementing cross-curricular strategies, the school believes that pupils are able to explore the attitudes and concepts relating to the nature of oppression, racial stereotyping, prejudice and racism. Through religious education and the pastoral curriculum, one aim of the school is to raise pupils' awareness and deepen their understanding by studying various religions, their customs, beliefs and value systems. Finally the school includes the following recommendations within their policy:

- The identification of racial harassment or abuse
- Procedures for responding to the incident
- Procedures for dealing with the perpetrators
- Involvement where necessary, of outside agents (e.g. parent, the LEA, or police)
- Procedure for helping the victims of such incidents (School for the Excluded, Anti-racist Policy, 2007).

Education in Newcastle-upon-Tyne

Newcastle City Council caters for all services for the public from businesses to community living, from education through to transportation and roads. The structure of the Newcastle Local Education Authority (LEA) is divided into three regional areas. According to the Newcastle Learning Partnership (2005), together they provide a high standard of education for up to 37,000 pupils of all abilities and nationalities. One significant role of the Local Education Authority in Newcastle is the monitoring and evaluation of the performance of all schools. The Local Authority undergoes this process by utilising a range of indicators, including performance data from tests and teacher assessments at each key stage. This is to allow the LEA to help schools evaluate their strengths and weaknesses, compare their performance with other schools and to develop plans to raise their standards.

In the Newcastle area, currently there are ninety nine schools divided into the three regional areas: north, east and west end of Newcastle-upon-Tyne. In the City, there are seven independent secondary schools with sixth forms, four special needs schools, one hospital school and one pupil referral unit. As Newcastle is a regional capital, these schools draw their pupils from across Tyne and Wear and beyond Durham and Northumberland. (Newcastle Learning Partnership; 2005:8).

At present, there are three types of schooling system in the city. These are:

    i.   Feeder school system
    ii. Two and three tier schooling system
    iii. Excelsior Academy

The feeder school system consists of Newcastle Community Schools. These do not have catchment areas, and therefore, the Local Education Authority operates a 'feeder school' system. This means that each community First, Primary and Middle School is fed into a designated Middle and Secondary or High School (a 'Receiver' school). Church of England, First and Primary Schools are fed into designated Community Schools. The Roman Catholic schools in Newcastle also operate a feeder school system. However, Roman Catholic Primary schools feed into designated Roman Catholic Secondary Schools and not into Community Secondary Schools.[1]

Historically the city of Newcastle-upon-Tyne operated a two-tier system until the Local Government boundary changes in 1974, in which

---

[1]   Pupils in feeder schools are not guaranteed a place in the receiving school, if the receiving school is oversubscribed.

areas of Northumberland were brought into the remit of Newcastle (Gosforth, Newburn, Westerhope, Chapel House, Throckley, Walbottle and West Denton). Northumberland operated a three-tier system and this tier system of the first-middle-high school type emerged in the late 1960's when local authorities reorganized schools on comprehensive lines. Originally, all pupils were transferred from the age of 11 to either secondary modern or grammar schools (Newcastle City Council Consultation Report 2003: 3). By 1980 the three-tier system was already being replaced in certain places in England and Wales by the two-tier system, such as in Wirral, Stoke and Brighton (Newcastle City Council review report 2002: 4). By 1983 there were 1,810 middle schools in England, however, by January 2002, there were only 432, in January 2003, this further decreased to 428. Thus the two-tier system is now the dominant mode of schooling in England. However, currently in 2011, both Northumberland and North Tyneside in the region continue to have a mix of two and three-tier schooling system (Newcastle City Council review report 2002: 4).

There were a number of reasons why local authorities, and in particular, Newcastle Local Authority reorganised most schools back to the two-tier system. Firstly, there was a belief that the two-tier system would raise school standards, following a detailed examination of the three-tier versus two-tier system by the North Tyneside Commission. The measured outcomes were that on average, 11 year olds in middle schools performed less well than they did in primary schools (NCC 2002:4). Secondly, it was believed that a change would offer a greater beneficial use of resources; and thirdly, local authorities wanted to limit the number of times a child would have to transfer schools. Finally, all new initiatives in the curriculum were based upon the assumption that pupils were in a two-tier system and that adapting the curriculum to a three-tier system may not work as efficiently (NCC Consultation Report 2003:3). Today in Newcastle, the only remaining three-tier schools are in Gosforth and Dinnington. There are currently no plans to change this to a two-tier. I was informed by one of the Team Managers School Organisations and Capital Access Divisions, Children's Services Directorates at Newcastle City Council that this was a political decision.

The two-tier school system in Newcastle-upon-Tyne consists of sixty four primary schools for children aged from four to eleven. Within these primary schools there are forty three community schools, eighteen Roman Catholic schools and three Church of England schools. From here, pupils are transferred into Secondary schools. In Newcastle-upon-Tyne there are ten Secondary schools, for pupils aged from eleven to eighteen. These include six Community schools, three Roman Catholic schools and one Church of England school.

The three-tier school system consists of eight First schools for children aged from four to nine. In Newcastle-upon-Tyne, there are seven Community First schools and one Church of England First school. From here pupils (aged 9-13) are transferred into the three Middle schools within Newcastle-upon-Tyne. After attending Middle school, there is one High school for pupils aged from thirteen to eighteen.[2]

More recently, a third schooling institution opened in Newcastle-upon-Tyne, called the Excelsior Academy. This is a brand new state-of-the-art academy, situated in the west end of Newcastle, which opened its doors to pupils on 1st September 2008. This modern concept in secondary education features the innovative 'five schools within a school' model, providing education and learning opportunities to 1800 pupils aged 11-18. Excelsior Academy is a public (no fees) institution for pupils from families of all faiths.

The age of admissions to schools are reception classes in a First or Primary School, year 5 (aged 8-9) in a Middle School; year 7 (aged 11) in a Secondary School and year 9 (aged 14), in a High School.

At present, Newcastle-upon-Tyne also consists of five Nursery Schools, two Early Years Centres and fifty-three Nursery Units that are attached to the First and Primary Schools. There are approximately four Special Needs Schools and a school for children whose special educational needs cannot be met in a mainstream school. The latter school in particular educates pupils living in Newcastle who have been permanently excluded from mainstream schools (Newcastle

---

[2] The entry and admission procedure is the same as that of the feeder school arrangement.

City Council, 2010). In addition pupils are also referred to it on a temporary basis via the Placement Review Council where after a period of time, based upon their behaviour and performance, these pupils can be reintegrated back into mainstream schools (Newcastle City Council, 2010). Furthermore, a small outreach facility operates within the school. Most pupils have their needs met within their local school, or a school of the parents' preference in the city. Where necessary, pupils may also be placed by the local authority, in consultation with their family or carers, in an additionally resourced centre within a mainstream school, or a special school. A number of schools also have additionally resourced centers (ARC) which provide a range of specialist staff and facilities for children with SEN, including educational psychologist services (Newcastle City Council, 2010).

Anti-Bullying and Equality for All

It is mandatory that each school in England and Wales follows the anti-bullying policy and equality policy guidelines that have been provided by and which are set out by the Department for Education. Under the new coalition Conservative and Liberal Democratic government, the Equalities Act 2010 was introduced which incorporated all discriminative legislation into the one Act. The new duty came into force in England and Scotland in April 2011 and in Wales in Spring/Summer 2011(Anti-Bullying Alliance, 2010). Under this new act, secondary schools have had to incorporate this new legislation with the main rationale statement is to make every effort to provide equal opportunities to all. Furthermore, under this new act, schools have a duty to protect young people against all discrimination which include, disability; gender; race; religion or belief; sexuality; gender reassignment and pregnancy and maternity (Anti-Bullying Alliance, 2010). Under this new act, it includes ensuring that each pupil has the opportunity to achieve the highest possible standard and attain the best possible qualifications in order to enable them to access the next phase of education and preparations for future life.

Over the last few years, the LEA has been active in seeking to develop a range of responses to support pupils, schools and communities to address this complex issue. According to the Newcastle Plan (2009/10), the LEA were successful in gaining substantial funding from both the

Children's Fund and the Neighbourhood Renewal Fund to develop specific projects focussed on the Primary and Secondary Sector. According to the Newcastle City Council Anti Bullying Strategy report (2006), these projects, Children Against Bullying in Schools (CABS) and RESPONSE, have provided valuable resources to pupils, their families and to schools. They have also played a leading role in raising the profile of anti-bullying work as well as developing effective practice in the field (Newcastle City Council, 2006: 7). Newcastle-upon-Tyne's own anti-bullying team, 'Response', is part of Newcastle Children's Services, located with the Early Intervention and Pupil Support Division. It comprises of a multi-disciplinary team of professionals who draw experience from Health, Education, Police and Youth work. They work with all schools, communities and young people in Newcastle and their aim is to ". . . respond to bullying in Newcastle schools and communities, working together to create a safer environment" (Response, 2007:2). They also represent Newcastle at a regional level as a member of the National Anti-bullying Alliance organization. In relation to bullying, it is an issue covered by the Newcastle Plan for Children and Young People (Newcastle Plan for Children and Young People, 2006-2009:13). Under the Every Child Matters Agenda, the main target is to reduce the percentage of children bullied from the previous year. The current report, (Newcastle Plan for Children and Young People, 2009-2010:47), reveals that the Tellus Survey 2008, reported 46.3% of children and young people in Newcastle admitted to experiencing bullying at least once in four weeks. Whilst this is nearly half of all young people, the report reveals that it is a lower proportion than nationally (48%) and neighbouring LEA's (49.4%) (Newcastle Plan for Children and Young People, 2009-2010:47).

Since September 2006, the Newcastle Children's Service, supported by Response, launched the 'Anti-Bullying Good Practice and Award Scheme Accredited for Action' programme. This was designed to offer schools a highly efficient framework to follow when developing anti-bullying policy, practice and ethos for the whole school community (Newcastle City Council, 2007:2). The fundamental principles were drawn directly from the 'Bullying A charter for Action' (Department for Education and Schools 2003) document and the structure was designed to support schools through a process of self-evaluation and a range of guidance notes. This award scheme aimed to simplify the process for schools to develop an environment where all pupils would feel safe to learn and achieve their full potential. The document introduced key issues derived from directives from the then DfES as well as the Department for Children, Schools and Families guidance including the 'Children's Plan' (2007), 'Charter for Action' (DfES 2003), 'Bullying around Racism, Religion and Culture' (DfES 2006), 'Safe to Learn—Embedding Anti-Bullying work in Schools'(DCSF 2007) and 'Healthy Schools Anti-Bullying Guidance for Schools' (DCSF 2008). Furthermore, schools in Newcastle that have led the way nationally by assisting pupils to become healthier, have been presented with a special plaque in recognition of their achievement (Newcastle Primary Care Trust [PCT], 2008:1). Some examples of the work schools have had to undertake in order to gain status have been: Written policies in place and put into action for sex and education, drug education, anti-bullying education and work undertaken, confidentiality, food in schools and physical activity. Such policies have also led to a high quality curriculum providing Personal, Social and Health Education and the national healthy school programme. Overall these policies have explored beyond physical health, which have included considering the emotional health and wellbeing and involvement of the whole school community to become involved in improving health and wellbeing (Newcastle PCT, 2008:2).

In order to qualify for the award, schools have had to show that they are committed to submitting quarterly data returns for bullying and racist incidents within published timescales (Newcastle City Council, 2007: 4). For the most part, across Newcastle-upon-Tyne, the anti-bullying policies mirror each other respectively for all three schools within the research sample. In particular, the objective of each schools' anti-bullying policy was to ensure that each pupil learn in a safe, supportive, friendly and caring environment. Nonetheless, within each school's anti-bullying policy, differences remain.

All schools in the UK are required to follow an anti-bullying policy and now with the Equalities Act, 2010 policy, set out by the government, to ensure equal opportunity for all pupils. Furthermore, in September 2006, the Newcastle Children's Services launched the 'Accreditation for Action' programme which was designed to offer schools a robust framework to follow when developing anti bullying policy, practice and ethos for the whole school community. The fundamentals of the programme were drawn directly from the 'Bullying—A Charter for Action' (DfES 2003) document and was designed to support schools through a process of self evaluation and a range of guidance notes. The anti bullying award is formal recognition by Newcastle Local Authority of a school's efforts and positive results in anti bullying policy and practice development (Newcastle City Council, 2009:3). Whilst both Old East End Community College and Modern Eastern Suburban School have been approved for anti-bullying accreditation, the School for Social Exclusion have not yet confirmed details of approved accreditation.

Schools Sampled in this Study

This section describes the schools accessed in this research. In particular, this section focuses upon the relevant policies, demographics and appropriate data pertaining to each school.

Old East End Community College

The College is large and situated in the east end suburbs of Newcastle-upon-Tyne. The College was founded in 1932 as two Central Schools that were designated as Technical Schools in 1946. The original bricks making the main building at the College are date-stamped 1930—two years after the Tyne Bridge was officially opened and in the same decade as much of the housing stock in the east end area. The School was designated as a specialist Technology College by the then Department for Education (DfEE) from 1 September 2000 and this provided an opportunity to build on the technological investment that had been made (OEECC Prospectus, 2009/10:2). The school area is one of high unemployment, with only a small fraction of families living in private housing. Local facilities are relatively poor, people generally travel to find work and social problems present significant challenges. Nearly all pupils live close to the college, an area of extreme social deprivation. Science laboratories, PE facilities including sports hall and gym, plus music rooms were added in the 1980s. However, a £2 million building programme in 1998 created a new technology centre and facilities for sixth form students. Finally, the College is moving to a £28 million building in September 2011 (OEECC Prospectus 2009/10: 2).

Old East End Community Centre is located in the Walkergate ward which is in the east end of Newcastle-upon-Tyne. Walkergate is one of the city's socially and economically deprived areas as there is a high population who live in close knit, inner city and manufacturing town communities with 27%. Similar to Walkergate, Elswick also has a rather high percentage of close knit, inner city and manufacturing town communities with 27.4%. Furthermore, as one of Newcastle's inner city ward, Elswick consists of one of the largest minority ethnic group population with 25.7%. Walkergate also possesses a significant asylum and refugee and minority ethnic group communities. This could suggest that in areas of high inner city and manufacturing communities where social deprivation is also high, the poorer ethnic minority communities and refugee and asylum seeker communities tend to be housed in these areas. Thus this could also reflect upon similar attitudes towards these groups, by the lower white working class communities.

Within Walkergate, 8.2% of older people living in social housing with high care needs reside there. Yet, 7% of independent older people have relatively active lifestyles. Despite this, Walkergate also houses the younger generation as 7% of younger families live in newer homes and interestingly, 13.2% of upwardly mobile families live in homes bought from social landlords (Rowntree, 2010), indicating that there may be areas where deprivation is less.

Old East End Community College is surrounded by five other wards which all differ from each other. These are South Heaton; North Heaton; Ouseburn; Byker and Walker. The relatively affluent side to Walkergate that is increasing in presence by younger families and upwardly mobile families as well as independent older people can possibly be influenced by South Heaton and particularly, North Heaton as a large percentage of the population are also upwardly mobile families who live in homes bought from social landlords. There is also a small percentage of independent older people residing there who possess relatively active lifestyles. Yet with Ouseburn, Byker and Walker, there is a large population of people residing in social housing, deprived areas where unemployment is uncertain, 31.6% in Ouseburn, 35.7% in Byker and 36.3% in Walker (Rowntree, 2010). Furthermore, where there is a large percentage of low income families living in estate based social housing, 33.9% in Byker, 49.9% in Walker, such contrasts in the surrounding wards to Walkergate can assist in explaining the moderate neighbourhoods to the considerable level of social deprivation within the Walkergate community that has increasing chances in high statistics in crime (Rowntree, 2010).

Table 1: Old East End Community College

School Category	Community College
Location	East End Newcastle-upon-Tyne
Age group	11-18
Gender	Mixed
Numbers on roll	1,219 pupils, (140 pupils in 6th form)
Race:	Mainly white, 5% from various minority ethnic groups
Approximate number of teachers	Approximately 23 House Staff per year, one head teacher and one pastoral care teacher

Table 1 outlines the generic social make-up of the school. The number of pupils who speak English as an additional language is approximately 3%. For many of these pupils, according to the Schools 2007 Ofsted Report, their English speaking is extremely poor. Under the Government Ofsted Inspection Report, it details how the standards on entry are well below average, including very low level of literacy (OEECC Ofsted Report, 2007:2). More than half of the pupils are known to be eligible for free school meals, a feature shared by only 4% of secondary schools nationally. Nearly a third of the pupils have identified special educational needs, a figure above the national average and this proportion of pupils with statements of special educational needs, 2.2% is broadly average. Never-the-less the proportion continuing in full time education beyond the age of 16 has tripled since the last inspection (2002) and the College is involved in the Excellence in Cities (EIC) initiative and is part of a developing, Small Education Action Zone (SEAZ) (OEECC, Ofsted Report, 2007:2).

The school's primary policy is to provide a college where all pupils are able to experience success, gain knowledge and enjoy their educational experience; thus sanctioning them to make a positive contribution to the quality of the life in the East End area of Newcastle and finally by working as a partnership with parents, pupils and teachers. (OEECC Prospectus 2009/10:2).

With regards to the pupils' attitudes and values, the Ofsted report (OEECC, Ofsted, 2007) indicates that there is an overall good behavioural response in and out of the classroom and that the college is an orderly community since most pupils observe the agreed codes of conduct. Subsequently, exclusions seldom occur; however, the report emphasizes a need for improvement with regards to pupils' performance. With regards to the pupils' personal development and relationships, there is an overall harmonious attitude found at the school. Yet, despite this, many pupils fail to readily show initiative and small minorities are disaffected, especially in years ten and eleven (OEECC, Ofsted report, 2007: 4).

The Newcastle Local Authority Response team as well as Children Against Bullying in Schools (CABS) have provided valuable resources to pupils and families and worked with nearly all schools in Newcastle-upon-Tyne, including Old East End Community College by assisting with anti-bullying initiatives. It could be speculated that such initiatives are tailored for each particular school type. A youth worker for the Response team (Old East End Community College Meeting, 2009:2), discussed a project with a principle aim to develop dialogues that changed attitudes, hearts and minds and a project on intergenerational that looked at issues which focused on getting to the root of prejudice, stereotyping, community cohesion, community pride and heritage. The project, which lasted for approximately two months, was about exploring ideas about growing up then and now (Old East End Community College, Meeting, 2009).

Furthermore, Old East End Community College utilizes a variety of anti-bullying initiatives, specifically establishing an ABC—Anti Bullying Culture. Consisting of members of the student council, the ABC group meet each term to discuss all issues regarding bullying and also to generate literature on bullying awareness (Old East End

Community College anti-bullying policy, 2010: 6). The ABC has introduced the concept of 'bullying boxes' in each house room, to report incidences of anti-social behaviour. Inset, is an anti-bullying toolkit for teachers at schools, carried out in order to train thirty peer mentors. Initiatives also include completing anonymous questionnaires by the student body (Old East End Community College anti-bullying policy, 2010). Further, the Parent-Teacher Association meetings are also used to relay bullying information and finally, the partnership between parents and the college staff is recognized by the school as invaluable in eradicating bullying behaviour. This recognition is nurtured by the college staff and the parents.

Modern Eastern Suburban School

The school is a large community comprehensive school situated in an eastern suburb of Newcastle upon Tyne. In September 2004 the school re-opened in a new state of the art building on three floors and is surrounded by approximately 2 acres of land and two large playgrounds. Although most pupils live in an area around the school, there are an increasing number of pupils that are travelling from other parts of the city of Newcastle.

Modern Eastern Suburban School rests within the North Heaton ward. In comparison to Old East End Community College in Walkergate, Modern Eastern Suburban School is relatively affluent and the majority of the population in North Heaton are from middle class backgrounds, and therefore, the area is less likely to have problems with crime. The population comprises of 32.6% of people in older families living in the suburbs and of which 9.6% are independent older people with active lifestyles. The affluent community can be demonstrated by the population of career professionals (8%) who are living in the most sought after locations, whilst 19.2% represent upwardly mobile families living in houses bought from social landlords (Rowntree, 2010).

Much of the affluent socio-economic make-up can be linked to the neighbouring wards to North Heaton. These are Dene; South Heaton; East Gosforth; North Jesmond and South Jesmond (Rowntree, 2010). In the ward Dene, 18.6% of the population are younger families who are living in newer homes. Whilst in East Gosforth, 16% are career professionals living in the most sought after locations, in North Jesmond, this is 18.7%. Furthermore, 82.6% (and the largest in Newcastle-upon-Tyne) make-up the educated, young, single people living in areas of transient population and student population. Finally, the older population in North Jesmond (6.5%) and South Jesmond (6.7%) are independent with relative active lifestyles (Rowntree, 2010). These characteristics within North Heaton and surrounding wards strongly indicate that there is more social and economic prosperity with a community that possess more middle class values. It can be further suggested that North Heaton consists of career professionals with families with middle class outlooks and lifestyles and are surrounded by wards that are of similar socio-economic status and position. There are some wards which are even more affluent than North Heaton, such as East Gosforth, which is neighbouring to South Gosforth, and consists of the largest population of career professionals living in the most sought after locations situated in relatively affluent wards, Thus, the socio-economic affluence and middle class societal values of Modern Eastern Suburban School will strongly be influenced by these traits.

Table 2: Modern Eastern Suburban School

School category:	Large Comprehensive School, designated technology college-specialist computing and mathematics school, and has a second specialism in humanities.
Location:	Eastern suburbs of Newcastle-upon-Tyne.
Age group:	11-18.
Gender:	Mixed.
Numbers on roll:	1,910 pupils, (345 pupils in 6th form).
Special Education Needs:	Yes, but below average.
Ethnicity proportion:	High.
Ethnic background:	Mixed, small numbers of Asylum & Refugees.
Approximate number of teachers:	Over 130 teaching staff with more than 80 support staff who provide additional learning, technical and clerical support.

This school is driven by its main educational policy, that is to develop pupils' potential to the full, through identifying and developing each pupil's individual strengths and providing a differentiated 'entitlement curriculum' capable to meet with their needs (Modern Eastern Suburban School Prospectus 2009/10:2). Very few pupils join or leave the school during the academic year. There is an average proportion of pupils eligible for free school meals. The national data indicates that when pupils are aged 11, their attainment is average. The school is closely linked with the Local Authority Excellence in Cities programme and part of a 'Leading Edge' partnership. Finally, the school was awarded the 'Healthy School' status in July 2007 (Ofsted report, 2007:3). The latest Ofsted Inspection Report, (September 2007), indicates that the school is a socially harmonious community and provides significant opportunities for pupils to take responsibilities and develop social understanding. In particular, the sixth form is the schools' prime success, largely because of the high rate of achievement (Ofsted Inspection Report, 2007:15). Table 2 reveals that the school has a high ethnic minority population and according to the Ofsted report, all pupils are equally valued and included in all aspects of school life and the report details that pupils show respect towards each other (2007: 5).

From the report, (Ofsted 2007:5), pupils enjoy being at the school. Pupils behave well during classes and the school can be considered safe enough for them to move around. Finally, the report emphasizes the school's awareness of the importance of the spiritual, moral, social and cultural development of its pupils and the impact that it has on their progress, attitudes and achievement. The report details how pupils show confidence and strongly discuss their opinions relating to their local community and worldly issues, especially during citizenship lessons (2007:6).

The school works with the Local Authority RESPONSE Team who assist with providing further anti-bullying initiatives in order to ensure that all pupils feel comfortable and safe in and around the school environment. Particularly in February 2008, pupils from Modern Eastern Suburban School had their voices heard at the highest level when they discussed how their school had tackled bullying with Sir Al Aynsley Green—the then Children's Commissioner for England.

Specifically Modern Eastern Suburban School, working with the Response team set up focus groups to discuss how pupils and staff could eliminate bullying (Response Anti-Bullying Newsletter, May 2008:2).

Where bullying exists, it is the school's responsibility to make sure that the 'victims' feel confident enough to activate the anti-bullying systems operational within the school. The school utilizes a range of proactive and reactive strategies which include anti-bullying discussions. For example the school's anti-bullying citizenship and PSHE booklet consists of prompts for discussion with the class and the teacher is able to set various tasks for pupils to undertake before following up with a classroom discussion. One of the tasks, for example is around name calling (MESS Anti-bullying policy, 2008:22). Other proactive and reactive strategies take place during tutorial time and assemblies. The school also works to prevent bullying by raising awareness through drama and creative writing and creating poster displays of pupils' anti-bullying work around the school. Furthermore, the Student Support Centre works with small groups to promote anti-bullying, for example, training year 12 pupils on a peer mentoring programme who then mentor one to two pupils during the year (Peer Mentor Programme 2005) there is also a lunch time peer support group, operated by year nine pupils. The support group produces materials to highlight certain issues; surveys are used to pin point key areas around the building and duty staff are positioned accordingly. Finally, the Health 4 U drop in service can prevent bullying from taking place. Routes around the building have been planned carefully so pupils can move around safely. During breaks and lunchtimes, there are safe areas created for year seven and for the more vulnerable other pupils (MESS, Anti-bullying policy, 2008).

Reactively, where any reports of bullying are made, according to the school's anti-bullying policy, the reports are taken seriously. Investigations are carried out as soon as possible and witness statements collected. If the school concludes that bullying has taken place, procedures are in place and finally, if the incident(s) are extremely serious, stages can be omitted. The police may also become involved.

School for the Excluded

The School for the Excluded opened in September 1999 following a local authority reorganisation. The School for the Excluded is a modern small unit located within a socially and economically deprived area in the East End of Newcastle-upon-Tyne. The school is small, colourful and has a good security system. There is one large dining area and one gym/sports hall and one lab with basic technological facilities.

The School for the Excluded is located in the Denton ward, which narrowly borders between the East and West end of suburban Newcastle-upon-Tyne. Similar to Walkergate, Denton is relatively socially and economically deprived as 24.8% of the population lives in estate based social housing, which is a significant percentage throughout the city of Newcastle (Rowntree, 2010). Furthermore, much of the population residing in Denton are older people, with 8.8% of older people living in social housing and 7.5% of them have relatively active lifestyles. Yet there are a small percentage of younger families who live in newer homes. Whilst the School for the Excluded is located within a socially and economically deprived area, the social ethos within the unit is a relatively strong and supportive one, and with a smaller number of pupils on roll, this enables for the school to invest more time and funding into addressing anti-bullying issues.

Much of the socio-economic and population type make up of Denton can be characterized by its surrounding wards; which are Kenton; Wingrove; Blakelaw and Newburn. Blakelaw; Kenton and Newburn are situated in the west end suburban of Newcastle and these wards also have a significant percentage of low income family residing in estate based social housing with 28.7% in Kenton; 22.9% in Newburn and 36% in Blakelaw (Rowntree, 2010). Furthermore, both these wards have a higher population of the older generation residing in social housing compared with the other wards in the west end of Newcastle-upon-Tyne. Denton reveals younger families living in newer estates, similarly, in Blakelaw, 15.4% of the population make up for those families that are upwardly mobile. This indicates that there may possibly be pockets around Denton where social and economic deprivation is less. Additionally, Wingrove, which is located in the east end of Newcastle, similarly has a close knit, inner city and manufacturing town community (27%, Rowntree, 2010), which is significant as it could therefore be speculated that whilst there may be more working class than middle class communities in Denton, there is a close connection between each community whom interact and support each other. Therefore, young people involved in groups of delinquent behaviour are more likely to be influenced and/or supported by their peers.

Table 3: School for the Excluded

Location:	East End, Newcastle-upon-Tyne.
School Type:	Community.
School Category:	Pupil Referral Unit.
Age group:	5-16.
Gender:	Mixed, majority boys.
Numbers on roll:	112 pupils.
Race category:	Predominantly white.
Approximate number of teachers:	12 in total. Six in key stages 2 and 3, four in key stage 4, one deputy head and one head teacher.

The School for the Excluded main educational policy is to provide outstanding care, moral guidance and support to the pupils (Ofsted Report 2008: 2). Table 3 details that pupils on roll are from years 1 to 11 and have been excluded from mainstream education (Ofsted Report 2008). The entire focus of the school is devoted to developing the personal, social and moral education of the pupils. According to the most recent government inspection report (Ofsted Report, 2008), this has been so effective that in Key stage 2, many pupils have been reintegrated back into mainstream schools. Furthermore, the report indicates that pupils gradually have gained their self-confidence, self-esteem and that their attendances have also improved (2008: 4).

As the School for the Excluded serves all Newcastle high schools, it has a diverse population and is over-subscribed (Ofsted Report, 2008:3). From the government inspection report, over 70% of the numbers of pupils are entitled to free school meals, which is rather high compared to the national average and many children reside in extreme socially deprived areas. All the pupils are identified as having social, emotional and behavioural difficulties and many have additional literacy and numeracy needs. In particular, eight pupils have a Statement of Special Educational Needs, six pupils are in the care of the Local Authority and a high percentage of pupils have been involved in the criminal justice system (Ofsted Report, 2008:3). On a higher note, pupils have been taught to live a life of healthier eating and the unit attained the 'Healthy Schools Award' and 'Basic Skills Quality' (Ofsted Report, 2008: 3).

The School for the Excluded works with Children Against Bullying in Schools (CABS) to provide support for the School for the Excluded through the Behaviour Improvement Project, an initiative which is government funded to provide full time, supervised education for all excluded pupils. The project provides key workers for all pupils at risk of truancy and criminal behaviour, improvement in behaviour, as measured by exclusion levels and other indicators and a reduction in the levels of truancy and improvement in attendance levels (CABS Behaviour Strategy, 2009:9).

Under its anti-bullying policy, the school employs various preventative strategies (School for the Excluded, Anti-bullying Policy 2008) and there is increasing collaboration with CABS under the behaviour strategy programme. One such approach asserts that pupils are not to be left without a staff member at anytime during the school day. Furthermore, there must be regular and effective communication between staff, as this results in a quicker response to any incidents of bullying and prevents the problem from escalating. As the anti-bullying policy states, perpetrators of bullying tend to target newcomers for bullying as a scapegoat as they are easy prey (School for the Excluded, Anti-bullying policy, 2008:3). All staff are well aware of this danger, and raise positive aspects of the newcomer, raising their self-esteem and allowing the potential bully to view them in a different light. The unit ensures that there is a school environment where issues of concern to children are discussed; including bullying and that parents are kept fully informed. The school works with pupils and staff to develop a more 'Whole School Approach' and believes in operating with a 'support' approach with intentions of wanting pupils to feel safe whilst at the school. This, the School for the Excluded believe, works better than issuing a sanction/punishment approach (School for the Excluded, Anti-bullying policy, 2008:5).

The whole school approach involves a basic seven step procedure as follows: (i) the teacher meets with the victim to discuss how they are feeling. The teacher does try to discover all those involved in the bullying incidents. (ii) A meeting is then convened with all individuals involved, including bystanders and friends of the victim who joined in, but did not initiate the bullying (SfE, Anti-bullying policy, 2008:5). (iii) In an attempt to alleviate the feelings of the victim, these are discussed and the teacher then proceeds to place the burden of responsibility on the feelings of the group in an attempt to make the group realize that their actions were wrong. However, the teacher takes great care not to discuss the details of the incident or allocate blame to the group. (iv) Responsibility is then shared amongst the group as well as aiming to bring about positive change for the victim. This then is followed by (v) the teacher encouraging the group to devise ways in which the victim could be helped. As the school's anti-bullying policy points out, whilst there is always hope for improved behaviour, the teachers are well aware that this may take time to come about (Ofsted report, 2008:6). (vi) The meeting concludes leaving the burden of responsibility on the group for a limited period of time to see if the problem can be resolved. However, the teacher arranges a follow up meeting to check the status. This culminates with the final step. (vii) After a brief respite of about a week, the teacher meets with the group and discusses how the situation has been coming along. This follow up meeting not only enables the teacher to monitor the bullying; however, it also assists to keep pupils engaged with the process in an attempt to make them reflect upon their actions and not repeat them in the future (SfE, Anti-bullying policy, 2008: 6).

In the management of the pupil's behaviour, the school uses praise and recognition of good behaviour. Pupils are given the opportunity to fulfil their potential through a differentiated work programme in order to allow each pupil to achieve success emphasizing collaboration and not competition. Where preventative measures can be addressed through discussions, pastoral work, PHSE (Personal Health Social Education), drama, classroom charters and other school based initiatives, the Ofsted report implies that there is a solid resource base to provide the needs of all pupils (SSD, Anti-bullying policy, 2004:313).

Summary and Discussion

This chapter began with a brief historical review of the North East region and discusses the demographic and socioeconomic profiles of each ward in the three main areas to Newcastle-upon-Tyne. This had been followed by an overview of education in Newcastle-upon-Tyne and detailed the LEA's role and duty to the schools. This was further followed by a review of the schooling system in Newcastle-upon-Tyne offering a discussion on anti-bullying, race and equality policies. It next had examined the schools that were sampled, including the demographics of each school, a discussion of the surrounding wards to assist in understanding the social and economic position to each ward. Finally, the chapter offers a discussion on the general performance of each school, educational policies and their anti-bullying policy.

From this chapter, two themes can be drawn upon. It is clear that the level of social and economic deprivation varies across the schools sampled. With such differences in socio-economic make up and location of the schools and neighbourhood environment, this would interestingly allow the PhD to obtain differences in perceptions of school bullying and racist bullying by pupils and teachers. It would also offer opportunities to explore shared as well as individual perspectives that pupils and adults would have when discussing bullying and racist bullying. Due to the socio-economic background of the school as well as the home and community environment this would strongly influence how participants view the nature and particularly the explanations for bullying and racist bullying.

Modern Eastern Suburban School is more affluent than Old East End Community College and the School for the Excluded. Furthermore, Modern Eastern Suburban School is more ethnically diverse than Old East End Community College and the School for the Excluded. In addition, the geographic and socio-economic make up and social class and age population of the catchment areas to each ward in which the schools are located in provides an understanding to varying deprivation levels of each school ward. Out of both secondary schools, Modern

Eastern Suburban School overall academic performance is higher, furthermore, the school has more funding and resources and a stronger ethos embedded in dealing with bullying and racist bullying. Yet, whilst the School for the Excluded is located in an area of social deprivation, similar to Old East End Community College, the ethos was also strong, yet the fewer numbers of pupils on roll can indicate the school's success due to having more time and money in order to effectively deal with pupils social welfare. Thus, a methodology that employs qualitative semi-structured focus groups and individual interviews, with the above varied factors, this would make it possible to obtain data on shared attitudes as well as individual perspectives by pupils and adults towards bullying and racist bullying.

A qualitative methodology employed that is able to obtain shared and individual perspectives on bullying and racist bullying, this will be discussed next in the Methodology chapter.

CHAPTER 4

Methodology

Introduction

THE AIM OF this chapter is to detail the research methodology selected for the PhD, and the process of fieldwork and data analysis. The purpose to this chapter is to reveal that semi structured qualitative research methodology was used, via focus groups and individual interviews, but also to justify why this method was employed. In doing so, it reveals that there remains a gap in the wider academic literature that examines school bullying and racist bullying using qualitative research and that most research employ quantitative research, largely through questionnaires and survey based methods. Therefore, the PhD provides a different approach to other studies in this area and exerts authority to the use of qualitative research. Another purpose to this chapter is to show by using qualitative research, it achieved the main aim and objectives of the PhD, which is to examine young people's perceptions of bullying and racist bullying and through this methodology employed, it allows for an arena where young people's voices can be heard, another gap in the literature.

The structure of this chapter is as follows. First it describes the research aim and objectives and reflects upon the factors that motivated the pursuit of the research in the subject area. It also describes how the aim and objectives changed and provides the research questions that the thesis is interested in exploring. Second, it explores the groundwork surrounding actually gaining access to the schools and how they were sampled. Third, the data collection section discusses the methods used in the research; key to this argument is that by using semi structured qualitative research methodology allows for deeper exploration of young people's perceptions and ideas on the subject of bullying and racist bullying. Fourth, the data handling and analysis section discusses how the data was handled and secured. Finally, the section on political and ethical issues discusses all the ethical and political concerns that were taken into account when designing and delivering the research.

Research Aims, Objectives and Approach

The aim of the PhD is:

- To examine pupils' and adults' perceptions of bullying and racist bullying and how they were manifested in a school environment in Newcastle-upon-Tyne.

Within this aim, a number of research questions arose and which the thesis was interested in exploring, including: how did young people explain bullying and racist bullying? What factors impacted upon their thinking? What role did socio-economic factors, if any, play on young people's perceptions, both of bullying, and of school responses? What were young people's perceptions of the responses of victims to experiences of bullying? What did adults perceive to be the main issues relating to bullying and racist bullying and how did these compare with that of young people?

These broad questions helped narrow and focus the overall PhD aim, and informed the findings immeasurably, as discussed below; and as a consequence, two of the original objectives, discussed below were refined:

- To examine, the dynamics of and responses to school bullying and racism amongst pupils aged between 11 to 18 years in the city of Newcastle-upon-Tyne.

The age range of participating pupils was reduced from 11-18 to 11-15 years, (Years 7-9) as this appropriately mapped onto the findings from the broader review of research, which suggests that school bullying mainly begins during the last year or so at Primary School and is much more apparent during the early years at Secondary/Middle school. There tends to be an age decline in bullying after it peaks in early adolescence and then tails off throughout secondary school (Sullivan *et al.,* 2005:8; Salmivalli, 2002). The decrease is as a result of a number of factors. At earlier years; new pupils are prey to the older and more experienced pupils, with the younger being less aware of the school culture and rules. Furthermore, younger pupils are physically smaller and psychologically tend to be less confident and therefore, are more vulnerable as targets of bullying (Sullivan *et al.,* 2005). This has been demonstrated by academic research (Sullivan, 2004; Train, 1995). In addition, the methodological approach changed over the course of the research. Another original objective included:

- The use of questionnaires, in addition to interviews.

However, during the literature review it was noted that survey/questionnaires was a traditional choice of method amongst many researchers of bullying, and following further discussion with my supervisors it was decided to adopt a more qualitative methodology.

Where quantitative research methodology rely on collecting data that is numerically based, largely carried out using questionnaires, surveys and experimental research, (i.e. research seeking to determine if a specific treatment influences on outcome) (Creswell, 2009:12), also quasi experimental design; case study design; cross-sectional design; longitudinal design and comparative design (Punch, 2005:136). Whereas, with qualitative research techniques, they rely more on language and the interpretation of its meaning, therefore, data collection methods tend to involve close human involvement and a creative process of theory development rather than testing (Walliman, 2006). Such as using a variety of forms of interviews, such as, structured, semi-structured, unstructured whether face-to-face or via the telephone, internet. Qualitative research also can be carried out through the use of focus groups, overt and covert observation, ethnography, grounded theory studies, phenomenological research and narrative research (Creswell, 2009). Most often researchers learn and discuss research following one of two logics (i) reconstructed logic (the logic of how to do research, highly organised and systematic) or (ii) logic in practice (logic of how research is carried out, messy, ambiguous, tied to specific cases and orientated towards practical completion of a task (Neuman, 2006:151). With quantitative researchers, there is a tendency to apply reconstructed logic to their work; however, qualitative researchers are most likely to apply the logic in practice (Neuman, 2006).

Despite the many strengths of studies on school bullying that have employed quantitative methodologies, they often have lacked depth. Furthermore, a key limitation with all quantitative research design approaches concerns the validity in the data. Various problems may arise regarding the ability of the researcher to conclude that the intervention affects the outcome and not some other factor (Creswell, 2009: 162). Other limitations that can be applied to quantitative research are the risks posed to the statistical conclusion validity (Creswell, 2009), which can arise when inaccurate inferences have been drawn from the data as a result of inadequate statistical power (Creswell, 2009:164). Yet, it is no more difficult to achieve a representative sample with a questionnaire than with any other form of data collection, the difficulty tends to be that there is a low response rate.

In contrast, the academic literature on racism, racial harassment and violence largely uses a variety of qualitative research methodologies, for example, Troyna and Hatcher, (1992); Mills, (2001); Mishna *et al.,* (2004); Barter, (1999); Ray and Smith, (2004) and Sibbit, (1997). It was hoped that a qualitative approach would offer a greater in-depth understanding of pupils' perceptions and experiences of bullying in school. It was also hoped that this approach would also offer a more detailed study on the motivations for school and racist bullying. There were also practical reasons associated with the decision to concentrate on qualitative rather than quantitative data and particularly questionnaires. Questionnaires are notoriously difficult to secure representative samples and offer little depth of analysis. There are financial and time constraints associated with questionnaires.

Qualitative research proves to be advantageous on various accounts. One of the central characteristics to qualitative research is that data can be collected through a holistic approach (Creswell, 2009:176). Where qualitative researchers try to develop a complex picture of the problem, this involves reporting multiple perspectives, identifying the many factors involved in a situation and generally drawing the larger picture that emerges (Creswell, 2009). A key objective with selecting semi structured focus groups and individual interviews was to gather and discuss multiple perspectives from young people on bullying and racist bullying and to enable them to identify numerous factors around both subjects, such as how bullying would be identified, how they recognize various issues that cause bullying. Through this approach, qualitative research benefits further over quantitative research as it enables for the data to delve much deeper in detail. Furthermore, the roots of qualitative research can be related to complex issues falling under multi-disciplinary areas, such as philosophical, psychology and sociological discourse revolving around, as Davies clearly asserts (2007:135):

> "How do we know what we know? How do we know what other people feel? Is what people say different from what people do? How can researchers interpret their findings without bringing into play their own prejudices, perspectives derived from their own gender, age or life experiences?" (Davis, 2007).

As such, the decision to use qualitative research derived from the core aim to discover what young people perceived bullying and racist bullying to be, how they believed it occurred and why and further explore how they felt about the existence of bullying and racist bullying. Drawing upon Davis's argument about researchers interpreting data without including own prejudices, qualitative interviews more than for example, observation would work as particularly participative observation maybe idiosyncratic, as well as difficult to replicate (Bryman, 1993:2). Using semi-structured qualitative interviews would be a more appropriate method to employ in gaining a higher response rate. Furthermore, few quantitative researchers agree that research can be 'value free' (Bryman, 1993) and place a great deal of importance upon the replication of data. Therefore, replication can help as it can investigate on any excess. Kiddr and Judd (1986: 26 in Bryman, 1993:38) so argue, "The researcher's biases inevitably affect how observations are gathered and interpreted. The only way to avoid these biases is to replicate the research . . ."

Therefore with semi-structured data collection, this aims to overcome some of the disadvantages to both approaches. Ensuring that pupils expressed their perspectives freely was an objective of the research and delved deeper in discussion. Yet, ensuring that the topic would not divert, selecting semi-structured qualitative type research was deemed the most appropriate choice. The pre-structured data falls short as respondents are unable to express themselves in their own terms. Yet, with unstructured data collection, this can present difficulties when it comes to analyzing the data collection, this aims to overcome some of the disadvantages to both approaches.

As qualitative research methodology can be conducted through a number of ways, as already identified above, a further benefit are the numerous qualitative 'empirical materials' that can be used, including interview transcripts, recording and notes, observational records and notes, documents and the products and records of material culture, audiovisual materials and personal experience materials (for e.g. artifacts, journals, diary information and narratives), (Punch, 2005:57). The qualitative researcher thus has a much wider range of possible empirical materials than the quantitative research and able to apply multiple data sources in the project. Furthermore, where quantitative data have a predetermined structure (see fig.2, pp 120), qualitative research data can sit anywhere within this continuum (Punch, 2005). Thus, as figure 2 demonstrates below, qualitative research data can be well structured, as in case of standardized interview questions with response categories, or observations based on a predetermined observation schedule. Qualitative data can also be totally unstructured at the point of collection, as in the transcript of an open-ended interview, or field notes from participant observation. In this situation, there would be no predetermined categories or codes (Punch, 2005).

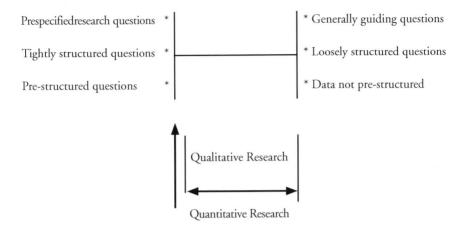

(Fig 2. Prespecified versus unfolding: the timing of structure. Punch, 2005:23).

Similarly, the research aimed to take advantage of the various opportunities provided by qualitative research with children as described by Mishna *et al.* (2004: 450):

> "Qualitative research provides an opportunity to tap into the richness of children's thoughts and feelings about themselves, their environments and the world in which we all live. Through qualitative interviewing, we are able to step outside the bounds of adult thinking and discover unexpected differences in the perceptions of adults and children."

There were relatively few self-identified perpetrators or victims in the focus groups. Nevertheless, there was a small number of self-identified perpetrators and victims who provided their own perspectives into the dynamics of the perpetrator and victim relationship. As a result, there are limited actual accounts of lived experiences taken directly from victims or perpetrators. Rather the PhD examines pupils and adults perceptions and views of bullying and racist bullying.

A significant drawback to qualitative research, specific to focus groups and individual interviews is 'interview effect' (McNeil and Chapman 2005: 59) or interview bias, which cannot be ignored. All interviews are interaction situations and result in those who participate in the interview attaching meanings or interpretations to what they see going on in and around the interview. Therefore, the researcher has to ensure that their values, attitudes and opinions do not influence the respondent's answers (McNeil and Chapman, 2005).

One issue that was considered from the outset was that of my gender and ethnic status. I am a British born Asian female entering three schools, one that was predominantly white and economically deprived; one that was highly ethnically mixed, but more affluent than the first school and one that consisted of highly deviant pupils, all white, and undertaking research on bullying and racism. This raised major ethical issues of how I would be perceived by pupils, how participative the interviews would become and what influence as a researcher, may have on the group. As an Asian female, a level of hostility was occasionally apparent, notably from Asian pupils, (male) in Old East End Community College. One hypothesis could be that this unreceptive and often intimidating reaction on the subject of racist bullying was due to the fact that it was a sensitive issue for these particular pupils. As Berg (2007:121) suggests, interpretations of the interviewee should be based upon the type of interaction they portray, such as moods, sentiments and role portrayals. Furthermore, Vogt *et al.* (2004: 234), claim that in relation to sensitive topics, focus group participants' comfort and candidness may depend upon the person asking the questions. Whilst agreeing that in general female interviewers are more preferable, Vogt *et al.* (2004) also emphasize that certain topics maybe more appropriate if delivered by a male moderator.

A further issue arose at the end of one focus group session, when pupils who arrived in the class, although not part of the sample, were curious about my ethnic background and asked where I came from. A brief response detailing that I was British born was given at which point they continued to delve deeper into my original background and origin. As this was the end of a session and a new class beginning, it was decided to not say anything, but leave the classroom. There were reservations in admitting being of Pakistani origin, due to recent terrorist events on July 7th 2005 and ultimately there was a feeling of discomfort. Subsequently, upon reflection, this revealed that the researcher was perceived as being different. This could also assist in explaining why the researcher was at the receiving end of hostility by the Asian pupils in the focus groups. As such biasness that may occur because of the role of the researcher cannot be avoided in the research; they instead need to be incorporated when analyzing the data. For example, any racial prejudice by a pupil may have been restrained from being viewed because of my physical and ethnic make-up and also because it is not considered politically correct.

Punch (2005:57) therefore recommends that with qualitative research:

> "Like all other such choices, it needs to be analysed, and there are advantages and disadvantages in each way of doing it. Thus, it will often seem good to begin with the data in respondent's own terms and concepts. But the systematic comparisons which structure and measurements permit are also valuable, and they require that the same terms and concepts be used across different respondents, that they be standardized . . . combining the two approaches in such a way as to retain the advantages of each" (Punch, 2005).

Upon reflection to Punch's (2005) argument, that by collecting data by means of semi-structured interviews, group and individual, would allow for combining the two approaches and retaining the advantages of each method.

Gaining Access

Preparation for gaining access to schools involved networking through meetings and building up credibility with various local organizations in Newcastle-upon-Tyne including; ARCH (Agencies Against Racist Crime and Harassment); WRAP (Working with Racially Aggravated Perpetrators); YOT (Youth Offending Team); Streetwise 4 Victims; the LEA and Victim Support. All meetings with organizations were scheduled over the telephone. The purpose of these meetings was to establish a rapport as well as to determine the most appropriate manner of gaining access. Representatives from these organizations advised sending out written correspondences to schools addressed to the Head Teachers. Preparation also included background research into the Ofsted reports of all the schools' that had been originally targeted and undergoing Criminal Background Checks.

Written correspondences printed on Northumbria University letter heads were sent to all ten secondary schools and one high school in Newcastle-upon-Tyne. They were addressed to Head and Assistant Head Teachers. These letters included my details, evidence of a successful Criminal Background Check and supervisor's contact details, along with a copy of the initial project approval (IPA). These ten schools were the only schools at secondary level located in Newcastle-upon-Tyne and were therefore targeted as the rest were primary or middle schools. Letters were followed up with telephone calls. Four schools rejected access through letters or emails and four did not respond to any of the written or telephone communications. The schools that granted access responded to the initial written correspondences with telephone calls.

Another school that accommodates children who have been excluded from mainstream schools also granted access. These were then followed by meetings with the Head Teachers and pastoral staff in order to discuss age groups to be sampled, consent letters and the process of data collection. The fieldwork was conducted in two secondary schools and a school for the excluded which consented to the research. The rationale for selecting these three schools is primarily due to being accepted by the schools to conduct the fieldwork. A further reason lay with the difference in the social make-up of each school as well as differences in socio-economic background, particularly between both secondary schools. It is also anticipated that due to the demographic context and socio-economic differences between each school and the smaller sized school for the excluded, there may be considerable differences in young people's perceptions and attitudes towards the causes and explanations for bullying and racist bullying.

Schools were provided with a copy of semi-structured questions for focus groups and individual interviews as well as drafts of consent letters to be addressed to pupils and parents. The consent letters briefly discussed the background to the research, documented the seriousness of the nature of bullying and racist bullying and requesting permission to interview pupils in focus groups. It was explained, that interviews would be recorded, and that all information was to be held sole and in confidence. These documents were approved by the schools. Furthermore, each school acknowledged that bullying was a serious problem and expressed a wish to see if the research findings could better assist their current anti-bullying and race equality policies or actually change any of them.

In Old East End Community College, the response rate from pupils was high as there was a lot of willingness to participate during focus group sessions and in individual interviews. However, with Modern Eastern Suburban School the response rate from pupil to consent in interviews was lower, yet there were more variety of interviews. For instance, there were more interviews conducted amongst a range of key educational stakeholders at this school than the other two due to the greater range of teacher type and its ethnically diverse population. At School for the Excluded, the response rate was moderate; however, unlike Old East End Community College and Modern Eastern Suburban School, there were less than 126 pupils on role. The School for the Excluded provided the opportunity to obtain access to excluded pupils with a greater prospect of interviewing those who may have been perpetrators and victims of bullying, as well as obtaining their perceptions, lived experiences and insights into the subject. For each of the above-mentioned schools, in order to protect their identity, the names given to the schools are pseudonyms.

Data Collection

The aim of using more than one method or a triangulation of methods is to increase the depth and breadth of understanding that an investigation can yield (Berg, 2007:8). As Denzin (1978: 101, in Berg, 2007:8) suggests that triangulation includes "multiple data collection procedures, multiple theoretical perspectives and multiple analysis techniques". This PhD study therefore employed a triangulation of methods of qualitative data collection; focus groups and semi-structured interviews, in order to increase the depth and breadth of understanding to the investigation. Interviews were documented through the use of a tape recorder and desk microphone and a note-pad.

Focus Groups

Focus groups are seen as "group discussions organised to explore a specific set of issues such as people's views and experiences of contraception, drink driving, nutrition or mental illness" (Kitzinger, 1994: 103). In the context of this study, the specific set of issues involved bullying and racist bullying. Focus groups are under-used in social research; although they have a long history in market research (Morgan 1997: 17). There are a number of benefits associated with the use of focus group research which involves organized discussion with a selected group of individuals to gain information about their views and experiences of a topic. According to Langford and McDonagh (2003: 314):

> ". . . focus groups have the additional advantage in that group members can react to and build upon the responses and comments of others, an effect which could lead to the emergence of information or the creation of ideas that would otherwise not have occurred" (Langford and McDonagh, 2003: 314).

Focus group interviewing is particularly suited for obtaining several perspectives about the same topic and is suitable for use with children. (Gibbs, 2005:1). There is also the importance of interaction and the need for a group to have something in common. Finally, focus groups assist to negotiate individual interviews.

The purpose of using focus groups for this research was primarily to obtain a deeper knowledge of pupils' perceptions of bullying and racist bullying as well as gaining multiple perspectives from pupils on both topics. The focus groups were structured around four key areas, (i) what was bullying and racist bullying and how did it occur? (ii) why does bullying and racist bullying occur? (iii) what did the pupils do? Tell a teacher, intervene or do nothing? and (iv) how do schools respond to preventing and intervening when incidents were reported and in pupils opinion, were they effective? Responses to questions in each of the four areas were provided, however, multiple perspectives were given when pupils would elaborate on various responses. Particularly so, this occurred when discussing issues such as why bullying and racist bullying occurred, why victims largely preferred to remain silent and why fewer pupils preferred to inform the teachers (See findings chapters 6 and 7).

In addition, the researcher was able to observe interactions between pupils, for example, during the group sessions when pupils interacted with each other when completing the spider diagrams. It was interesting to observe their comments, their reactions from what they scribbled and the questions they asked each other as a result of what they had written. Another purpose of using focus groups was to negotiate access to those pupils who subsequently would be involved in individual interviews. One main reason for this was to gain enriched data on their perceptions of school bullying and racist bullying as well as any possible lived experiences of pupils.

For the majority of the focus groups, pupils shared their understandings of bullying and racist bullying, particularly at Modern Eastern Suburban School and School for the Excluded. For example, pupils would reveal the nature of bullying, how it occurred and many pupils even illustrated their answers through actions, particularly when describing physical bullying. Shared understandings such as these would not necessarily come from individual interviews as often many pupils responses would instigate a reaction from other members in the group who would either agree or follow up with more detail in the initial response. Therefore conducting focus groups was important not only to negotiate to lead to further individual interviews, however, also to obtain detailed responses by pupils which were ad hoc. At Old East End Community College, at times, views did often come from dominant group members and then others would follow the same answer, many providing examples. This was particularly so during the discussions on bullying. Due to the sensitive nature of the subject, the possibility of gaining data on any lived experiences during the focus group interviews was obviously limited.

Despite the reasons why focus groups were used, it is acknowledged that there are various weaknesses with the use. The small number of respondents limits generalization to the wider population (Stewart and Shamdasani, 1990 in Burton, 2000:193). Also, the results may be biased by a particularly dominant group member and the open-ended nature of responses may make interpreting results difficult. Where similar situations had arisen, this was dealt with by managing the group to allow each pupil to voice their opinion. This often involved stopping other pupils who began to talk to each other, whilst another pupil in the group was answering a question. Where the conversation drifted too far out, quick intervention was made to steer the discussion back to the original question. It was noted that the researcher as interviewer may influence the responses of the group members (Stewart and Shamdasani, 1990 in Burton, 2000: 194). For example, as Berg (2007: 148) points out, the quality of the data is deeply influenced by the skills of the researcher to motivate and moderate. As an inexperienced researcher to the field, despite the activities used, generating quality data proved a challenge at times, in particular from Old East End Community College, where some pupils in the earlier focus groups did not cooperate sensibly with the session. This was overcome by requesting those pupils who were persistently disruptive to leave the classroom and rejoin their form class.

Meetings with the Head Teachers and pastoral care workers allowed for the negotiation of focus group style, year groups and sampling numbers. Academic research consistently reveals that the peak age for school bullying is between 10/11 through to 14/15 (Salmivalli 2002; Sullivan *et al.,* 2005) and therefore this was the age group it was most useful to target. Punch (2005) stresses that the sample must fit in with the other components of the study.

> "There must be an internal consistency and a coherent logic, across the study's components, including its sampling. The sampling plan . . . should line up with the purposes and the research questions of the study" (Punch 2005: 188).

As the subject is sensitive, the sample had been selected by negotiating the most appropriate classes with the head and pastoral teachers. Individual interviews with focus group members were then conducted with the consent of the pupil themselves, their parents and the school.

Preparation involved researching the various school anti-bullying tool kits, which helped to gain an awareness of the aims and objectives of school anti-bullying prevention. Furthermore, tools were used in order to assist pupils to comprehend what the core issues of bullying and racism were, develop their awareness of the subject and an easier method to steer the questions onto any lived experiences. A search was undertaken of the Department for Education and Skills (DfES) website and published literature following which a list of eight to nine basic questions were devised for the focus group interviews: (i) From this video can you tell me what this means to you? (ii) How would you define bullying? (iii) What ways do you think bullying is carried out? (iv) Have you seen anyone being bullied? Where? (iv) If you did, what did you do? (v) Why do you think this happens? (vi) What is racist bullying? (vii) How is it carried out and why? What are your thoughts on bullying/racist bullying? (viii) In what ways do you think this kind of bullying and racist bullying behaviour can be stopped? How? (ix) What do the school teachers do to stop this?

All questions used were previously approved by the supervisory team as well as the schools. Planning also included in-depth discussions with supervisors on the particular tools for activities that would be appropriate, manageable and stimulating to carry out with the focus groups.

Old East End Community College

The process for sampling pupils in years 7 to 9 involved discussions and negotiation with the pastoral health and education teacher. As shown in Table 4, ten focus groups, including a pilot focus group were arranged. For feasibility and manageability purposes, sampling numbers were negotiated by requesting to interview up to two groups per year. Focus groups with pupils were arranged during their Personal Social Health and Education classes. Extra focus groups were arranged for years 7 and 9 in order to negotiate and secure individual interviews, because few pupils initially volunteered. Although there was no explanation given for the low response, it can be assumed that it may have been due to the sensitivity of the subject. Important patterns were emerging in particular between year 7 and year 9. A pattern began to develop on common attitudes on the dynamics of bullying and racist attitudes and the new immigrant population in the city of Newcastle-upon-Tyne. Pupils in year 7 displayed a greater understanding of bullying; in contrast, pupils in year 9 demonstrated not only an understanding of bullying, but also an increased awareness of racist bullying and the related issues.

Focus groups began with no more than ten pupils in each session. However, after conducting one pilot sample and two unsupervised focus group sessions, it became increasingly difficult to manage the group and capture everyone's voices and views on tape. In order to overcome this, it was requested to interview no more than six pupils in future focus groups. Therefore, after the pilot sample and first two focus groups, which contained 10 pupils, thereafter, the remaining 7 focus groups consisted of no more than 6 pupils. Table 4 lists not only the year group, but also the date in which each focus group was conducted and at the time they were conducted. The focus groups lasted between 35 to 50 minutes, however, 40 minutes on average. A total of ten focus groups, including the pilot sample were conducted at this school from November 2005 to February 2006 (see Table 4).

Table 4: Focus Groups in Old East End Community College

Year:	Date:	Time:
Pilot sample (yrs 8 and 9)	17th November 2005	1.15pm
Year 9	24th November 2005	10.30am
Year 8	29th November 2005	1.05pm
Year 9	1st December 2005	10.30am
Year 8	13th December 2005	1.05pm
Year 7	19th January 2006	1.05pm
Year 7	26th January 2006 (n/r)	12.45pm
Year 9	27th January 2006	11.50am
Year 7	2nd February 2006	1.05pm
Year 9	10th February 2006 (n/r—not recorded)	11.50am

Modern Eastern Suburban School

The process for sampling pupils in year's 7 to 9 was primarily through discussions and negotiations with the Assistant Head Teacher and pupils were interviewed in focus groups during their Citizenship classes. Based upon the experiences at Old East End Community College, it was requested that the groups should consist of no more than 6 to 7 pupils. A total of six focus groups of those who volunteered were conducted at this school during March 2006 as can be seen in Table 5. Except for the focus group which was conducted on March 9th 2006 at 2.10pm, which had 7 pupils, the remaining 5 focus groups had no more than 6 pupils. Again table 5 lists the dates of the focus group sessions and times they began, the group sessions lasted between 40-45 minutes approximately.

The participant rate of response from Modern Eastern Suburban School was poor and whilst no explanation was given, it can be assumed that the reluctance to participate was due to the sensitive nature of the subject. It is interesting to note that more boys than girls volunteered to take part in the focus groups. This reaction was quite unlike Old East End Community College. Here, all pupils from years 7 to 9 were quite comfortable discussing both bullying and racist bullying, including those from minority ethnic backgrounds.

Table 5: Focus Groups in Modern Eastern Suburban School

Year:	Date:	Time:
Year 8	9th March 2006	1.30pm
Year 8	9th March 2006 (n/r)	2.10pm
Year 9	10th March 2006	1.30pm
Year 9	10th March 2006	2.10pm
Year 7	15th March 2006	2.10pm
Year 7	22nd March 2006	2.10pm

School for the Excluded

Two focus group interviews were carried out in this school which was arranged by the Head Teacher and class tutors. The focus groups were conducted in January 2006, as shown in Table 6 and there were 6 pupils in each group session and in order to ensure an effective delivery, the class tutors were present throughout the focus group session. Table 6 also details the dates of the focus group and the time each session began and ended. The Head Teacher advised that year seven pupils were not suitable to take part. In view of the size of the school and number of pupils on roll, the response was adequate and analogous to Modern Eastern Suburban School. As here, like Modern Eastern, the pupils were at ease during discussions. Many of the pupils had witnessed incidents of racist bullying at their previous mainstream schools; such experiences had allowed them to develop an innate insight of the dynamics of racist bullying.

Table 6: Focus Groups in the School for the Excluded

Year:	Date:	Time:
Years 8 & 9 (group 3)	16th January 2006	12.20-1.05pm
Year 9 (group 6)	20th January 2006	12.20-1.05pm

Delivering Focus Groups

The process of fieldwork began with a pilot focus group study on November 17th 2005 in Old East End Community College. It was recommended by the supervisory team and the pastoral teacher that a pilot sample be conducted. This is in accordance with Wilkinson (2004:349) who believes focus group projects should not be attempted without a practice session or a full-scale pilot sample. She further argues that new researchers make many mistakes due to nerves; such as failure to listen and follow-up appropriately, talk too much and use sequential questioning (2004). Whilst the pilot sample did draw out nerves, some mistakes were made, although none of those listed above, except for sequential questioning. The pilot sample comprised of six pupils ranging from years 7 through to 9 and the pastoral teacher was present. Unfortunately, the anti-bullying video had been left behind in the office drawer. A sketch-pad for pupils to complete the spider diagram, however, was utilized. The idea to use post-it notes to allow pupils to write down racist terminologies they had heard, rather than vocalize them, was realized following the pilot sample. This had the effect of making the participants both uncomfortable and hesitant, thus avoiding any breach of the code of ethics against ensuring the comfort and safety of participants at all times (See pp 149).

The questions and moderating the focus group were delivered with relative ease as the presence of the teacher was morally supportive as the teacher assisted in controlling the group as well as asking any follow up questions to the group. During the initial first fifteen minutes of the discussion it was realized that the tape was on to play rather than record. Nevertheless some discussion on attitudes towards racist bullying and refugee/asylum seekers and minority ethnic communities turned out to be of reasonable data. Issues that arose from this pilot group were understanding how to moderate the group efficiently so whoever was talking was listened to by the group. As a result of the pilot, there were lessons learned as to the preparation for the focus groups, which were; checklists were made on all necessary materials prior to leaving for the school, spending a few minutes to set up activities to ensure order of delivery and arriving for each interview approximately ten minutes before the focus group. As Wilkinson (2004: 350) argues, "Proper preparation for and efficient planning of, the focus group session itself is just as essential as moderator's skills for obtaining high-quality data"(2004: 350).

Another lesson learned from the pilot sample included setting a time limit on each question answered so as to ensure all important issues were covered, while not interrupting the flow of the discussion. Moderating the time pupils spent on the spider diagram needed careful thought and adjustment and this process took up to two or three focus group sessions before the researcher was able to organize pupils efficiently, especially the younger pupils in year 7. A final reflection on the pilot sample that was fed into subsequent focus groups was that the researcher should pose fewer questions and allow the participant to speak in an informal way in order to allow the discussion to flow, rather than restrict the discussion by a more sequential style of delivery.

Every focus group began with a short introduction detailing, what the research entailed and each pupil was asked to identify themselves and one thing they liked to do. This allowed the researcher, as a facilitator to command control, while putting the pupils at ease. The intention was for them to realize the session involved a subject that is serious and sensitive, but could also be informal, thought provoking and interesting. As Langford and McDonagh (2005: 174) claim "It is extremely important that each participant feels comfortable and secure at all times". Reactions from nearly all pupils were co-operative, although some would use the session as an opportunity to relax and show off to their peers. It was crucial that each pupil felt and believed that their presence was valued and that their comments were of the utmost importance (Alderson and Morrow, 2004:115). To ensure that all pupils felt comfortable and important throughout the focus group, each was given the chance to speak and the group was informed of the importance of what they had to say.

Mechanisms to engage pupils in discussion were used throughout the focus groups, for example, the use of a five minute video encouraged discussion. Other than the focus groups conducted at the School for the Excluded and the first two conducted in Old East End Community College, all focus groups were carried out without any staff member present. This was mainly because the focus groups were held during the year groups PSHE or Citizenship class time and therefore, no teacher was available to be present during the session. Another explanation given for conducting the sessions alone, as the pastoral teacher from Old East End Community College suggested, was that pupils may not feel comfortable discussing issues relating to bullying and racist bullying in the presence of their year tutor, but would do so in front of an outside researcher. In all three schools, as the class time given was one hour, on average, each focus group lasted between 35-50 minutes, depending upon how quickly pupils took to settle down, how quickly they interacted with and responded to questions. With year 7 in particular, the transition between activities took slightly longer as pupils were considerably more hyper compared to those in year's 8 and 9.

The first prompt used was the five minute video "Kick It Bullying", and it's main use, as Langford and McDonagh agree, clearly focuses participants on the issues in question and provides a "useful stimulus to subsequent discussion" (2005: 179). The purpose of the anti-bullying video was to stimulate pupils' discussion from the outset and allow them to engage with the video and explore issues around bullying. As a point of commencing the discussion after viewing the video, it was put to all pupils in each focus group, years 7-9, immediately what their initial thoughts were of the video, "what did you think of this?" Whilst not phrased exactly in the original set of focus group questions, the purpose was to discover how many pupils paid attention, if any showed emotion towards the issues raised in the video, particularly the role-plays and to answer without any influence of others as Berg

(2007:157) also recommends that "Exercises and activities also allow the moderator to determine what subjects individually know or believe without the influence of others in the group" (Berg, 2007). As experienced from the pilot focus group, the video also enabled me as a moderator to settle into the focus group session and be more prepared to effectively launch the group into an engaging discussion. This part to the focus group usually lasted between 2-3 minutes with all year groups. The first question from the focus group list presented was "what do you think is bullying?" with the purpose to explore the depth of pupils understanding on the nature of bullying and if pupils could identify bullying in a few words or along with examples of how it occurs.

Following on from this, the second prompt used was a sketch pad with the spider diagram entitled "Bullying, what is it?" was presented to the group asking them to write down what they understood what constituted bullying. For every focus group, a fresh sketchpad sheet for the spider diagram with the same title written had been used (for a select sample, please see appendices 1-4:i). The rationale behind the spider diagram was to discover how pupils initially identified the characteristics of bullying, how well they engaged with the subject of bullying, to allow them to explore the subject more in their minds whilst writing, as well as to observe how pupils interacted with each other during the activity. The exercise was also a lead into a deeper exploration on what pupils believed bullying to be, who was the perpetrator, the victim, why the particular individual was selected, how much bullying had they witnessed, and if anyone was able to share any lived experiences. The exercise led to an overall discussion on pupils' perceptions into the nature, extent and manifestation of bullying. These were for general exploratory purposes to gain an understanding of what forms of bullying occurred and where it generally occurred in the school.

Statements about bullying were written on a sketch pad and used to stimulate opinions and discussion, with an objective to develop pupils' perceptions and discussion on the subject of bullying. These were presented to each year group at each school as it was understood that since bullying occurred from an early age, pupils' comprehension would be stronger. Statements included: (i) None of us deserve to be bullied); (ii) Just having a laugh is not bullying; (iii) Girls bully more than boys do; (iv) If you are being bullied don't tell anyone, it will make things worse; (v) Bullying is part of growing up (vi) People who get bullied should change themselves, they wouldn't get bullied if they weren't different! The bullying statements were primarily to further stimulate pupils' opinions and explore their individual perceptions behind each situation.

Post it notes were distributed to pupils, targeted to each year, in order to allow them to write down various racist comments they have come across in the school, the main purpose for this was to allow them to feel comfortable disclosing what they had heard rather than vocalizing racist terminologies. The rationale behind giving each pupil post-it notes was to allow them to feel comfortable in relation to sharing sensitive information, with the knowledge that this would remain confidential and therefore refrain from causing any harm (to be discussed in further detail in the Political and Ethical Issues section, pp149).

Pupils were then questioned as to what and how they identified what racist bullying was and how it occurred. Whilst nearly all pupils from each year were able to identify the general characteristics of racist bullying, pupils from years 8 and 9 were able to explore further, rather than just skin colour. Identifying the nature of racist bullying and causes were further prompted by discussing particular popular television programmes and how the media influences racist behaviour. Another purpose for the discussion was also to identify the depth in knowledge pupils had about the nature and characteristics of racist bullying.

Finally, a quiz was presented to the groups which were used in order to obtain a deeper insight in to their knowledge and attitude on the subjects and to prompt the discussions further. The short quiz comprised of 4-5 scenarios which were read out to pupils, asking them to identify if the situation was either a case of bullying, racist bullying or merely a joke. A primary purpose to this quiz was to particularly explore how much pupils were able to distinguish between a situation that involved bullying and what was not considered to be bullying. Furthermore, the quiz sought to establish how far young people deemed bullying and racist bullying as being normal, particularly as the literature suggests that much of young people's perceptions and prejudicial attitude derives from the influence of families at homes and from the communities (Sibbitt, 1997; Troyna and Hatcher, 1991; Cockburn, 2007).

Questions revolving around racist bullying were purposely asked to explore pupils' reactions and forms of response as to whether they disapproved or would say nothing. The scenario questions asked included the following: (i) A boy in year 7 is walking to school when three boys in year 10 come up to him and corner him and they demand that he gives them his money or mobile phone or else; (ii) Three white girls are playing together during lunch break when an Asian girl who is also in the same class comes up to them and she wants to join in. One of the girls turns around and says in a nasty tone, "Get lost you dumb P***"; (iii) Sally walks into the playground during the lunch break, Janet, whom Sally argued with the day before is playing with some friends. Sally goes up to them and asks to join in. Janet turns around and says; "I think Sally is a real nerd with those glasses on, she smells and I don't think that anyone should talk to her". They all then walk away from her . . . ; (iv) Someone is laughing and teasing you by calling you names such as "stupid" and saying things like "you don't have any friends". But, when they are saying these things to you, they ARE NOT saying it in front of anyone, so not to embarrass you; (v) Anil, this kid, he is late for chemistry class and as he is runs down the corridor, standing outside of one classroom are 4 White boys, one of them sticks his leg out and trips him up. As Anil goes crashing to the floor, the kid who tripped him up yells out: "Enjoyed your trip, you f*****g darkie!!"

Whilst this quiz was targeted to all years, this was not delivered to every focus group. Pupils were either already engaged in a deep discussion about both subjects and therefore the quiz was not seen as being necessary, this was applicable to year 9 focus groups in Modern Eastern Suburban School (table 5) or, there was no time. The latter was particularly the case for year 7, 19th January 2006 (table 4).

Whilst the core aim of using all the prompts were to stimulate and engage pupils into a meaningful discussion around the subject of bullying and racist bullying, particularly, the video, spider diagram

BULLYING AND RACIST BULLYING IN SCHOOLS

and the post-it notes generated data which were used in the findings chapters. Data generated by the video through pupils' discussion were analyzed by categorizing the data in various themes and headers and subsequently incorporated into the necessary sections in the findings chapters, such as, pupils identifying the nature and characteristics of bullying. The spider diagram, which also generated data was analyzed by using the most common written responses and used in chapter five which discusses pupils' identification of bullying. The post-it notes whilst also generating data, was analyzed by using the most common responses given and various terms were incorporated in chapter five where pupils identified the nature of racist bullying. The main issue which arose, particularly with the post-it notes were to justify the ethics of their use, and not to appear to be eliciting any racist language from pupils.

Following on from this, in the concluding segment to the focus group session, pupils from each year were then asked what had they done or not done when witnessing incidents of bullying and racist bullying, if in their opinion teachers did anything and what preventative measures could be taken. The rationale behind such questions were to explore their perceptions and opinions in greater depth and to explore if they found informing a teacher effective or what preventative and intervention measures worked or did not work in the school.

It became apparent during the initial focus groups that pupils were more engaged when their responses were further explored and also when the atmosphere of the discussion was more relaxed. They engaged with each other more during the activities that involved them writing and thinking about what they understood bullying to be. None of the focus groups from the three schools was the same; however, key themes were drawn out in every session. For the most part, pupils did not discuss direct experiences of bullying, but rather their perceptions on the subject as witnesses.

As a researcher, it was important to be able to reach out to pupils on a level where the age gap between them and the researcher did not matter. Explaining to pupils how important their role was to the research and conducting informal discussions enabled the facilitator to try and bridge this gap. Consent in the form of written consent letters was obtained at all stages of the fieldwork from the focus groups to the semi-structured individual interviews, particularly at Modern Eastern Suburban School. A detailed discussion on consent is provided in the last section of this chapter.

In addition to cassette recording all focus group interviews and noting general issues down in a note-pad, such as pupils' names, common patterns in response, personal reflective diaries detailing experiences and feelings after each interview were recorded, first by tape recorder on leaving the school premises, and then in a written diary. These diary entries assisted in reflecting upon my immediate reactions. Some interviews unfortunately did not record due to minor technical problems with the desk microphone and in these instances; detailed reflective journal notes were taken. The initial two or three focus groups were not as well delivered as the rest due to a number of issues. Primarily, the first three focus groups consisted of up to ten pupils, which, at times, made it difficult to provide adequate attention to all of them and often when one pupil was speaking, two or three others would interrupt. Secondly, it proved extremely difficult to capture what every pupil was saying and thus the transcription process was extremely lengthy. Thirdly, my lack of experience in focus group control showed through in the early ones. It was important to develop a relationship/ rapport with students which were positive. Yet to agree with Berg (2007:116),

> "with regard to rapport, which can be defined as the positive feelings that develop between the interviewer and the subject, it should not be understood as meaning there are no boundaries between the interviewer and the subject . . . The dramaturgical interview should not be a dialogue, with more or less equal time allocated to each participant, because the whole point is to obtain information from the subject. In many ways, the ideal situation would be to assert the subject in conveying almost a monologue on the research topic" (Berg, 2007:117).

Such rapport came with experience, however moderate rapport was established with pupils almost from the outset of the focus groups interviews, in that pupils engaged immediately after viewing the anti-bullying video and since the initial few were conducted at Old

East End Community College, this varied per group. However, there was more rapport established at Modern Eastern Suburban School and School for the Excluded. Pupils from Modern Eastern Suburban School and School for the Excluded were more willing and more knowledgeable in developing upon why bullying occurred and therefore rapport came easier, however, experience with the initial few focus groups at Old East End Community College allowed for reflect and make changes, which resulted in a more successful rapport with pupils and obtaining data.

Such changes came about with discussions with supervisors and with further reflection, it was decided to allow pupils to talk more, with the purpose to allow pupils to engage with each other and feel more comfortable, yet also to ensure the topic did not deviate. This technique improved establishing rapport with pupils significantly with time, practice and confidence.

Semi-Structured Interviews

Semi-structured individual interviews were the second method to be used as part of the research. The purpose of the interviews, as a result of the focus groups was to allow for more in depth assessment of individuals perceptions on the subject of school bullying and racism and enhance the purpose of exploratory research. A further purpose was to allow for an exploration of the lived experiences of individuals *as* victims, onlookers and perpetrators of racist school bullying. Another purpose of the individual interviews was to discuss individual experiences and much of the questions in the semi structured interviews were focused on these experiences, for e.g. Have you been bullied before? When? How long? Do you want to tell me about it? How did it make you feel? (For a full set of questions, see pp 138). Pupils who agreed to participate in the individual interviews as a result of the focus group sessions may not have been easily individually identified as either being a victim, perpetrator or simply a spectator. A final purpose of the individual interviews was to assert more authority on qualitative research in this area as it is largely underused.

Although this type of interview style allows the interviewees to digress and explain their answers in more depth, the quality of the data depends greatly upon how well the researcher prepares in advance and also how well they are able to respond to issues raised. Semi-structured interviews require more training and more mental preparation before each session. In order to be successful semi-structured interviews require three main ingredients; (i) preparation prior to the interview; (ii) discipline and creativity during the session and (iii) time for analysis and interpretation after the session (Wengraf, 2002:5). These three requirements were met through careful preparation of the individual interview questions together with appropriate use of anti-bullying and anti-racist photographs and pictures during the interviews. This was followed by a constant review of the data during the analysis stage, including many amendments to the data analysis. The entire data analysis and interpretation process took almost seven months. Semi-structured interviews were conducted amongst pupils from years 7-9 from all three schools who consented to the interview. Interviews were also carried out with teachers in the schools, two youth workers and a parent of a pupil from the School for the Excluded.

Individual interviews lasted approximately between fifteen to thirty minutes. The interviews were structured around four key areas, (i) pupils identification of bullying and racist bullying (ii) any lived experiences of victimization or witnessed; (iii) pupils actions, either informing an adult or remaining silent; (iv) effectiveness of adult (parent or teacher) intervention.

Pupils were encouraged to speak freely about their perceptions and were not pressurised into revealing any information that made them uncomfortable. Therefore, the design of the interviews was informal. As McNeil and Chapman (2005, 58) assert, "Semi-structured interviews are perceived as a unique type of conversational interaction and issues are prepared with a semi planned script with the intention to go into matters 'in-depth'" (McNeil & Chapman, 2005). Planning for the individual interviews fieldwork involved many discussions with supervisors. Much of the preparation involved researching various school anti-bullying resources such as from the 'Planning and Preparation' the then, Department for Education and Skills (DfES) website, now Department for Education (DfE) and published literature. This resulted in a list of twelve to thirteen basic questions: (i) From these images/pictures what does this mean to you? What do you think is going on here? What does bullying/racist bullying mean to you? (ii) Have you been bullied before? Racially bullied? When? How long? (iii) If yes, by which gender/age group? (iv) If no, do you know anyone who has been bullied or racially bullied? (v) Do you want to tell me about it? (How did this happen? What happened? Where did this happen? Why?); (vi) How did you feel? (vii) Did you tell anyone about it? Who? (I.e. parents, teacher, friend); (viii) What did they do about it? (ix) Did the bullying/racism stop as a result of their intervention? (x) Have you ever bullied/racially bullied someone before? (xi) What did you do? (xii) Why did you do this? Did no-one do anything to stop the bullying/racism from happening? (xiii) Did that person tell anyone? The questions were intentionally kept as simple as possible; however, they were sufficiently open for pupils to develop their views. The rationale behind the questions was primarily for narrative purposes and to explore pupils' perceptions and where necessary, lived experiences.

All interviews in the secondary schools were secured as a result of distributing consent letters to pupils in years seven to nine requesting participation in semi-structured individual interviews. These letters were given to the year tutors who distributed them to each pupil and teachers confirmed with the pastoral teachers that each pupil had been given letters. Some of the pupils' from each school, who consented to the individual interviews, did so because of their participation in the focus groups. With the School for the Excluded however, consent letters were only given to each class from which the focus group interviews were conducted.

The prompt used were a series of images/pictures downloaded from Google Images, that were targeted to all year pupils during the interviews, and pupils were questioned on their immediate perceptions as a result of viewing the pictures. These images/pictures of various young people indicated they were being victimized or pictures of minority ethnic pupils were primarily utilized in order to assist in generating the pupils understanding and interest in the subject and also as an ice-breaker to lead into the questions. As most of the images were characterizations, other than pictures of minority ethnic groups, copyright issues were considered and therefore, each image/picture was duly referenced. This process took no longer than 2-3 minutes. Following on from this, the main part of the interview began. Depending upon whether the participant revealed whether they had been victimized or witnessed incidents of bullying or racist bullying, most of the original questions listed above were covered. However, for those who had identified a victimized state, there was more emphasis placed around their lived experiences, how they felt, whether they informed an adult and, as a result, what forms of action were taken, or neglected and whether in their opinion, the outcome was positive or not. Questions posed to the pupils were intentionally kept brief and open in order not to restrict any answers, nor to detract the participant's enthusiasm.

In Old East End Community College, nine pupils from year's 7 to 9 volunteered to take part in the interview (4 girls and 5 boys, see Table 7). One girl who participated in the focus group volunteered for the individual interview, the others volunteered as a result of an invitation letter and year tutor's' request as can be seen in Table 7. In Modern Eastern Suburban School only one individual interview was conducted (Table 8). This was with one girl year 8, who also volunteered to participate in the focus group research. Furthermore, table 8 includes an interview with a group of peer mentors, (year 11) who were interviewed on their perspectives of bullying and racist bullying in the school, however, there were no prompts used for discussion like there were for the focus groups. In addition, five peer mentors (year 9), who operate a lunch time peer mentoring system within the school, were interviewed in relation to their association with peers who were being bullied. This group interview was primarily conducted to gain a background perspective of the school type of response, there was no consent letters required as this was not a formal interview and was not recorded. At the School for the Excluded, a total of five interviews were conducted (Table 9). All five pupils (2 girls, 3 boys—years 8 and 9), were interviewed as a result of volunteering at the focus group sessions. Table 9 reveals how interviews were spread across three dates with two interviews held on two occasions and a single interview at the end on 6th February 2006. Therefore a total of fifteen individual interviews with pupils across all three schools were conducted.

Table 7: Individual Interviews with Pupils in Old East End Community College

Year:	Date:	Start Time:
Year 7 (1 pupil)	8th February 2006	11am
Year 7 (2 pupils)	15th February 2006	11am
Year 7 (1 pupil)	29th March 2006	11am
Year 8 & 9 (5 pupils)	17th May 2006	11am

Table 8: Individual Interviews with Pupils in Modern Eastern Suburban School

Year:	Date:	Time:
Year 11 (peer mentors)	13th February 2006	11am (n/r)
Year 8 (1 pupil)	6th April 2006	11.50am

Table 9: Individual Interviews with Pupils in the School for the Excluded

Year:	Date:	Time:
Year 8 (2 pupils)	23rd January 2006	1pm
Year 9 (2 pupils)	25th January 2006	1pm
Year 9 (1 pupil)	6th February 2006	10.30am (n/r)

Individual interviewees allowed for the interviews to be recorded and for the most part participants spoke at length. One interview with a pupil did not record (Table 8) and in another interview a pupil refused permission for it to be recorded (Table 9). Upon reflection, it was hoped that overall more individual interviews could have been consented to and carried out. However, this depended upon consent by both pupil and parent and the nature and sensitivity of the subject had to be taken into consideration. Although not many pupils talked about their direct experience of being victims of bullying, the individual interviews involved pupils with a range of experiences some of whom, in their introduction, had identified that they had experienced victimization.

At Old East End Community College, out of the nine interviews, five were self-identified victims and they recounted their experiences. One did not self-identify as a bully, but was identified as such by another pupil. This information was revealed during the individual interview with one pupil who identified a focus group participant as a bully (for ethical issues, see pp 145). As this was an ethical issue, the rule of confidentiality had already been explained to all participants. Furthermore, all participating pupils were asked not to discuss the contents of the interview with anyone. Therefore this pupil was allowed to continue as she had been a victim of bullying, had participated during the same focus group as the pupil she identified as a bully and a main purpose for her agreeing to the interview, is because she wanted to share her experiences. Immediately after the information was disclosed she was encouraged to speak to an adult but it emerged that she had already spoken with her house tutor as well as her parents. The remaining three interviewees were bystanders. However all pupils were able to express an opinion on school bullying and racism. In Modern Eastern Suburban School, the only pupil who volunteered for an individual interview was a bystander. At the School for the Excluded, out of five interviews, two were victims, one of whom was also a self-identified bully. Another participant volunteered because her sister had been victimized and wanted to share her experiences with me. The other two were neither a victim nor a bully, but presented accounts of incidents that they had witnessed. Subsequently, at this school, a wide range of data was collected. Participants were very relaxed and for the most part, open.

Semi-Structured Interviews with Teachers, Parents and Youth Workers

The sampling process for negotiating interviews with teachers was convenience sampling, i.e. those who agreed to be interviewed and who were available to participate (Berg 1996). Berg (2007: 43) describes this sampling as including all those close at hand or easily accessible. As a convenience sample, the method was weak, there were limited numbers of teachers available who were willing to participate, yet the sample allowed the researcher to make contact with teachers who had direct contact with pupils that were interviewed. Berg (2007:43) further argues that such a strategy as the convenience sample is an excellent means to obtain preliminary information about research questions quickly and inexpensively and therefore, "convenience samples must be evaluated for appropriateness of fit for a given study" (Berg, 2007).

Similarly, the weakness of using the convenience sample can be acknowledged in that it was discovered how representative the views expressed by teachers were. Where the data from the teachers' interviews has been evaluated, only the appropriate data has been used in findings chapters, 5, 6 and 7. The teachers included, head and assistant head teachers; head of citizenship; pastoral care and learning mentors; year and form tutors. A breakdown of these categories is illustrated below. Table 10 reveals that four teachers were interviewed, including the pastoral teacher as well as the deputy head in Old East End Community College. Table 11 reveals that in addition to interviewing one head of year 7 and two learning mentors, the head of citizenship and a year tutor were also interviewed in Modern Eastern Suburban School. Table 12 further shows a mixture of teacher types including a parent at the School for the Excluded. These teachers included three class teachers and an assistant teacher as well as the head teacher. In addition to this, interviews were conducted with two detached youth workers as shown in Table 13. Each interview took up to twenty five minutes, except for one of the learning mentors and one youth worker both of which took up to forty five minutes. In total, seventeen interviews were conducted. The interviews were structured around four key areas, (i) how adults identified the nature, characteristics of bullying, gender and age differences and how it occurred around the school; (ii) in their opinion, how much bullying and racist bullying occurred and why (iii) any lived experiences by adults, or through their children/pupils; (iv) what forms of anti-bullying and anti-racist prevention and intervention measures were used, sanctions implemented and in their opinion, enough was being done by the school to effectively respond to incidents reported. For the adult interviews, there were no activities used to prompt the discussions.

The list of semi-structured questions devised was brief (no more than seven basic questions); however, they were formulated in order to allow for lengthy discussions and any necessary follow up questions, they were also designed to target both teachers, parents and outside agencies, such as youth workers. Questions included: (i) How would you define what bullying is? What racism is? What does it mean to you? This relates to area 1 with identifying the nature, characteristic of bullying and prevalence of them. (ii) Do you know if your child has been a victim of bullying? This relates to area 3 on any lived experiences (iii) Can you tell me about their experiences? Again associating with area 3 (iv) In what ways do you think the nature of bullying is different now than when you were growing up Have you ever been a victim of bullying? This can be associated with key area 1 (v) Has the school written to you with regards to bullying? Racist bullying? What are they doing to eradicate the problem? Do you think the school is doing enough to tackle the issue? Such questions as these can be linked with area 4 which deals with all forms of how schools respond to bullying and racist bullying (vi) Have you been invited to attend any training sessions/meetings on this subject? This can be linked in with key area 4 (vii) What do you think can be done/should be done to tackle this problem? This question can also be associated with the fourth key area, however, this was more directly related to obtaining teachers perceptions and opinions of the anti-bullying preventative measures that the school and if in their opinion if they considered such measures effective enough, and if not, how would they like such measures to be improved upon. The purpose for these questions was primarily for perception and exploratory reasons. Another purpose was to allow for facilitation into an examination of adults perceptions and attitudes towards school bullying and racism and of the ways in which these issues can be addressed.

The questions however, did vary between teachers, youth workers and the parent. When interviewing the parent, the discussion largely focused upon how their children were victims and perpetrators of bullying, the lived experiences, and how the schools responded. In contrast, with teachers, there was much more discussion on identifying what bullying and racist bullying was how the nature of bullying differed between gender and age, what forms of sanctions were used and preventative strategies employed by the school. Much of the teacher's discussion centered around what drove pupils to bully and for those teachers who witnessed racial prejudice, what reasons drove pupils to be racist. There were few teachers however, who did provide personal experiences of bullying and that of their children. These interviews came from teachers from the School for the Excluded. The two youth workers however, provided fuller discussions in that all key areas were covered in the interviews, including perceptions and opinions on the effectiveness/inefficiency of school response and lack of anti-bullying training in teachers. The rationale behind the way these interviews were steered, lay in assessing in the first few minutes how adults responded to key questions, such as "Do you know if your child has been a victim of bullying?", "Can you tell me about their experiences?" and "What are they (the school) doing to eradicate the problem (bullying/ racist bullying)? Do you think the school is doing enough to tackle the issue?" Where adults appeared to be more responsive to questions such as these, follow-up questions were asked, with the intention of exploring facts and perceptions of the adults in much greater detail, so to allow for comparisons with the pupils responses when it came to the data analysis and conceptualization process.

Consent letters were sent out to pupils from all three schools, years 7 to 9, asking them to pass the letter on to their parents. This was followed by telephone calls and enquiries to the school. Continual attempts were made to access more parents throughout the duration of the fieldwork but with little success. Unfortunately, only one parent, whose child attended the School for the Excluded, agreed to take part in the interview. During the follow up in both secondary schools, the teachers revealed the fact that despite reminding pupils to speak with their parents, there was no response. It can be speculated that parents were either not given the consent letters or that they simply did not want to participate in the interviews.

Table 10: Interviews with Teachers in Old East End Community College

Date:	Time:
15th February 2006 (2 teachers)	11-1pm
14th March 2006 (2 teachers)	3pm

Table 11: Interviews with Teachers in Modern Eastern Suburban School

Date:	Time:
13th February 2006 (1 teacher, 2 learning mentors)	11am (n/r)
14th February 2006 (1 teacher)	8.50am
7th March 2006 (1 teacher)	2.10pm

Table 12: Interviews with Teachers and a Parent in the School for the Excluded

Date:	Time:
23rd January 2006 (2 teachers)	1pm
25th January 2006 (2 teachers)	1pm
6th February 2006 (1 teacher)	10.30am
2nd March 2006 (1 parent and daughter)	10.30am

Table 13: Interviews with Detached Youth Workers

Date:	Time:
23rd May 2006 (1 detached worker)	12 noon
21st June 2006 (1 detached worker)	1pm

Data Handling and Analysis

Interview cassettes were clearly labelled, with date, year group; interview type and school name (Wilkinson, 2004: 353). They were transcribed verbatim and verbal expressions, such as laughter at an issue were noted in brackets. It was decided to do this as it was felt that it contributed towards a fuller understanding of the meanings involved. For example, when pupils talked about cumulative bullying, and referred to one pupil targeted regularly, they described the example with such hilarity, that this revealed attitudinal perceptions of the subject. The first four interviews were transcribed shortly after they had been conducted; however the entire transcription process took seven months due to the short spacing of the interviews.

Once all interviews had been transcribed, it was decided to analyze the data using themes. An essential first step of analysis for semi-structured qualitative data involves a close reading of the data (Berg, 2007). This involved identifying aspects that may be significant (Boulton and Hammersley, 1996:290). Therefore, close repeat reading of the data and drawing out the main findings was a significant process in the data analysis. Furthermore, after examining the data, the analysis also involved going back to the literature in order to draw out themes. The process of the data analysis was carried out in two stages.

During stage one the data analysis followed the process described by Macnaghten (2004:74); that is of looking for main and repeated themes. Macnaghten (2004) reported that he marked quotable themes with a highlighter, folded down the corner of the page and indexed the page number on the front of the transcript. A similar process was used in this research; the transcripts were initially marked with various coloured highlighters in order to draw attention to repeated themes. From the transcripts, the process of analysis moved from reading a set of interviews to analyzing the data by school. This was further broken down by analyzing transcripts of pupils by year, with focus groups per school, and individual interviews per school. This process also included analyzing data from adults by school. It was decided to use a thematic process for the data analysis.

Initial analysis used the themes referred to in the transcripts. However, prior knowledge on the subject based on academic research was taken into account when searching for themes. There were also some specific research questions and objections in mind, for example, who is the bully? After several readings of all transcripts, the process of thematic data analysis involved creating a number of headers. These were arranged per year, per school for focus groups. For individual interviews, separate headers were created for pupils, teachers/parents and detached youth workers.

The process then involved reading through each transcript again matching headers and readjusting their titles. This was followed by a process of colour coding the headers and then colour coding the transcripts. To Bryman, (2004: 401), coding is one of the most central processes of data analysis. It entails reviewing transcripts and/or field notes and giving labels (names) to component parts that seem to be of potential theoretical significance and/or that appear to be particularly salient within the social worlds of those being studied (Bryman; 2004: 402). As Charmaz (1983:186), puts it, "Codes . . . serve as shorthand devices to label, separate, compile, and organise data . . . Coding in qualitative data analysis tends to be in a constant state of potential revision and fluidity . . . ." (Charmaz, 1983:186). Similarly, the colour coding was used in order to assist in identifying and differentiating which quotes would go under which heading.

From this stage, dialogues were copy/pasted electronically under relevant headings. For the focus groups each document was arranged per year per school; for the individual interviews amongst pupils, they were arranged by grouping pupils from both mainstream schools; this process was done in the same manner for pupils from the School for the Excluded, but on a separate document. Finally, copy/pasted dialogue was placed on separate documents for the individual interviews amongst adults, teachers per school, including the School for the Excluded and a separate document was prepared for detached youth workers.

For stage two analysis, the dialogues were analyzed under each header in all the grouped documents and further analysed by writing notes on the side of the electronically copy/pasted transcript. This assisted in drawing out the main themes. Six main themes were drawn from these transcripts and notes were also written separately in order to further interpret and analyse the dialogue, and interpret notes about any vocal expression by pupils. Finally, the headers were grouped under each theme and dialogue rearranged under the collapsed headers. This was in order for the headers to be categorised under the relevant theme and also to further narrow the dialogue and to avoid any overlap under each header. Flick et al. (2004:256) emphasize that if more than one description fits, the dominant one is used. They feel it is crucial at this stage of the process of categorization that descriptive labels are formulated very distinctively, so that there is no overlap (Flick *et al.*, 2004). This process was a crucial aspect to the process of the data analysis. The headers needed to be specific and clear in order to paste the relevant dialogue and therefore vague headers which did not relate to many themes were discarded.

During the process of interpreting the data, the main challenges were overcome by matching similar results from each focus group and individual interview.

Political and Ethical Issues

The research was undertaken in accordance to the British Sociological Association (BSA), the British Society of Criminology (BSC) and Northumbria University guidelines on ethics in research. This means that the research adhered to various ethical codes of conduct. Prior to the fieldwork, a full Criminal Record Background (CRB) check was conducted and a copy provided to head teachers at all three schools. The main ethical issues that need to be considered when conducting research with pupils are selection and sampling (for discussion, please refer to pp 123); respect for children's rights; safety of participants and researcher (minimizing harm); maintaining child confidentiality and informed consent.

Respect for Children's Rights

A key political and ethical issue with regards to conducting research with pupils is to respect children's rights. The government report, 'Every Child Matters' states that "Real service improvement is only attainable through involving children and pupils and listening to their views" (Borland *et al.*, 2001: 10). Respect for children's rights has grown since the United Nations Convention on the Rights of the Child (UNCRC) in 1989 which inspired countless new policies and projects around the world. One key right is under article 12 where children have a right to express their views on all matters that affect them (Alderson and Morrow, 2004: 10). Woodhead (2005:12) develops this right under Article 12, which clearly stated that children's competencies had to be acknowledged. Article 12 expressed the full principle under the UNCRC that:

"States parties shall assure to the child who is capable of forming his or her own views the rights to express those views freely in all matters affecting the child, the view of the child being given due weight in accordance with the age and maturity of the child" (UNCRC, 1989, Article 12 in Woodhead, 2005: 13).

The research therefore showed relevance with this article because it repeatedly encouraged children to express their views on bullying and racist bullying. Pupils were encouraged to explore various characteristics on bullying and racist bullying and to express their opinions on the subject, assuring them that their response would comprise the main data to the thesis and therefore, their views were important.

Safety of Participants and Researcher

In carrying out the research, considering the ethical issue of safety and potential harm to the participants, especially when dealing with young people, as well as considering the safety of the researcher, is crucial to the researcher at all times. As Walliman (2006:155) clearly states; "A prediction must be made by the researcher about the potential of the chosen research methods and their outcomes for causing harm or gain".

According to Berg, (2007:74), it is not unheard of for a participant to become upset or unsettled during a group session and therefore, it is crucial to debrief the "subjects and to determine if they require any assistance, counselling, or explanations for questions they have been asked during the course of the interview". This information was addressed to all participants at the start of each focus group. During a focus group session with year eight pupils in Old East End Community College, a victim was identified by other members of the group. Out of support for this person, other pupils began to question what happened to her. She was asked if she wanted to talk about her ordeal, which she did briefly. However, it was becoming apparent that she felt uncomfortable and was visibly upset so the subject was immediately changed and the discussion moved on to avoid any further attention being drawn to her. Again, this action was taken in order to ensure that the participant was subject to minimized discomfort and harm. Had this been an individual interview, any potential harm or risk could have been alleviated by voluntarily participating and informing participants again, that they had the right to terminate the interview whenever they wanted to and if they required any counselling. However, for focus groups, this option would have been more difficult to pose as others were willing to continue with the session. Therefore, changing the subject immediately was the clearest and appropriate option at that time, yet it was with intention to approach the pupil after the group and request if any assistance was required, as in accordance to the British Sociological Association, researchers have "a responsibility both to safeguard the proper interests of those involved in or affected by their work" (BSA, 2004: 1). After the focus group, I was approached by the pupil who informed me that she did not feel comfortable discussing this in front of strangers. She was then asked if she had told a teacher or wanted to speak to a teacher, the pupil did not respond, however turned and left the classroom. The subject was raised with the class tutor who confirmed that they would look into the matter.

A further complication arose during an individual interview with one pupil from year 8, (see pp.140), who responded to the interview questions with a certain level of hostility. In order to subject her to minimum discomfort, the questions asked were brief and there was no probing of any responses that she did not volunteer to go into depth. Upon reflection, as a new researcher, such experiences were unexpected and a little uncomfortable; however, they were not daunting. As Neuman (2006: 131), so questions, "When, if ever, are researchers justified in risking physical harm or injury to those being studied, causing them great embarrassment, or frightening them?" (Neuman, 2006). In relation to this PhD, there was no justification for any intentional or unintentional risk or harm to any minor, however to take appropriate actions such as by informing the participant that they could terminate the interview whenever they desired, or by changing the subject during the interview and therefore minimizing any harm. In this situation, the participant was informed of their rights to terminate the interview at any point and since this was not acted upon by the participant, any questions that were met with hostility, the subject would then be changed.

When asking pupils directly what racist terminologies they had come across, this would be eliciting racist language when pupils would have no intention to do so. Yet, discovering what racist terminologies occurred as they had witnessed, would only be able to be retrieved through distributing post-it notes for them write down individually, as pupils were well aware that the focus group interviews were being recorded. As ethical issues relating to harm and risk and confidentiality had to be taken into consideration, by allowing pupils to privately write racist terminologies on the post-it notes and informing them that all information would be held in the strictest confidentiality, this could be suggested to be the safest means to minimize any harm. Moreover, it had to be considered that "any decisions made on the basis of research may have effects on individuals as members of a group, even if individual research participants are protected by confidentiality and anonymity" (BSA, 2004:4). In this PhD, despite informing and assuring participants that all information given would be kept strictly confidential, the decision to request for this information on post-it notes may possibly have had an effect on individual participants after the focus group. Yet, obtaining information pertaining to racist bullying by pupils was one of the key objectives in the initial project approval/ethical approval form and all aims and objectives were duly examined and approved by the University Ethics Committee/School Research Committee.

Child Confidentiality and Informed Consent

Informing pupils of their rights to confidentiality and to express their views worked in both the focus groups and individual interviews. There were two reasons for stressing confidentiality. First, it prevented pupils from becoming self-conscious or afraid to reveal anything private. Second, informing the participants that all interviews would be kept strictly confidential was also key to the British Society of Criminology; British Sociological Association and Northumbria University ethical guidelines. With regards to the rights of participants, the Northumbria University ethical guidelines (Northumbria University Ethics Committee, 2003:2), clearly state that participants should be guaranteed their right to privacy. Furthermore, both the British Sociological Association Code of Ethics and the British Society of Criminology Code of Research Ethics (2003) affirm that the researcher has specific responsibilities towards their research participants, such as striving to protect their privacy. For instance, in this PhD, pupils were requested not to share whatever was discussed during the focus group sessions with any other pupil outside of the focus group. However, this could not guarantee that pupils would not repeat outside of the sessions what had been said in them, yet the responsibility to inform them of this information to protect their privacy were met.

Furthermore, additional measures were taken to protect pupils' privacy by not sharing any details of the focus group and individual interviews with any teachers, unless a child protection issue emerged. In addition, a boy in Old East End Community College, year seven, refused permission for the interview to be recorded, even though he had previously agreed to the interview being taped. Respecting this pupil's rights to confidentiality and the right to change his mind, the interview was not recorded, and a few brief questions were asked. As David and Sutton (2004: 19) so critically assert, "If sensitive topics are to be addressed (and it is important to remember that what is sensitive may be understood differently by the research participants than it is by the researcher), the research subject's right to withdraw must be respected". When it appeared that the pupil was becoming restless, although he did not ask for the interview to be terminated, this right was presented to him, at which point he then requested to leave, the interview lasted no longer than six minutes.

Privacy and confidentiality are essential ethical issues in the field of research. A person's time and information can also be construed as their personal property and therefore, breach of this privacy and confidentiality could be one of the strongest ethical issues where the information could be used against subjects, or used in ways they would disapprove or if they were fully informed (Neuman, 2006:141). Yet this poses a problem as the researcher is ethically bound to reveal any information pertaining to child protection issues to the appropriate adult. Breaching the child's confidentiality may also result in data bias or a refusal from that child to further participate in the research. One example occurred in this respect during a focus group session at Old East End Community College when an individual in year eight was identified as having been stalked by a family member who attended the same school. This was a potential child protection issue, as was realized during the transcription. The matter was dealt with appropriately by contacting the relevant school staff immediately, emphasizing the importance of the situation and requesting that they look into the matter; the researcher also consulted with the supervisory team and cleared with them that this was the correct action to take. There was further follow up with the relevant teacher who was investigating into this matter. As Walliman (2006: 155) advocates, "The implications of involving people in your research are not always obvious, so if there are issues about which you are uncertain, you should consult with experts in the field who have had more experience".

Furthermore, complex issues of confidentiality were considered during the focus group sessions when pupils explained situations of bullying or racist bullying when referring and talking about other pupils. Whilst pupils were asked if they had witnessed any incidents of bullying or racist bullying, they were not asked to identify any particular individual, however, they automatically began to identify other pupils when discussing bullying. When this occurred, their attention was diverted by asking another question. However, whilst emphasizing the need for confidentiality, if any further discussion or identification of pupils occurred outside of the focus group sessions, this would be beyond the researcher's control.

Data Handling

All recorded focus groups and semi-structured interviews with pupils by cassette were kept securely locked in a drawer at home (Huberman and Miles 1994 in Berg, 2007:46). All interviews were transcribed in full and all transcriptions from the focus group and semi-structured interviews, notes taken during the interviews; reflective journal notes and post-it notes where pupils wrote familiar racist terminology in confidence were securely placed in a locked drawer at home. Individual interviews were gained through formal written requests to parents and telephone requests to teachers and other relevant persons.

According to Richards (2005:59), recorded data does not only include that transferred to computer-based or paper storage, and decisions need to be made on how large the data record should be and whether original tapes/data be kept. It was decided that since there were only 51 interviews in total, the audio data would be kept and stored securely and would not contribute to excessive data recording. Furthermore, it would, "maximize the complexity and context one would be storing" (Richards, 2005). Finally the sketch pads with pupils' input have been securely placed at home. One final ethical issue to consider involves the researcher ensuring that participants are subject to minimal discomfort and harm (Macklin, R. 1992 in Mishna *et al.*, 2004: 452). Addressing this issue involved assuring pupils that everything they said would be kept in strict confidence, that they were under no obligation to reveal anything that they did not feel comfortable about and that no-one would have access to the tapes other than myself. This was to reassure pupils that they were safe.

Gate Keeping and Consent

Denscombe (2002:71-72) emphasizes the importance of gatekeepers and asserts that:

> "Gatekeepers are people who can grant permission and allow access. In formal settings, they exercise 'institutional authority' to permit or deny access. In the world of education, for example, access to a school requires permission from the head teacher and probably from the LEA as well. With authorization to research in a school having been obtained, access to the staff will need approval from the head teacher and access to the pupils will require the approval of teachers and, possibly, parents and school governors. Each level of contact requires the approval of someone with the authority to allow access to the people, and events from which the data will come" (Denscombe, 2002).

Access to schools was secured through written correspondences, detailed information relating to the research and permission to interview pupils was secured through signed consent letters by parents and pupils. This also involved subsequent negotiation with relevant staff and there were mixed responses from each school. The research was explained thoroughly at each stage, because as Bailey (2007:17) states: "only after the potential participant understands each of the items in an informed consent document and agrees to participate, can the research begin". For the focus group sessions in Old East End Community College, the form tutors selected the forms and the number of pupils at random, but parental consent was not required at this stage of the fieldwork. At this school it was requested that there should be no more than six pupils per group, the teachers chose six pupils per year group to take part in the focus group research.

From the outset, it was crucial to ensure that pupils understood the nature of the research programme and exactly what their role entailed as participants in the focus groups as well as in the individual interviews. This was dealt with by a brief personal introduction and an explanation about the nature of the research, providing an opportunity for pupils to ask any necessary questions. Pupils were continually questioned if they understood the process or had any queries pertaining to the research. It was important to find some common ground with the pupils in order for them to feel at ease and participate in the focus group sessions without feeling obliged to do so. Pupils were informed of their rights to withdraw from the interviews and focus groups, even after granting consent. This was secured through distributing consent letters addressed to pupils and parents.

In Modern Eastern Suburban School all interviews (focus group and individual) were based upon pupil and parental consent. Therefore, consent letters were distributed to each class in year's 7 to 9. At the School for the Excluded, there were only two groups in years 8 and 9, which were sampled for the focus group sessions. Again the teachers specified that consent letters would not be mandatory at this stage and all parents would be informed by the school.

Upon reflection, there was a major weakness in the way the focus group data was accessed in Old East End Community College and the School for the Excluded regarding the focus groups. In hindsight, after having conducted the focus group interviews in Modern Eastern Suburban School—which were conducted after most of the focus groups had been carried out in Old East End Community College and completed at the School for the Excluded, it was clear that it would have been much more appropriate to have obtained signed consent forms from the parents and pupils for all focus group interviews. Despite the fact that teachers at both these schools clearly stated that consent forms at this stage were not necessary and that they would duly inform all parents and pupils of the research, it can now be acknowledged that not obtaining consent for these focus groups was an error. This was rectified by ensuring that the subsequent focus groups, carried out with Modern Eastern Suburban School, were only conducted upon the production of signed consent letters by pupils and their parents as Walliman (2006: 154) so argues that, "An important aspect about participant's decisions to take part or not is the quality of the information they receive about the research, enabling them to make a fair assessment of the project so that they can give 'informed consent'".

At the outset of the research, there was a concern that it would take far too long to wait for consent forms to be returned, that the overall sample would be too small and therefore the data would have been much weaker. If fieldwork was to be conducted in the future, there would be significant changes, primarily, the insistence of obtaining signed consent forms for all types of data collection.

Summary and Discussion

This chapter discusses the research aim and objectives of the PhD including the research questions which the study was keen to explore. It also reveals how access was granted into the schools. The chapter further demonstrates that the qualitative approach adopted, which was semi-structured focus groups and individual interviews, were felt most appropriate in order to allow pupils and adults to explore their perceptions, opinions and experiences of bullying in a moderate environment. Furthermore, using a semi-structured approach would enable for participants to express their views freely but without much diversion. The chapter further discusses how the data was handled and analysed and how this was handled and secured. Finally, the section on political and ethical issues discusses all political and ethical concerns that were taken into account when designing and delivering the research.

Two key themes emerge in relation to the methodology employed. First and with reference to focus groups, the use of qualitative research is beneficial as an approach to obtaining data on pupils' perceptions towards bullying and racist bullying. Participants are able to provide a shared understanding, listen to one another and the use of a qualitative approach offers a greater in-depth understanding of pupils' perceptions and experiences of bullying in school as well as offering a more detailed study on the motivations for school and racist bullying.

Qualitative research allows pupils to identify shared as well as multiple perspectives on issues regarding bullying and racist bullying. It also enables them to identify numerous factors around both subjects, such as how bullying is identified and recognizing various issues that cause bullying to occur. Through this approach, qualitative research benefits further over quantitative research as it allows for the data to go much deeper into detail. As such, the decision to use qualitative research derived from a number of research questions that arose during the literature search and which the study was keen to explore. These include: how do pupils explain bullying and racist bullying and what factors play on influencing pupils' perceptions both of bullying and of the school response? What were pupils' perceptions of the responses of victims to experiences of bullying? What do adults perceive to be the main issues relating to bullying and racist bullying and how do these compare with that of pupils?

Second, using qualitative research provides a different approach to many other studies that have examined school bullying and racism. Currently, most of the academic research on school bullying and school racism conduct their research through quantitative research methodologies, usually through surveys and questionnaires. There is a significant gap in the literature that has focuses upon school bullying and racist bullying giving authority to qualitative research methodology. Yet, this PhD also compliments the few studies which do examine school racism particularly using qualitative research (Troyna and Hatcher, 1992, Connolly and Keenan, 2002, Kailin 1999).

Thus, the use of focus groups and individual interviews has facilitated an analysis of both personal and shared understandings. It is the perceptions of pupils and adults on bullying and racist bullying that form the basis of the three findings chapters that follow.

CHAPTER 5

The Nature of Bullying and Racist Bullying

Introduction

THE PURPOSE OF this chapter is to examine pupils' and adults' perceptions of the nature of school bullying and racist bullying. There are three main themes which run through this chapter.

First pupils' understanding of the nature and characteristics of bullying are not dissimilar to the nature and characteristics of racist bullying. However, when discussing bullying, pupils focus largely on the individual characteristics of the perpetrators and how they were responsible for their actions. Yet when discussing racist bullying, pupils' focus shifts towards a narrative of the victims and racist bullying is identified by describing the attributes of victims.

Second, there are differences in how pupils talk about the nature and characteristics of bullying and racist bullying; pupils' identification towards bullying and racist bullying are determined by the socio-economic environment of the school as well as the home, community and neighbourhood surroundings in which they live. Pupils from Old East End Community College acknowledge one off incidents to be bullying, whilst pupils from Modern Eastern Suburban School and School for the Excluded recognize that bullying is an accumulative process. Pupils from Modern Eastern Suburban School are able to discuss racist bullying in more depth and with an empathetic attitude.

Third the presence and influence of peers is the main driving force for of bullying. It is acknowledged by all pupils that peers have the power to control the bullying or to prevent the bullying from continuing.

The chapter is structured as follows. It begins with a discussion of pupils' perceptions of the nature of bullying and racist bullying. This is followed by an analysis of pupils' and some teachers' perceptions of the context provided by the socio-economic and demographic profile of each school. This is to allow for an understanding of shared and individual perspectives. The chapter then explores teachers' perceptions of bullying and racist bullying. The last section of the chapter provides an examination of the relationship between the bully and victim and makes an assessment of the location of bullying and the significance of the relationship between peers as bystanders and perpetrators.

Pupils Perceptions of School Bullying and Racism

Pupils responded that bullying appeared in a variety of forms and that it was often a cumulative process. They primarily perceived bullying as involving both verbal name calling and physical acts. These ranged from minor to more severe acts. Verbal and physical bullying have often been identified as the two most popular forms (Boulton and Underwood 1992; Cranham and Carroll 2003; Coloroso 2008; DfES 2007; Rigby *et al.,* 2004; Naylor *et al,.* 2001; Smith 2004; Smith *et al,.* 2003; Sullivan *et al.,* 2005; Ma *et al.,* 2001).

Pupils perceived that verbal name calling was common around the school environment and there were lengthy discussions into the nature of verbal bullying. Pupils explained that victims were name-called due to, for example, hairstyle, or for simply wearing glasses. As pupils from various focus groups in Old East End Community College and Modern Eastern Suburban School remarked:

> ". . . name calling . . . . . . when you name call people for what they look like and what they speak like and what they wear" (Transcription 2: focus group, year 9, Old East End Community College: 2).

". . . one of the worst forms of bullying, like name calling and things," (Transcription 22, focus group, Modern Eastern Suburban School, year 7: 4)

". . . you hear, even when you walk around, you hear name calling . . ." (Transcription 18, focus group, Modern Eastern Suburban School, year 9: 12)

Pupil 1: ". . . calling someone an ugly smack head!

Pupil 2: Spotty b****** . . . . . . Ugly tramp. You UGLY tramp!" (Transcription 4, focus group, Old East End Community College, year 9: 2)

Physical acts of bullying were, for the majority of pupils, viewed more or less as part of everyday life and ranged from one off minor incidents, such as pushing or shoving, 'squatting' (i.e. pulling pupils ties tightly to choke them) to actual physical fights. It was suggested by pupils that physical fights were not necessarily actual 'bullying', although, pupils agreed that it was bullying when a fight occurred in front of a group of peers. One pupil articulated that:

". . . you know when you see that someone is . . . . . . like having a fight, they're not on their own doing it, there's always a massive gang round them" (Transcription 17, focus group, year 8, Modern Eastern Suburban School: 5).

Pupils in Modern Eastern Suburban School suggested that fights could occur spontaneously between two pupils who knew each other. Much of the serious fighting began inside the school through arguments and then plans would be made between the pupils to 'take it outside' and settle the 'score'. Unlike pupils from Old East End Community College and School for the Excluded, pupils from Modern Eastern Suburban School were able to distinguish when a regular fight became a bullying situation, especially once peers surrounded both pupils who were fighting. Under the circumstances where one pupil wanted to stop fighting, peers would support the pupil who was still fighting, as this scene was providing entertainment for their peers. The dynamics of the fight would change where one pupil supported by peers deliberately continued fighting in order to seek approval. Under this circumstance, it would be considered as bullying as this demonstrated an imbalance of power. The weakest pupil would then be subjected to bullying, as pupils' from Modern Eastern Suburban School described such a scenario:

> Pupil 1" . . . if there's been arguments in the school they say, 'oh after school, I'll fight you!' and they meet up after school and they fight and all their fans are there . . . . . . you wouldn't just have the people fighting after you, you'd have all these people wanting to see it,

> Pupil 2: it's like the worst of them out of the ring (likening the situation to that of a boxing match) . . . . . . I think that's what's bullying like, if you've been put into this fight then you, you don't get the best and you get beat . . . . . . then like the next day if you come into school everyone's going to say 'ha, you rot! . . . . . you want training!'" (Transcription 19; focus group, year 9, Modern Eastern Suburban School: 12/13)

Pupils also talked about 'happy slapping', which involves witnesses recording bullying incidents and circulating images/video recordings amongst friends. The term 'happy slapping' was originally given its name as many bystanders often perceived the bullying act to be a joke (Campbell, 2006). By sending the recording to other people, however, it humiliates the victim even more. For Schrock and Boyd (2008) cyberbullying is:

> "an overt, intentional act of aggression towards another person online, or a wilful and repeated harm inflicted through the use of computers, cell phones (mobile phones), and other electronic devices" (Schrock and Boyd., 2008: 22).

Campbell (2006: 1) asserts that happy slapping is the name given to an event where at least two people surprise a third by slapping them and then videoing the event on a mobile phone. Furthermore, Coloroso (2008:211) refers to this as Photo Bullying, whereby pupils use their mobile phones to take humiliating photographs or videos of the victim being attacked and subsequently send these to everyone in their address book and or post the pictures on a file-sharing service so more people can download and view them (Coloroso, 2008). The phenomenon began in the UK in late 2004 and subsequently spread through Europe. However, she also argues that happy slapping has become more violent as the first reported case was published in Australia in September 2006 (Campbell 2006).

Pupils identified that 'happy slapping' was highly popular. One pupil in Old East End Community College described a typical happy slapping scene:

> ". . . people hit you then they record it on their phones to show off to other people." (Transcription 7, focus group, year 7; Old East End Community College: 7)

In the study by Smith *et al.* (2006:18), happy slapping was also described as additional methods of cyberbullying. However, as it involves individuals recording the incident and then circulating the recorded event to other people, it falls under the category 'picture/video clip bullying' (Smith 2006) or 'photo bullying' as referred to by Coloroso, (2008). To some pupils, particularly from Old East End Community College, happy slapping was perceived as a less serious form of bullying, as there was no 'real violence' and the perpetrators genuinely intended on having fun. This was in contrast to the views of adults. However, other pupils argued that the victims may feel hurt and offended by this behaviour and therefore they perceived this to be bullying. Pupils in a focus group from Old East End Community College argued that:

> Pupil 1: "it's just like people are like some people think it's funny and like when people run up and happy slap them like this (demonstrates a happy slapping motion with his hand),
>
> Pupil 2: it's true but, some people take it the wrong way" (Transcription 7, focus group, year 7, Old East End Community College: 13/14).

At Modern Eastern Suburban School, pupils discussed perpetrators who bullied the victim by using their mobile phones. This involved sending specific text messages to or texting others about the victim as well as through the use of the internet and, in particular, MSN chat rooms. Two pupils at Modern Eastern Suburban School tried to explain that:

> Pupil1: "I think that a lot of name calling and rumours go round . . . there's . . . . . . like name calling and stuff like that . . . .
> . . .
>
> Pupil 4: I think a lot of it might go over emailing, like MSN and, like texting" (Transcription 17, focus group, year 8, Modern Eastern Suburban School: 3).

Cyberbullying is becoming increasingly popular as it is a new fad (Schrock and Boyd, 2008: 22; Coloroso, 2008; Varjas, *et al.,* 2009; Kowalski *et al.,* 2008; Rigby *et al.,* 2008). Cyberbullying also reaches out to a wider audience than would be possible during a traditional face to face incident of bullying. Furthermore, the perpetrator is also able to retain some form of anonymity. Coloroso (2008) also argues that cyberbullying has the potential to cause more harm than face to face bullying, and the intent with cyberbullying is to harm.

Indirect bullying (Rigby 2004) was identified by pupils largely at Modern Eastern Suburban School, as involving staring, that is, an individual or group looking hard and long at the victim, as a means of isolating or excluding the victim from situations. This bears resemblance to the work of Smith *et al.* (2002:1120) who regard this as an aggressive act in order to create an imbalance of power (Smith *et al.,* 2002: 1120). Sullivan *et al.* (2006: 6) and Reid *et al.* (2004:242) also agree but choose to identify this as indirect bullying. To them, indirect bullying can involve spreading rumours or unpleasant stories about the victim behind their backs. Furthermore, constant staring has also been classified as indirect bullying, especially if the look frightens or intimidates the victim. As such, Reid *et al.* (2004) particularly emphasise the manner of behaviour in which 'intention and context' is used and view this as an important determinate in defining indirect bullying. This is in order to allow adults and pupils to interpret what is and what is not bullying (Reid *et al.,* 2004). Similarly, pupils from Modern Eastern Suburban School presented such characteristics of bullying on a spider diagram as: "Exclusion—Leaving people out" (Transcription 23, spider diagram, focus group, Year 7, Modern Eastern Suburban School). They were also able to construct the characteristics of indirect bullying through other actions such as threatening and intimidation of the victim. For example, pupils in one focus group in Modern Eastern Suburban School revealed that some bullies in their school had reconstructed their own version of the movie 'The Ring'. They personally delivered seven life threatening letters to their selected victim's house, one a day for seven days. This was purely to play pranks and intimidate the victim.

An incident such as this raises the question as to how far the line can be drawn between establishing the parameters of bullying; that is what differentiates bullying as 'intent to harm' from harmless activities. When it came to discussing such differentiations during the focus groups, pupils, in particular from the School for the Excluded recognised that certain behaviour with the intention to joke, was not bullying, because the individual would laugh along with them. Two pupils interestingly remarked that:

> SQ: "When do you think that teasing is just having a laugh and it's not bullying?
>
> Pupil 1: only when the other person's having a laugh with you.
>
> Pupil 2: aye, because if someone like says like 'oh you got a proper big square head' . . . like **** watch (turns to pupil 1): '**** you got a proper big square head'
>
> Pupil 1: Have I? So have you!
>
> Pupil 2: see what I mean?
>
> SQ: Yeah.
>
> Pupil 2: and they just say it back to you" (Transcription 6, focus group, year 8 and 9, School for the Excluded: 17).

Pertinent to the above distinction on what is bullying and what is not bullying is through the work of one esteemed academic, Rigby (2004:5), who defines bullying as a systematic abuse of power which is repeated and with the intention to harm. In the context for school bullying, the term 'power' includes the perpetrator gaining power for popularity, reputation as well as already possessing it and as Lines (2008) has identified, the bully seeks out their victim in a calculating manner. Furthermore, Smith (2004:98) suggests bullying applies where an individual cannot readily defend themselves and as such, bullying can happen in many contexts. For example, Smith (2004:98), along with Underwood (2002), describe 'joking' and, 'nasty teasing' as prototypical verbal bullying. Rumour spreading was also identified as typical indirect, relational/social bullying. Smith (2004) identifies that less direct forms of bullying occur although they are often not fully recognised as bullying. Only 62% of English 14 year old pupils in his surveys believed the less direct forms were bullying, compared to the 94% and 91% who identified physical and verbal forms of bullying (Smith 2004: 98). Thus in the above dialogue, pupils from the School for the Excluded similarly believed that teasing could be seen as prototypical verbal bullying, as this was illustrated through the use of the term, 'square head'. Furthermore, they acknowledged that the 'joking' could actually be seen as bullying when the intention behind the joke was malicious. In another focus group, pupils referred to one situation and explained:

SQ: "Why do you think it is bullying?

Pupil 1: because they're having a laugh . . . . but they're on to them, they're picking on someone to get them bust . . . . . . They're laughing about hitting someone,

Pupil 2: say they'll hit him that bad, that he ends up in hospital but they laughed about it" (Transcription 8: focus group, year 9; School for the Excluded: 9/10).

Whilst these pupils recognized the indirect forms of verbal bullying, they also associated bullying with physical violence. As Coloroso (2008:32) discusses in her work, children and young people find it difficult to distinguish between what can be classed as joking and 'teasing'.

In addition, pupils perceived that teasing for fun could be considered as bullying if the treatment was carried out in front of other people and caused embarrassment to the victim. Lines' (2008:20) research support this claim as he argues that pupils' lack of awareness of their actions means they are often misinterpreted as teasing and not bullying. Furthermore, Lines (2008) argues that the problem with focusing too much awareness upon the 'intent' to harm as constituting bullying, means that often the situation would be less easy to diagnose as bullying and therefore open to misconception. This is a role which Lines believes to be crucial as he theorises that many pupils are unable to recognise what behaviour is appropriate and what is not. The example in the dialogue above reflects this dilemma of what can or cannot be constituted as bullying. However, in this dialogue (pp 160), pupils clearly understood that this form of a 'joke' was bullying.

The Nature of Racist Bullying

Racist bullying was identified by all pupils as actions involving racist verbal name calling through to physical violence. Although there were fewer forms identified, the way in which pupils described racist forms of bullying was specific and direct. Furthermore, pupils were more descriptive and able to articulate that verbal and physical bullying was directed against the individual because of their ethnic make-up. A person's ethnicity was directed against them in the following way:

Pupil 1: "like name calling,

Pupil 2: like calling people (pauses) I don't want to say . . . . . . like calling Chinky's,

Pupil 3: have heard them say 'Paki' . . . . . . like singling them out because they've got a different coloured skin" (Transcription 23, focus group, Modern Eastern Suburban School, year 7: 18)

". . . like when if a white person calls the other . . . like a 'nigger' or something" (Transcription 19, focus group, Modern Eastern Suburban School, year 9: 16/17)

Similarly, Connolly and Keenan's (2002:349), research revealed that the pupils in their sample identified examples of racist bullying using specific and illustrative language. For example, in their sample, pupils used expression such as 'Chinky, Paki and coco-pops' as names they had heard people being called. The use of such racist terms tended to play a role in contributing towards and reinforcing an environment within which pupils in their sample felt degraded and humiliated (Connolly and Keenan 2002).

Similarly, in this study, pupils presented themselves as non-racist. However, they were very descriptive and illustrative when they tried to explain racist bullying. Pupils' illustrated typical racist names that they had come across as:

> "Ginger; packy; darky" (Focus group 2, year 9, Old East End Community College, 11/2005, notes).

> "Paki; black b******; chinki; Jew; chocolate drop; nigger" (Focus group 4, year 9, Modern Eastern Suburban School; 01/2005, notes).

Pupils identified racist verbal terminologies that they had heard and presented these on written notes (For a full justification, please refer to ethical section on pp 155). Again, pupils used belittling language quite easily and this supports Connolly and Keenan's (2002) argument that the use of such language places the victim in a position where they are greatly insulted and humiliated. Pupils notes included the following:

> "Black boy; black currant; black b******; People call coloured people Black c**** and B******* . . ." (Written notes by focus group, year 7, Old East End Community College).

> "Jew; Paki; chinki; Jew; Nigger; Paki; Chinky; Nigga; Jew; Paki; Chinky; Nigga; Black b**tar*; Chinky; Paki; Nigger; Paki; Chinky; The Paki B*****d; Nigger." (Written notes by focus group, year 7, Modern Eastern Suburban School).

In the research findings by Kelly and Cohen (1988:14), verbal name calling was revealed to be the most popular form of racist bullying.

Their findings revealed that more black/Asian pupils reported racist verbal name calling than any other form of racist abuse. They also raised the argument that the use of racist name calling located the victims most firmly into stereotypes and depersonalized categories (1988). Furthermore, Richardson and Miles (2008:34) also talk about prejudiced-related words, such as the ones noted above, and emphasize that such words are experienced as an attack on the "values, loyalties and commitments central to a person's sense of identity and self-worth. Often, therefore, they hurt not only more widely but also more deeply" (2008). In agreement with Richardson and Miles, therefore, Lane (2008:229/230) declares that the use of prejudiced-related words, for example 'black' have particular implications for children who are black. She further asserts that when they are being ridiculed for being black, their family and whole ethnic community are also being ridiculed. Therefore, the experience is over and above specific personal insults (Lane 2008). This is a direct comparison to the nature of regular bullying which is targeted at the individual alone.

Troyna and Hatcher (1992:195) found similar findings in their study, which were revealed when using the model they specifically devised to locate racist name calling in schools. These findings arose from an examination of pupils' beliefs and attitudes towards race. Their findings revealed that 'race' and 'racism' were significant features of the cultures of children in mainly white schools and that the most common expression of racism was racist name-calling. Troyna and Hatcher (1992:196) continued to assert that whilst the frequency level varied for racist name-calling, for all victims, it was the most hurtful and humiliating form of racist aggression. This corresponds with the main argument by Richardson and Miles (2008).

Another example where pupils identified racist verbal bullying in order to humiliate the individual was by mimicking the accents of pupils from minority ethnic groups. As pupils in one focus group identified:

> Pupil 1: "and these Koreans go 'ye what? Yeh whitey!' (All start laughing) . . .

Pupil 2: I think, it's when you're calling them and are taking the mickey out of them" (Transcription 3; focus group, year 8, Old East End Community College: 13)

Moreover, it is clear that, ignorance and a lack of understanding of minority ethnic groups provoked the white young people to imitate the accents and mock minority ethnic groups. As emphasized during a focus group:

Pupil 1: "if they can't speak fully English,

Pupil 2: some people might take the mick out of the way they talk

Pupil 3: like a really strong accent,

Pupil 4: like you can't really understand them" (Transcription 17, focus group, year 8, Modern Eastern Suburban School: 8)

Whilst pupils from both schools emphasised that minority ethnic groups were mocked by their accents, the ways in which pupils articulated this issue differed considerably. Pupils from Modern Eastern Suburban School were much more informative and articulate whilst pupils from Old East End Community College could only explain this by verbally illustrating how accents were mocked. The varied socio-economic background to each school could speculate such difference in the form of response given.

In all focus groups conducted with pupils from year seven in Old East End Community College, an interesting perspective arose when pupils referred to one particular individual who was targeted for racist bullying. This pupil was targeted according to pupils because he was black and possessed a strong accent. Indeed the language pupils used appeared to be ingrained in the wider contexts of culture as different from the way they would identify white victims. As one pupil remarked:

". . . There's this kid called Elijah . . . and I don't know what this means, but they call him 'chicken dipper' . . . and now they've started to call him 'burnt chicken dipper'" (Transcription 14; pupil, year 7, Old East End Community College: 19)

It was difficult for pupils to establish exactly why this pupil was a constant target; however, they were described as a loner. It was interesting to observe that pupils showed no feelings of guilt or disgust when repeating the name used for this individual. This dispassionate attitude indicates a lack of understanding of victimization when pupils discussed racist bullying; they demonstrated a lack of understanding of the negative impact of the stereotypes they used. The data also suggests the possibility that such racist attitudes are more entrenched than schools would commonly be aware of or care to admit.

Richardson and Miles (2008:34) claim that one distinctive feature of a prejudiced-related attack is that the intent is to attack and insult the individual as a representative of a community or group. Pupils' explanations during a focus group in Old East End Community College support Richardson and Miles claim as they articulated that racist bullying and the intent of harm was to humiliate. This intent was exemplified as:

> Pupil 1: "when you're called a Paki!
>
> Pupil 2: It's when you're being called things about your skin colour, religion; you might call someone a Black Ugly Bastard or something like that.
>
> Pupil 3: a Jew! (They start laughing)
>
> Pupil 4: . . . Taliban Bastard, Paki Bastard etc" (they all continue laughing) (Transcription 4, focus group, year 9, Old East End Community College: 7/8).

Pupils' discussions, particularly those from Old East End Community College, on how verbal racist name-calling was carried out often had religious and political associations. As the discussion moves beyond physical difference it becomes a distinctive element of racist bullying. What is interesting here is despite detailed and articulate responses to questions on racist bullying by those from Modern Eastern Suburban

School, only pupils from Old East End Community College were able to make this particular distinction. Whilst Pupils from the School for the Excluded resided in an area of high social deprivation, there were no pupils from minority ethnic background present at the unit.

Where pupils' discussion of bullying focused on its various forms, pupils' discussion of racist bullying, involved the use of specific language in order to illustrate their views. For example, pupils repeated comments and names that they heard which referred to a religion by country of origin. For example, if an individual was from India, they would be mocked by being called a 'Hindu'. Furthermore, if individuals were known to be from a Muslim country, then the racist taunts would appear as political links to, for example terrorism, by means of anti-Muslim jokes or humiliating retort. As pupils from a focus group in Old East End Community College explained:

> Pupil 1: ". . . well like when you call someone like, Hindus or something like that,
>
> Pupil 2: for example, it's like if you got a different coloured skin then they call you something really horrible like, if you from Pakistan, they might call you something horrible like,
>
> Pupil 3: they might call you Taliban and other things like that, (others begin to laugh).
>
> Pupil 4: and suicide bombers and all that, (others laugh)
>
> Pupil 2: If you're from Germany, they call you Hitler (they all laugh)" (Transcription 5, focus group, year 8, Old East End Community College: 13).

Pupils also defined and discussed racist bullying through forms such as racist imagery. For example, pupils mentioned incidents wherein, white pupils would write racist comments on paper and then attach these to the individuals' backs without their knowledge, therefore making them vulnerable to public mockery. Pupils commented that:

SQ: "they write things and stick it on the back, like what kind of things?

Pupil 2: names and things like that, they go like 'oh there right . . .'

Pupil 1: . . . they just write things like 'give me a kick up the bum' and things like that, 'ching chong'" (Transcription no. 8, year 9, School for the Excluded: 15).

However, pupils at the School for the Excluded agreed that these incidents were rare at the school.

One source of anger among white pupils was their perception that they also experienced staring and name calling by the non-white community. However, they declared that if they retaliated, they (white pupils) would be punished by the school. As pupils retorted:

". . . well, aye, but they just call you and if you call them back then it's you who's wrong and not them!" (Transcription 2, focus group, year 9, Old East End Community College: 15)

Pupil 4: ". . . It's difficult . . . . . . they call you names and stuff . . . . . . we get called because . . . . . . they have never heard of our names, so we get called like.

Pupil 1: . . . . . . in the school when you're walking past them, they turn around and look at you and you look at them then, and when you tell a teacher, they just say that 'oh well but I didn't see anything, so you can't do nothing about it!'

Pupil 4: all they can say is that they've got a right to look at people across the classroom, new faces and stuff like that" (Transcription 1, pilot sample focus group, Old East End Community College, years 8 & 9: 4/5).

Nayak's (2003:147), data reports a similar sentiment. During his research, one disillusioned young person complained that their school was "racist against their own kind" and that this was ignored by the teachers.

Racist bullying was further identified through physical fights. At the School for the Excluded, pupils believed the physical fights that occurred at their previous mainstream school were racially driven and extreme and that these fights went beyond the teachers' control. Similarly, Kelly and Cohen (1988:26) also found that teachers' admitted to experiencing great difficulties in dealing with racist violence at the school.

With regards to the frequency of racist bullying, pupils across the board from all three schools generally concurred that their school was not particularly racist; yet, pupils had admitted to witnessing some racist incidents. This was particularly so, with pupils at Modern Eastern Suburban School. Their responses to the frequency of racist bullying were:

> Pupil 1: "there isn't much of that in this school . . . . . . there's very little,

> Pupil 2: no, there's nothing serious,

> Pupil 1: no I don't think that there's any racist bullying in this school" (Transcription 18, focus group, year 9, Modern Eastern Suburban School: 21).

Perceptions in Context: Socio-Economic and Demographic Consideration

What can be noted from each of the three schools are the considerable differences with the socio-economic backgrounds, particularly between Old East End Community College and Modern Eastern Suburban School between the neighbourhoods within which the schools are located. Old East End Community College, for example, located in the east end suburbs of the city, has significant social and economic deprivation with a high population of lower working class people who live in close knit, inner city and manufacturing town communities.

The crime rate is high. In comparison, Modern Eastern Suburban School also located in the east end of the city, is relatively affluent and the majority of the population is from middle class backgrounds, and therefore, the area has less problems with crime. As there are variations in class backgrounds between both schools, there were differences between pupils' perceptions of bullying and it can be suggested that the socio-economic and demographic backgrounds provide an understanding to these differences.

Where pupils, revealed shared perspectives, it was for the most part where they identified and understood bullying to be an act that was ongoing, persistent and often cumulative. However, pupils from Modern Eastern Suburban School were the only ones to constantly recognize that bullying was often an ongoing process. One pupil articulated the ongoing process using the example of physical bullying:

> ". . . yeah anything and beating someone up is beating someone up . . . . . . but beating someone up and then going back the next day and doing it again and again etc, etc, I'd class that as bullying" (Transcription 18, focus group, year 9, Modern Eastern Suburban School:3).

The Department for Education (DFE, 2010:4), recognizes bullying as an act that is repeated. Rigby (2002) suggests that bullying is persistent. Persistency was discussed across the focus groups and interviews with pupils and involved:

> ". . . being picked on day after day"; "people being nasty to one person all the time" (Spider diagram: Group 1: year 8, Old East End Community College: 29/11/2005)

> ". . . it has to be persistent, I don't think like, some people like just mess around . . . . . . and not even beating them up like, saying, 'you're a NERD!!' and then the next day, "you're a NERD!!" and then the next day, "you're still a NERD!!" (Transcription 18, focus group, year 9, Modern Eastern Suburban School: 3)

Such persistence in behaviour reveals a sense of school culture where bullying behaviours become engrained. The pupils discussed this with great hilarity:

> Pupil 1: "she gets like; everyone calls mushroom (and starts giggling)
>
> Me: why do they call her 'mushroom'?
>
> All: because of her hair like, looks like a mushroom!"
>
> (Pupil 1 demonstrates by circling his head) . . ." . . . well it grows down here and then they cut it all the way round!
>
> Pupil 2: "but there's a bit that still comes around here" (pointing to the back of her neck) (she laughs) (Transcription 8: focus group, year 7, Old East End Community College: 8/9).

Interestingly, one pupil in particular from Old East End Community College identified bullying as a cumulative process that first began with verbal name calling but which often turned into physical fighting. Bullying was noted as:

> ". . . carried out in like different stages like one day you get called a name and the next day you get called something else and then, over a period of time they would start getting more physical, like hitting you more and more"
>
> (Transcription 12: focus group, year 7, Old East End Community College: 5)

The work of Griffin and Gross (2004:382) is important to the issues raised above as they agree with other academics, such as that of Olweus (1993) that the nature of bullying largely appears as a repeated process. Furthermore, their work emphasises the issue of intent to harm an individual and uses Olweus' definition of bullying to explain this. Bullying is defined as a negative action when someone intentionally and repeatedly inflicts discomfort to injure another individual, whether this is mental or physical injury (Griffin and Gross, 2004:

382). Therefore the above example exemplifies the gradual process of bullying becoming increasingly aggressive in nature with the intention to harm, as Griffin and Gross (2004) describe. One pupil from the School for the Excluded described how his bullying ordeal continued:

". . . about, all the time I was there. And I was there for about a year" (Transcription 10, individual interview, year 9, School for the Excluded: 17).

Pupils at Modern Eastern Suburban School recognized that bullying was an ongoing process. Yet interestingly, pupils from Old East End Community College identified that one off incidents were also bullying, especially when it came to physical bullying. Where pupils at Modern Eastern Suburban School recognized such incidents to be a fight, pupils at Old East End Community College saw otherwise:

"Pupil 1: . . . you get squatted and that, well ah haven't been squatted once!

Pupil 2: well ah have,

Pupil 2 to Pupil 3: well ye don't need to go in to them 20 times a day and that!

Pupil 1: well this happens as well as all the name calling bullying

Pupil 2: I know" (Transcription 7, focus groups, year 7, Old East End Community College: 5).

It was however, clear during the individual interviews with pupils that one off incidents were also perceived to be bullying as one pupil reported:

". . . they sometimes just go up and just start fighting with them for like no reason sometimes . . . and most of the time they just let it slip, most people . . .

SQ: who lets it slip? The victims?

Pupil: no like, the people who are trying to fight some people, just let it slip . . . because sometimes, they get expelled from school" (Transcription 24, individual interview, year 7, Old East End Community College:6).

To Sullivan *et al.* (2005:7), physically aggressive behaviour can often be mistaken for bullying as it occurs in the open, but does not involve an imbalance of power. For instance individuals or a group may set out to create a situation where it appears that both have equal responsibility, but this could be part of a plan to discredit a targeted person (Sullivan *et al.*, 2005). Although an individual may be targeted, as demonstrated in the above example, there is no evidence that this physical behaviour would continue, however, pupils still believed this to be bullying because the individual was selected. Sullivan *et al.* (2005) therefore recommend that schools take the responsibility to be able to distinguish between what is a conflict and what is bullying and recognize such web of deceit that normally surrounds bullying (2005:7).

As reported from chapter 3, the community living in the North Heaton ward, in which Modern Eastern Suburban School is situated, is affluent and, the community is comprised of many young career professionals living in the most sought after houses, independent older people with active lifestyles and upwardly mobile families living in houses bought from social landlords. As such the area is surrounded by the 'middle class' community values and attitudes and the school thrives on high academic performance. It can be speculated that the standards at Modern Eastern Suburban School in comparison to Old East End Community College were far higher in the anti-bullying preventative support provided. Thus, pupils' attitudes towards the nature of bullying at Modern Eastern Suburban School were more articulate than pupils at Old East End Community College. This was partially because of the types of experiences they faced; located within the area where crime was barely non-existent and bullying was discussed more as verbal than physical

Although the socio-economic environment for both Old East End Community College and the School for the Excluded were similar in that they are socio-economically deprived, have a high unemployment and crime rate, pupils' depth to their responses on bullying differed.

Whilst pupils from Old East End Community College considered all negative incidents to be bullying, those from the School for the Excluded recognised that bullying is a cumulative process as did pupils from Modern Eastern Suburban School. Whilst pupils from Old East End Community College acknowledged the high frequency of bullying within the school environment, pupils from the School for the Excluded identified that bullying occurred more outside the school gate. Two main factors can be attributed towards these differences; firstly the class sizes are much smaller at the School for the Excluded with less than 126 pupils on roll. Secondly, anti-bullying preventative education and support was strong. Thus, this allowed teachers sufficient time to devote towards pupils' social and welfare needs. Further, there were a lot of outside agencies that regularly worked with pupils at the school, for example, CABS, who developed a behavioural strategy programme. These factors have assisted in explaining the depth of pupils knowledge. Where Old East End Community College have larger classes and minimal resources to teach against bullying, this could account for pupils lack of depth, accuracy and detail than talking about bullying.

With Old East End Community College, there was no issue regarding a high fighting culture, however, where physical bullying occurred, it was more severe, as identified by one teacher, yet there was a larger bullying problem within the school. One teacher discussed the nature of the typical form of bullying which occurred a lot and posed as a problem as:

> "I think there's quite a lot of bullying in the school, Claire: I think that just normal bullying . . . every day bullying . . . . . . it can be quite in your face, they don't hide it necessarily, I mean if it's going on and it can be hidden, but they're not so like that, devious about that bullying, so they would call somebody a name across the room, you know, "ah your little ***, your haircut", whatever, or "your mam's a ***", whatever, erm, or other things as well like other types of bullying, I have seen in the corridor or whatever . . ." (Transcription 20, teacher interview, Old East End Community College: 1).

When identifying and discussing the nature of racist bullying, the depth of discussion was largely provided by pupils from Modern Eastern Suburban School, which operated on a zero tolerance approach to racism. The detailed discussion about racist bullying as well as adopting a more empathetic approach to it can it may be suggested attributed towards the social and economic prosperity with a community that possesses more middle class values as well as stronger likelihood for social cohesion. Furthermore, given that this school had multi-racial pupils, it can be speculated that this zero tolerance approach is influenced by the affluent socio-economic makeup of the school as well as the neighbourhood environment. Empathy towards the feelings of minority ethnic groups was particularly emphasized by pupils during the focus groups:

> "Pupil 1: I know people can call dark, black people like . . . really bad names,
>
> Pupil 2: but what do they think, what do they think about people's colours?
>
> Pupil 1: I mean like, we've got aware that they have names . . . but we've got no reason to call them anything . . . . . . because they don't, is known but, is not normal,
>
> SQ: but why do you think it happens? Why do you think Asian people get called, "P***", even if they're Indian they still get called it, or something else?
>
> Pupil 3: cos their different,
>
> Others: yeah different,
>
> SQ: because they're different? Okay,
>
> Pupil 4: like it's physical down to England or whatever, and there's not many black, black people live here, white people will call them that because they're different and because they have like,
>
> Pupil 5: ah got upset like,

Pupil 4: it's like Jack said,

Pupil 5: ah got upset one time when I was walking home and I was, I've got like a friend whose like Asian . . . . . . and a grown up stuck his head out of the window and said 'Paki'! I was like, 'urrggh!!' (Others begin to giggle), and I ran after the car. I got really upset because like, because I've got some good close friends, and . . . . . . I just thought, that's S***." (Transcription 22, focus group, year 7, Modern Eastern Suburban School: 19).

On a similar stance, another focus group raised a rather interesting issue about the notion of hierarchy of races as they discussed the ways in which racist bullying occurred:

"SQ: who would be singled out?

Pupil 1: like people who have come from like another country and that . . . . . . like not like me, not all of them have been born in the country like . . .

SQ: okay, why, why do you think that people would be like that?

Pupil 2: cos like,

Pupil 3 (imitating a scene): "ah here's like a Paki", but . . . . . when they, they don't understand like . . . . . . they think like, erm, white people or whoever is bullying, like their colour and like their right and like the other colour is wrong" (Transcription 23, focus group, year 7, Modern Eastern Suburban School:19).

Pupils, largely from Old East End Community College described racist forms of bullying that was specific and direct. Much of this tactless form of behaviour can be attributed towards the ethnic make-up of the already socially and economically deprived neighbourhood located in the Walkergate ward. The hostile attitude towards such groups was further attributed to the limited social contact between the large asylum and refugee community that existed, and the white working class community. Not only was there a problem of a lack of social cohesion between both communities in the Walkergate ward, however, there was no real understanding amongst the white community as to why the immigrant, asylum and refugee community were present and misconceptions of services received by these groups from the local government.

In comparison, at the School for the Excluded, there was moderate discussion on identifying different forms of racist bullying. Much of which concerned experiences at previous mainstream schools; however, again, regarding the victims, there was very little empathy by pupils, but the description of forms of racist bullying was less direct. Despite the schools' race-equality policy, at the time of the research, the school was all white. Similar to Walkergate, the Denton ward was also socially deprived, and in similar conditions. Thus, any hostility found in the home and within the community, directed towards such groups, were based on similar characteristics that were found in the Walkergate ward.

Adults Perceptions of Bullying and Racist Bullying

Interviews with teachers showed many differences from those with pupils. In comparison with the interviews with pupils, interviews with teachers provided an insightful discussion of bullying through the use of technology and gender differences. When discussing racist bullying however, a key issue that arose from interviews with teachers was that racist bullying was perceived as a minor issue and that the teachers' views did not necessarily mirror with the pupils. Primarily teachers perceived that racist bullying did not occur as they had not witnessed many incidents, in reality however, pupils' admission was that many victims largely preferred to remain silent.

Where some teachers in Old East End Community College believed that one off incidents could be described as bullying, most teachers especially at Modern Eastern Suburban School suggested that incidents has to be persistent in order to be classified as bullying. As one teacher from Modern Eastern Suburban School identified:

> ". . . from my own experience . . . . when it becomes a persistent problem, that's when you see it as 'being bullied'" (Transcription 16, teacher, Modern Eastern Suburban School: 1).

Furthermore, when discussing physical bullying and associated this with the fighting culture at the school, a teacher from Old East End Community College stated that this form of bullying appeared with pupils in groups who were opposed to another youth group. The general nature of the bullying scene involved the group targeting an individual from the opposed group, should they be seen alone. This teacher explained that such bullying behaviour was:

> "a learnt behaviour in how they actually get on and you get a little bit of one group versus another group and if they get one individual by themselves they'll pick on those and the other group will pick back, there's a bit of that mobish type bullying culture involved in some of the individuals that occur in******" (Transcription 21, teacher, Old East End Community College: 2).

O'Brien (2007: 298) illustrates this as group-based bullying that occurs against a targeted individual belonging to an opposed group (O'Brien, 2007). Overall, during the discussion of fighting, teachers identified this as typical mob type of culture.

For those teachers who identified the growing problem of cyberbullying, they did so by perceiving that with the increased use in mobile phones and the internet, perpetrators were able to hide behind the technology and still conduct a maximum degree of bullying whereas previously the manifestation of bullying could only be done face to face. Although none of the teachers were able to offer examples of cyberbullying with one teacher from Old East End Community College described the use of such technology:

> "they are being used and . . . are increasing the sort of breach of bullies to some extent, because now, when I was younger you almost had to be face to face with the bullies to hear them call you names and stuff like that, ... you can be at the other side of the world now, ... and they can send you emails and text messages and all the rest of it, ... with the sort of nasty comments with it, isn't it?" (Transcription 21; teacher, Old East End Community College: 15).

Teachers, in particular from Modern Eastern Suburban School emphasised that the nature of bullying had become more diverse through the constant use of new technology. Similarly, Li (2007: 1778) asserts that one drawback of new technology, such as mobile telephones and the internet is that it has provided new opportunities for harassment. A major attraction for perpetrators of cyberbullying is that they can remain anonymous and still continue to bully the victim as Li's (2007) research study revealed. His 2000 survey conducted in schools in New Hampshire, Canada showed that out of 177 grade seven children, the highest percentage of victims did not know who their attacker or attackers were. In this study, teachers also discussed happy slapping as a form of cyberbullying. As one teacher emphasized:

> "they do things like that and the mobile phones, they're sending texts and stuff, that comes into it because it has to . . . . . . but it's just, I think that's like a technology isn't it, along the lines where when we were at school, it wasn't around then. It would probably if it had have been . . . . . . I know they would have used it just the same" (Transcription 16: teacher, Modern Eastern Suburban School: 12).

The use of mobile phones and the internet was recognised by teachers as creating severe bullying. Schrock and Boyd (2008:28) developed a report 'Enhancing child safety and online technologies' that supports this claim in that cyberbullying has the potential to be severe. They argued that cyberbullying or 'online harassment' could be reported to increase in severity as the nature of bullying could become much more aggressive and threatening (Schrock and Boyd, 2008).

However, one teacher discussed the varying nature of internet bullying as:

> "you know some of it is just tit for tat, but other sort, not obviously, the more severe it is, the more likelihood there is for using new technology like mobile phones and internet, all that kind of stuff" (Transcription 20, teacher, Old East End Community College: 4)

What is interesting with the above discussion is that teachers seemed to perceive virtual and internet bullying as an issue more than pupils.

Schrock and Boyd (2008:29) argue that the increasing sophistication in technology has opened up more avenues for abuse. For example, in Kowalski *et al.'s* (2008:193) research the teachers' identified that cyberbullying appeared in many forms (Kowalski *et al.,* 2008). A further element to cyberbullying is that victims are under attack at all times and most are unaware of who their attacker/s are. During the interviews teachers indicated that cyberbullying can be more threatening, because of what it involves. The theme of national Anti-bullying week 2009, was also cyberbullying. This is pertinent given that when these interviews were conducted, teachers identified cyberbullying as a growing problem, as well as the physical relations between the bully and victim. Increasingly, schools and local authorities have recognized cyberbullying as a serious problem (NEABA meeting, 2009).

Teachers also perceived that persistent and calculating bullying was carried out by girls. As an example, when teachers talked about gender and bullying, one teacher from Modern Eastern Suburban School differentiated the nature of bullying:

> ". . . it varies between boys and girls. Boys are very, what you can call, stupid, they call each others mam's . . . . so the boys do that, the girls, girls are much nastier, girls do it very much exclusion, and they would just exclude their friends . . . . they ignore their friends, they completely shut them out, or they might do something like . . . . . . if they are going to do group work or something, they'll deliberately make sure that one friend isn't part of it." (Transcription 16: teacher, Modern Eastern Suburban School: 2)

Similarly, one youth worker agreed that girls tended to possess a cruel and vindictive streak in their bullying treatment towards the victim. This often would include involving their friends and the treatment would continue for a long time. Noaks and Noaks, (2000:72) and particularly Reid *et al.* (2004) reinforce this perception when they indicate that research reveals that girls "tend to channel their aggression socially, using indirect, subtle methods such as slander, spreading rumours, social exclusion and manipulation of friendship relations . . ." (Reid *et al.,* 2004: 244); see also Ahmed and Smith (1994); Ahmed and Braithwaite (2006); Batsche and Knoff (1994); Berthold and Hoover (2000); Carney and Merrell (2001); Coloroso (2008); Craig and Pepler (1997); Gini and Pozzoli, (2006) and Olweus (1997). Their findings also suggest that whilst girls may appear to bully less than boys, this may not necessarily be the case, as girls are less obvious and more subtle in their style of bullying female bullying has been largely underestimated by researchers in the past (2004: 245). Gini and Pozzoli (2006), particularly emphasise this and attribute this lack of research to societal stereotypical views where girls are least expected to bully. Furthermore, teachers from Modern Eastern Suburban School commented that social exclusion as a form of bullying, also termed as 'relational bullying', or 'indirect bullying' as identified by Smith (2004), was more likely to occur amongst girls. One teacher from Modern Eastern Suburban School identified a typical way in which this form of bullying appeared:

> "I think it's just a girls' mind . . . . . . they see that not talking to each other . . . . . . is more of a, sort of a nasty thing to do, than to call somebody. So I think . . . . . . women as a whole we tend to use communication and talk about things, we talk about how we feel and we share all our intimate thoughts and you tell your best friends all your secrets don't you?

> SQ: yeah,

> Teacher: and suddenly, that's taken away from them, that's much more hurtful" (Transcription 16, teacher, Modern Eastern Suburban School: 3).

Therefore, such treatment also imposed maximum mental and emotional anguish upon the victim:

> "so the gender thing is, I think girls can be a lot more cruel actually bullying . . . . . . and it tends to be like a pact based thing as I said and like a group thing . . . . . . and it can be very, very . . . . . . vindictive, mental, emotional . . . . . torture in some cases and it can be very long winded as well" (Transcription 28, youth worker: 23).

The findings from Deakin (2006:380) and Crick *et al.* (1997) assert that girls are much more aggressive relationally than boys (Crick *et al.*, 1997). From this discussion, one can argue that adults, in particular teachers suggest that persistent bullying is carried out more by girls. Ahmad and Smith (1994: 77) provide one explanation for such behaviour and equate it with girls developing a competitive attitude over a certain male partner. They also explain that often where best friends fall out with each other, they come away with knowledge of the other person's secrets, as the teacher in Modern Eastern Suburban School so identified. Thus, there is much to lose and as Ahmad and Smith (1994: 81) also explain; the revengeful nature of bullying is demonstrated through spreading gossip in order to hurt and isolate the victim.

Teachers, in particular from Old East End Community College, emphasised that whilst violent bullying was not the most common form that occurred at the school, when it did occur, the nature of physical bullying involved so much violence, especially amongst girls that even parents became involved in the actual violent acts. As one teacher emphasised:

> ". . . some of the most serious bullying that I've had, where I've excluded five students have been girls . . . . . . it's all these girls, relationships between girls,
>
> SQ: and is that more serious on the verbal side or?
>
> Teacher: no. it is violent . . . . . . the level of violence involved and it's been them and their parents getting involved is just horrendous at ****** . . . . . . days and days go by and they knock down doors and break in and beat up kids and all sorts of stupid things . . . . . . it's very, very serious stuff . . ." (Transcription 21: teacher, Old East End Community College: 12)

It is evident from this teacher's comment that girls deliver physical bullying quite differently to the ways boys do. Garandeau *et al.* (2006) argue that girls who use such extreme aggression are more likely to lack social intelligence and social skills and argue further that these deficiencies in girls are higher than boys (Garandeau *et al.*, 2006: 615).

Garandeau *et al.* (2006) therefore suggest that girls bully in different forms. Pupils however, did not acknowledge or discuss this difference. Yet, one teacher acknowledged:

> "The boys on the other hand are followed through and if they've decided to have a fight, they would follow it through . . . . . . and then, once it's done though, that's it, they'll shake hands, that's the end of it, it's forgotten about . . . . where the girls may keep it going for months, they're still a bit mean (laughs)," (Transcription 16: teacher, Modern Eastern Suburban School: 4).

Teachers responded to questions about racist bullying by suggesting that they did not perceive that much occurred within the school. Particularly, a teacher from Modern Eastern Suburban School perceived that racist bullying was virtually non-existent. This suggests that teachers are either less aware or victims remain silent. As one teacher identified that:

> Teacher: ". . . in terms of racism, I haven't seen any in the classes that I teach,

> SQ: okay, how about around the school or a situation that you've heard from maybe other teachers from other years, as well,

> Teacher: I have, well, from the experience of the pupils who I teach and from what I've heard, I haven't personally heard of any, in that sense. But I'm sure there will be, but it's probably more if you ask other year groups, you know you would get more of a clearer picture of that thing, ... because, personally I, I haven't, I just haven't come across that, as such. Probably very luckily, (laughs). I would say, definitely.

> SQ: So, you're not aware, or nothing actually takes place in your own classrooms at all?

> Teacher: no. Not in my classrooms, no, no, no" (Transcription 16, teacher, Modern Eastern Suburban School: 2).

Furthermore, this was the only mention of racist bullying throughout the whole interview.

A major problem with such a response is that it is open to many interpretations. Richardson and Miles (2008:51) argue that it would be unrealistic for any school to expect that no racist bullying will ever occur; they claim that a school's population does not exist in a different world far removed from society and neither is it unchanging. A low response may imply that pupils are less confident about reporting incidents or that the staff have failed to understand the nature or seriousness of prejudice-related incidents (2008). Another explanation for this can be similar to the findings by Connolly and Keenan's (2002: 351), research that highlighted the level of unwillingness to acknowledge the seriousness of racism, which left parents feeling that at best the school was ". . . willing to tolerate such behaviour" (Connolly and Keenan, 2002). Their findings help to explain why pupils talked less about racism in the school. For one teacher in this study:

> ". . . it is very, very difficult, sometimes we might have two students who have just fallen out and one has called another one a nasty name and . . . if one of them is from a different ethnic background and one of them sort of uses a name it might sort of come over though as racist bullying . . . ." (Transcription 21, teacher, Old East End Community College: 2)

This teacher expressed some doubt as to whether, in this situation, incidents of name calling were caused by racial hatred amongst pupils and therefore, were 'actual' racist bullying. Raby (2004) comments in her research that a common pattern existed with the interviews where participants argued that racist comments or stereotypes were part of building up personal popularity and of joking with friends (Raby, 2004). This is in contrast to pupils' discussions, who were very clear that racist name-calling was bullying. Yet to this teacher, 'race' or ethnicity was just like any other characteristic; they explained that unfortunately, this is the way pupils carry on and the situation is such that the attitude is more or less accepted by all the pupils.

In contrast one teacher from Modern Eastern Suburban School revealed that pupils knew that using certain racist terminologies was wrong, and were challenged. This teacher went on to explain that:

"the students . . . . . . know that they're wrong . . . . . . they'll acknowledge things like 'nigger' is wrong, 'wog' is wrong, those kind of terminology because we do a lesson where we look at language, yet they will say 'Paki' and 'Chinky', not all of the students, you know it's a minority of them . . ." (Transcription 13, teacher, Modern Eastern Suburban School: 3).

However, this teacher also perceived that pupils did not fully understand the impact behind these terminologies.

A further contrast appeared with teachers at the School for the Excluded who recognized that much racism occurred. Whilst there was no pupil from any minority ethnic background attending the school at that time, there was much evidence of racist attitudes. One teacher clearly emphasized:

"Oh yes, definitely, there's a lot of racist comments goes on here . . ." (Transcription 9, teacher, School for the Excluded: 13).

Furthermore, another teacher explained that much occurred outside of the unit, however, the forms in which it did take place in the unit were:

"I think, when they do make racist comments its mostly amongst themselves and in amongst the community, how they use slang, just general piece of language, but not so much around the class because there is no minorities . . ." (Transcription 9, teacher, School for the Excluded: 25)

One main difference between the pupils and teachers was that pupils were more specific with their use of language when they identified racist bullying. Teachers were less illustrative. Furthermore, teachers' general consensus with fighting was that it was more one off and placed less emphasis on viewing it as bullying. Pupils on the other hand perceived that the fighting was bullying as they perceived name calling to be verbal bullying. This would indicate that the belief of what constitutes bullying differs between child and adult. Generally fighting is the culmination of a period of sustained verbal bullying. So while the physical acts may be sporadic, pupils associated them both as they felt that both physical and verbal bullying are related. Finally, in the opinion of some teachers, especially from Old East End Community College, bullying was part of the school culture and that all pupils had now become used to it.

Bullying, Victimization and Place

Interviews with both pupils and teachers interestingly revealed that a relationship existed between bullying, victimization and place. Not only did these discussions involve the differential power relationships between the offender and victims, but also the importance of bystanders and the impact of the location upon the bullying incident.

Pupils from Modern Eastern Suburban School and the School for the Excluded identified the bully primarily as the cowardly and spineless type of perpetrator. The bully, as pupils articulated, would only perpetrate when with a group of people as support was received by their peers. Pellegrini (1998:167) explains that such bullies use physical assertive behaviour as a way to publicly display dominance over their weaker victims. His review suggests that observations of boys in early adolescence provide further support for this claim and particularly for the importance of support by peers (Pellegrini, 1998). Indeed, to Sullivan *et al.* (2005:17), peer support was a vital condition for bullying. It was identified during one individual interview at the School for the Excluded that:

> Pupil: "what the ones who are bullying? Well nothing, they're just trying to be hard and they're not, but they do it just because there are more of them . . . . . . just because they can and it's all a big gang, that's what they do it for, if they were by themselves, they'd be scared.
>
> SQ: Right. So you think that the gang actually gives them more, strength, more power to go ahead and . . .

Pupil: aye! Because if they were by themself, it would be a different thing because they would be one on one. But the person's not goanna chin them if there were loads and loads of them is it? He's not goanna fight back is he? I would though!" (Transcription 9, individual interview, year 9, School for the Excluded: 4).

The majority of pupils interviewed suggested that bullies usually move around in groups that bullying, whether it is carried out verbally or physically, is always done in front of a group of people. As some pupils from the School for the Excluded recognised during a focus group:

". . . but it's not one on one, it's always three onto one and that, and four onto one" (Transcription 8, focus group, year 9, School for the Excluded: 5).

One key characteristic of the bully as perceived by pupils was the physical presence and physique of the bully. It was suggested that the stronger and larger framed perpetrator is more likely to be supported by peers to bully. The bully strives to look strong in front of their peers. Goody's research (1997:408) illustrates such behaviour as appearing as 'masculine bravado' and in her questionnaire findings, the high frequency of anonymous questionnaires revealed the extent of boys fear, but also a process whereby being stronger hindered the boys as their physicality meant that they were expected to be physically strong in order to impress their peers. Particularly this is due to boys' experience stemming from every day social interactions and social expectations, they are expected to be fearless (Goodey, 1997:403). Pupils at Old East End Community College placed particular emphasis upon identifying the bully as being strong, tough and powerful, not only in physique, as they were taller and bigger, but also in their mannerism. Reid *et al.* (2004:241) support pupils' perceptions and claim that the 'bully' benefits from more physical or psychological power than the 'victim', and applies this power in order to devalue the victim and make himself/herself appear superior (Reid *et al.*, 2004). In an atmosphere where bullying is condoned, Reid *et al.* assert that this encourages the bully to continue with their anti-social behaviour (Reid *et al.*, 2004: 247). Pupils from Old East End Community College articulated the rationalization of bullying as:

SQ: "Okay, why do you think the bully picks on people?

Pupil: because they are . . . stronger and harder" (Transcription 3, focus group, year 8, Old East End Community College: 5)

". . . the stronger, older people," (Transcription 2, focus group, year 9, Old East End Community College: 3)

In general, bullies' characteristics were stereotyped as being older, bigger in size, as having a poor upbringing and that such types usually targeted those who looked smaller, weaker and were quiet. During one focus group at the School for the Excluded, pupils identified a situation in which the bullies selected the ideal victim, that is one who is a loner, smaller in size, weak looking and easily intimidated (Olweus, 1993). It was identified how the victim would be first cornered and then attacked as:

". . . they'll isolate you though . . . . . . hunting for like . . . . . . the weakest animal and then they'll pick on that one. That's what bullies do, they tend to do that. There's no way that a bully would go and pick on a 7ft rugby player" (Transcription 8, focus group, year 9, School for the Excluded: 8)

In relation to the characteristics of the victim, pupils identified these as the traditional meek type. Cranham and Carroll (2003:114) identified the characteristics of the victim as being passive and submissive (Cranham and Carroll, 2003). They claim that victims usually are more introverted, anxious, insecure, cautious, sensitive and quieter than other pupils (Cranham and Carroll, 2003:114). Furthermore, whilst often possessing low self-esteem and having difficulty in asserting themselves, they argue that victims also experience social isolation as well as alienation. This was highlighted by pupils in Old East End Community College and the School for the Excluded. Pupils perceived the basic nature of the victim to be extremely vulnerable, weak and viable to stand up to the perpetrators. Reid *et al.* (2004:249) explain that this may possibly be as a result of victims not acquiring the appropriate skills for handling conflict because of a lack of exposure or because they have become over-reliant on parents/carers. Thus, they argue that this increases their sense of 'helplessness' and 'victim thinking' (Reid *et al.,* 2004). This issue was further developed when pupils explained that on average, most victims were unable to fight back because they were intimidated by the size of the bully or bullies, who were usually bigger. Similarly, Deakin (2006:376) found based upon the Children and Young People's Safety Study Survey, that victims who reported their bullying experiences admitted to feeling fear of the bullies in addition to feeling anxiety, intimidation and worry about experiencing bullying (Deakin, 2006). Pupils tended to use the example of the role play in the anti-bullying video to illustrate their point about how the victim's mental state would be:

Pupil 1: ". . . she was scared because, he was, she was dead little and they were all really, really taller than her,

Pupil 2: taller than her

SQ: okay. Anything else? Any other reason why she was just standing there and taking it?

Pupil 2: because one of them in the group knew that if she tried to defend herself, they would like just jump on her" (Transcription 12, focus group, Old East End Community College year 7: 16).

Pupil 1: ". . . because they were just ganging up on her, she couldn't do anything.

Pupil 2: because their bigger than her,

SQ: She could have screamed,

Pupil 1: I know, but then they would have just hit her harder then

Pupil 2: they would only hit her harder if she did like" (Transcription 6, focus group, year 9, School for the Excluded: 6).

It was understood by pupils that most victims' general mental state at the time was to allow the bullies to have their own way; screaming for help or physically fighting back, would only deepen the nature of the bullying. Pupils from Old East End Community College discussed this issue and used an example from the role play in the anti-bullying video to support their argument:

> ". . . she thinks if she does something, it might get worse.

> Others: she . . . . . . might get jumped on" (Transcription 5, focus group, year 8, Old East End Community College: 5)

> SQ: "Do you think that had she said something they would not bother her?

> Pupil: nah because if she had said something, then they would just pick on her even more, because if she called them something, it would make it worse!" (Transcription 4, focus groups, year 9, Old East End Community College: 6)

Such victims can be classified as 'passive' victims (Olweus, 1978 in Ma *et al.*, 2001: 253). Furthermore, the physical size of the victim plays an important role in bullying. Pupils also reported that victims were selected as they looked academic or like a 'geek'.

Pupils perceived that victims believed that by doing nothing, they could ensure that the length of the bullying incident would be brief and they would not be bullied in the future. Pupils further explored reasons as to why victims did nothing:

> ". . . they'll think, 'ah he's got friends and' and they'll think that he's got friends and people who'll stick up for him, because some people only bully other people because they think they've got no one to help them. So then if he shows them his mates and then they're not going, they're not going to stop them are they?" (Transcription 6, focus group, School for the Excluded, years 8 and 9: 8)

Furthermore, some pupils in Modern Eastern Suburban School argued that the perpetrators would go for particular victims who were weak, known as 'easy prey', and since the victims were more likely to be 'loners', the bullies were aware that they were likely go unpunished for their behaviour. Smith's (2004:100) research on bullying affirms that low friendship quality of the victim puts them in a more vulnerable position to be targeted for bullying. During one focus group at Modern Eastern Suburban School, pupils indentified that victims were selected because:

> Pupil 1: ". . . they'll go for a particular person for a reason, but then go back to that person because they've done it before and they know that they didn't fight back that time, so they probably won't the next either,

> Pupil 2: they probably go for them because they're easy targets" (Transcription 18, focus group, year 9, Modern Eastern Suburban School: 5)

In addition to the dynamics of the victims and perpetrator and their relationships, pupils also identified the environment where bullying occurs as an important element in sustaining or reducing the incidence of bullying. They acknowledged that the locations for bullying are in general places where there are no guardians such as a teacher present. As Ojala and Nesdale (2004:20) note, bullying often takes place in places unsupervised by adults. Pupils identified corridors, changing rooms, toilets, school playground, astro turf/grounds and links as the major areas where the bullying occurred. This was because for the most part, pupils believed the location meant bullying could occur without detection and therefore, without punishment. The location where bullying occurred was acknowledged by a few pupils from Old East End Community College as:

> Pupils 1 and 2: "toilets and outside

> Pupil 3: Miss in the corridors . . . . . . out there, (referring to the link), where we have our break time and dinner times

> SQ: So the links, toilets, where else do you think?

> Pupil 3: outside, changing rooms, anywhere where there's no teachers" (Transcription 5, focus group, year 8, Old East End Community College: 23).

Pupil 1: "anywhere,

SQ: anywhere?

Pupil 1: in the corridors and that,

Pupil 2: corridors,

Pupil 3: or like outside,

Pupil 1: classes . . . . . . when the teacher's there, some teachers cannot do nothing . . ." (Transcription 11, focus group, year 9, Old East End Community College: 9)

SQ: "where does most bullying take place?

Pupil 1: outside . . . . . . like standing in the basketball courts,

Pupil 3: outside the main entrance" (Transcription 18, focus group, year 9, Modern Eastern Suburban School: 7)

Pupils also recognized that bullying would often appear in the classroom, yet subtly behind the teachers back, or if the teacher walked out of the classroom during the session. One pupil illustrated the way in which the bullying incident may spiral out of control inside the classroom just after the teacher walked out:

SQ: "So what happens in the class?

Pupil: somebody might twig something off somebody and then the other person might start on them and it creates often a fight" (Transcription 11, focus group, year 9, Old East End Community College: 9).

Following on from this theme of the location of bullying, open space and lack of adult supervision, it was agreed by pupils that the lack of adult supervision or attention strongly influenced the nature of bullying. Similarly, part of Boxford's (2006:62) research on school crime discusses the school location as a venue for behavioural setting.

His large scale surveys revealed how particular locations of the school had one form of behaviour setting at one time during the day and another form at a different time of the day. For example, when referring to the school hall, Boxford (2006) identified that this would be used as a gym in the morning, a school canteen during lunchtime and then a play area after lunch. However, he argued that whilst the spatial structure remains the same, pupils behaviour that occurred in it changed through the day. For instance, when teachers were present, he discovered that pupils exercised more control in their behaviour. However, when the same location was used for play time, and with little supervision, Boxford (2006: 63) reveals that pupils' behaviour towards each other changed. When asked about such behaviour, pupils' from Modern Eastern Suburban School responded:

> SQ: "why do you think bullying occurs in these particular areas? Are they unmanned?
>
> Pupil 2: because people can do it there . . . . . . I think because it's a big space,
>
> SQ: what about teachers, are there any teachers present there?
>
> Others: yeah sometimes,
>
> Pupil 1: not all of the time,
>
> Pupil 4: yeah sometimes when there are loads of people,
>
> Pupil 2: yeah, but they're around the corner," (Transcription 22, focus group, Modern Eastern Suburban School, year 7: 8)

Pupils at the School for the Excluded highlighted that much of the bullying occurred outside the school gates because perpetrators were aware that they would be less likely to be caught by teachers. The research findings by Deakin (2006:383) revealed an affiliation between victimisation and location. Her findings showed that bullying occurred more on the way to and from the school. Deakin adds that street victimization accounted for half of all incidents of harassment, including bullying, between 18% and 28% (Deakin, 2006). The school location was found to be the second most common location for bullying and victimisation, between 11% and 18% (Deakin, 2006). Pupils in Modern Eastern Suburban School identified any areas where the security cameras did not monitor could become a venue for bullying. They claimed that:

> Pupil 1: ". . . there's a couple of corners where you could see . . .
> . . . it could be a target spot . . . . . . they're basically out of sight from cameras and
>
> Pupil 2: yeah the corner near the memorial quads," (Transcription 18, focus group, year 9, Modern Eastern Suburban School: 7).

When discussing peers as bystanders, pupils and adults recognized the importance of the influence peers had over the bully and the nature of the bullying activity. Peers were identified as being potential enablers or detractors for bullying. For instance, the perpetrator can either be encouraged by peers to continue or may be deterred from perpetrating if they are not given the support. Sullivan *et al.* (2005:109) reinforce this view as their research explains that the presence of peers/bystanders acts as an audience. They assert that if the peer group reject the bullying, the direction and motivation for bullying disappears; the perpetrator is less likely to continue without support. They argue that "All they (the peers) have to do is move away from the sidelines, become active, and withdraw their support of the bullying. Once they do this . . . the bully ceases to be a bully and the victim is no longer a victim" (Sullivan *et al.*, 2005).

Across the board in all three schools the discussion was unanimous that the role of peers was vital in understanding the occurrence of bullying. They perceived that the role and impact that bystanders had upon the bullying situation dictated whether the bullying would be permitted or actually encouraged to continue. Salmivalli's (1996) findings revealed that bystanders had numerous roles and preventing bullying was one of them. As one pupil identified:

> "I think . . . it can really be like, like for both on allowing it, because they could be watching to see like what's going on, so they can go and tell a teacher, or they could just be watching and just

like egging the person on to like . . . . . . beat you even more," (Transcription 24: individual interview, year 7, Old East End Community College: 5).

Pupils further indentified bystanders as those who merely watched, those who intervened and those who encouraged the bullying to continue. For most pupils in all three schools, the presence of bystanders usually had a negative aspect in that they would be more likely to encourage the bullying to continue. Sullivan *et al.* (2005:112) refer to these type of bystanders as 'reinforcers', who may not actively attack the victim, but laugh and encourage the bully and the bullying to continue. Sullivan *et al,* (2005) assert that becoming part of the action arouses feelings of excitement in them (2005:114). (See also Cranham and Carroll, 2003; Cowie, 1998; Baldry, 2005; Rigby and Johnson, 2006).

Many academics agree that most bystanders do nothing, due to the fear of being targeted next (Roldier and Ochayon, 2005; Garandeau and Cillessen, 2006). Whilst pupils acknowledged that they felt for the victims, they preferred not to get involved as they feared being targeted next: it was naturally expected of them to support the gang leader. As they said:

> ". . . aye, and they don't want to pick on the person who's being bullied in case it happens to them" (Transcription 23, focus group, Modern Eastern Suburban School, year 7:15). Furthermore, pupils discussed those bystanders:

> ". . . like, the people who are witnessing it, all stick up for the bully because, they usually pick on someone who's by themselves like, and then they call them" (Transcription 23, focus group, year 7, Modern Eastern Suburban School: 15).

Pupils from Modern Eastern Suburban School also identified that bystanders help to keep persistent bullying going. This is especially so if there was a personal grudge brewing between the bully and victim pupils perceived that perpetrators found it much easier to continue to target their enemy if they were with a large group of people. Sullivan *et al.* (2005:19) agree that bullying only continues if the bystanders allow it to (Sullivan *et al.,* 2005). For instance, pupils at Modern Eastern Suburban School discussed the extent of bystanders support for the perpetrator when they are bullying the victim. As pupils remarked:

> Pupil 1: "you know when you see that someone is picking on somebody or like having a fight, they're not on their own doing it, there's always a massive gang round them . . . . . . and their singling out one person,
>
> Pupil 2: well, I think they're just too afraid to do it on their own . . . . . . and they get loads of friends to come with them, so that they back them up,
>
> Pupil 1: and also when people see like bullying going on, they think of fights and then everybody just follows,
>
> Pupil 2: yeah everybody just follows" (Transcription 17, focus group, year 8, Modern Eastern Suburban School: 5).

There is also a sense that bullying becomes a form of entertainment for peers. Coloroso (2008:216) discovered that bystanders influenced the bullying behaviour by cheering on the bully as they derived pleasure from the victim's humiliation (Coloroso, 2008). Pupils in Modern Eastern Suburban School explained that the bystanders were not in a neutral role, but actually encouraged the bullying:

> SQ: "and the people who are standing beside them, how important do you think their role is on how the bully performs?
>
> Pupil 1: well depends how bad,
>
> Pupil 2: well how yeah, because if they're cheering them on and they're going 'fight, fight, fight' and stuff . . . well there was a fight and I was watching it and everyone was like,
>
> Pupil 3: K*** and D*****,
>
> Pupil 2: and I was watching them and . . .

Pupil 1: loads and there was this big and everyone was shouting 'fight, fight!' and then, but D***** was, like K*** wasn't going to fight and D***** kicked him and K*** started" (Transcription 23, focus group, year 7, Modern Eastern Suburban School: 26/7).

Pupil 1: ". . . with people, you get a lot of people egging each other on . . . . . . people like to see fights,

Pupil 2: yeah,

Pupil 1: in a fight everyone's calling or they're cheering,

Pupil 2: you know there might just be an argument and you'll get a lot of people who are just doing fights like, do you know what I mean, 'go on, hit him!' . . . . . . some people just like, they enjoy seeing fights . . . . . . they wouldn't stop it" (Transcription 19, focus group, year 9, Modern Eastern Suburban School: 12).

However, pupils at the School for the Excluded made it quite clear that bystanders were helpless towards the victim and would only intervene if it was their friends being bullied, whether it was verbal or physical bullying. As two pupils emphasized:

SQ: "But if you saw one of your mates being bullied by one or two boys then,

Pupil 1: I would go and help them

Pupil 2: I would go and help them, because he's me mate.

SQ: . . . . . . What would you do?

Pupil 1: go and help me mate

Pupil 2: go and dig one of them me!" (Grins) (Transcription 6, Focus Group, year 9, School for the Excluded: 8).

This section provides a strong indication that further work is required to target peers and motivate them to be more positive about their role and lend more support towards the victim.

Summary and Discussion

This chapter explores a variety of ways in which pupils and teachers make sense of bullying and racist bullying. This has been supported by a discussion of pupils' perceptions of the nature of bullying and racist bullying. The chapter then provides a background to the socio-economic and demographic character and profile of each school and threading through the chapter specific differences and similarities between pupil groups. Following this was an analysis of teachers' perceptions of bullying and racist bullying. The chapter finally examines the relationship between the bully and victim, assessed location of bullying and discusses the significance of the relationship between peers as bystanders and perpetrators.

Three main issues emerge from this chapter. First the ways in which pupils identify the nature and characteristics of bullying are not so dissimilar to their perceptions nature and characteristics of racist bullying. However, with regards to bullying, pupils' focus their discussion largely on the individual characteristics of the perpetrators and the bully is unanimously perceived as being responsible for their actions. Yet when discussing racist bullying, pupils' shift the focus of their discussion towards the victims. In particular, pupils from Old East End Community College are able to provide more depth to their descriptions and illustrations when explaining racist bullying than pupils from the other two schools. The school is embedded in an environment where poverty is the dominant factor and there is a high crime and unemployment rate. Preventative and intervention mechanisms compared with the other two schools were relatively weak. The presence of a large immigrant community residing amongst the lower white working class, where there is little or no social cohesion is not a positive prospective either. These socio-economic and structural factors are most likely to contribute to and influence the ways in which, pupils perceive and discuss how immigrants are viewed in their school and community.

Second, there are fundamental differences as to how pupils talk about the nature and characteristics of bullying and racist bullying. Pupils from Modern Eastern Suburban School have a deeper knowledge and understanding of bullying, and are able to establish that accumulated incidents amount to bullying and not one off incidents. Modern Eastern Suburban School not only is relatively affluent, but also located within a middle class and largely career professional neighbourhood. Thus the attitude by the school to prevent bullying as well as racist bullying would be stronger. The social ethos at Modern Eastern Suburban School reflects its middle class surroundings as financial support is strong. This enables the school to employ a variety of preventative and intervention mechanisms to support all pupils as well as allowing the schools to give bullying and racist bullying priority within the curriculum. Pupils from Old East End Community College reveal prejudices through their hostility towards victims of racist bullying, unlike pupils from Modern Eastern Suburban School who show more empathy and understanding towards victims. This suggests that the more socio-economically deprived a school and neighbourhood is, the stronger the resentment would be towards minority groups. Similar to Modern Eastern Suburban School, pupils from the School for the Excluded also recognize that bullying is an accumulative process. Yet whilst the school is also located in a socially and economically deprived area in Newcastle-upon-Tyne, anti-bullying support and preventative education is strong and the school ethos towards eradicating bullying was positive. This is due to the smaller numbers of pupils on roll therefore enabling teachers to devote more time towards pupils' social and mental wellbeing. This suggests that the stronger the preventative and intervention mechanisms are, the stronger the awareness and understanding will be amongst pupils (See chapter 7 for a fuller discussion).

Third, the presence and influence of peers act is a driving force for the occurrence of bullying, whether as an enabler or detractor of the bullying act. Across the board in all three schools, pupils are able to establish that peers have the power to control the bullying or to prevent the bullying from continuing. Interestingly, despite socio-economic factors contrasting greatly between the schools, this view is shared by all pupils, therefore, suggesting that further work needs to be done to encourage pupils to act more frequently as positive bystanders and/or guardians.

In conclusion, the chapter has provided insight into the ways pupils and adults identify the nature of bullying and racist bullying. Much of which are shared opinions, yet there are multiple perspectives given and the socio-economic and geographic factors can be argued to contribute towards differing opinions. Chapter six therefore explores pupils and adults explanations as to why such bullying and racist bullying occurs.

CHAPTER 6

Explaining Bullying and Racist Bullying

Introduction

THE AIM OF this chapter is to explore the rationalization of bullying and racist bullying from the perspective of pupils and adults. This chapter shows both individual and shared perspectives on why bullying and racist bullying occurs and how the socio-economic and geographic environment contributes towards pupils' responses. Two main themes emerge from this chapter: Firstly, pupils hold the perpetrator responsible for the bullying and perceive that it is their individual and psychological problems that drive them to bully. Secondly, when explaining racist bullying, victims are often held accountable for their victimisation. Those pupils from Old East End Community College, in particular believe that different cultural lifestyle of the victims that are to blame for the racist bullying. These pupils believe that hostile reactions to the victims of racist bullying are born out of provocation; as they feel that victims, who they perceive are in receipt of government benefits, enjoy an unfair advantage over the indigenous white community. In comparison, pupils from Modern Eastern Suburban School reveal a more empathetic response to the victim when explaining for racist bullying. The socio-economic environment and geographical location makes an important contribution towards the contrasting opinions.

The chapter is structured as follows. First it reveals pupils' explanations of wider bullying as being concentrated on four broad issues. (i)

Status, power and reputation; (ii) family experiences and childhood victimization; (iii) relative deprivation and (iv) the negative influence of the media and social context. Second, their explanations for racist bullying, concentrates on individual and cultural differences and perceptions of unfair advantage. The chapter also includes a discussion of teachers' perceptions of bullying and racist bullying. Finally, the chapter explores the differences between schools through a discussion of their socio-economic and geographic characteristics.

Explanations for Bullying

A number of reasons were put forward to explain bullying by pupils. These reasons are grouped and discussed below. Explanations of the perpetrating behaviour drew upon broad concepts such as status, power and reputation while some of the reasoning was rooted in family and childhood experiences. There was some discussion of ideas supporting a relative deprivation theory as well as the negative influence of the media and social context. What is interesting throughout this discussion is that pupils, when explaining school bullying, based their discussion solely on the characteristics of the perpetrator.

Status, Power and Reputation

One way in which pupils explained bullying was by reference to the theme of status, power and reputation. A simple example arose in one individual interview with one pupil from Old East End Community College. It was clear from the interview with the pupil that it was believed that the bully had to continue to perpetrate in order to preserve his or her image:

> "I think because if someone calls them a name, they think they have to do it, I think they think that they have to do it, to stay . . .
> . . . in the group and look hard" (Transcription 26, individual interviews, years 8 and 9, Old East End Community College: 31).

Pupils suggested that once labelled, a bully had to sustain the reputation in order to fit in with their peers, preserve the image of being 'hard' and maintain a leadership style status. This theory is supported by Woods (2009:224) who talks about social stratification and hierarchy in the peer group and argues that children, in particular boys, employ aggression in order to achieve status and dominance. Woods further claims that individuals who have achieved a higher status in the peer group through the use of aggression continue to use aggression in order to maintain this status and target those who are lower down the hierarchy (Woods, 2009).

Exploring this issue further during the focus groups, pupils maintained that perpetrators who previously had family members at the school with a reputation were expected to follow their footpaths. Pupils explained family reputation in the following terms:

> Pupil 1: "Well Miss if you have a family member here who's got a reputation of being hard, well you have to try and carry on the family name as if you are solid and that . . . . . . so you can keep the name going on and that

> Pupil 2: aye, it's the reputation of your family!" (Transcription 2, focus group, year 9, Old East End Community College: 9/10).

Pupils in Modern Eastern Suburban School used this concept and applied it to a situation where family members supported a younger sibling if they were being threatened by anyone. One pupil in year 8 clarified that:

> "if the younger sister's friends or if they've got like a younger sister or brother in year 7, they've got their worst enemy, but they're scared to go and pick on them, so they get their older brother or sister to go . . . ." (Transcription 17, focus group, Modern Eastern Suburban School, year 8: 11).

> "If you get bullied and . . . you're from a ****** family . . . . . . and you don't less know anything . . . . . . if you got a big brother here who is hard, you know what I mean" (Transcription 2, focus group, year 9, Old East End Community College: 9).

The research of Sullivan *et al.* (2005:17) and Haynie (2001, in Sullivan *et al.*, 2005), is consistent with the above construction of the bully particularly with pupils at Old East End Community College. In keeping with maintaining this leadership status, in order to continue receiving the power and prestige granted by their peers, the bully has to continue with the bullying and not feel any possible empathy towards the victim (Sullivan *et al.*, 2005: 17). Furthermore, Olweus (1991) argues the importance for the bully to maintain a physically strong and non-empathetic image. Yet despite the differences in attitudes, pupils have clearly indicated that under no circumstances can a particular reputation be compromised. It is obvious from pupils' perceptions that the perpetrator has much to gain by bullying:

> Pupil 1: "the bully bullied them because it makes them feels big and strong and,

> Pupil 2: Miss when they bully it gives them more attention and makes them look hard (others, 'aye, aye!')" (Transcription 3, focus group, year 8, Old East End Community College: 5)

The pupils' comments demonstrate how important it is for the bully to show off and impress their friends and pay no regards to the fact that the victim is hurt, belittled and embarrassed. This view is supported by academic writers: Lines (2008:66) claims that impressing peers is one crucial common characteristic of bullying and further claims that they are able to show off their power by humiliating the reserved and weaker individuals (Lines 2008: 105). Frisen *et al.'s* (2007: 759) findings revealed that one of the most common explanations as to why bullies perpetrated was that they suffered from low self esteem, in addition to feeling provoked by the victims. From the interviews it was evident that pupils believed that bullies felt good about themselves as they targeted an individual who was smaller. Cranham and Carroll (2003:113) suggest that bullying largely is an act of aggression against an individual who is either physically or psychologically weaker than the perpetrator. As one pupil from the School for the Excluded expressed:

> ". . . some of them think they're good because they pick on you . . .
> . . . they think they're good because they're bigger" (Transcription 9, individual interview, year 9, School for the Excluded: 2).

A further reason was:

Pupil 1: "to show off,

Pupil 2: because they think they're rock solid (girls start laughing)". Transcription 5, focus group, year 8, Old East End Community College: 6).

In addition to the above, pupils, particularly from Old East End Community College expressed the view that individuals were targeted because they looked defenceless, as victims were often by themselves. This explanation of bullying implicitly suggests that the motivation behind the bullying behaviour is calculating. As two pupils put it:

". . . if someone comes in and hasn't like got any friends with them, then some people might choose them" (Transcription 18, focus group, year 9, Modern Eastern Suburban School: 5).

". . . some people only bully other people because they think they've got no one to help them" (Transcription 6, focus group, year 9, School for the Excluded: 8).

For some pupils, the importance of having peers or family members present demonstrated that bullies were cowards. In particular, pupils from Modern Eastern Suburban School explained:

SQ: "do you think that the bullies are hard or they are just like,

Pupil 1: nah! They're like poodles!

Pupil 2: they're just like cowards because, they're not exactly going to,

Pupil 3: show offs. Their big show offs!

Pupil 1: nah, exactly because they have family who would do something to them, so they'll say that, 'I'll grab,' whoever, 'on you!' . . . . . . they also get them to do the dirty work for them,

Pupil 2: and hide behind them,

Pupil 1: they're like assassins, they've got like assassins" (Begins to giggle) (Transcription 23, focus group, Modern Eastern Suburban School, year 7: 16)

Yet, pupils at Old East End Community College believed:

Pupil 1: "whenever they're in a group, they might show off and feel hard in front of their friends.

Pupil 2: but when there're by themselves, they just leave you alone

Pupil 3: aye, exactly

Pupil 1: when they are by themselves, they don't bother you" (Transcription 3, focus group, Old East End Community College, year 8: 5)

An interesting comparison of the same answer between both schools is revealed here. Where pupils at Modern Eastern Suburban School involved family members, pupils at Old East End Community College expressed the importance of bullying occurring in front of peers. These views are supported by Rolider and Ochayon's (2005:39) research which indicates that bullying nearly always took place in the presence of peers, as peers would make a point of witnessing the bullying act by simply standing there, rather than walking away. Sutton *et al.* (1999:120) similarly suggest that the perpetrator joins in with their peers to bully the victim in order to raise their social status.

Family Experiences and Childhood Victimization

A second way in which pupils explained bullying was through a discussion of the bully's background. This focus on family and childhood background derives from a perception among many of the pupils that were interviewed alone or in a focus group that a bully's psychology and/or personality can explain their behaviour(s). Particularly the social environment in which pupils live in also assists to characterise the bully/victim persona. As Bradshaw *et al.* (2009:206) contend that the home and community contextual environment tends to have an influence on aggressive bullying behaviours at school.

Whilst the social background of the perpetrator was not discussed, only the social psychological, it can be suggested that the differences between each ward, the degree of inner-city social deprivation could indicate that the higher social disorganisation and domestic abuse, the more likely this is to occur amongst families of low income than those from an affluent and upwardly mobile family background. Pupils also suggested that the behaviour of some bullies was linked to the bullying that they themselves experienced at home.

Yet Coloroso (2008:19) maintains that children who have been abused and bullied by adults (usually parents) repeat these acts in order to gain some relief from their own feeling of powerlessness and self-loathing. These views were shared in particular by pupils from Old East End Community College and Modern Eastern Suburban School. During one focus group at Old East End Community College, pupils commented:

> Pupil 1: ". . . they are probably getting bullied at home off their dad or their mam and that . . .
>
> Pupil 2: they probably think it's alright to do it . . ." (Transcription 2, focus group, year 9, Old East End Community College: 14).

It was suggested by pupils at Old East End Community College that a victimized background shaped the personality of the perpetrator. A similar view was echoed by pupils in Modern Eastern Suburban School:

> Pupil 4: ". . . they might have something going on at home and like their parents might be abusing them or something.
>
> Pupil 2: well, they might have a problem or something, and . . . instead of curing it, they're just making it worse by trying to hurt someone to make them feel better . . . . . . which is just totally taking it the wrong way,
>
> Pupil 1: well most bullies . . . . . . they've been bullied before and then they think, 'Well I've been bullied, so someone else should

be, deserves to be bullied'". (Transcription 17, focus group, Modern Eastern Suburban School, Year 8: 22).

Pupils expressed their belief that bullies needed to behave in this manner because:

". . . they're angry and that. They're upset and that's why they still might want to take it out on younger people." (Transcription 10, individual interview, year 9, School for the Excluded: 6).

It was interesting to note that pupils emphasised the urgency for parents to pay more attention towards their children and understand the ramifications of their abuse over their children. This was particularly articulated in further depth by pupils from Modern Eastern Suburban School. Here pupils clearly acknowledged that family background directly contributes towards the bullying behaviour. During one focus group with pupils in Modern Eastern Suburban School, they ultimately expressed their concern by blaming the parents, thereby revealing a deeper understanding:

". . . maybe their mams and dads . . . . . . didn't really bring them up that well . . . . . . so then their mams and dads would just let them see what their mam and dads did, so then, so their mams and dads might like have just ignored them and just done what they like . . . . . . so then maybe they (the bullies) just like took control and like said like 'right, I'm going to do this and do whatever I like because they're not going to tell us off because they don't really care'" (Transcription 23, focus group, year 7, Modern Eastern Suburban School: 25/26).

Pupils also suggested or implied that psychological and medical disorders may contribute. As one pupil expressed:

"I do believe that to bully, to be doing something as serious as cases in bullying, to be doing something in that, cruel and ambitious, you've got to have, there's got to be something going on in your head as well. You know the way I think, I think it's disgraceful bullying as well" (Transcription 6, focus group, year 9, School for the Excluded: 4)

This opinion is in line with academic writers such as Olweus (1993), who suggests that most bullies are highly insecure and often need help with psychiatric disorders. Griffin and Gross (2004:384) discuss bullies who are exposed to a harsh and aggressive upbringing with 'inconsistent parental discipline strategies'. Their view supports that of Carney and Merril (2001 cited in Griffin and Gross, 2004:384), who suggest that bullies, "often have a positive outlook on the use of violence to solve problematic situations". Furthermore, Griffin and Gross (2001:385) suggest that, since bullies who are victims at home are less likely to retaliate due to helplessness, they are quite adept at identifying victims who reveal the same characteristics, or will be ineffective in their efforts to retaliate, thus making them more desirable targets.

Teachers from the School for the Excluded also professed the opinion that bullies may have been bullied and abused at home and subsequently treated other pupils the same way. They commented that many bullies were too embarrassed to discuss their own ordeals and that many who bullied out of aggression needed assistance to control their behaviour. Similarly, Rigby (2003:1) suggests that perpetrators of bullying not only tend to experience depression and engage in suicidal thinking, but often they bully in response to aggression and violence at home.

Support for the bullies requiring individual help which could be attained through services such as counselling, mentoring and anti-bullying education was also a popular option. Pupils also believed that bullies required punishing, for example by detention or being sent to the cooler. In particular, pupils at the School for the Excluded perceived bullies as psychological delinquents who needed punishing:

> Pupil 1: ". . . . like there must be something wrong with them . . . .
>
> Pupil 2: they need to learn their lesson!" (Transcription 6: focus group, year 9, School for the Excluded: 11).

This desire by some pupils to see bullies punished is an issue that is highlighted and discussed further in chapter seven.

BULLYING AND RACIST BULLYING IN SCHOOLS

Coloroso (2008:104) argues that if bullies are to feel responsible for their behaviour then empathy is the key characteristic that needs to be developed. She asserts that "the feeling of guilt won't be there unless the feeling of empathy has been cultivated. Empathy and guilt go hand in hand" (Coloroso, 2008). This is not dissimilar to the view of Ahmed and Braithwaite (2006:350) who argue for shame and restorative justice processes to curb bullying and provide the appropriate support for the perpetrators as well as the victims. Similarly, according to pupils, the bullies needed to be educated and understand the immorality of bullying.

Relative Deprivation

A third reason given by a handful of pupils as to why some people bully was that of relative deprivation. For some pupils, largely those from Modern Eastern Suburban School, the bully's deprived social and economic background often shaped a higher level of expectation for material possession and resentment or covetousness towards others who, in their opinion, unjustifiably had obtained these possessions. Victims who possessed expensive items, such as shoes, jewellery or clothes were often bullied because the perpetrators were not able to afford these things themselves. Pupils in focus groups from Modern Eastern Suburban School and Old East End Community College reflected upon the idea that:

> ". . . if somebody wasn't as well off and they thought, well they'd bully the more well off person and they would take the property off from them . . ." (Transcription 19, focus group, year 9, Modern Eastern Suburban School: 5).

> "They could be just jealous and then start picking on you . . . . . . like you might have something and they don't have it, so they could try and pick on you and stuff and try and get it off you" (Transcription 17, focus group, year 8, Modern Eastern Suburban School: 1).

> ". . . some people get bullied because if their parents can't afford stuff, they get bullied because they get called 'tramps' and that, and they can't afford and have to shop at Netto and that because they

can't afford to go anywhere else. To shop anywhere else either" (Transcription 12, focus group, year 7, Old East End Community College: 6).

Graham (1996) and Chaux *et al.* (2009:523), strongly assert that bullying bred more rapidly through inequality than absolute poverty/ deprivation.

Whilst no pupil from the School for the Excluded raised this issue, one teacher suggested that pupils were bullied if they appeared richer than other pupils, or if they appeared poorer. As the teacher commented:

> "the way children pick on each other is something that worries me a lot and . . . . . . that's to do with material possession, what they look like . . . . what they're wearing, what they're not wearing, what they can afford, what they can't afford . . ." (Transcription 10, teacher, School for the Excluded: 20).

Negative Influence of the Media and Social Context

In the wider social context, the media holds a significant amount of negative influence over the way pupils treat each other. Research has suggested that with regular exposure to violence young people are likely to become desensitized to real life violence and have less understanding of the suffering inflicted upon victims (Coloroso 2008:120). Similarly, pupils from Old East End Community College and the School for the Excluded acknowledged this and discussed 'copy cat' bullying, by reflecting upon popular television programmes, such as EastEnders and various violent play station games. When discussing how EastEnders played a part in influencing bullying, pupils from Old East End Community College used the following example:

> ". . . did you see when Dennis got killed because Johnny Allen goes round beating people up! . . . . . . well, yeah there's someone in year 9 who goes around calling himself Johnny Allen . . . . . . all violent and beats people up!" (Transcription 7, focus group, year 7, Old East End Community College: 11).

Furthermore, pupils from the School for the Excluded referred to one popular play station game that depicted all forms of violence:

> Pupil 1: ". . . San Andreas like! Proper learns you everything after that, don't it?

> Pupil 2: definitely, too right

> SQ: What was that?

> Pupil 1: San Andreas learns you everything, EVERYTHING right!!

> Pupil 2: drugs, prostitutes, hit man" (Transcription 6, focus group, year 9, School for the Excluded: 13/14).

Similarly, Coloroso (2008:121) identified Grand Theft Auto III as inviting young people into violence and argued that "Kids who are regularly exposed to media violence are apt to become 'intimidated' . . . . . . and imitate the violence they see and hear". Eron and Huesmann (1984:159) argue that, in addition to peers, the media becomes increasingly important in influencing a child's social development. They believe that the media holds long-term effects as it portrays aggression and violence as attractive attributes to copy. Teachers also commented that the media, especially with computerised games, had gained considerable influence over younger pupils, leading to bullying and disrespect. Coloroso (2008:123) agrees with the theories set out by Comstock and Paik (1991), that the more young people are exposed to television violence, the more likely they are to become anti-social and display aggressive behaviour.

Explanations for Racist Bullying

In contrast to the explanations pupils offered for school bullying, when asked to explain racist bullying, pupils offered a range of explanations some different than those discussed above. Instead of focusing upon the individual characteristics of the bully, pupils' explanations for racist bullying often focused on the victim's individual and cultural traits. Their explanations for racist bullying appeared to indirectly hold the victims responsible. Kailin (1999:724) found that the majority of white pupils "blamed the victim" and used their individual and cultural presence as a justification for racism. In addition, whilst pupils declared that they were not racist many were unable to discuss racist bullying without using either a range of racist language or prejudicial descriptions.

Individual and Cultural Differences

A major factor associated with the motivations for racist bullying identified by the pupils related to the individual characteristics of victims, namely their physical traits and characteristics. For example, pupils often brought up images of minority ethnic groups such as different coloured skin and wearing headscarves, turbans, etc. Pupils in a focus group from Old East End Community College described racist bullying as:

Pupil 1: "Racist? It's when you call someone when they're skiv!

Pupil 2: name calling and making fun of them.

SQ: Okay. So it's making fun of their colour,

Pupil 1: The way they talk, they way say that they're from . . . . They way they look like, how they talk and where they're from and all that!" (Transcription 2, focus group, year 9, Old East End Community College: 12).

During a focus group session in Old East End Community College, pupils disclosed their anger and frustration towards the non-white community, as they perceived that they were present in 'their' streets, attending 'their' schools and yet, in their view, not integrating. Although the vast majority of minority ethnic groups reside in the ward areas of Wingrove and Elswick, a percentage, particularly from the asylum and refugee population from Eastern Europe reside in the Walkergate ward and therefore attend this school. As pupils from one focus group in Old East End Community College suggested:

Pupil 1: "I don't mind them coming to our country, but I don't like it when they just sit there and don't say anything to us.

Pupil 2: aye there's about 17 good families on my street and the rest are just blooming Chinese!" (Transcription 2, focus group, year 9, Old East End Community College: 17)

The comment of pupil 2 from the above dialogue demonstrates an uncomfortable feeling about living in an ethnically mixed area, where there tends to be a lack of integration and social cohesion. These views are consistent with Cockburn's (2007:548) finding that the white community feels vulnerable and isolated. Elsewhere, Cockburn (2007:548) argues that a failure of society to recognize this has serious consequences for challenging racism and fostering community cohesion. His findings also associate racist attitudes with fear. Pupils justified a defensive attitude amongst the white community by discussing perceived provocation such as:

Pupil 1: "they swear in their own language and

Pupil 2: yeah and they talk to each other in their own languages and like". (Transcription 1, focus group, pilot sample, Old East End Community College: 4).

Raby (2004:377) identified this type of response as 'white defensiveness'; respondents in her interviews discussed their whiteness as a form of 'disadvantage'. The white community felt victimized and this shared view provoked growing levels of 'mutual racism' (Raby, 2004). Pupils from a focus group session in Old East End Community College used the physical differences of the ethnic minority groups, as a way to justify racist bullying:

Pupil 1: "Miss can I say something first? . . . . . . Right, if you got dark coloured skin right, you might not be born in a foreign country . . . . . . but Miss there's this family and their kid goes here right, and they've got a corner shop right, and they do anything they want right, and they are from India right, and they go right, and with his mam right, she like looks at you right, and . . . .

Pupil 2: she stares at you,

Pupil 3: and, but they talk to you in that Indian voice and you don't know what they are saying right, but you know it's about you because she says your name and that, and she pure stares at you.

Pupil 2: ah nah, she talks in that language and gives you pure dodgy talks and that . . . . . . she gives you dodgy looks and that . . . . . . (In an Asian accent): You give me back that shopping and I'll give you ten dollars!! (They all start laughing)" (Transcription 5, focus group, year 8, Old East End Community College: 14).

A further interesting assumption was made during a focus group at Old East End Community College where one pupil claimed that the minority ethnic groups felt inferior and jealous of the white community because they did not have white skin colour and because of this she believed that they would retaliate towards the white community. As she remarked:

"Oh because they are jealous of us, because we are white and they aren't!" (Reflective diary 1: 17/11/2005).

In another focus group with Old East End Community College, year 9, only one boy openly disclosed his true racist feelings based upon his frustration with the presence of minority ethnic groups. He perceived that the presence of such groups, their lifestyle differences had a deep impact on the living conditions of the white community. He adamantly expressed a desire for all immigrants to return to 'their own' country and showed no remorse or guilt in his attitude. The pupil in year 9 expressed:

"I don't know why dark people just don't go back to where they came from, they just come over here and cause fights for white people and then the white people just get in trouble for them. Well I think it's wrong and they shouldn't be here! . . . . ." (Transcription 2, focus group, year 9, Old East End Community College: 15)

Such racist hostility and attitude shocked the class tutor who was present throughout the focus group. Furthermore, in the class no one challenged his racist remarks. The same pupil expressed his racism openly:

> ". . . they should just go back to Nigeria, I'm sorry though, but I just don't like them! They are just very different! . . . . . . I think they should just leave all the dark people alone and let them get on with their own lives, but for me, I think they should all just go back to where they came from!" (Transcription 2, focus group, year 9, Old East End Community College: 15)

Cockburn's (2007:551) findings suggest that white young peoples' dislike or animosity towards minority ethnic groups had increased as they felt the decrease in their economic wellbeing and that there was a loss in their sense of identity. These mindsets were born out of fear of unknown cultures, anger and in particular, frustration. Cockburn's findings further revealed that these feelings had developed as a result of the white community feeling overwhelmed by the increasing numbers of asylum seekers and refugees coming into their neighbourhood (Cockburn, 2007). Pupils acknowledged the growing numbers of asylum seekers and refugees coming into their neighbourhood; but did not feel that this was a positive change. As the teacher and pupils discussed:

> Teacher: "I think we have quite a lot of black and Chinese and Kosovo's
>
> Pupil 1: Miss, we got Chinese, Asian, Afghanistans, Pakistans . . . and whatever!
>
> Pupil 2: and Bosnians,
>
> Pupil 1: Bosnians!
>
> SQ: what's the ratio of Asylum seekers and refugee's in the school?
>
> Teacher: I don't know but I can find out for you, but we're getting more.

Pupil1: We're getting more and more and more!!" (Transcription 1, pilot focus group, Old East End Community College: 3).

In contrast however, during one focus group interview in Modern Eastern Suburban School, pupils discussed one incident where a young Muslim girl had her headscarf pulled off by some boys. The dialogue below demonstrates that some pupils acknowledged and accepted cultural differences. As they remarked:

SQ: "why were they attacking her, those boys?

Pupil 3: maybe it's because of her colour,

Pupil 4: colour and her head scarf and she's really nice as well . . . . . . she's American, but she's coloured and she's got a headscarf and she's really friendly.

Pupil 2: they might have been brought up where they haven't seen anyone with a headscarf, and then they might think, 'oh well, she's not like us is she', so they might just try to take it off her . . . . . . break her, making her cry

Pupil 3: but that's her religion and she has to wear it". (Transcription 17, focus group, year 8 Modern Eastern Suburban School: 7)

This response which showed sympathy towards the Asian girl can be contrasted with previous responses that have only shown hostility. This can be linked with Cockburn's (2007) view that young people are able to accept non-white people at an individual level whilst maintaining racist views. Sympathy was shown here as pupils in this group indicated that they knew the individual who was targeted and that they genuinely liked her. Furthermore, this more sympathetic view can be associated with the social make-up of the school, which is strongly multiracial and practices zero tolerance towards racism. Furthermore, emphasis is given to performing and achieving academically well at this school only which serves for one to understand that anti-bullying and anti-racist support would also be strong and given high priority. Two pupils praised the school's effort to deal with incidents of racism:

Pupil 1: "I think it's quite a good school for, I think teachers seem to be on scene almost instantly if you like . . .

Pupil 2: you know there's two lunch times here, either earlier you know, some teachers will be teacher at the time, they do seem to get on the scene quickly, you know there's only like half of them there.

Pupil 1: also in bullying like, if two children have been involved in it, like one child is bullying another through racism . . .

Pupil 2: family members get into it . . ." (Transcription 19, focus group, year 9, Modern Eastern Suburban School: 21).

Pupils considered that racist language was avoided in the school not necessarily because perpetrators thought it to be wrong, but from fear of the consequences. One pupil who was appalled by this racist behaviour raised the issue:

Pupil: "it is just something that I think people have started to think twice now about racism . . . . . . because, like they know the consequences and the police and everything can be brought into it. So I think that they think before they act.

SQ: yeah? And you said they think twice in the sense that they think it's wrong,

Pupil: might do a little,

SQ: or that they don't want to get into trouble?

Pupil: well I feel that's appalling but . . . .

SQ: so they don't want to get into trouble?

Pupil: they'd just think, 'calling them is wrong, but, well should I do it or not?' . . . . . . and more because 'oh I might get into trouble so I'll it some other time' . . . . . . like depending where you are, if you're in school, the teachers might find out, but then you'd think, 'I'll wait till I'm outside the school'" (Transcription 19, focus group, year 9, Modern Eastern Suburban School: 20/21).

During the interviews at this school, there were no racist overtones or attitudes expressed by any pupils. This could also be associated with the idea that the school sought to raise awareness of racial verbal stereotype and would challenge any racially prejudiced attitudes from pupils.

Unfair Advantage

A second explanation given by pupils for racist bullying related to what they perceived to be preferential treatment afforded to immigrant and asylum seeker communities by the government. The presence of minority ethnic groups, asylum seeker and refugee populations was perceived to have generated major changes within the local community. In some pupils' estimation, the government has made "unnecessary" changes in order to assist particular groups, which were perceived to be unfair and unwarranted. As two pupils discussed:

> ". . . Miss the government's been changing things here because of them, like Christmas, they're changing that and that's not for any reason . . . . . . well that makes people more racist like". (Transcription 11, focus group, year 8, Old East End Community College: 22)

> "I mean schools don't call it Christmas anymore, it's called festivities" (Transcription 11, focus group, year 8, Old East End Community College: 23)

Pupils in one focus group in Old East End Community College complained that the name was changed from black board to dry white board so as not to offend any minority ethnic groups. They agreed that implementing such drastic changes would:

> Pupil 1: "well it makes people feel racist

> Pupil 2: well people might effect to that, like just because of the name, like ah wouldn't think that calling it a black board is being

racist towards anyone. . . . I mean it's a black board and Christmas is Christmas" (Transcription 11, focus group, year 8, Old East End Community College: 23)

During these discussions, pupils became more vociferous in their articulation of the disparity. For instance, during one focus group session at Old East End Community College, pupils complained at the advancement in the quality of life for minority ethnic groups, which was believed to have been achieved largely by attaining their own businesses. In the opinion of some pupils, minority ethnic groups were favoured by the government by being given first choice of housing. Furthermore, as Webster (2007:86) argues, areas where social deprivation and poverty is high, so too are racist hostility towards minority ethnic groups. His research is located in the North East of England, in an area of mass de-industrialization and many young adults were hindered by this. The decline in any decent stable jobs and poor economic plight assisted in shaping their perpetrating behaviour (Webster 2004:3). Cockburn (2007:553) claims that while racism is undeniably a prime cause of community conflict, there is a failure by policy makers to carry some parts of the white community with them and this perpetuates a cycle of resentment. For example, his data reveals that the young people who were interviewed perceived that "nothing is being done for them and plenty done for others" (Cockburn, 2007:553). Echoing a similar view, pupils' complained that:

Pupil 1: "about immigrants having corner shops . . . . .yeah every corner shops have got them in them and flats, they all are in the flats, and they just keep on bringing more and more . . . .

Pupil 2: there's like flats behind mine (house) and they get first option of flats, coloureds moving in before us". (Transcription 1: focus group, pilot sample, Old East End Community College: 2).

One parent explained pupils' attitudes further:

". . . well what they're saying is that 'how come they can get more important and this and that and we English people can't afford stuff like that? How can they get stuff for their houses and the English people can't get that?' . . . and they get the same money . . . . . . and like, . . . S**** was one of them, S**** got told off his teacher not long ago, and the teacher had to say to S**** that he was a racist, and S**** went, 'well how?' he says 'because you shouldn't be saying, well this persons getting this money and this English person's getting nothing' and they class S**** as a racist, now S**** hit the roof when they classed him that" (Transcription 15, parent interview, School for the Excluded: 17).

Whilst no pupil at the School for the Excluded revealed any resentment towards minority ethnic groups, there was equally no remorse or sympathy shown for victims of racist bullying. Had the school been ethnically mixed, it can be speculated that this attitude may have been more pronounced.

Pupils in Old East End Community College displayed a great deal of resentment about the way they were being treated by the school and the government. Their discussions revealed an overwhelming opinion that they felt neglected. They linked this neglect to the schools' role, which consisted of an extensive asylum and refugee population. Pupils perceived that there have been many changes made by the Government and the school in order to accommodate such groups and this was deemed to be unfair. Pupils' frustration was particularly acute because they believed that they had witnessed the immigrant/asylum seeker/refugee community receiving material goods from the local council. Becoming increasingly emotional, pupils asserted that:

Pupil 1: ". . . I think it wrong because we only have small things off the council, but when they come over here, they get big Mercedes and stuff and it's not fair!

Pupil 2: aye, in my street they get everything done for them." (Transcription 2, focus group, year 9, Old East End Community College: 15)

Clearly, the presence of these groups and the services that they were believed to receive angered the white pupils. Particularly those present at Old East End Community College, unlike pupils at Modern Eastern Suburban School, they failed to understand why asylum seekers and refugees were in the UK and believed the treatment towards them to be unfair and used this to justify racist comments. Whilst no pupil at Old East End Community College made any open declaration, they appeared to suggest that the non-white community should almost expect racist retaliation.

When discussing what strategies could be employed to eradicate racist bullying, most pupils had little or nothing to offer. There were suggestions from pupils in Old East End Community College that all pupils should be treated the same and that the government and school system was unfair. However, at this school, other pupils in other focus groups articulated a desire for segregation. This desire for segregation has been manifested in many different ways elsewhere. Feagin and Vera (1995:4) note that widespread segregation remains in the USA, ranging from blatant acts reminiscent of the legal segregation period to subtle and covert forms that have flourished under the conditions of desegregation (Feagin and Vera, 1995). Bonilla-Silva and Forman (2000:51), suggest that white Americans claim to believe in racial equality and yet oppose programs that reduce racial inequality, thereby subtly suggesting the existence of widespread segregation. Pupils' desire for segregation however, was more formal than informal, in that they openly declared the desire to have separation between white and non-white pupils during breaks. This attitude is clearly opposite to the idea of community cohesion. As two pupils clearly expressed:

> SQ: "okay, a final couple of questions, how do you think this kind of behaviour can be stopped/prevented?
>
> Pupil 1: well like, in some ways it can like, if they build separate little blocks for breaks for their friends, (that is, separate playground areas during break time) for when people come in new, put them in separate classes, boxes . . .
>
> SQ: you mean like to segregate them?
>
> Pupil 1: aye, but still have them mixing at classes,
>
> Pupil 2: but everyone should be equal,

Pupil 1: but, yeah, but if they don't want to get called then, they should. I suggest that . . ." (Transcription 1, pilot focus group, Old East End Community College: 2).

Interestingly, when this question was asked to pupils at the School for the Excluded, pupils' response were only in reference to bullying. As there was no mixed ethnic groups present at the school, pupils discussion on racist bullying was minimal, despite as mentioned earlier, very little empathy was given towards the plight of victims of racist bullying. This could suggest that racist bullying was not deemed to be a major problem as they would not have to interact with them on a daily basis whilst at school. In contrast however, pupils from Modern Eastern Suburban School also talked less about racist bullying; however whatever was discussed during the interviews was more positive. This issue is discussed at length in the school response section in the following chapter.

Pupils blaming the non-white communities for prospering may suggest that they feel ashamed of the lack of progression in their own lives and resentful of the development in the lives of these communities. One pupil remarked during the pilot focus group that:

"There's loads of Asian people, black people . . . . . . well there's too many of them in this country and they take over the corner shops since the 70's" (Transcription 1, focus group-pilot, years 8 and 9, Old East End Community College: 2).

The stereotypical example of all corner shops being owned by immigrants suggests that in a short space of time minority ethnic groups have managed to prosper economically, whilst white people appear to be lagging. These findings are similar to those of Ray *et al.* (2004:360) who suggest that often communities are ashamed of their lack of achievement in life in comparison to the achievements of ethnic minority communities. Ray *et al.* (2004)'s findings interpreted the racist reactions of their interviewees as capturing both rage-emotions along with unacknowledged shame that stemmed from the belief that minority ethnic communities were receiving benefits and advantages. Ray *et al.* (2004: 356) argue that:

"The accounts that interviewees gave of their offending and their attitudes . . . reveal a sense of grievance, victimization, unfairness and powerlessness when they compare their situation with that of Asians, as they perceive it . . . . . . they saw themselves as weak, disregarded, overlooked, unfairly treated, victimized without being recognized as victims (by the government and local police), made to feel small; meanwhile, the other—their Asian victims . . . . was experienced as powerful, in control, laughing, successful, 'arrogant'".

Studies of shame (Scheff 1990; 1994; 1997 and Retzinger 1991, in Ray *et al.,* 2004: 350) have shown that perpetrators carried out racist violence due to their own deep emotional roots that were caused by alienation, shame and rage (Ray *et al.,* 2004:364). Ray and Smith's (2001: 217) research into racist perpetrators in Oldham, Greater Manchester, suggested that there was much support for the National Front due to their stereotypical attitude that minority ethnic groups were at an unfair advantage. They argue that much of the racist perpetration was due to using minority ethnic groups as scapegoats, "for their own sense of failure and resentment" (Ray and Smith, 2001:216). Ray *et al.* (2004:350) therefore suggest that racist violence may be motivated by 'unacknowledged shame'. Whilst the sentiments of the pupils at Old East End Community College were the same as those in Ray *et al.* research, there was no direct evidence from any interviews at this school that this drove members from their community to racist violence.

Adults' Explanations for Bullying and Racist Bullying

The teachers involved in this study were of the view that bullying is a combination of lack of respect, tolerance, understanding and discipline amongst pupils that contributes to their bullying behaviour. Yet, despite this, teachers simultaneously perceived that pupils do not know or understand the ramifications behind bullying. For many of the bullies, teachers suggested that they see it as a joke and therefore, are less likely to take bullying seriously. As one teacher from the School for the Excluded emphasised:

"I think kids are becoming very desensitized and don't quite comprehend the consequences of their actions. I don't think they quite realize the ramifications they have over other people. It's just a laugh and you see the kids do that in the catchment area in the front, they are very desensitized. I don't think that they are being malicious; they're just having a laugh. Or they don't realize how destructive they can be . . . . They just don't seem to . . . well they know when you sit down and talk to them about it. But actually putting it into practice in their own minds is just, probably very difficult" (Transcription 9, teacher, School for the Excluded: 27).

This teacher also suggested that the occurrences of bullying were more to do with opportunity than premeditation. The teacher explained this in relation to hierarchy:

". . . bullying does occur, but I think that its more opportunistic, it's not something that's systematic, I think people will flex their muscles with kids and they will try to intimidate younger ones, less dominant ones in the class, but it's not systematic, it's not really bullying, but there is an element of posturing, and that is to be expected, you know the hierarchy of the client group, the top dogs. I don't think that it's much more bullying than the pecking order within the school" (Transcription 9, teacher, School for the Excluded: 26).

Indeed as Olweus (1992:74) characterises that particularly amongst boys than girls, a hierarchy existed in these groups where the younger pupils would be targeted by the older pupils at the school.

This view mirrored many of the views of the pupils in that bullying was a consequence of the search for power, status and reputation. Similarly, within the School for the Excluded teachers believed that pupils were often coerced into bullying the victim in order to integrate with the rest of the group:

Teacher 1: ". . . the bullying that they sort of, like if you're not seen to insult somebody here within two weeks of arriving, you'll start getting picked on . . . .

Teacher 2: you've lost your street cred really" (Transcription 10; teachers, School for the Excluded: 32).

Similarly, Sullivan *et al.* (2005) assert that many individuals are coerced into bullying in order to seek approval by their peers which were deemed more important than anything else.

Teachers from the School for the Excluded also suggested that bullies did not take pleasure in tormenting others. They perceived that many bullies needed help as they did not know how to stop bullying others. Referring to one individual who was a bully, one teacher from the School for the Excluded commented:

> "I can see that he wants help, ***** doesn't like that side of him, he doesn't like to bully, I see that in him, he doesn't want to bully, but it's like he can't, it's almost like a demon he . . . . . . can't handle it. . . . it's like Jekyll and Hyde with *****, you start questioning him about it, start sort of really on his case about it, and he can be very defensive" (Transcription 10, teacher, School for the Excluded: 34).

In the case of racist bullying, unlike the pupils, teachers were able to see beyond the individual and cultural differences and recognized that such differences serve no justification. However, all teachers and youth workers interviewed identified pupils' racist attitudes as stemming from the wider family and from the surrounding community. Teachers in this study perceived that pupils lacked an awareness of the implications of their racist comments. Similarly, Troyna and Hatcher (1992:49) discovered that much of young people's racist attitude emanated from the home and wider community and ultimately believed that whilst pupils' terminologies were racist, they themselves were not.

Racist behaviour was alleged by teachers to be a result of socialization in the home and the consequence of a 'fear' mentality which resulted in aggression towards the non-white community. One teacher from the School for the Excluded articulated the racism of parents and the subconscious way this influenced their children:

> SQ: "Do you think that the racist elements have gone up?

Teacher: I do, yeah. How could they not? I mean, in an ideal world we wouldn't have done, but in a world that we all live in, how could they not go up? I think you'll find a lot more people will be racist and when they say it, they don't realize that their two year old child is standing there and they don't think that they understand . . . . . yeah, they're not going to understand word for word, but they're going to have an idea, and if that child gets older and continues with these comments, then you've got another racist, and that's the worrying thing about it" (Transcription 9, teacher interview, School for the Excluded: 21).

Teachers at the School for the Excluded particularly believed that a lack of multicultural exposure existed not only amongst the pupils, but also in the community and home environment. Subsequently they articulated that adults held racially prejudicial attitudes as there was little or no contact with minority ethnic groups; pupils adopted similar attitudes. Sibbit (1997: ix) found that the views of perpetrators that she interviewed were shared by the wider community to which they belonged. Rather than condemning young people's racist perpetration, the wider community actively reinforces their behaviour. Similarly Cockburn's (2007:551) research suggests that parental influence shapes pupils racist beliefs. However, Hirschfeld (1996, in Cockburn, 2007: 552) criticizes this conclusion, arguing that, the idea of parental influence perpetuates the model of young people as being 'passive recipients' of education and knowledge from parents, teachers or the media.

One teacher from the School for the Excluded expressed the extent of racial prejudice in the community by relating a recent incident:

". . . but it's not just the kids, there was an adult on the bus behind me and she went on and on and on about this kind of thing and then we got to the bus at Gallowgate . . . . and there was this gorgeous ornamental Chinese arch that they've just built and she said, 'and these lot as well, you know they're putting up bloody arches here and it's not their country either and' and I had to say something before I got up and I said to her 'you know, this is not OUR country, we all share this planet and it's to people like you that I have to put up with' and then I just walked away from her but there is an awful lot of racism that goes on within schools and within the community as well" (Transcription 9, teacher, School for the Excluded: 12/13)

According to this teacher, pupils maintained the belief that minority ethnic groups and asylum seeker/refugee communities were receiving more help from the government than the white community. She explained that this conviction, therefore, fuelled further resentment towards these groups. Yet some teachers also perceived that once pupils became familiar with individual pupils from these groups, they were able to socially mix with them and accept them. This was especially the case at Old East End Community College. Teachers otherwise were more doubtful suggesting that pupils were racist and resentful towards the whole 'concept' of immigrants, asylum seekers/refugees and BME groups. As one teacher from Old East End Community College expressed:

"I mean it's *******'s one of the gang and ******* is so cool and is he smoking? I don't know, but you know, he's one of the gang, so he does aim for that, but the concept of asylum seekers and refugees for the kids in this school, is I think, something that they don't like". (Transcription 14, teacher, Old East End Community College: 4).

Lane (2008:142) suggests that, for parents and families to have a role in ensuring that their children learn positive attitudes to differences between people and cultures, they must unlearn any negative attitudes that they (the parents) may have already learnt. The youth workers suggested that, without such unlearning, negative attitudes are passed down to the younger generation. One youth worker who had spent a vast amount of time working with pupils at secondary schools in Newcastle and particularly at Old East End Community College maintained this firm belief. The second youth worker whose youth centre attracted young people from schools across the city, developed upon this idea. The question of teaching adults against racism arose during the interview:

SQ: "so you think it's probably more the adults, the parents who need more of an education especially with race rather than the children?

Youth worker: hmm, mm, yes because you will, you would sit with the Bosnian project; there was very much the stereotypical . . . . . . image they had, at the time, and I think it was because there was a lot of the outside influences . . . . . . it was like, refugees coming in and taking people's houses and the concepts of taking people's houses . . . ." (Transcription 28, youth worker: 13/14).

During interviews with teachers the discussion shifted towards the local community's attitude towards Muslims. This discussion took place primarily amongst teachers from the School for the Excluded who articulated that the local white community maintained a feeling of fear towards the Muslim community after the September 11th 2001 and July 7th 2005 bombings. Liese (2004: 65) comments that in post September 11th 2001 America, prejudice towards the Muslim community, especially students, appears to derive from social stereotypes. He continues to assert that "This is of special concern because the pejorative stereotypes against Muslim students are often justified . . . . in the guise of patriotism". Liese (2004:65) argues that where the white community feels pain or perceives a threat which is out of their control, they often come to experience frustration and resentment towards the social groups whom they blame for their feelings. Similarly, one teacher commented:

"Well people are more afraid now aren't they? And, you know, whatever you're afraid of you come to hate it, because that's what it breeds, fear breeds hatred, basically. And it's, it's very highlighted that, you know, it was a told that it was a Muslim thing," (Transcription 9: teacher, School for the Excluded: 21).

Teachers at the School for the Excluded suggested that adults who fear the practicing Muslim lifestyle have feelings that breed hatred; in turn these feelings drive them to make racist comments which often take place in front of their children. It was emphasized that whilst no minority ethnic groups were on roll the school is located in an area where social deprivation is high and a percentage of the Muslim community are present in the local neighbourhood. Children are therefore most likely to adopt such racist attitudes and replicate the expressions despite not knowing exactly what they mean. For example, teachers from the School for the Excluded revealed how one pupil admitted that his community was petitioning to get one family out of their street because they were Muslims; their attitude was that all Muslims are terrorists. Furthermore, the teacher remarked that:

> "So I said to him, 'So you're trying to tell me that anybody with a different coloured skin is a terrorist?' He only said, 'Well, yeah!'" (Transcription 9; teacher, School for the Excluded: 12).

Another teacher from the School for the Excluded highlighted this view by describing the current social climate in Metropolitan London. By using this example, he tried to articulate that the white community in the North East of England held similar beliefs to those of the white community living in London, in that there was much antipathy towards minority groups, especially the Muslim community:

> "it's a propaganda thing, I mean its suspicion now obviously and . . . the people have, I mean I've been down to London since July 7th and I have obviously been, I've even worked in London since 9/11 stuff and that, the suspicion of people just on a tube and everyone looking daggers at each other, it's a weird feeling" (Transcription 10, teacher, School for the Excluded: 28)

Oka (2005:34) contends that since September 11th 2001, most of the public have a real awareness of the non-white community, in particular Muslims. She declares that this has conditioned people to fear Muslims. The findings presented here suggest that this fear is also present among young people in the North East of England.

The lack of social acceptance towards minority ethnic groups was attributed by the teachers in particular from Old East End Community College and the School for the Excluded, to a lack of multicultural awareness. Bulmer and Solomos (2004:113) argue that members of the white community who deem their culture to be superior are inhibited from aspiring to learn and embrace different cultures. In a similar vein, one teacher from the School for the Excluded commented that some pupils were:

> "Far removed from a situation, say where they would encounter someone, from a Muslim community, whatever, that's just not, the only people they would see for racist bullying is like some of the Chinese or from the 'Paki' shop. That's the only contact that they would really have, they know very little of the culture. They would know, I would say next to nothing about the culture," (Transcription 9, teacher, School for the Excluded: 28)

This also suggests that where there is a lack of contact between the white community and the non-white community this helps to rationalize the hostility towards the cultures. However, unless any real integration takes place, isolation and seclusion undoubtedly plays a significant role in creating the lack of empathy or desire for a harmonious melting pot. Lane (2008:156) argues that children are encouraged by parents not to talk or trust people from different communities and that they are unable to accept that their fears might be exaggerated or imaginary. One youth worker suggested that multicultural events could help to change misconceptions:

> ". . . in our play programme . . . we would do sessions where it would explore different themes or around different countries, different cultures, different aspects of society, ... like just open up their broader minds to things like art, crafts and specific celebrations, and to always remember like, the Chinese New Year, we have done work in the past and Eid and things like that, also, around open children to like different foods from around the world as well, so it's like broadening like their taste buds, and they were very popular . . . . . . many children who would go, 'oh, I'm not going to eat that' . . . . . . and once you've actually tried it, it was nice actually . . ." (Transcription 28, youth worker: 15).

In the wider social context, youth workers argued that the media assisted in the proliferation of racist feelings. For example, the constant portrayal of the dire political and social welfare situation in the immigrants' home country can have a negative effect. This has developed the impression that immigrants desperately need the British government's help and has led the public to rank them as second class and undeserving citizens. Lane (2008:47) asserts that people living in mainly white areas may have no 'countervailing' information about such communities to present a different and more positive view. Thus, negative attitudes flourish unchallenged (Lane 2008). One youth worker expressed that:

> ". . . the concepts of like how communities are portrayed like they talk about the Bosnian project as well . . . and a lot of the parents attitudes towards these families you know, ... like will come from, horrific backgrounds to a new country and what they perceive and what benefits they were receiving, what they were getting and things like that, and I think sometimes the society feels as though they have to have a target group" (Transcription 28, youth worker: 39).

The explanations given for racist bullying by teachers and youth workers drew on two main threads. Firstly, teachers perceived that racist bullying occurred due to ignorance and a lack of acceptance of minority ethnic groups and their cultures, amongst the white community and this often turned into a feeling of fear of the unknown, particularly towards the Muslim community. Secondly, teachers firmly believed that pupils' racist behaviour and attitude derived from antipathy displayed within the home and the wider community and therefore viewed young people as 'passive recipients'. One such example of passive learned behaviour was pupils believing that minority ethnic groups, in particular asylum and refugee communities were receiving preferential treatment.

Explaining Bullying and Racist Bullying from Socio-Economic and Geographic Perspective

Pupil's explanations for bullying drew upon three contrasting perspectives. Primarily findings from Old East End Community College and Modern Eastern Suburban School emphasized maintaining a family reputation and the importance of reputation amongst friends as well as bullying occurring as a result of relative deprivation.

Whilst pupils narrated that bullying occurred in order to maintain a particular reputation and status, comparisons can be drawn between pupils' attitude from Modern Eastern Suburban School and Old East End Community College. At Modern Eastern Suburban School such a situation only occurred to defend a family member, whilst at Old East End Community College, bullying to maintain a reputation was more associated with emphasizing aggression. As Modern Eastern Suburban School is located in the North Heaton ward, which is affluent with a middle class community and school, this can assist for the two comparisons. There is less emphasis placed upon aggression at Modern Eastern Suburban School. This could also be attributed towards the low crime rate in the area, unlike Old East End Community College which is located in the Walkergate ward, an area of significant crime, so too aggressive attitudes filter into the school environment.

The contrasting display in attitudes suggests that the social demographic environment shows some significance. Modern Eastern Suburban School is located within an affluent and low crime rate ward where there is also a large community of elderly people as well as young single professionals. Yet, Old East End Community College is located in a neighbourhood that is significantly socially and economically deprived. There is also a large population that lives in close-knit, inner city post manufacturing communities and much of the population are low income families living in estate based social housing with uncertain employment (Rowntree 2010). Furthermore, the area in which this school is located in has a high rate of crime. Aggressive behaviour at this school was implied during the focus groups and this could largely be determined by the socio-economic deprivation not only in the school, but also the home and community environment. Stewart (2003:579) considers crime through social disorganization both in the school and home environment as a major characteristic that influences the behavioural development of the adolescent. He further argues that "while neighbourhood context and delinquency received a great deal of empirical attention, the school level context and its influence on school misbehaviour remains one of the least studied areas" (Stewart, 2003:580).

As pupils from Modern Eastern Suburban School reside in a ward and surrounding wards that are considerably more affluent than pupils from Old East End Community College and School for the Excluded, it was an interesting observation that they would highlight upon the issue that bullying occurs due to relative deprivation (see pp 194). The school and its geographical location that is situated in the east end suburban side to Newcastle-upon-Tyne suggests that poverty was less common. As it is, in the North Heaton ward, many career professionals reside there in the most sought after homes, as well as a large percentage of upwardly mobile families living in houses bought from social landlords (Rowntree, 2010). Yet this does not reasonably indicate that pupils were referring explicitly to bullying out of relative deprivation solely within the school. Graham (1996:185) claims that relative deprivation is more important as a cause for violence, including physical bullying, than absolute deprivation in children, in particular at schools, as pupils feel frustrated due to not having the same material items as others. Relative deprivation was an obvious association to Old East End Community College and School for the Excluded given the vast socially and economically deprived neighbourhood and where regular employment was an uncertainty, in these two wards, particularly Walkergate. Elliott *et al.* (1996); Pitts (2001); Chaux *et al.,* (2009), David, (2010) and largely Espealage and Swearer (2009:155), similarly associate deviant and bullying behaviour in areas that are impoverished both economically and socially.

Racist Bullying

When it came to explaining racist bullying, there were vast differences in pupils' attitudes towards the victims, yet the topic diverted attention from a discussion often of perpetrators. With Old East End Community College, there was clearly hostility shown towards victims and their individual and cultural presence was seen as a justification for their victimization. Given the ethnic make-up at this school and in the community, and the extent of socio-economic deprivation, where the white community are less willing to understand why the asylum and refugee community are in the UK, this only reinforces the white defensive attitude. It is this thought which provokes the white community to react in a racially stereotypical manner (see pp 197/98). Old East End Community College is located in an area of high unemployment, and where there is a high population who live in close knit, inner city and manufacturing town communities. Webster's

(2004) research revealed that in areas of mass deindustrialization, young people's lack of employment opportunities only reinforced their hostility towards the presence of minority ethnic groups as poverty allows for minority ethnic groups to be used as scapegoats for the working class people's lifestyle. There is also a high percentage of asylum seekers and refugees who live in the same community. Thus witnessing these groups living in their neighbourhoods, receiving benefits, many Asian families who have their own businesses, these elements provoke resentment amongst white working class people due to the notion of unfair advantage. Ray *et al.*(2004) suggest and argue that offenders' are ashamed of their own lives and this shame is deep rooted in "multiple disadvantages and that rage is directed against south Asians who are perceived as more successful, but illegitimately so, within a cultural context in which violence and racism are taken for granted" (2004: 350). Therefore, it can be speculated that due to the socio-economic environment in which they live, racist perpetration is motivated by shame. Furthermore, this perception of unfair advantage, witnessed by the white communities, who already are struggling, only reinforces the hostile attitude towards them. As such, when pupils provided explanations for racist bullying, these often incorporated elements of white defensiveness as a prime cause for racist bullying. Furthermore, those pupils who presented a hostile attitude towards victims of racist bullying were very stereotypical in their explanations.

The school ethos may also contribute towards racist hostility amongst the victims. The teachers at Old East End Community College appeared by pupils to favour the minority ethnic groups, asylum seekers and refugee pupils, neither was there much mentioned in anti-racist education, however, teachers at this school were of the firm belief that young people were not racist once getting to know individuals, yet agreed that prejudicial attitudes emanated from the home environment. As one teacher from Old East End Community College emphasized:

". . . the same applies with racism . . . because I happen to work with kids who are not from the UK and some kids will actually find it difficult to accept that we have other people who look different . . . . . . I believe it's according to what they hear from the home. I have read in papers that go into their homes and they believe what they read. They'll often be like 'oh, we don't like that' and as time goes by they change . . . . . . They have different names, and when you explain to them like in year 9 last year, the teacher did explain so many things to them because I remember when one of the girls just went on saying, 'I don't like foreigners', but the teacher would explain that 'nobody knows exactly where these or' . . . . . . when told how different we can be, in terms of physical appearance, in terms of skin, accent, they end up accepting that we are different" (Transcription 14, teacher, Old East End Community College:2).

Indeed the youth worker who had spent time working with pupils at Old East End Community College also discussed racism as being passed down from the home and assisted in shaping pupils prejudicial attitudes towards victims of racist bullying. Thus, the notion of 'unfair advantage' could be further explained in that it particularly affects the deprived White communities where racism is passed on inter-generationally. Again this could all be attributed to the socio-economic factors and with less funding at the school, it could be speculated that teachers were only able to provide minimal support when to efficiently address racist bullying.

In comparison, pupils at Modern Eastern Suburban School were much more empathetic towards victims of racism. There was also more acceptances towards such groups (pp 198/99). As Modern Eastern Suburban School is located in an affluent ward, North Heaton where the majority of the community are of middle class career professional backgrounds living in the most sought after homes, so too is the affluent attitude and school ethos. The school operates on a zero tolerance attitude towards racism; there is a vast ethnic minority population present within the school, which can assist in understanding young people's tolerant behaviour towards minority ethnic groups, asylum seekers and refugee communities. As noted by one teacher from Modern Eastern Suburban School, any pupils' racial prejudice would be challenged (see chapter seven) and then addressed. In this situation, this would assist in lowering prejudicial attitudes and assist in developing a more harmonious atmosphere, where pupils can learn to accept and integrate with each other. Furthermore, the school is given much funding, therefore allowing pupils to be taught efficiently.

With the School for the Excluded, there was an interesting exchange in perceptions. Whilst teachers were more open to admit racism occurred more in the community, they admitted that prejudices filtered in the school yet pupils' attitudes were less clear. Whilst there were no racist incidents at the school, as at the time of the fieldwork there were no pupils from minority ethnic groups on roll, however, the school is located in an area with a large Muslim population. Most pupils however, were less empathetic towards victims of racist bullying, therefore, adopting a similar attitude as those in Old East End Community College. As the school is located in a deprived ward, much of the population live in estate based social housing, which is a significant percentage throughout the city of Newcastle. As such, much of the population is of lower working class, where similar attitudes towards minority ethnic groups, asylum seekers and refugees reflect those in Old East End Community College. Furthermore, with a lack of social cohesion amongst both the white and non-white communities, this only increases in the lack of knowledge of different cultures. Thus this creates a fear of the unknown, a lack of acceptance amongst both groups as well as increased racist prejudicial thoughts and racist acts. As Back (1996) and Sibbitt (1997), argue, integration is essential in order to alleviate people's fear of unknown cultures.

Summary and Discussion

This chapter explores the various explanations given by pupils, teachers and youth workers for the root cause of school bullying and racist bullying. In doing so, it demonstrates individual and shared perspectives of pupils as to why bullying and racist bullying occurs. Explanations of bullying concentrate on four broad issues. (i) Status, power and reputation; (ii) family experiences and childhood victimization; (iii) relative deprivation and (iv) the negative influence of the media and social context. Further, the chapter reveals pupils' explanations for racist bullying which focuses on victims' individual and cultural differences and perceptions of unfair advantage. Next an examination of teachers' perceptions of bullying and racist bullying is offered. Finally, the chapter provides an explanation for differences between schools findings by exploring the socio-economic and geographic characteristics.

From this chapter two main themes emerge. Firstly and across the board from all three schools, pupils hold the perpetrator responsible for their bullying actions. Yet when discussing bullying in order to maintain a reputation, the differences between Old East End Community College and Modern Eastern Suburban School are evident and can be explained by the socio-economic environment of the school and neighbourhood. The social deprivation, high unemployment and high criminal activity by young people that is manifested around Old East End Community College could explain the volume of aggressive behaviour that existed within the school. The school is also located in a ward where a large population live in close-knit, inner city manufacturing communities and much of the population are low income families living in estate based social housing with uncertain employment. Bullying in order to maintain a family reputation reveals inward aggression, implying spontaneity, and this pattern could be associated with the surrounding environment. Whilst at Modern Eastern Suburban School, bullying in this context was emphasized to protect a family member, so whilst aggressive behaviour was implied, this was more for defence. Modern Eastern Suburban School is located in an affluent ward, consisting of many career professionals living in the most sought after homes and upwardly mobile families with middle class values. These factors can assist understanding the differences between both schools. The lack of aggression associated with bullying behaviour at Modern Eastern Suburban School could also be attributed to the low crime rate in the area, despite the high fighting culture which existed at the school.

Secondly, in relation to explaining racist bullying, pupils from Old East End Community College and, indirectly from the School for the Excluded blame the presence and cultural lifestyles of victims for provoking racist behaviour. The perception that victims of racist bullying are responsible for their victimization is further linked to pupils' belief that minority ethnic groups are at an unfair advantage over the indigenous white working class community. Much of the pupils' rationale for their hostile thinking can be associated with their deprived school and neighbourhood/community. In comparison, pupils from Modern Eastern Suburban School reveal more empathy towards victims of racist bullying; the affluent and middle class environment in which the school is situated could contribute to this difference.

To conclude, the chapter has examined pupils' and adults' explanations for bullying and racist bullying. Issues pertaining to under reporting and perceptions of the schools response are examined next in chapter seven.

CHAPTER 7

Bullying and the School Response

Introduction

THE AIM OF this chapter is to explore the under-reporting of incidents and of schools to bullying and racist bullying and the response of schools. The chapter demonstrates pupils' perspectives on the effectiveness of schools preventative education and the schools response to bullying. Another purpose of this chapter is to explore different perspectives on this. In this regard, two main themes run through the chapter. First, despite the progress in developing schools' response to reported cases of bullying and racist bullying, victims largely prefer to remain silent. Second, pupils have clear views on the importance of school mechanisms to prevent and intervene in reported cases of bullying.

This chapter is structured as follows. First, it reports pupils' explanations as to why victims prefer to remain silent. Second, the chapter examines pupils and teachers' perceptions on punishment, retribution and deterrence. Third, the chapter explores various preventative and intervention measures which schools employ. Finally, there is an examination of the socio-economic and geographical the differences between each school and their means of addressing and responding to incidents of bullying and racist bullying.

The Reporting and Under Reporting of Bullying

Since 1991, National Government Guidelines (the then Department for Education, 1991), have required all bullying incidents at school to be recorded, but not necessarily reported to their local authorities, except for incidents of racist bullying (DCSF 2008). However, despite this, as the findings in this section suggest, victims of bullying prefer to suffer in silence and not report their experiences outside of very close friendships. This finding is corroborated by Oliver and Candappa, (2007); Smith and Shu, (2000); Nicolaides, Toda and Smith, (2002) and Naylor *et al.* (2001).

However, in February 2009, following a consultation with a number of representatives, the DCSF stated that they would meet and consult over the issue of whether schools should be required to continue reporting racist bullying and indeed report all forms of bullying (Miles, 2009:32). This consultation began on December 10th 2009 after the DCSF simultaneously released a press notice wherein a twelve week consultation period would allow discussion of the new duty indicating that schools would have a mandatory duty to record and report serious or recurring incidents of bullying to their local authority. This also includes incidents of bullying and racism between pupils, and abuse or bullying of school staff (Coaker, 2009:1). Under the new Equality Act 2010 guidance (Equality and Human Rights, 2011), it is the schools responsibility and they are liable for the actions of schools employees and agents unless the school can show that it has taken 'all reasonable steps' to prevent the discrimination, harassment or victimization which includes racism from taking place (2011).

A teacher from Old East End Community College disclosed that:

> "I mean at some stage, we're going to be asked by the Local Education Authority to log and record on a database all incidents of bullying and harassment . . . . . . so that's going to come very shortly. So then they'll pull all the figures and find out, whose done what, why and where, and where it happens, I'm not sure, what they're going to ask us to log in yet" (Transcription 21, teacher interview, Old East End Community College: 7).

Although the teacher did not strongly oppose this system, he was of the opinion that this was determined by the government; schools had less authority in deciding if reporting cases to the local authority would be effective. The prospect for reporting was considered as follows:

> SQ: "And what implications do you think this will have for the teachers, I mean, this is going to be an extra burden of work, or is it something they will actually support?
>
> Teacher: I think they would have to pass it onto the house staff and house staff would have to enter it on to the database . . .
> . . . and I don't think it comes down to anything as to whether they are going to support it or not, I think this is going to be an instruction in the DfES, I don't think we've even got a choice . . .
> . . . quite how it would work, is I'm not sure . . . . . . if it's just the case, say collecting data, not sure how difficult that could be . . . . . . it would be useful for identifying victims and useful for identifying students, who are repeat offenders . . . . . . which, for some reason if they are slightly racist, we can have that through ARCH" (Transcription 21, teacher interview, Old East End Community College: 7).

Agencies against Racist Crime and Harassment (ARCH), formerly known as Multi-Agency Panel to Combat Racist Incidents (MAP) was founded in 1996. ARCH is a group of organizations located in the city of Newcastle-upon-Tyne that work together to assist victims of racist incidents. They also initiate proceedings against perpetrators of racist incidents. Schools and individuals are able to report racist incidents by calling the 24 hour free helpline provided by ARCH or by dropping in to one of the ARCH incident reporting centres. As one teacher reported:

> ". . . we have a system where we use the Arch system for reporting racism . . . . . . so there's not a lot that comes to light to be honest. That's not to say that it doesn't happen and I know there's a lot of stuff that goes on in the community . . . . . . but it doesn't appear to come into school . . . . . . and whether things have been reported or not, I don't know . . . . . . I don't perceive that there's a big issue, to do with racist incidents within the school. I know we

do get them, we do lodge them" (Transcription 21, teacher, Old East End Community College: 6).

This school kept records of all incidents that were reported to them and would then report these to ARCH. In contrast, during the discussion on racist bullying, pupils were able to explain that any incident of racist bullying that may have occurred and was subsequently reported to the school, the school would respond by recording the details and then reporting each case to the Civic Centre. Pupils clearly stated and without any form of criticism that:

". . . for any racial comment has to be sent off to the Civic Centre to be investigated, anything, no matter what it's about" (Transcription 19, focus group, yr 9, Modern Eastern Suburban School: 21).

This claim has been authenticated by the schools Equal Opportunities Race Equality Policy (2007) where clear procedures have been put into place to ensure that all staff deal with all forms of bullying and harassment promptly, firmly and consistently.

The government, anti-bullying and children's organizations and schools all advocate that victims should speak out about their bullying experiences. However, despite the positive messages and intensive work, during the focus group and individual interviews with pupils, many articulated views that most victims were less likely to share their experiences of bullying. This view was maintained by pupils in all three schools. Pupils from focus groups in Modern Eastern Suburban School responded as follows:

SQ: "Would you say that in the school most victims would either keep it to themselves or tell a friend or they would,

Pupil: they would keep it to themselves,

SQ: do you think that anybody would tell a teacher?

Pupil: no they won't, no" (Transcription 22, focus group, year 7, Modern Eastern Suburban School: 12).

SQ: ". . . do you think that people here would or they would just keep it to themselves?

Pupil 1: most of them would keep it to themselves,

Pupil 2: I would as well" (Transcription 19, focus group, year 9, Modern Eastern Suburban School: 10).

Various explanations as to why victims chose not to inform an adult were presented from those pupils engaged in focus groups and interviews. What was interesting during this particular discussion and also during the individual interviews was that pupils' socio-economic background had no real reflection in their responses about underreporting, unlike it did when pupils explained for the causes of bullying and racist bullying. This suggests that 'keeping silent' as a major coping strategy for victims is the cultural norm throughout all schools. Keeping quiet was explained in many ways. Despite the schools attempts to raise awareness and to encourage victims to speak out, many pupils felt that most victims preferred to keep quiet as they would otherwise feel embarrassed or ashamed to speak out. For example, one pupil discussed this reaction from victims who were targeted by bullies:

"I think that . . . . . . because the people, who are doing it, take it so slightly, they make it seem like it's a joke . . . they (the victim) might feel embarrassed to tell someone". (Transcription 19, focus group, year 9, Modern Eastern Suburban School: 10).

This was illustrated during a focus group with year nine at Old East End Community College. Here, pupils identified one individual in the group that had been bullied. When asked if she wanted to share her experiences, she briefly mentioned that she had been bullied through verbal name calling. After the focus group she approached me and discussed that she had not gone into detail because she felt uncomfortable talking about her ordeal.

Coloroso (2008:214), presents a number of reasons as to why victims feel less comfortable about talking about their ordeals. Amongst many reasons, she details that victims feel ashamed of being bullied, preferred not to tell due to fear of retaliation from the perpetrators and also learned that by 'grassing' on a peer was bad. Many victims believed that no one could do anything to help them and finally, some victims believed that being bullied was a normal part of growing up (Coloroso, 2008). A core explanation given as to why victims remain quiet was a fear of the consequences of telling someone. Pupils perceived that victims kept quiet because they were scared. The possible consequence of 'grassing' was expressed by many pupils, but particularly during the focus groups in Old East End Community College. Pupils emphasized that:

". . . if they grass on them, then it just makes it worse. The person is gonna get bullied even more". (Transcription 2, focus group, year 9, Old East End Community College: 7).

SQ: What about telling a teacher?

Pupil: nah that would make things worse, they would say you're grassing them and would pick on you even more" (Transcription 5, focus group, year 8, Old East End Community College: 6).

Similarly, Smith and Shu (2000:194) found that victims who informed a teacher ran a risk of the bullying becoming worse than if they told a friend. Their survey of 2,308 pupils aged 10-14 years, from 19 schools across England reported that a culture of silence still remains in that 30 percent of victims had told no one of the bullying. However, for those who had reported an incident, the outcome was usually seen as positive, although there was a small risk of matters worsening especially when teachers were informed. Boulton and Underwood (1992) found that victims kept quiet for fear of reprisals and lacked confidence in teachers' ability to help (1992 in Oliver and Candappa 2007: 72). Not satisfying the bully/bullies was a further reason why pupils, in particular at the School for the Excluded, considered that victims would maintain their silence. This view is similar to Camodeca and Goossens' (2005:103) research findings, where they suggest that pupils, especially younger pupils, often favour nonchalance as it could be a good way to avoid harassment. However, their findings also revealed that older pupils preferred to use assertive and pro-social strategies as coping mechanisms than retaliating through aggression. Similarly, during one focus group from the School for the Excluded, pupils indeed argued that showing some reaction provoked (or motivated) the bullying to continue. Pupils' typically explored the advantages from doing nothing:

> Pupil 1: ". . . don't let them show you, don't show that you're scared. If you show them that you're scared, then they'll do more, if you don't show you're scared, then they'll not do it to you, because . . . . they'll
>
> Pupil 2: get tired after,
>
> Pupil 1: yeah tired after a while and if you show them that you're not paying any attention then it will show them . . ." (Transcription 6, focus group year 8/9, School for the Excluded: 7).

Pupils explained that perpetrators often realize that when victims inform an adult, they sense a kind of victory as the tormenting has impacted them. Subsequently, pupils perceived that this motivated the perpetrators to bully the victims further:

> ". . . if they tell the teacher . . . . . . then the teacher would talk to the bully about it and the bully would . . . . . . bully them more because they know that's getting to them" (Transcription 11, focus group, yr 9, Old East End Community College: 14).

Much of the wider academic literature discusses the coping strategy to "ignore the bullies" (Kristensen and Smith, 2003; Naylor *et al.,* 2001; Oliver and Candappa, 2007; Naylor and Cowie, 1999; O'Connell *et al.,* 1999). They indicate that victims widely preferred to use this strategy as they considered this as self-reliant and a problem solving approach.

Another reason why victims kept silent was given by pupils who also suggested that, victims were not taken seriously by either the teachers or their parents; therefore pupils felt that they along with other victims were not receiving the correct moral support. This was a major finding from interviews especially at Old East End Community College and

School for the Excluded. Pupils from one focus group explained a typical situation where they believed that the teachers failed them. They responded:

> SQ: ". . . have any of the teachers taken any action? Do they do something about it when you tell them?
>
> Pupil 1: Sometimes the teachers do, but sometimes they don't do nothing. They say 'ah we'll see what happens' and then, we just get bullied further and . . .
>
> Pupil 2: yeah, you just get bullied more and that,
>
> Pupil 3: you could be getting bullied and the teachers just stand there with their cup o'tea's! (All begin to giggle)
>
> Pupil 2: and their biscuits and scones!" (Transcription 5, focus group, year 8, Old East End Community College: 10).

These findings are supported by other scholars, such as Coloroso (2008:173-174) who confirm this view. She states that pupils, in particular preteens and teenagers have little faith in reporting to an adult as they believe the adult is apathetic or if they take some action, it will only make matters worse. She suggests that young people also prefer to find their own path in life without the intervention of adults. Pupils expressed the indifferent attitudes they received from teachers when they did gather the courage to inform them:

> Pupil 1: ". . . see if you went and told the tutors right now, say that someone here was picking on me . . . . . . and say that '**** was bullying us', if I went to the tutors now, she might not believe me because what's the teacher going to her, 'haven't heard what she said', and . . . . .
>
> Pupil 3: because 'has she ever been naughty or something?'" (All start laughing) (Transcription 5, focus group, year 8, Old East End Community College: 9).

Pupils place an emphasis upon the teachers' attitude or moral reasoning towards certain pupils. That is, pupils suggest that teachers fail to believe that a 'good' pupil is able to commit the act of aggression and are less likely to believe what has been reported to them, until they have been presented with both accounts. Whilst teachers want pupils to confide in them, it is essential that they remain neutral and hear both parties. It can also be speculated that teachers believe minor incidents reported can soon be resolved and therefore, taking the situation too seriously can be counterproductive. This could help explain why teachers hold a more casual attitude to occasional reported incidents. Ellis and Shute, (2007:650), argue that a teacher's moral reasoning is confronted by a choice of whether and how to respond to a bullying incident. Their findings revealed that for an incident which teachers rated as less serious compared to those rated as more serious, a relatively large number of teachers believed that it was best to allow pupils to sort the problem out for themselves. Furthermore, their findings showed that teachers attitude towards minor incidents and whether to deal with it were more influenced by the decision as to whether they had the time to deal with it (Ellis and Shute 2007: 660).

As stated above, pupils argued that by speaking to a guardian, the seriousness of the bullying condition was likely to worsen. As one pupil remarked:

> "I wouldn't tell me Ma or Da, because they would just come to the door and make it worse" (Transcription 6, focus group, year 9, School for the Excluded: 19).

Furthermore, pupils presented the argument that adults, especially parents, often took the situation to extreme measures when contacting the school. Not only was this embarrassing for the victim, but it would also anger the bullies as they would discover that the victims had spoken out against them. It was suggested that parents often allowed the situation to get out of hand. It was revealed during one focus group session with Old East End Community College that victims therefore, would probably prefer to tell a friend. As one pupil expressed:

> ". . . if you told your parents, then they'd want to do something about it, whereas, your friends would try to help you about it. You

would feel more safe telling a friend than a parent because your parents would get in touch with the school" (Transcription 11, focus group, year 9, Old East End Community College: 8).

Confiding in friends, as expressed by pupils, seemed like a better and safer option for the victim. Oliver and Candappa's (2007:74) research findings revealed that victims were more comfortable when approaching their friends than adults as it was less risky and this coping mechanism tended to increase with age. Yet the participants in the focus groups, who discussed this approach, also revealed that this had no impact on the degree of bullying experienced (Oliver and Candappa, 2007). It was largely revealed during a focus group in Old East End Community College that as bystanders most pupils would not inform a guardian. Pupils emphasized that supporting victims often resulted in trouble for them, in that they would be targeted next. One pupil from this focus group explained what would happen if they tried to intervene:

SQ: "you get into a lot of trouble? In what way do you get into a lot of trouble?

Pupil: because sometimes the teacher doesn't notice in what you do if you try to stop it then you get in with it, and it's you who gets in trouble for trying to stop it" (Transcription 11, focus group, year 9, Old East End Community College: 10).

This view is supported by Coloroso (2008:67) who claims that bystanders are more afraid of becoming the new target of bullying and she offers that even if the bystander was able to successfully intervene they would be singled out at a later date for retribution as bullies are quick to "disparage and malign anyone who tries to intervene". Yet support at this school was limited in resources, particularly with peer mediated resources in comparison with Modern Eastern Suburban School.

However, pupils attitudes differed when it came to helping a victim who was a friend. During this interview, pupils said that they would tell someone if it was a friend who was being bullied. Therefore, this shows that pupils are willing to take a risk, however, only to help their friends. Pupils from one focus group with year 7, Modern Eastern

Suburban School blatantly articulated the problems created for them as a result of helping the victim. As they expressed:

> Pupil 1: "if I don't know the person, I don't want to get involved . . . . . because as soon as they (the bully) come out of the behaviour unit, I'm like legging it around the school and they're following you around (all laugh)

> Pupil 2: yeah, (others still giggling), but if it's someone I know, I would try and find a teacher" (Transcription 22, focus group, yr 7, Modern Eastern Suburban School: 9/10).

Pupils agreed that one should only inform a teacher if the bullying becomes really serious. This subsequently indicates the formal need to confide in an adult, but only as a last resort. Cowie *et al.'s* (2008:70) study advocates peer support and in their research findings participants revealed that they would inform someone if serious or "bad" bullying was occurring at the school. Most pupils suggested that there were risks associated with telling an adult. One pupil expressed:

> ". . . sometimes it stops completely, but sometimes it gets worse" (Transcription 22, focus group, yr 7, Modern Eastern Suburban School: 12).

Roberts and Counsel (1996, in Ma *et al.,* 2001:254) believed that victims often do not report bullying incidents, for fear of being found out by the perpetrators.

From these discussions, it is clear that pupils worry about being discovered, being labelled a 'grass', and the intensifying of their bullying experiences. Pupils largely from Modern Eastern Suburban School, revealed that, despite a worry of being discovered, on the whole, it was agreed that the situation did improve, over time, for those victims who had reported the incident to an adult. They concurred that notifying an adult was the best course of action.

Lines' (2005:20) research findings reveal that primarily those victims who tell teachers, only do so once they have suffered extreme bullying. Pupils censured teachers for their apathy/indifference. They stated the need for paying special attention to the pupils. They reinforce this by stating:

> ". . . they should pay more attention because I think sometimes the teachers just don't pay enough attention to them . . . . . . to the bullying that is going on . . . . they just walk out right there" (Transcription 17, focus group, yr 8, Modern Eastern Suburban School: 14/15).

Similarly, from the findings in their workshop, Richardson and Miles (2008: 119), suggest that teachers need to consult with pupils and listen to their answers as to what would work for them. On a similar stance, a parent of a pupil at the School for the Excluded believed that the schools and teachers ought to listen to the voices of pupils, take in what they have to say and then get them the help:

> ". . . ah think the staff should listen to the kids more . . . . and if they do think the kids have got a problem, they should . . . get some help for the kids . . . ." (Transcription 15, Parent, School for the Excluded: 21/22).

It can be argued therefore that pupils perceptions to the school's response conflicts. There are some pupils mostly from Modern Eastern Suburban School who give some acknowledgment to the schools, however, for the most, the reaction is negative. Most pupils argued that teachers did not deal with the bullying problem effectively. They complained that mere reprimands did not work with perpetrators as they would return to bully the victim further. Therefore, pupils still questioned whether these remedies were of any use to stop bullying. As one pupil implied that:

> ". . . they get put on report, you can get suspended on it . . . . . . but they'll still do it in front of their mates" (Transcription 26, individual interview, yrs 8 and 9, Old East End Community College: 24).

One pupil described the futility of reporting bullying to a teacher in the following terms:

"the teachers . . . say that they're taking like notice, but they just say that 'ah if you really like call them again, you going to get wrong' . . . but, that's all they say then an hour later they're like calling you again, and you go and tell them, 'ah but', and the teacher's are saying, I've already told them, what can we do'" (Transcription 26, individual interviews, yrs 8 and 9, Old East End Community College: 18).

This indicates a major disadvantage in reporting to an adult and explains why many victims simply keep silent about their ordeal. As Oliver and Candappa (2003:72) reveal, pupils complained that teachers failed to thoroughly investigate incidents of bullying. Furthermore, pupils also complained how teachers were biased or unresponsive in their responses or failed to take pupils seriously unless, for example, they saw any bruises (Oliver and Candappa, 2003). Therefore, pupils' displayed an indifferent attitude when considering if informing a teacher was of any long term benefit. During the focus group with Old East End Community College, in their view, it made no difference either in the long or short term for the victim to report to an adult, which is in contrast to the views held by the pupils at Modern Eastern Suburban School. Again this indicates that the stronger the anti-bullying support and particularly given at Modern Eastern Suburban School, this has some reflection upon their response.

Furthermore, youth workers maintained a belief that most victims remain silent due to the teachers' lack of awareness of the scale of bullying and the inefficiency in their response. Moreover, Oliver and Candappa (2007:80) argue that the willingness of pupils to tell and the capacity of the teacher to listen appear to represent an important factor to make schools a safer place for pupils. One youth worker linked this lack of awareness to a lack of clarity over reporting mechanisms:

"I think it's one of these things where they've just got absolutely no idea of the scale of it . . . . . . because of reporting is very difficult, you know, there's no reporting mechanism . . . . . . and clearly defined way of doing it, there's no clearly defined responses . . . . . . to it, and I would think that it is very, very under reported" (Transcription 27, youth worker, YOT: 16).

Teachers at Modern Eastern Suburban School also highlighted that learning and peer mentors were another avenue for pupils to go and confide in and feel comfortable about sharing confidential issues. However, despite these positive measures, the reality remains that most victims still fail to report their ordeals to the appropriate member of staff. Finally, the off-putting reaction of victims to remain silent is interesting given the wealth of policy, procedure and practice developed and implemented over recent years in schools, including the three schools sampled for this research.

Punishment, Retribution and Deterrence

Whilst immediate punishment was not the sole discussion of how to resolve the problem of bullying and racist bullying, many pupils displayed the stance that the perpetrators should be immediately punished. During the focus group at Modern Eastern Suburban School pupils desired punishment as a form of immediate retribution. It was suggested that teachers:

> ". . . can give them a detention, or like a small form of . . . or a one off thing . . . . . . but like if they come back and do it again, like the worst they can do is stick with that information and stick them in the . . . unit for the day. So I suppose they can put them in for longer" (Transcription 18, focus group, year 9, Modern Eastern Suburban School: 14).

> Pupil 1: "if you arrest everyone who's being horrible

> Pupil 2: or tie them to the chair

> Pupil 1: and a big fireman comes and chucks you out of the school!" (Transcription 5, focus group, year 8, Old East End Community College: 24/ 25).

The pupils' reaction reveals a sense of frustration with the perpetrators, in that pupils very rarely felt that the bullies received adequate punishment. Pupils in particular from Old East End Community College believed that the perpetrators need harsher punishment:

Pupil 1: "30 years in jail . . . . .In school they should wear the same clothes . . . . . . get punishment like a C1, C2, C3 and C4 and that. But they should do that if they were being bullies and that . . .

Pupil 4: get expelled for like a week or so" (Transcription 5, focus group, year 8, Old East End Community College: 24).

Pupils suggested that sometimes the teachers did not issue the appropriate punishment. They explained that once an incident of bullying was reported, the teachers tended to give verbal reprimands to the perpetrator and then talk to the victim. It can be suggested that this rather lax approach indicates that where minimal preventative and intervention support is used, often teachers are overwhelmed and unable to deal effectively with bullying. Some pupils believed that the bullies needed to be punished either by detention or through temporary suspension.

Another immediate response was to punish the perpetrators through after school or lunch break detention or to put them in the schools' 'unit' or 'cooler'. However, one pupil questioned the value of the unit, asking whether leaving someone 'by themselves in silence' was appropriate for bullies who were disruptive and needed help or who bullied because they 'don't understand'. Rather than simply placing the individual in the unit to reflect upon their actions, some pupils argued that such individuals need the right kind of attention. Pupils in a focus group at Modern Eastern Suburban School maintained that:

Pupil 2: "I just think it's not ideal, but just the way of putting,

Pupil 1: it's isolating people who might be disrupting classes because they might need some help . . . . . . and sometimes people like disrupt lessons and pick on people because they don't understand or something like that and I don't think that putting them in a room . . . . . . by themselves in silence, is ever going to help them, and I think that you need to engage with people, you can't just, yeah, people have to realize that detention and units and things, aren't really going to help them, you have to just stop to talk to people and I know that the teachers do that, but

I just don't think that, it's still enough, I mean, I know it's not the teacher's job really, it's like . . . . . . to get sort out quarrels or whatever, it's their job to teach us, it must be really annoying if they are being prevented from doing that, but I think, part of the job should be making sure that everyone is happy and making sure that the lessons are being enjoyed, because if they're not being enjoyed then, people are blatantly going to bunk off and things" (Transcription 18, focus group, year 9, Modern Eastern Suburban School: 16).

Lewis *et al.* (2005: 730) examined classroom discipline and pupil misbehaviour and compared these relationships in three different national settings; Australia, China and Israel. A particular finding when they examined schools in Australia, unlike China and Israel, was that the use of unnecessarily harsh and punitive disciplinary practices against students (for example unfairly picking on pupils and the over use of the cooler), had the potential to create a climate contributing towards school violence. They further argue that those teachers' who sought harsh punitive measures, especially those adopting punishment with an aggressive approach (yelling, sarcasm then punishing), increasingly distracted pupils from work and became more disruptive (Lewis *et al.*, 2005).

Pupils also recognized that often teachers were unable to control and prevent the bullying situation because there were simply too many pupils. For an immediate and temporary solution, it was easier for teachers to send the pupils to the unit. Particularly at Modern Eastern Suburban School, one pupil felt that teachers relied too much on the unit and that the purpose for the unit was becoming obsolete. He expressed that:

". . . going just quickly back to the unit . . . . . . I think a couple of teachers take it a bit too seriously, I think possibly to have a larger scale of consequences . . . . . . there's been some cases when, someone has beaten someone up, well in a fight, not . . . . . . and they'll be in the unit and some people get put in the unit for something that's not half as bad as that" (Transcription 18, focus group, year 9, Modern Eastern Suburban School: 16).

Again, this comment raises the subject of the size of the school and teachers effectiveness in handling bullying.

Further, pupils at the School for the Excluded discussed the idea of corporal punishment and that it should be reintroduced into schools. Pupils felt that this form of immediate retribution would assist in teaching a lesson in that the perpetrators would be dealt with instantly and therefore would feel some repercussion. Durrant's (2000:450) research revealed an increase in anti-social behaviour, especially violence amongst youth in Sweden, since the 1979 ban of corporal punishment amongst children. Although other research does not confirm that banning corporal punishment was the sole cause of the rise in anti-social behaviour. Here, pupils were serious with their opinions to reintroduce corporal punishment, however, also joked as they expressed that schools should:

> Pupil 1: "bring back what they had years ago . . . . . . cane, the cane! . . . . . . the ruler or the belt!

> Pupil 2: or the black board rubber, they used to stomp it off yeh head! (Giggles)" (Transcription 8, focus group, yr 9, School for the Excluded: 18).

Teachers from each school described the process of how they responded to incidents of bullying and racist bullying. This involved investigating the reported case and then issuing the appropriate punishment. As teachers from Old East End Community College discussed, for regular incidents at:

> ". . . all levels . . . we pick up name calling and taunting and something like that, and then we'll deal with it, through the House staff and classroom staff, the teachers will pick it up in the classrooms and they will go through those" (Transcription 21, teacher, Old East End Community College: 4).

Teachers at the School for the Excluded also claimed to verbally challenge perpetrators, especially on racial incidents, in order to try and get them to understand what they said or did and why they said or took this action. As one teacher from the School for the Excluded commented however:

> ". . . it's more about situations that have happened in the community rather than saying this happened to you . . . . and as for bullying . . . . . . we will get parents involved, talk to both parties involved and take it from there" (Transcription 9, teacher, School for the Excluded: 29).

In relation to persistent bullying or racist bullying at Old East End Community College, teachers discussed how eventually parents and educational welfare officers would become involved. For more extreme cases, authorities such as the police and street counsellors become involved. As Sullivan *et al.* (2005:58) claim, some schools maintain a 'whole-school approach' which allows staff and students to develop anti-bullying strategies and remain vigilant about bullying. Other schools adopt a zero tolerance response which is associated with the more authoritarian schools that believe bullying behaviour can be contained and controlled by discipline and rules (Sullivan *et al.*, 2005).

Teachers, in particular at the School for the Excluded and Modern Eastern Suburban School believed that corporal punishment ought to be reintroduced into schools as this would assist in teaching pupils how to respect teachers and one another. For instance, one teacher from the School for the Excluded claimed:

> "I think they should have corporal punishment. It's a respect thing . . . . . . People are becoming a little more cheeky, a little bit where they say, 'oh you can't tell me what to do' type of thing . . . So there's a great wealth in getting their opinions and views on things, but when they use it as a weapon" (Transcription 9, teachers' interview, School for the Excluded: 34).

Teachers' perceptions to immediate punishment can be noted as follows. First, teachers valued or recognized the use of punishment in the form of detention as a means to deal with anti-social behaviour. Second, the teachers in Modern Eastern Suburban School maintained the belief that the school reacted and responded immediately and effectively to cases that were reported:

BULLYING AND RACIST BULLYING IN SCHOOLS

"well I think the biggest thing is that we're very approachable and we have got that level of awareness and we do know what's going on . . . . there are things in place for them, you know, there's so many different things, . . . and it's not swept under the carpet and forgotten about" (Transcription 16, teacher, Modern Eastern Suburban School: 15).

The above comment is in such contrast with pupils' views who strongly believed that teachers were less aware of the bullying that took place. Furthermore, to pupils, even when teachers were informed, they took a nonchalant attitude. Third teachers believed that, if the schools have solid evidence of bullying, permanently excluding the perpetrator would be making an example out of them towards the rest of the pupils. Lewis *et al.* (2005:731) suggest that discipline was considered to be of the utmost importance to teachers and therefore, and issuing the harshest form of punishment, was considered by teachers to be highly effective (Lewis *et al.*, 2005). Finally, teachers believed that the school responded effectively to bullying and managed the problem well. One teacher described the process in the following terms:

". . . as soon as it's reported really, that's when it starts being acted upon, the house staff move very quickly on any incident, because they know if you leave them, they absolutely grow . . . . . . they don't go away, ... so the sooner you can deal with it, the better . . . and that works for all of them" (Transcription 21, teacher, Old East End Community College: 7).

In addition, teachers in Old East End Community College believed that varying detention levels helped pupils to understand the meaning behind each stage of punishment that had been given to them. One teacher from Old East End Community College described how the records kept were important when dealing with issues such as appeals against exclusions:

"it's all on the computer then that's for us going to the appeal saying 'well come on, such and such has never had a C3, he's had 50' and you know being excluded however else, so it's good from that point of view . . . and it's, and it's a fair system, the kids know why they've got it" (Transcription 20, teacher, Old East End Community College: 19).

The teachers' response suggests that they view punishment as an immediate action that is effective. Parents and youth workers however, agree with pupils' that perpetrators need to be spoken with, behaviour understood and not simply pushed into the 'cooler'. Similarly, Christie (1999:10) argues in her research that traditional responses are ineffective for many students with severe or chronic behaviour problems. Furthermore, she claims that for most pupils, they will abide by the school rules in order to avoid punishments, however, for pupils with behaviour disorders they will not escape the reactive management cycle. Christie argues that quick fixes such as placing pupils in the unit or suspension are unlikely to be successful in the long-term (Christie, 1999).

Prevention and Intervention

This section identifies a variety of holistic and restorative prevention and intervention measures that each school used. Such support took the form of classes including Personal Development, Citizenship, Personal Social Health and Education and Circle Time. At Old East End Community College, anti-bullying support included Personal Development and Circle Time. At Modern Eastern Suburban School this included anti-bullying education delivered through Citizenship classes and Personal Social Health and Education classes. Finally at the School for the Excluded, anti-bullying preventative education was also conducted as part of the Personal Social Health and Education curriculum. The purpose for such classes was to raise awareness of all issues pertaining to bullying and to educate pupils against bullying. For example, one preventative measure would be to show pupils anti-bullying videos that addressed all forms of bullying, including racist bullying. This would assist in engaging pupils in stimulating discussions and debates.

During an interview with one teacher from Old East End Community College; she articulated that the schools personal development classes intended to increase pupils' awareness of bullying and racist bullying by reaching through to pupils empathetic side. The increase in holistic delivering through emotional literacy also ensures that schools are doing all they can to prevent bullying from occurring (Smith *et al.,* 2008:10). This is a similar approach in the work by various academics (Goleman, 1995 in Sharp 2008); (Bocchino, 1999; Elliot and Faupel, 1997; Miller, 2001). Goleman (1995 in Sharp, 2000:8), developed the idea of using emotional literacy as a form of delivering education to support schools in their anti-bullying teaching. His main hypothesis was that improving pupils emotional literacy resulted in higher academic achievement, pupils felt better about themselves and were able to learn and be more focused (cited in Sharp 2000:9). This feeling of satisfaction was achieved by developing plans, initiatives and materials on anti-bullying work for schools, delivered through the style of emotional literacy.

Samara and Smith (2008:673) suggest that such development classes allow pupils and teachers to identify and discuss issues to do with bullying together. Furthermore, they claim that during the classes, teachers and pupils find themselves able to discuss issues in an open and positive atmosphere which encourages children to come up with solutions. One important factor to these sessions are that they help pupils to learn how to listen and how to consider the feelings of others. Samara and Smith (2008) assert that these skills not only aid individual children but also help to make the whole school a more caring and positive place. Another purpose of the classes was to teach pupils the significance of inclusion, acceptance and understanding. In particular, a teacher from Old East End Community College related this to pupils' stereotypical attitudes towards those from the asylum and refugee community:

> "I suppose it's more of trying to give the pupils the knowledge and understanding, the proper knowledge and understanding of where those pupils have come from maybe . . . . . . what troubles they have had to face and the true fact about whether they do get a list of what they are supposed to get for free or is it just a fallacy? I don't know . . . . but just to educate them so they're fully aware of the whole situation and hopefully by doing that they might improve their treatment" (Transcription 20, teacher, Old East End Community College: 7).

One teacher from Modern Eastern Suburban School described how the system worked at their school:

> ". . . all students get one lesson a week on citizenship and that's taught by a specialist team of teachers . . . . . . and issues of bullying, racism all the things that we've been interested in looking at are covered within citizenship lessons . . . ." (Transcription 5, teacher, Modern Eastern Suburban School: 1).

Similarly Reid *et al.* (2004) discuss that where the DfES provides support and training to schools, in the form of anti-bullying preventative education and intervention programmes, this has focused raising awareness amongst pupils and teachers. Overall this support assists to improve the school environment (Reid *et al.,* 2004).

Furthermore, anti-bullying training also takes place in specialized schools such as the School for the Excluded:

> SQ: "Is there anything in this school that's being done to tackle the situation on bullying and on racism?
>
> Teacher: Oh definitely because, we do quite a bit of PHSE and we're doing a whole topic on bullying" (Transcription 9, teacher, School for the Excluded: 19).

When questioning the regularity of anti-bullying classes, the teachers however, put forward the point that the school has little funding to devote to regular anti-bullying education. Other than discussing it during the Personal Social Health and Education, Circle Time, Personal Development classes, etc, the national curriculum was so tight, that the teachers had little time to spend on anti-bullying education and/ or to take pupils away from their regular classes to attend anti-bullying sessions that may be conducted from outside researchers.

However, the research also identified that outside agencies, such as youth workers collaborate with the schools and undertake various activities with pupils, such as role plays and group discussions:

". . . on the bullying aspect, ... we do mediation work, we do group support work, we do personal development work with the pupils who are showing difficulties with their relationships particularly, because that's where most of it stems from really . . . there is the case where you end up with young people who have a problem within the school and they kind of offload them on you, for the right reasons we ask what aspects of the school do they have a problem with and we often get many aspects of the school," (Transcription 27, youth worker, YOT: 13).

This youth worker agreed that when the teachers saw pupils enjoying the group sessions and actively engaged, the teachers became more motivated, and encouraged by this. As the youth worker commented:

Youth worker: ". . . all the teachers who were involved were really, really positive . . . . . . what, I think they got out of it was that they saw the young people differently . . . . . . you know,

SQ: in what way?

Youth worker: well they saw them being very positive, they saw them being very, very actively engaged because that's one thing about that process, it really, really engages the young people, and I think that everyone sort of reacts is that the national curriculum is not particularly engaged . . . . . . you know? You've got to be very, very, a really, really sexy teacher, you know . . . . . . you know what I mean when I say that . . . . . . who engages with it, students at every level tend to make that national curriculum work . . ." (Transcription 27, youth worker, YOT: 20/21)

This shows the importance of the presence of outside agencies, in the school environment. Their collaboration with the school shows that they are able to provide emotional support as well as actively working with pupils against bullying and racism. Pupils in particular perceived the long term benefits of a regular presence of an outside agency working within the school. To pupils, it provides an additional support network for victims who are rather scared to approach anyone else for help, including a teacher. As Coloroso (2008:180) states, the presence of outside workers and educators can assist in teaching tolerance and provide support to those victims who prefer to talk to them.

In addition, pupils, in particular from the School for the Excluded professed a greater need for more specialized education delivered by anti-bullying specialized workers. Salmivalli (1999:456) refers to this as 'assertiveness training' from trained outside professionals that not only target victims, but all pupils. From her findings, she believes that this form of training effectively assisted in reducing aggression (Salmivalli, 1999). Something not so dissimilar was noted by one pupil from the School for the Excluded:

> ". . . that's why we need . . . someone like you should go to all the schools, just to learn them a bit and that" (Transcription 9, Individual interviews, yr 9, School for the Excluded: 7).

Pupils believed that this form of intervention would develop the perpetrators knowledge and understanding of the negative impact of bullying. Furthermore, pupils believed that this would provoke the perpetrators to actually think about what it is they are doing to other pupils, rather than simply being told not to do it. Another desire for having specialized workers was to enable pupils to have the confidence to speak out and confide in a designated person. By this the pupils referred to those who were new to the school and therefore were the most vulnerable targets of bullying.

Teachers also welcomed the use of outside workers engaging with pupils at schools as they believed that their collaboration helped to reduce the fear and vulnerability of bullying in the school. As one teacher from Old East End Community College commented:

> ". . . he's fantastic with the kids. And he's done work on bullying with them and he's done one to one sessions with them. He, he's the same as the teachers and he can easily identify who the victim is . . . . . . you know, not always a perpetrator . . . . . . on a personal level, he's much better at spotting them then, yeah, so you can usually spot who the victim is" (Transcription 14, teacher, Old East End Community College: 10/11)

The teacher continued that the presence of youth workers or researchers helped. For instance, a teacher from Old East End Community College explained that some pupils found it challenging to appear at the school on time and treat others with respect. This teacher explained that youth workers assisted by conducting outreach work that better assisted pupils social norms and that this provided an added support for the rest of the staff at school, as:

> ". . . one of the bigger issues that I have is where you have students within school and they don't appear to respond to most of the social norms that other students do . . . . . . that they're outside of that . . . . . . and it's through the inclusion generally that most of the students will see as emotional behavioral difficulties into mainstream schools, some of these students can't function at the same way the vast majority are and don't see the boundaries and don't see, you know, the rights and wrongs and some of the things that they do and see" (Transcription 21, teacher, Old East End Community College: 9).

Fekkes *et al.* (2005:89) findings suggest that the presence of outside workers provide education and support to enhance the emotional, social and physical well-being of all pupils and gives additional support to school staff. Fekkes *et al.* (2005) findings also reveal that outside research work assisted to promote anti-bullying as they communicated with and encouraged pupils to talk. For that reason in this study, with the regular presence of youth workers in each school, they were able to deliver strong messages, some of which would get through to pupils and assists in reducing bullying. However, teachers highlighted that issues of time and cost arose when considering when youth workers and researchers could be brought into the school.

In comparison, parents and teachers at the School for the Excluded understood the gravity of the bullying behaviour, and preferred specialized staff to be employed at schools in order to teach and counsel both the perpetrators and victims. Indeed, Camodeca and Goossens (2005:93) findings suggest that it may be that some interventions demand too much from teachers. Furthermore, they suggest that the right interventions with long lasting effects may not have been designed yet, or that current interventions do not address all potential bullying situations. They therefore, strongly recommend that outside workers be employed to demonstrate effective intervention schemes, such as assertive training and prosocial responses from pupils (Camodeca and Goossens, 2005:104). Thus, for this reason, teachers, in particular at the School for the Excluded saw the need for specialized staff:

> Teacher 2: "I personally would like to see specialist staff in schools. Employed, counselling for bullies and . . . victims as well,

> Teacher 1: a lot more involvement with the parents and a lot more regularly coming in" (Transcription 10, teachers' interviews, School for the Excluded: 39).

Another reason why teachers welcomed outside professionals was because they agreed that teachers were not adequately trained to fully deal with pupils' social and emotional needs. Teachers agreed that very few are adequately trained and capable of effectively dealing with bullying incidents, which occur frequently. Similarly, Fekkes *et al.* (2005:90) claim that, teachers do not always effectively deal with many bullying incidents because they do not know what to do. Therefore, they argue that schools must include outside workers and organizations that can help to improve interventions and prevent bullying (Fekkes *et al.,* 2005). As one teacher commented:

> "we haven't specifically had any training on . . . . because we only get about 2 or 3 training days a year . . . . . . that would be covering the whole school training," (Transcription 20; teacher, Old East End Community College: 7).

Youth workers who collaborated with the schools also believed that the teachers required adequate training and needed to act upon their policies. However, whilst teachers agreed they needed more training, especially those at Old East End Community College, they did not believe that they did not follow the school policies. In Smith's (2004:101) review on bullying, he claims that teachers have "good knowledge about bullying, but do not feel fully equipped to tackle it". He continues to assert that all schools have anti-bullying policies and from his research findings, schools found the Department for Schools and Education (DfES) 'Don't suffer in silence' pack very useful (Smith,

2004). Youth workers complained that for many of the schools, the policies simply exist on paper; however, very few teachers fully adhere to these policies:

> ". . . the staff needs training, they need policies that actually mean something, and that everybody understands . . . . . . not just a dusty document" (Transcription 27, youth worker, YOT: 18).

Mentoring

Mentoring was a particularly strong facet at Modern Eastern Suburban School and during interviews with learning and peer mentors, this system of support for all pupils was emphasized as to the positive difference it made. Mentoring is a system that takes the form of peer mentors as well as adult learning mentors. Pupils, from Modern Eastern Suburban School acknowledged in particular the role of peer mentors. For example, at this school there are peer mentors available for pupils in years 7 and 8. The pupils can go to them during lunch breaks and are able to confide in them on any issue, including bullying. When interviewing these peer mentors, they unanimously agreed that most pupils who confided in them were victims of bullying. As discussed in the first section to this chapter, pupils identified that they would largely prefer to confide in a fellow peer/friend than an adult. Pupils at this school agreed that this system was well publicized through advertising on walls and in assembly. As one pupil discussed:

> "I think they are really good and organized . . . . .when people tell . . . teachers, they handle it well, but, and they've got like the '*** ****' group as well if you don't want to tell a teacher, ... you can go and talk to them and they'll help you" (Transcription 25, individual interview, year 8 Modern Eastern Suburban School: 4).

Bishop's (2003:31) findings suggest that the role played by peers has become a salient issue in the recent literature on bullying. He further argues that the power of the peer group can be harnessed, leading to peers becoming moderators and capable of intervening via listening, supporting and counselling (Bishop, 2003). Much of Cowie's work (2008:70) has discovered that peer support is effective; her recent research reveals pupils ease in the knowledge that peer support was available. Pupils admitted that this sends out positive messages as it allows everybody to feel included and that it raises awareness about whom they can go to confide in. Lines (2005:23) further asserts that learning mentors and advisors encourage peer counselling and support. Indeed Knights' (1998) study reveals how positive peer counselling is. Her study revealed that most victims were too scared to inform an adult and that victims felt comfortable confiding in peers.

Within Modern Eastern Suburban School, mentoring in the form of adult learning mentors and staff training are provided to help deal with bullying issues alongside anti-social behaviour. Counsellors, that were not trained teachers, also exist in this school in order to further support victims. Pupils approved of the counselling service at the school as their presence was permanent. As one pupil responded:

SQ: ". . . what about specialized help, people with or who are specialized in that area so just to deal with victims or with bullies?

Pupil: they already have in the school with the teachers . . . . . . well there's someone that comes in, I think it's every Thursday . . . . . . and it's with the year 8's and 7's know about this . . . . . . she's called like Lucy and she does loads and loads of meetings . . . . . . and she takes students out of the class room and tries to sort things out . . . . . . and she's from the Newcastle Bullying thing and council.

SQ: do you think that's something which is quite effective?

Pupil: aye, because if someone was bullied, I think they could go to her and say to her, 'I'm getting bullied, what can I do?' . . . . . . I think that more than the people like her who are here every day, I think there would be less bullying" (Transcription 19, focus group, year 9, Modern Eastern Suburban School: 15).

Ma, *et al.* (2001:260) assert that school counsellors play a significant role in reducing bullying in the school as they have the advantage of working individually with students involved in bullying. Furthermore, they note that social skills training in small groups and classroom discussions on bullying, particularly intervention against aggressive behaviour are other effective strategies to be considered in order to modify pupils' strategies of social problem solving (Ma *et al.,* 2001).

Support for victims on a personal level primarily lay in the mentoring and counselling services available at each of the schools involved in the research. However, pupils noted that this form of support should be available to all pupils and not just the younger students as older pupils faced the problem of bullying. During the same focus group, pupils continued to comment that:

> Pupil 1: "if they could do it for rather than just year's 7 and 8, you're kind of still getting new to the school so yeah, you might be getting bullied, but in year 11 in stuff like that, I'm sure it would be a lot more serious because,
>
> Pupil 2: because people are getting more physical
>
> Pupil 1: yeah and people have to means to
>
> Pupil 3: they do, they go to them
>
> Pupil 1: aha, being able to hurt someone. So if they are able to do it, but they would have to be able to do it in a way like . . . . . . communicate like with bullies as well rather than just telling them off" (Transcription 19, focus group, year 9, Modern Eastern Suburban School: 15).

This discussion exemplifies pupils' desire for prevention and intervention support to all pupils. Their remarks are justified as there is a strong indication that bullying continues, yet as pupils grow older, they are less likely to speak out.

One teacher in Old East End Community College noted an important benefit of the house system and associated this to how well teachers got to know all the pupils:

> ". . . every kid and staff are all put in a house . . . . . . so for staff you've got a Judge, with you (and begins laughing), and them there's all the children put in one of the houses, and they stay

in that house throughout the whole school . . . . . . and so you then get to know the brothers and sisters and they get to know what's going on, what the boundaries are and their house system is really good and sometimes they'll pick up because anybody who wore glasses and now because they go in and say to the tutors 'oh you know such a person is being nasty to such a person' . . . . . . some tutors will deal with things on a tutor level and they may come to you as a form teacher and say 'hey look Ms. ********, will you keep an eye out for such and such, because we think that something is happening'" (Transcription 14, teacher, Old East End Community College: 11/12).

Whiston and Sexton (1998:413) discuss the setting up of such support services. They describe the counselling or school support system providing special assistance to pupils with their health, personal, social or educational development. This includes bullying (Whiston and Sexton, 1998). Furthermore, teachers, particularly in Old East End Community College, emphasized how pupils are encouraged to approach their personal tutors and pastoral/house staff believing that this would allow pupils to feel safer:

SQ: "what about victims themselves, if they want to approach somebody?

Teacher: oh yeah, they're encouraged to see their form teacher . . . . . . Their form teachers are always, always the first point of reference, the form teacher then they inform the form tutor or perhaps if they feel safe, they go to the house and speak to the house tutors. Or as a form teacher they might say 'have you spoken to house staff about this?'" (Transcription 14, teacher, Old East End Community College: 12).

Upon reflection, it could be speculated that teachers preferred to support pupils by counselling them rather than encouraging them to become peer mentors, given the poor socio-economic background to the school, local community and neighbourhood where the criminal statistics were high. For instance, as identified in chapter five, cumulative bullying was viewed by pupils with much hilarity. The teachers also complained of little time to devote to dealing with bullying education and adequate funding for training courses. This is discussed later in the chapter.

At the School for the Excluded, counselling took the form of dealing directly with the victim and involving the child's parents. Since the School for the Excluded has significant smaller numbers of pupils on roll, teachers are able to spend more quality time in dealing with an incident as one teacher discussed:

> ". . . if we see anybody being bullied in any way, shape or form, then they're taken to Mr. ***** where they are sent home, phone calls are made, we've got zero tolerance. Obviously, what we don't see, you know and what the kids don't tell us, we're not psychic, you know, but if we see a child being quiet for any reason, we'll say to him, you know, 'how are you . . . what's wrong?' and that's not only forthcoming in these children because they haven't got many people who they can trust in their lives, but if they trust you, then they will tell you" (Transcription 9, teacher, School for the Excluded: 19).

Whiston and Sexton (1998) suggest that school counsellors believed that their work was more effective when dealing with small groups or one to one counselling. From the above quotation, it is strongly suggested that having fewer pupils in the school allows the staff to be better able to detect children who may be bullied, counsel them and deal with their case in more depth. However, this is much more problematic for secondary schools and whilst pupils have the support, they have to take the initial steps to confide in the teacher and, as raised earlier, there are numerous reasons why victims prefer to remain silent.

Arguments For and Against the Use of Prevention and Intervention Measures

As part of the focus group discussions pupils were questioned regarding the effectiveness of the schools in raising awareness of bullying prevention. Pupils, in particular from Modern Eastern Suburban School, identified that anti-bullying education took place during their citizenship classes and they understood that such classes may assist in developing an understanding amongst peers about the immorality of bullying and racist bullying and had the intention of allowing pupils to reflect upon the seriousness of bullying. Bosacki *et al.* (2006:240) found that through anti-bullying education, pupils were capable of expressing how they would feel as the bully as well as the victim (Bosacki *et al.,* 2006). Furthermore, from their research, pupils expressed how a discussion of moral issues was vital to anti-bullying education as many aggressive perpetrators downplayed the importance of the extent of harm to the victim and underestimated the damage to victims (Bosacki *et al.,* 2006). One way in which pupils could be engaged during classes was suggested to talk about common anti-bullying situations where pupils could also seek advice. As one girl from a focus group agreed that:

> "they help you, because if you, if you're, in a situation where you're talking about a similar one and the teacher's 'well if this happens to you', or something, 'then this is what you should do, you should list things' because like, they give you a little bit of help going and they tell you what to do" (Transcription 17, focus group year 8, Modern Eastern Suburban School: 12).

Pupils from Old East End Community College appreciated the long term benefit of anti-bullying classes as it enabled them to contemplate and deal with the pertinent issues of racist bullying. During one individual interview, one pupil expressed:

> ". . . most of me and my friends just like to listen to PD . . . . . . because, like that's important because their missing about bullying and stuff. . . . and we just try to listen about facts to make it stop," (Transcription 24, individual interview, year 7. Old East End Community College: 14).

It was unanimously agreed amongst pupils at the School for the Excluded, that teachers at mainstream schools were unable to effectively deal with larger numbers in the class. One pupil agreed that the School for the Excluded was more effective in dealing with anti-bullying work, compared to most mainstream schools, as the class sizes were small. She commented:

". . . this school's done a bit more than they do at the other schools, because there's less people in the class and that . . . . . . because it's easier when there's like only 70 of you, but when like there's 32 in a class and that" (Transcription 10; individual interviews, year 9 School for the Excluded: 9).

For those pupils who were in favour of anti-bullying education, they identified the need for informal as well as formal instruction. This would take place either during break times or after school; and would allow the schools to advise pupils on preventative measures as well as avoid a confrontation:

> Pupil 1: ". . . bullying, like every month or something, they could kept, they could give out like, a questionnaire or something like saying like . . . . . . if they've been bullied and that and if they want a one to one talk or something,
>
> Pupil 2: bullying can be coached by people saying if you don't steal the cell chain it'll stop" (Transcription 12, focus group, year 7, Old East End Community College: 18)

Pupils also perceived the increasing need for more anti-bullying education in the form of lectures in assemblies, videos and role plays, so that pupils could understand why and how it was wrong. One pupil from Modern Eastern Suburban School discussed the bully's possible mentality, after attending an informal specialized session on anti-bullying:

> ". . . once they call someone, they don't think what effect it has on them, what they might think when they go away . . . . and if they go home, they don't know what they are going to do, like could they come back or not if they keep doing it" (Transcription 19, focus group, year 9: Modern Eastern Suburban School: 15).

Similarly, teachers saw a long term benefit of anti-bullying classes as they maintained that such classes would allow pupils to become more comfortable and build up their confidence by talking about the subject as well as applying what they had been taught during the sessions. As one teacher from Modern Eastern Suburban School emphasized:

". . . they'll say 'well no that's not right, you should have said something', and if somebody has said something towards you or somebody had said something and stopped it, there's definitely been a shift"(Transcription 16, teacher, Modern Eastern Suburban School: 6).

In addition to this, pupils particularly at Modern Eastern Suburban School believed that anti-bullying education and mentoring in the long term was beneficial as it gave victims the incentive and encouragement to disclose their feelings and fears. Bosacki *et al.*, (2006:242) claimed that anti-bullying education helped to make it easier for potential victims to enact some of the strategies suggested, such as telling a teacher. Pupils perceived the need for extra school intervention measures on a number of levels. They were of the opinion that provisions for counselling for both perpetrators and victims should be given and that pupils ought to have the option to have some space. As Salmivalli (1999) asserts the focus of counselling could be shifted from not only supporting the victim, but towards bullies and the whole group to enable them all gradually to understand bullying behaviour. Furthermore, it was interesting that pupils at the School for the Excluded believed that schools needed to enforce more anti-bullying techniques in order to educate the perpetrators. They also affirmed the view that school staff needed more specialized training in anti-bullying and anti-racist bullying. This view was articulated in the following way:

". . . you should like, tell the schools to do loads of things about it . . . know loads of things about bullying, like put videos on and . . . shows what people feel like when they getting bullied!" (Transcription 6, focus group, School for the Excluded years 8 and 9: 16)

Finally, pupils maintained that more staff needed to be placed on supervision around the school in the most vulnerable areas. Coloroso (2008:6) asserts that the bully surveys the location where adults are either not present or less likely to be paying attention. To pupils, this would provide added security as one pupil expressed:

"if we had like people on the corridors, like adults . . . just like watching people, like when they're going like past . . . . and saying 'who's, who's starting the stuff?' . . . and then they'll just think 'well, well, he's started it so we're gonna get the both people together to see why they started it'" (Transcription 24, individual interview, year 7, Old East End Community College: 12).

Some pupils were not in favour of anti-bullying education, in particular from Old East End Community College. Here the pupils reflected that, for example the Personal Development, Citizenship classes and discussions on the nature, causes and how morally wrong bullying was, often had the reverse effect and would antagonize the bullying situation. This contrasting view was held by pupils on the basis that they thought such classes had little or no impact upon the attitude of pupils, especially the bullies. Ferguson *et al.,* (2007:401) suggest that overall anti-bullying programs produced little discernible effect on pupils. They further argued that whilst anti-bullying programs may encourage equality in problem solving, helping bullies to reduce their social dominance, there may simply be no incentive offered to entice bullies or violent children to follow such strategies (Ferguson *et al.,* 2007: 411). As one pupil from Old East End Community College expressed:

> ". . . they cannot really say anything, how's the teachers going to be able to stop it? Kids don't listen to the teachers anyway" (Transcription 11, focus group, year 9 Old East End Community College: 8).

During an individual interview at Old East End Community College, one pupil indicated that the personality of the teacher who took the anti-bullying classes was of significance in relation to the overall response by the class. As this pupil perceived that:

> ". . . people just see these as a joke . . . . . . because of the teachers who we've had, they're just too soft and no one likes that" (Transcription 26, individual interviews, years 8 and 9, Old East End Community College: 25).

The above view polarizes the positive perceptions maintained by, for example pupils especially at Modern Eastern Suburban School who believed that such classes prompted pupils to think about the issue of bullying and racist bullying. Samara and Smith (2008:673) claim that such classes enabled pupils to openly raise and discuss issues and problem solve issues in groups. Some teachers those particularly at the School for the Excluded considered that such classes may not always be successful as, in their opinion; pupils do not take the issues of bullying seriously enough, despite the issues being highly sensitive. Hunt's (2007:24) research findings revealed from her sample that pupils did not change their attitude towards bullying or victims and predicted they did not have much of a sympathetic attitude towards victims of bullying. Hunt's findings also revealed that pupils showed a decreased acceptance towards bullying that occurred at the school (Hunt, 2007). Teachers at the School for the Excluded emphasized how most of the pupils had severe anti-social behavioural problems and lacked the intellect to respond positively to the anti-bullying education that took place within the school. As one teacher commented:

> "they tend to be better at one to one or two or very small groups to talk to sensibly . . . . it just takes one person to make a stupid comment then, whoosh, they all make a comment and they use sensitive material . . . It's very difficult . . . . to get them to address it in a mature way" (Transcription 9, teacher, School for the Excluded: 29/30).

Many teachers and youth workers shared this opinion and preferred to work with smaller groups. In particular, teachers at Old East End Community College preferred to target vulnerable pupils who were both perpetrators and victims and had low self-esteem. Teachers also drew attention to a number of obstacles for such an idea, such as the shortage of time and government funds. Similarly, youth workers were of the opinion that the system would work better for teachers who dealt with fewer pupils. Hunt (2007:25) also indicated in her research that teachers, who worked with smaller groups on anti-bullying education/intervention, gradually saw a decreased reporting of bullying and a stronger effect in positive behaviour amongst pupils. One youth worker commented:

> "I think it has to, I think the smaller it is, the more the personal development will work" (Transcription 27, youth worker, YOT: 11).

Moreover, such a system enabled the teachers to spend more time with the pupils and allowed for more personal development on a specialized subject, as the same youth worker discovered that:

> ". . . if you work with 30 pupils you've got such a variety of matches and that's a big space and . . . it would take someone who was highly skilled to work very consistently with them . . . because it definitely is a specialism . . . and I don't think many teachers have got that" (Transcription 27; Youth worker, YOT: 11).

Therefore, to teachers, the key factors that affected the effectiveness of anti-bullying education included the delivery of the education, the person responsible for who delivered it, whether or not pupils were emotionally equipped to receive it and finally, the size of the group made all the difference.

School Response and the Socio-Economic and Geographical Perspective

Old East End Community College had a relatively weak response system, in comparison to Modern Eastern Suburban School. Whilst preventative education took shape through Circle Time classes, there was no specific curriculum for anti-bullying or anti-racist education at Old East End Community College. From pupils' responses at this school, underreporting by victims and not speaking out on the victim's behalf was heavily implied. Particularly as Old East End Community College is located in an environment that is socially and economically deprived, with the lack of funding and time given by teachers to be effectively trained, there was much disgruntlement amongst pupils as to the effectiveness of the teachers' response (pp: 224). As in the research findings by Ellis and Shute (2007:661), there was an inconsistency between pupils reporting bullying to teachers and the teachers' level of intervention (Ellis and Shute, 2007). They claim that this discrepancy may, in part reflect the inconsistency between teacher recognition of bullying and the harm evident in pupils (Ellis and Shute, 2007).

As reported in the findings in chapter 5 (pp:167), a fighting culture at Modern Eastern Suburban School existed yet whilst rare, some of the physical fighting which took place at Old East End Community College, was at times extremely violent. Furthermore, the physical bullying at Old East End Community College was more pronounced. This could strongly be attributed towards the social and economic environment in the Walkergate ward where most families live in low income or unemployed status and in estate based social housing (Rowntree, 2010). Furthermore, where there is a large percentage of low income families living in estate based social housing in the surrounding wards, such as in Byker, and Walker, these can assist in explaining the considerable level of social deprivation within the Walkergate community that has increasing chances in high statistics in crime (Rowntree, 2010).

Whilst teachers in Old East End Community College also discussed how they have learning and peer mentors, unlike at Modern Eastern Suburban School, this resource was not utilized as much and less emphasis was given by teachers as to its effectiveness. The school has tutors and pastoral staff who play the role of adult mentors and are available for pupils to go and talk to them in private about any matter, including issues of bullying. Unlike Modern Eastern Suburban School that emphasized the use of peer mediation through mentoring and peer support, the teachers at Old East End Community College perceived that the school possessed a strong and durable house system which included counsellors. They believed that there remains adequate support for pupils and more importance was given to this system. The teachers therefore relied more heavily on the house system for peer support rather than for mentoring. As one teacher emphasized:

> SQ: ". . . okay. And what kind of support does this school provide? I mean I know they have the PSHE education but how well aware are the children to know who to go to approach?
>
> Teacher: . . . well because of the type of school that we've got and the type of pupils that we've got, the only way this school survives is through our really, really strong house system . . ." (Transcription 20, teacher, Old East End Community College: 5).

Thus, in comparison, at Modern Eastern Suburban School, there was a strong anti-bullying support network that operated in the form of anti-bullying classes during Citizenship, Personal, Social Health and Education numerus mentoring from staff learning mentors, peer mentors and lunch time peer mentors for years 7 and 8. In addition, the school employed a counsellor who saw pupils frequently. This reveals a sense of positive interactions between pupils and adults as support for pupils are strong. In one of Hrschi's (in Greenberg,1999) elements to the social control theory a positive integration amongst pupils and teachers can contribute towards delinquent behaviour and in this context, bullying behaviour. The school posted numerous anti-bullying posters by pupils all around the school as well as contact details for professional help from organizations such as ChildLine. Racism would be challenged on all accounts as there was a zero tolerance approach by this school. Therefore, with greater emphasis upon peer support, it could be speculated that this is why pupils saw more value of reporting to an adult than pupils at Old East End Community College. Not only was there a strong stance against bullying and racism at Modern Eastern Suburban School, teachers made more use of immediate sanctions, in the form of the 'cooler' than Old East End Community College and to an extent, School for the Excluded.

As Modern Eastern Suburban School, located in the North Heaton ward in the eastern suburbs to Newcastle-upon-Tyne is an affluent part to the city, there resides a community which comprises of more career professionals living in the most sought after homes. There also exists upwardly mobile families with decent income and overall a middle class environment (Rowntree, 2010). Furthermore, the surrounding wards shared similar characteristics, some more affluent that even North Heaton, such as North and South Jesmond, Dene and East and West Gosforth. These socio-economic characteristics within North Heaton and the surrounding wards strongly indicate that further social and economic prosperity with more middle class values exists. Thus, the socio-economic affluence and societal values of Modern Eastern Suburban School can be speculated to be strongly influenced by these middle class traits. Despite the large fighting culture that existed at Modern Eastern Suburban School, there was a low crime rate in the neighbourhood. This could also assist why there was significant emphasis placed upon peer support through the form of mentoring, as physical bullying often stemmed from what was initially a fight.

At the School for the Excluded, anti-bullying preventative measures were addressed through discussions during pastoral classes: Personal, Social, Health and Education, drama, classroom charters and other school initiatives. Like Old East End Community College and Modern Eastern Suburban School, the school used a whole school approach to teach anti-bullying through emotional literacy. In relation to immediate sanctioning, this often involved parents and could possibly indicate that this contributed towards any effectiveness with immediate retribution.

The School for the Excluded located in the Denton ward, is also socio-economic deprived, with a relatively high crime rate and much of the population live in estate based social housing. This is a significant percentage throughout the city of Newcastle; therefore, like Old East End Community College, much of the population of Denton is of lower working class. Furthermore, the surrounding wards; Kenton; Wingrove; Blakelaw and Newburn, particularly with Blakelaw, Kenton and Newburn situated in the west end suburban of Newcastle, also have a significant percentage of low income family residing in estate based social housing (Rowntree, 2010). Even though teachers had few resources, but with fewer numbers on roll, they had more time to be able to effectively deal with pupils' social welfare and address issues to do with bullying in depth. Furthermore, pupils agreed that with smaller class sizes, the teaching delivery was much more focused and effective. However, there was little response offered towards how racism would be addressed. Given that all pupils on roll were white, this could possibly explain why more emphasis was given to bullying than racist bullying.

Summary and Discussion

This chapter explored the issues pertaining to under reporting of bullying and racist bullying and the ways in which schools respond to them. One main purpose has been to explore pupils' perspectives on the effectiveness of school preventative education as well as the efficiency of the schools response. The chapter reports pupils' shared explanations as to why victims prefer to remain silent. The chapter further explores pupils and teachers' perceptions on punishment, retribution and deterrence. There has been a discussion of the various preventative and intervention measures which schools employ highlighting the different support mechanisms used by each school. Finally, the chapter explores the impact of socio-economic and geographical factors on the differences between each school and their means of addressing and responding to incidents of bullying and racist bullying.

Two main themes emerge from this chapter. First, despite the progress in all three schools' response to reported cases of bullying and racist bullying, victims largely prefer to remain silent, whatever the socio-economic and geographical environment of the school. Yet the perception of long-term benefits of reporting have been considered by some pupils. Particularly at Modern Eastern Suburban School, which utilizes the most varied preventive and intervention form of response and is the most affluent of the three schools sampled. These factors could assist in understanding the responses from some pupils who believe that informing an adult, especially a teacher is the most appropriate and beneficial coping mechanism for victims. Some pupils at the School for the Excluded, pupils share similar sentiments that informing an adult is better for the victim in the long term. Although the school is located in a ward that has high unemployment, working class white communities and social and economic deprivation, the school itself has a strong anti-bullying support system for both victims and perpetrators. Furthermore, as there are less than 126 pupils on roll, this allows teachers to pay more attention to their social welfare needs. There is an indication, therefore, that the stronger the anti-bullying support, the more likely pupils are to acknowledge the benefits of confiding in an adult as a positive coping mechanism.

Second pupils have clear views on the importance of school mechanisms to prevent and intervene in reported cases of bullying. Whilst pupils desire restorative measures, they are also supportive of immediate punishment. Pupils also want a combination of sanctioning, preventative and intervention measures delivered over the long term. Particularly at Modern Eastern Suburban School, they perceive that there is an overuse of referrals of pupils to particular 'units' and are less supportive of this particular form of sanctioning. Pupils instead prefer preventative education and find peer support highly beneficial. The more affluent home and local community environment, at Modern

Eastern Suburban School appeared to influence a strong anti-bullying/racism approach taken by the school. As the school strongly encourages peers to support victims through mentoring as well as by being positive bystanders, this appeared to have an impact upon pupils' responses at Modern Eastern Suburban School.

CHAPTER 8

School Bullying, Racism and the School Response

Summary of Thesis

B ULLYING AND RACIST bullying in schools offer a diversity of issues that have been covered by academic research, including the problem of definition, understanding its nature, prevalence and causes (Moon, *et al.*, 2008). Providing effective responses to bullying present significant challenges to schools as a consequence of its varied nature and causes and the problems of underreporting (Ma *et al.*, 2001; Olweus, 1993). (Salmivalli, 2010). Indeed, the complex nature of bullying and racist bullying is reflected within numerous changes to government legislation, such as the introduction of the Equality Act 2010 to incorporate all forms of discrimination (Green *et al.*, 2010). There are also changes within policy guidelines to schools, including the most recent duty to investigate reported incidents of bullying that occur outside the school grounds (Department for Education, 2011). Despite such developments, academic research on school bullying has fallen short when investigating the causes and manifestation of bullying and racist bullying from the perspectives of young people and adults. Thus, this study has sought to examine the perceptions and experiences of school bullying and racist bullying across three schools in a northern city of England. It demonstrates variation in young people's perceptions according to the socio-economic background and locale of their home, community neighbourhood and the social make-up of their school. For instance, similarities include that the nature of bullying is considered to be an accumulated process. However, an example of pupils' perceptions differing is shown in their attitude towards victims of racist bullying. Where some pupils show resentment and hostility towards the individual and cultural presence of immigrants, pupils from affluent schools are more sympathetic towards their plight. The purpose of this chapter is to draw out the core themes of this thesis, and to make pertinent links back to wider academic literature.

This chapter is structured as follows. First it discusses the main aim of the study and how these were achieved. Secondly the chapter details how the fieldwork is carried out using qualitative research through semi-structured focus groups and individual interviews. Thirdly the chapter then summarizes the three key themes of the study. Finally, the chapter provides a broader assessment of these themes in relation to wider academic literature. The chapter concludes by summarising key findings and posing future directions for research.

Methodology

The PhD aims to examine pupils' and adults' perceptions of bullying and racist bullying and how they are manifested in a school environment in Newcastle-upon-Tyne. Within this aim, a number of broad research questions arose, which this study had been interested in exploring, including: how do pupils explain bullying and racist bullying? What factors impact upon their thinking? What role do socio-economic factors, if any play on pupil's perceptions both of bullying, and of school responses? What are pupil's perceptions of the responses of victims to experiences of bullying? What do adults perceive to be the main issues relating to bullying and racist bullying and how do these compare with that of pupils? These questions have helped the study to narrow and focus the overall aim. As a result, two minor modifications have been made to the original objectives: The age range of participating pupils has been reduced from 11-18 to 11-15 years, (Years 7-9) as this appropriately maps onto the findings from the broader review of research, which suggests that school bullying mainly begins during the last year at primary school and is much more apparent during the early years at secondary/middle school. Another original objective includes using questionnaires, in addition to interviews and focus groups. However, during the literature review it became apparent that survey/questionnaires was a traditional choice of method amongst most studies on school bullying and therefore it was decided to adopt a more qualitative methodology to capture better the voices of young people involved.

The fieldwork involved conducting semi structured focus groups and individual interviews. A number of research techniques are utilised during focus group sessions to stimulate discussion and debate. These include an anti-bullying video 'Kick-It Bullying', spider diagrams and post-it notes to enable pupils to comfortably share both their perceptions of bullying and any racist remarks they may have encountered. Furthermore, the use of anti-bullying and anti-racist statements and the use of a quiz are intended to encourage students to discuss and reflect upon their understanding of bullying and racist bullying and to provoke discussion and debate.

In total there are 18 focus groups conducted at these schools and on average, each focus group lasts between 35-50 minutes. The fieldwork was carried out between November 2005-June 2006. There are ten focus groups conducted with pupils in years 7 to 9 attending Old East End Community College. Initially the group began with 10 pupils, however, in order to manage the process; this was reduced to 6. At Modern Eastern Suburban School, there are 6 focus groups conducted with pupils in years 7 to 9, with 2 groups per year with an average of 6 participating pupils. At the School for the Excluded there are only 2 focus groups conducted with no more than 6 pupils in each group. These two focus groups have been supported by class tutors in order to minimise disruption and assist in the smooth delivery of discussions.

Fifteen interviews have been conducted with each interview lasting approximately 30 minutes. Semi-structured individual interviews have also been carried out amongst a range of key stake holders, such as educationalists, including year tutors, form teachers, pastoral staff, head and assistant head teachers. Interviews are also conducted with two youth workers and a parent and all interviews with the participants have been carried out on the school premises.

In addition to using key themes as prompts for discussion in interviews, pupils are also presented with a number of images (downloaded from Google.com) of young people who are victims of bullying as well as images that represent acceptance of all races and cultures. These were used as an ice breaker to place students at ease and also as a means of identifying immediate perceptions to bullying. At Old East End Community College, 9 pupils from years 7 to 9 volunteered to take part in the interview. However, in Modern Eastern Suburban School, there is only one pupil from year 8 who gave consent to the interview process. At the School for the Excluded, there are 5 pupils from years 8 and 9 who agreed to the interview.

Whilst the planning, preparation and conducting of the field work was carried out with due diligence, with hindsight, a few actions could have been conducted differently. Firstly, and as chapter 4 details the process of building up credibility and gaining access to schools, all interviews including focus groups should have been carried out based upon consent from pupils and parents, this being politically, ethically and morally correct. Even though Old East End Community College and the School for the Excluded assured me prior consent had been secured for the focus groups, my own collection of consent forms should have been secured. At Modern Eastern Suburban School consent is required at all stages of the field work, even though there are fewer interviews, these are of greater quality with pupils being more coherent.

Secondly, pupils could have been asked more questions regarding gender and bullying, as this topic has been touched upon when reading out various statements written on the sketchpad. It is certainly an area that can have been explored in further detail. Thirdly, during a focus group at Old East End Community College, one pupil had been identified as a being a victim of bullying, and was asked if she wanted to talk about her experience. In addition to this, she should also have been informed that should she not feel comfortable talking about her experience, it is her right to say no. This additional information repeated to the group again would have further minimized any potential for harm to this pupil. Finally, it should have been emphasized before reading out the bullying and racist bullying quiz that all the scenarios are purely hypothetical and not based on real life events. Some of the language used may be construed as being offensive. However, pupils wrote down similar language when documenting racist comments they had heard on post it notes before the quiz had been carried out.

Key Findings

The three data chapters identify a number of findings. In summary, the nature and characteristics of bullying and racist bullying are similar; the bully is held responsible for their actions, whilst for most pupils, victims of racist bullying are held accountable for their own plight. Whilst schools employ a number of support mechanisms, victims still prefer to remain silent. Furthermore, there is an overall consensus in support of sanctioning, preventative education and intervention approaches to be implemented in schools over a long term basis.

Chapter five shows that the ways in which pupils' identify the nature and characteristics of bullying are not dissimilar to the nature and characteristics of racist bullying. However, with regards to bullying, discussion focuses largely on the individual characteristics of the perpetrators, unanimously perceiving the perpetrator as being responsible for their actions. Yet when discussing racist bullying, pupils' shifted the focus of their discussion towards the victims. Chapter five also identifies fundamental differences in the ways in which pupils talk about the nature and characteristics of bullying and racist bullying. Much of pupils' identification towards bullying and racist bullying is determined by the socio-economic environment of the school as well as their home, community and neighbourhood surroundings. For example, pupils from Modern Eastern Suburban School and the School for the Excluded have greater knowledge and understanding of bullying, and acknowledge that accumulated incidents, not one off incidents amount to bullying. This contrasts to pupils from Old East End Community College who acknowledge one off incidents as being part of the bullying nature. Pupils from Old East End Community College reveal prejudices through their hostility towards victims of racist bullying, yet pupils from Modern Eastern Suburban School show more empathy and understanding towards minority communities. This suggests that the more socio-economically deprived a school and neighbourhood is, the stronger the resentment is towards minority groups. Finally chapter five acknowledges that the presence and influence of peers act as a driving force for the occurrence of bullying, whether as an enabler or detractor of the act or incidences.

Chapter 6 identifies that across all three schools, pupils hold the perpetrator responsible for their bullying actions. Yet when explaining bullying, there are notable differences between Old East End Community College and Modern Eastern Suburban School, suggesting that the socio-economic environment and neighbourhood of the schools may influence pupils' outlook. Pupils at Old East End Community College disclose that bullying may occur in order to maintain a family reputation, revealing inner aggression and spontaneity. This pattern can be associated with social factors. The social deprivation, high unemployment and high criminal activity by young people manifested around Old East End Community college could explain the volume of aggressive behaviour that exists within the school. For pupils at Modern Eastern Suburban School, bullying is seen as a means to protect a family member which implies that bullying is committed as a defence mechanism. Modern Eastern Suburban School is located in an affluent ward, consisting of many career professionals living in the most sought after homes and upwardly mobile families with middle class values. When talking about racist bullying, pupils largely from Old East End Community College and from the School for the Excluded discuss and explain that the cultural lifestyles of victims provoke racist behaviour, therefore indirectly blame the victims. Furthermore, it is perceived that victims of racist bullying are responsible for their victimization due to pupils' belief that minority ethnic groups are at an unfair advantage over the indigenous white working class community. In comparison, there is no hostility or resentment shown towards victims of racist bullying by those pupils from Modern Eastern Suburban School. These contrasting opinions may well be influenced by the affluent middle class environment in which the pupils reside.

Chapter 7 acknowledges a distinct problem of under-reporting despite the progress of the schools' response to reported cases of bullying and racist bullying. However, pupils, largely at Modern Eastern Suburban School are more willing to support the idea of reporting incidents of bullying and racist bullying to teachers, as the school utilizes the most varied forms of preventive methods and intervention. Therefore, the variety of support mechanisms for victims can contribute towards pupils who believe that informing an adult, especially a teacher, is the most appropriate and most beneficial coping mechanism for victims. Indeed, it can be suggested that the stronger the anti-bullying support, the more pupils believe that confiding in an adult is a positive coping mechanism. Chapter 7 also identifies that pupils have clear views on the importance of school mechanisms to prevent and intervene in reported cases of bullying. Whilst there is a desire for restorative measures, pupils are very supportive towards immediate punishment. A desire for a combination of preventative measures and intervention delivered over the long term is unanimous. This is particularly prevalent amongst those from Modern Eastern Suburban School, who complain of the overuse of the 'units' or 'cooler', a room where pupils are referred to immediately for sanctioning. Instead there is more emphasis given to preventative education and peer support.

Beyond these core findings, the thesis identifies a number of wider and broader themes. Firstly, there continues to be a need for high quality qualitative research undertaken on bullying and racist bullying, given that much research remains centred upon the collection of quantitative data and the analysis of generalised 'findings'. Secondly, the difference in perceptions of bullying and racist bullying, which reflects pupils' broader beliefs are often drawn from family and environment. When pupils discuss bullying, the focus is often upon the individual perpetrator and their characteristics and motivations, whilst the discussion on racist bullying focuses almost entirely upon the victim. Thirdly, socio-economic and structural factors frequently contribute towards the ways in which pupils perceive and understand bullying and racist bullying. The study also reveals the importance of a holistic restorative/whole school approach to bullying that incorporates preventative education in encouraging enhanced emotional literacy.

Key Themes

Using Qualitative Methodology to Study Bullying and Racist Bullying

The use of qualitative approaches and methods is important to this PhD as by and large, studies that have been conducted on school bullying (Olweus, 1993; Coloroso, 2008; Sullivan *et al.,* 2005; Rigby, 2004; Cranham and Carroll, 2003) and school racism, (Verkuyten and Thijs, 2002; Bonilla-Silva and Forman, 2000; Kailin, 1999) repeatedly use quantitative research methodology and in particular, questionnaires and surveys. Moreover, there is a tendency for these studies to offer only one perspective when examining bullying, namely a psychological perspective that explores bullying from the individual characteristics of the perpetrator (Ma et al. (2001), Cranham and Carroll (2003) Rigby, (2004); and Dixon, (2007).

This PhD employs a qualitative methodology that examines both the individual as well as the sociological perspectives, therefore offering a much broader outlook when explaining the nature, causes and motivations for bullying and racist bullying. In addition, using qualitative methodology allows the research to locate the experiences and perceptions of young people within their social, historical, political and economic context. This is particularly interesting, given that it can be suggested that context and environment dictates many pupils' *tolerance* towards victims of racism (Modern Eastern Suburban School), and *intolerance* (Old East End Community College). Had this PhD conducted quantitative research using surveys or questionnaires, such notable differences in pupils perceptions would not have been so apparent.

The use of qualitative research methodology enables this PhD to explore the personal experiences of victims and pupil's perceptions of bullying in some depth. It reveals during the focus group sessions that the preferred coping mechanism by most victims is to either remain silent, or at best, tell a friend. Had this PhD used quantitative research methodology, this depth and detail in the data would not have been obtained. By combining both semi-structured focus groups and interviews, the study achieves a deeper understanding of school bullying and racist bullying than offered by quantitative methodologies. Specifically, using a qualitative approach enables the study to move beyond focusing on the individual and offender to a much broader study of the social and economic context and perceptions of those involved in the fieldwork. Finally, by employing qualitative methodology through the use of semi-structured focus groups and individual interviews, young people's voices and perceptions are brought to the forefront.

Differences in Perceptions of Bullying and Racist Bullying

When pupils try to make sense of bullying and attempt to understand why bullying took place, their discussion always focuses on the individual perpetrator and his or her characteristics and motivations. For example, pupils' comments centre on the perpetrator's intention to secure power and control over the victim, often undermined by their own experiences of socialization. Yet interestingly, despite the perpetrators' circumstances, pupils always hold them responsible for their actions. The literature on bullying often focuses upon the perpetrator's individual nature and characteristics. The discussions and findings in chapters 2 and 5 also reflects upon these previous findings. In research conducted by Rigby (2002), Lines (2008) and Cranham and Carroll (2003), the perpetrator is largely identified as an aggressor exuding power and control over the victim and thereby emphasizing the deliberate intent to harm. The research by Sutton (1991) argues that the perpetrator's actions can be viewed as a deliberate and calculating attempt to gain power over the victim.

Bullying is also constructed by pupils as a socially learned process developing as a consequence of the bully's experience as a victim (Sullivan *et al.,* 2005 and Batsche and Knoff, 1994). During the focus group discussions, pupils identify that bullies often perpetrate because they have themselves been a victim of bullying. Those interviewed however, have very little sympathy for perpetrators who had been victims of bullying. Not only does the thesis examine the psychological factors, it also considers explanations for bullying as a result of the socio-economic environment of the school and the neighbourhood in which pupils reside, which many studies fail to consider.

During the focus group discussions there are some differences in opinion between pupils from each school. Whilst pupils across the board recognize the individual psychological characteristics of the perpetrator, when explaining the motivations for bullying, pupils at Modern Eastern Suburban School are able to articulate in greater detail that bullying occurs for 'relative' reasons, i.e. pupils who are poor or those who possess expensive items are likely to be bullied. This is perceived less of an issue at Old East End Community College. As Bradshaw (2009:2006) has suggested bullying out of relative deprivation is often more common than being bullied due to absolute poverty.

Another notable comparison between both secondary schools is pupils' depth of understanding of the nature of bullying. Particularly, pupils at Modern Eastern Suburban School are able to recognize that bullying is a cumulative process whereas pupils at Old East End Community College and the School for the Excluded identify that bullying is often about one off incidents. Again, the socio-economic perspectives of pupils has relevance; Modern Eastern Suburban School is of an affluent environment with a strong anti-bullying ethos which contributes in deepening pupils' understanding of the subject.

In contrast, whenever pupils talk about racist bullying and particularly the motivation for racist bullying, the perpetrator is lost in a wider discussion of the victim and victim characteristics, both individual and social. However, the ways in which pupils speak about victims vary. By and large, pupils from Old East End Community College talk about victims in ways that suggest that they contribute towards their own victimization. This is either through a lack of assimilation and integration, or as a consequence of 'unfair advantage' and support which they have been perceived as receiving. Further, pupils from Old East End Community College articulate this through the use of racist language, whilst at the same time noting that they are not personally racist. In comparison, discussions with pupils at Modern Eastern Suburban School demonstrate empathy towards the victims and a shared understanding and acceptance of different cultures. At the School for the Excluded, pupils have little to discuss on victims of racist bullying; whilst there is no outward resentment shown towards victims or to the presence of minority ethnic groups, asylum seekers or refugees, neither is any sympathy given. Similar to Old East End Community College, pupils from the School for the Excluded are in an environment which is heavily socially and economically deprived, yet, at the school, all pupils on roll are white. In contrast, pupils at Modern Eastern Suburban School are attending a school and living in an area which is considerably affluent and where pupils are more ethnically diverse. This indeed has an impact upon their perceptions as the school strongly values a zero tolerance approach to racism, which may impact upon attitudes towards those living in the immediate neighbourhood.

Much of the literature suggests that racist perpetration is driven by a variety of factors and not necessarily racist beliefs. Studies used in this PhD determine that, not all people are generally tolerant of different cultures and in addition have difficulty accepting their economic prosperity. This is so amongst particularly white socio economic groups. In this sense, minority ethnic groups have been used as scapegoats by those who view such individuals as the cause of all their own problems, this has been articulated repeatedly by Caucasian pupils from Old East End Community College. When Sibbit (1997) interviewed elderly people living in council housing, her findings reflected the same as above, that is the elder generation appear to hold minority ethnic groups responsible for all problems, particularly socio-economic factors. Therefore, it can be speculated that often such behaviour is learned and emanates from external influences. The literature also articulates that many Caucasian people maintain a belief that the "white" race is superior (Ray and Smith 2004) and it is with this belief that incites racist perpetration when they witness the many changes in their community and the relative economic success achieved by some members of minority ethnic groups. In chapter 6, whilst pupils from Old East End Community College did not admit to being openly racist, there are similar disgruntled reactions when pupils suggest that members from the South Asian community have achieved economic success and perceive this to be unfair.

Furthermore, from this study, racist bullying is driven by another factor, which is the home environment. The literature argues that where racist attitudes exist within the home and local community, these attitudes also tend to be adopted by young people. For example, Sibbit's (1997) study finds that there is little understanding in the white community of difference which breeds hatred and hostility towards particular individuals and groups. There is a widespread belief that immigrant and minority ethnic groups receive more help and benefits from the local government than the white communities. This perception of unfair advantage towards such groups leads white pupils and the white working class community to believe that they are unduly victimized. This perception is emphasized, in particular from the focus groups conducted in Old East End Community College, where many pupils expose their dissatisfaction with increased aid given to minority ethnic groups. This disgruntlement expressed by pupils, expose their viewpoint (or belief) that minority ethnic groups, asylum seekers and refugees are given superior treatment by the schools. In addition, resentment is also born from a belief that traditional activities change due to political corrections. For example, changing the name of Christmas to "festivities", omitting (or excluding) the nativity play and changing the name 'black board' to 'dry white board' so as not to offend particular groups. Pupils use examples such as these to explain and justify why the white majority community hold racist attitudes.

Drawing upon the work of Bonnett, (1997, cited in Gillborn, 2005:490) helps to explain why white pupils and the community blame victims for racist bullying. For Gillborn;

> "Whiteness has developed, over the past two hundred years, into a taken-for-granted experience structured upon a varying set of supremacist assumptions . . . Non-White identities, by contrast, have been denied the privileges of normativity, and are marked within the West as marginal and inferior" (Bonnett, 1997 cited in Gillborn 2005:490).

Gillborn (2005) claims that the critical race theory promotes a different perspective on white supremacy rather than the limited and extreme understandings usually denoted by the term in everyday language. Gillborn (2005) suggests that white communities are used to privileges, such as benefits from the government, but at the same time are unable to accept that non-white communities receive the same benefits. Gillborn's (2005) work also helps to put pupils' explanations for racist bullying into perspective, suggesting that pupils believe they are fighting back against an unfair disadvantage and striving to restore the natural hierarchy of the white race. Academics such as Nayak (2003) and Cockburn (2007) also argue that a large proportion of the lower working white class community struggle to accept the changing face of Britain. Findings from this thesis support Nayak's findings, namely that pupils (at Old East End Community College) hold prejudicial and hostile attitudes towards victims of racist bullying, thus revealing that the white community struggle to cope and accept changes within their community as well as changes in England. Indeed, previous studies fail to relate these wider perceptions of superiority to the motivations of racist bullying in schools. By examining pupils' perceptions of the motivations for racist bullying, this thesis provides another angle of knowledge, and contribution, offering an opportunity for further research. For instance, further research may explore if similar hostile attitudes towards immigrants exist amongst pupils in schools where the community is of low socio-economic environment and high socio disadvantage, schools situated within an area that is socially and economically deprived and with high statistics of crime.

Impact of Socio-Economic Factors

The ways in which young people see bullying and understand victim's experiences largely depend upon their experience within particular schools, at specific times and in particular parts of the city. We are informed much about the ways in which the socio-economic environment impacts upon how young people perceive bullying and racist bullying. For instance, bullying, both physically and verbally is much more of a widespread problem at Old East End Community College, whilst at Modern Eastern Suburban School, there is more verbal bullying occurring, despite the involvement of some pupils in physical fighting. At the School for the Excluded, bullying is more of a problem outside of the school gates than inside the school.

With Old East End Community College, the school is located in the Walkergate ward; an area of mass social deprivation, where unemployment is high and a percentage of the elderly live in social housing with high care needs. Yet there is also a large percentage of the population who are lower working class and live in close knit, inner city and manufacturing communities. The surrounding wards are also of lower working class communities that largely reside in social housing, in deprived areas with high statistics of unemployment. This may contribute to an understanding where bullying and particularly racial prejudicial attitudes are high. For instance, the findings chapters reveal that where resentment towards the presence of minority ethnic groups, asylum seekers and refugees is high, little is done in the community to overcome such prejudices. An examination of the social and economic characteristics of the Walkergate and surrounding wards assists in developing our understanding that the school has minimal resources to effectively respond to bullying, but also that there is minimal attention given for teachers to develop a deeper understanding into the nature and motivations for racist bullying. Where adult perceptions include merging bullying and racist bullying terminologies together, this can suggest that more support needs to be given towards teachers understanding of the differences between what is racist and what is not. Further research into exploring teachers' knowledge and pupils' perceptions of racist bullying according to the socio-economic environment they live in will be beneficial in tackling and preventing the problem.

In comparison, Modern Eastern Suburban School, located in the North Heaton ward is considerably more affluent than Walkergate. Where there is a large majority of people who are career professionals, middle class and living in the most sought after locations, so too are the class and category of people living in the surrounding wards, such as North Jesmond, South Jesmond and Dene. Thus, it is of little surprise to discover that at Modern Eastern Suburban School, more funding is available and considerable attention is paid towards anti-bullying prevention and responses and that the school operates a zero tolerance approach to any racist issue, including challenging any racist comments from pupils. Furthermore, the school is multi-racial and for much of the focus groups, many pupils are of minority ethnic background. Yet during the focus groups, they are comfortable and at ease when discussing issues on bullying and racist bullying, which is indeed the opposite reaction from the few pupils of minority ethnic background at Old East End Community College. They had been either silent or questions were met with hostility. This again suggests that the social environment and school ethos can dictate pupil's views and how they interact with one another. It may be possibly speculated that pupils from minority ethnic communities, asylum and refugee groups struggle to fit in with the white community. Such comparisons between both mainstream schools clearly indicate that there are notable differences in how young people perceive bullying and racist bullying according to the socio-economic environment and ethos of the school and of the home and community environment. The work of Stewart (2003) and Chaux et al. (2009) clearly associate that a school with a poor ethos contributes towards bullying and anti-social behaviour. Yet these studies omit to consider racist prejudicial attitudes, which this research examines upon.

The School for the Excluded, situated in a neighbourhood of considerable social deprivation, in the Denton ward, is a special needs school with less than 126 pupils on roll. This can explain the sufficient attention addressed towards anti-bullying and physical violence issues at the school. Yet the neighbourhood, and surrounding wards, consists of a large percentage working class, low income families living in estate based social housing. Within the Denton ward, the crime rate and unemployment levels are somewhat high. The presence of minority ethnic groups, asylum seekers and refugees is met with considerable prejudice, as is disclosed during the teachers' interviews. Yet at the School for the Excluded, this attitude is less apparent amongst pupils, as at the time of the research, the school was all white. However, greater empathy towards victims of racism is demonstrated by the teachers whilst pupils are less empathetic. Cockburn (2007) finds that many of young people's hostile attitudes emanate from the home environment, yet Cockburn's research is conducted in the community and not in schools. Unlike other studies that have examined school bullying (Olweus, 1993; Coloroso, 2008; Sullivan *et al.*, 2005; Rigby, 2004; Cranham and Carroll, 2003; Naylor *et al.*, 2001), this PhD draws upon notable differences and comparisons with pupils' perceptions, not only by taking into account the literature on the psychological individual factors to explain bullying, but by also examining the socio-economic factors. This PhD broadens our understanding as to why pupils have their perceptions, particularly towards explaining racist bullying. Indeed, currently much of the academic research, particularly the psychological studies, fail to explore in detail the social and structural factors that contribute towards bullying, how pupils think, interact with each other, and motivations to perpetrate. For those studies that do explain bullying from a sociological perspective, (Espelage and Swearer, 2009; Stephenson, 2007; Stewart, 2003; Bradshaw *et al.*, 2009; Chaux *et al.*, 2009; David, 2010; Goody, 1997), the socio-economic environment is particularly limited and therefore warrants further research. Indeed, there is a dearth of literature examining school bullying from both the psychological and sociological perspectives. However, further research into the socio-economic environment lead to stronger preventative and intervention measures, as this area strongly determines how pupils perceive and understand bullying and racist bullying.

DR. SAIRAH QURESHI

Increase in a Holistic Restorative/Whole School Approach

Although pupils seem to understand the range of punitive, preventative and restorative measures operational in their schools, they often contradict themselves when talking about them and when explaining what methods they support. While some pupils believe a combination of all three is the solution to the bullying problem, other pupils did not support any and their views of an effective response focus upon an immediate punishment even though they also support restorative measures. This perception occurs across of all three schools.

The broader literature on anti-bullying preventative measures argues that prevention using a holistic/restorative approach is effective through two methods. First, through a whole school approach and second, delivered through emotional literacy. Academic research has also highlighted that in order for a whole school approach to be more effective, it needs to be delivered through an emotional literacy style (Littlechild, 2009: 5). Earlier studies reveal a style of a whole school approach that merely involved teachers coming together with pupils and parents to develop their own anti-bullying initiatives based upon the main bullying problems that occur in the school. (Knights 1998; Samara and Smith 2008; Olweus, 2001 and Pitts 1999). Yet research also indicates that it is imperative to institute consultative exercises which allow members at all levels of the school to participate in the analysis of the problem, and the construction of a collective response to it (Pitts, 1999). The research demonstrates that this form of preventative approach is successful with levels of bullying falling as a consequence (Slee and Mohyla, 2007). Similarly, each school sampled in this thesis respectively adopts a whole school approach.

Within the broader literature on both bullying and racist bullying, there is an emphasis towards a 'guardian' in a positive role. Academic research argues that using peers in a positive role is probably the most effective means to reduce bullying. It has been suggested that peer leaders have more effect and authority over the bullying environment than pupils actually realize (Ahmed 2005; Knights, 1998; Salmivalli, 2005; Naylor and Cowie, 1999; Rigby 2006 and Lines 2005). Drawing from Salmivalli's work (1999; 2002; 2005), her findings specify that there is success in using peers as mentors and bystanders as her findings exemplify that many stepped in to stop the bullying. Academic research also argues that peers are able to model, reinforce, extinguish, and monitor bullying behaviours even at a primary school age. Research has emphasized that when it comes to bullying, support for victims largely derives from peers as mentors and bystanders (Salmivalli, 2005). Whilst recent research on preventing bullying examines the role of peers, there is a strong emphasis for further research to concentrate upon encouraging pupils to gain confidence in their multiple roles and in informing teachers. Yet by failing to examine preventative, intervention and sanctioning measures combined, there remains a gap in the literature. This thesis has discovered the use and desire by pupils for both a restorative approach that is long term and, the need for an immediate response, that the perpetrator should feel some immediate punishment. A restorative approach allows teachers and pupils to work together to educate the bully on where and why their actions are wrong and thus present an opportunity for the perpetrator to redeem themselves rather than purely receiving punishment (Ahmed and Braithwaite (2006). This approach can take place either through mentoring, peers acting as guardians, guiding victims to speak to an adult, or inform on their behalf, with the use of and classroom based exercises to encourage this. The difference with the earlier whole school approach technique is that the concept of forgiveness, reconciliation, and shame, which appeal to pupils emotional literacy are not present. However, as recent research indicates, (Littlechild, 2009; Morrison, 2002), schools using a whole school approach develop this by delivering through the use of emotional literacy. As the findings in chapter 7 reveal, a whole school approach that develops pupil awareness by teaching through emotional literacy occur largely at Modern Eastern Suburban School. To confer with Salmivalli's findings (2005), during the focus groups pupils are more willing to either intervene or inform and agree that telling a teacher is beneficial for the long term.

The second restorative approach is emotional literacy (Morrison 2002; Ahmed and Braithwaite 2006; Goleman 1995 in Sharp, 2000 and Lewis 2006). Academics such as Ahmed and Braithwaite (2006: 364) indicate that this is an effective means to reduce bullying as teaching pupils to become emotionally literate allows them to use alternative approaches towards violence and dysfunctional relationships (Ahmed and Braithwaite 2006). Both secondary schools in this study use an emotional literacy approach during pastoral care classes, such as in Circle Time and in Citizenship Class, with the aim of creating a harmonious atmosphere amongst pupils in the schools. During the interviews, pupils generally show their support for an increase in restorative education that was directed at all pupils, not just perpetrators. This would ensure that pupils have maximum awareness and understanding of the consequences of bullying.

When reviewing victims' experiences and coping mechanisms, the majority of pupils believe that the main option for victims is to do nothing, believing that most victims prefer to remain silent. The broader literature on bullying argues that victims prefer to remain silent, or at best confide in a friend, rather than engage with the formal school systems (Hunter *et al.,* 2004). Hunter *et al.,* (2004:378), particularly emphasize that confiding in a teacher was more common amongst younger pupils, but that this diminished with age (Hunter *et al.,* 2004) which indicates that under-reporting remains a big problem for schools. Yet, the broader literature has examined these factors through employing quantitative research and therefore fails to document why pupils believe that victims would prefer to remain silent or at best confide in a friend.

This thesis considers in detail the various explanations offered by pupils as to why many prefer not to tell an adult, and therefore, unlike the academic research, clearly suggests that under-reporting incidents exists and is a major problem for schools. However, a few studies (Oliver and Candappa 2007; 2003; Smith and Shu 2000), have similarly noted that primarily, victims fear reprisal of the incidents of bullying. Where the perpetrators have discovered that victims have informed an adult, this can often result in further and more serious bullying. Also this research highlights that many pupils feel that if victims inform a teacher or parent, there is a risk that the whole bullying investigation can be blown out of proportion. Pupils believe that victims are also reluctant to tell a teacher because many lack faith in them and the system. This is largely discovered at Old East End Community College and the School for the Excluded. This research identifies that many pupils believe teachers do not take reported incidents of bullying seriously unless there is some physical evidence, a characteristic that has briefly been noted in the wider academic research (Ellis and Shute, 2007: 660). Similarly, in their research, Ellis and Shute (ibid) find that teachers only respond to incidents they deem to be serious, and when dealing with reported incidents that they consider as minor, they use their morale reasoning as well as considering if they had enough time to deal with the incident. The teachers therefore prefer to leave what they consider to be less serious incidents to the pupils to resolve (Ellis and Shute, 2007). To pupils, all cases of bullying are serious and important, and the failure to prioritise all incidents only enhances under-reporting. There is however limited research to date exploring the relationship between prioritisation of incidents of bullying and reporting, demonstrating the need for further academic research. The socio-economic environment and ethos of the school can also assist to understand why pupils, particularly at Old East End Community College, hold such beliefs, that informing a teacher is ineffective. Minimal resources are devoted to dealing with bullying and racism where funding is restricted. Unlike Modern Eastern Suburban School, which utilizes a variety of support mechanisms, including a school counsellor, Old East End Community College is restricted primarily to House Tutors.

Academic research that examines school intervention argues that schools tend to intervene using punishment and the monitoring and recording of incidents that are reported (Samara and Smith, 2008; Ellis and Shute, 2007; Dake *et al.,* 2003 and Rigby, 2002). Schools also issue sanctions in the form of immediate punishment, such as detention, suspension, denying pupils small privileges and in many cases the requirement that the bully apologizes to the victim (Rigby, 2002). Research establishes that schools conduct their own forms of monitoring in order to raise awareness of the scale of the problem. The study by Samara and Smith (2008) identifies that many schools do this by encouraging pupils to complete anonymous questionnaires (Samara and Smith, 2008). The work of Ellis and Shute, (2007) also helps to put pupils' opinions, which favoured punitive measures, into perspective. Their findings reveal that where teachers believe the seriousness of the bullying incident, they would intervene. However, most often where they perceive minor incidents occurring, they would ignore taking any stringent actions. Similarly, pupils from Old East End Community College largely express that this is the case in their school. Where pupils lack faith in reporting bullying incidents to teachers, it usually derives from this perceived complacent attitude (Ellis and Shute, 2007).

The broader literature on anti-racist preventative measures identifies that schools implement these through multicultural approaches and anti-racist education (Ratcliffe 2004; Raby, 2004). The research identifies that these didactic approaches serve the purpose of raising pupils' awareness of other cultures and identities, as well as teaching pupils the importance of integration. However, criticism of teaching styles indicates that they can also lead to divisions amongst European and non-European pupils. Whilst researchers (Woolfson, 2004; Richardson and Miles, 2009) argue that MCE and ARE have limitations, eradicating anti-racism in schools would be a step back (Richardson and Miles 2009). Instead, academic research has argued that teaching strategies can be improved in order to allow pupils to understand, for example, why refugees and asylum seekers reside in the UK. Woolfson (2004) particularly argues that in order for substantial improvement to occur schools need to both recognize that the problem of racism exists and that teaching strategies and styles need to be implemented whole-heartedly. This helps to explain where findings have identified that the manifestation of racist bullying has been downplayed in schools.

Academic research has important implications for the way school bullying and racist bullying are conceptualized and treated. As identified by Connolly and Keenan, (2002) schools appear often to condone racist behaviour, as the teachers inadvertently hold racist prejudicial beliefs. They recommend a need for more effective anti-racist measures as well as more encouragement for social cohesion. Since the early 1990's government legislation has compelled schools to acknowledge that the problem exists. Existing research on anti-bullying prevention and intervention measures reveal that it has had some success, yet research also indicates that teaching strategies have room for improvement. Yet, few studies concentrate on combining a sanctioning approach along with a holistic preventative approach. The findings from this research study highlight pupils' desire for such a combination and one that is long term. For instance, counselling for the entire school and not the younger aged pupils has been desired by pupils. Furthermore, sanctioning is expressed to be used as an immediate action, but one that is not over used, instead regular education is desired to occur as part of the curriculum or during lunch time/after school sessions. This is an area where further research could be developed as it would be most beneficial to compare and contrast pupils' perceptions on the need for an increase in a combination of all three measures using schools.

At present, all schools follow the Department for Education guidelines and adhere to their anti-bullying policy and discrimination policies under the Equality Act, 2010. These policies formally require all schools to deal and work towards eradicating all forms of bullying by implementing preventative and intervention measures as well as appropriate sanctioning. As the findings reveal, pupils desire for a combination of all three approaches and for these to be employed on a long term basis. At Old East End Community College, the intervention approach is met through support by house tutors however, is limited to friendship exercises through 'Circle Time' classes, once a week for an hour. However, there are frequent appearances by youth workers who work with pupils and the school also uses a sanctioning approach. Yet at Modern Eastern Suburban School, a variety of the approaches have been used. As immediate punishment a 'cooler' for the delinquent pupil is used regularly. Anti-bullying education and awareness takes place during pastoral classes such as Personal, Social, Health and Education and Citizenship classes, yet the curriculum is limited to a term. The school is strong, however, in its intervention approach and implements a variety of mechanisms, such as learning, peer and lunchtime mentors. The presence of a counsellor and visual awareness of anti-bullying through posters designed by pupils are placed around the school walls. There are also posters with hotline numbers of organisations such as ChildLine. Whilst the support is varied and positive, much of this is targeted to pupils in years 7 and 8, for example lunchtime peer support and the school counsellor, therefore, there is a desire for support for all ages. At the School for the Excluded, sanctioning involves parents and is a process that is employed frequently. Anti-bullying education is also delivered during Personal, Social Health and Education classes during the term, yet the intervention approach is limited to teachers providing support. As this is a special needs school, all three mechanisms of support are targeted to all pupils. Currently various preventative measures that are class based, are short term group and individual based exercises. This thesis makes a contribution towards policy, as long term anti-bullying and anti-racist education would require developments and structural changes to be made within the national school curriculum.

Summary

Overall, the findings suggest that pupils' understanding of bullying and racist bulling are influenced by their own life experiences, located within their own neighbourhood, family and school environment. Specifically, they suggest that, whilst perpetrators are often seen as individual agents identified by particular 'individual' traits, the behaviour of perpetrators of racist bullying is often explained with recourse to a discussion of the victim traits, such as lifestyle, background and culture. The PhD has indicated that school responses need to involve the whole school and incorporate emotional literacy approach although young people also wish to see immediate and often harsh punishment.

There remains a need to further explore these themes and issues across different schools, age ranges and ethnic groups in England and Wales. This study reflects the research findings from one inner city. Additional areas of research that this PhD recommends are: Firstly, that racist bullying is an issue that requires further exploration in schools, especially in the context of school anti-bullying policies and the Equality Act 2010. Secondly, further research is needed into the ways in which different school policies impact on young people, particularly contrasting a narrower and a more holistic approach.

APPENDICES

Appendix 1: Spider Diagram, Focus Group, Year 8. Modern Eastern Suburban School

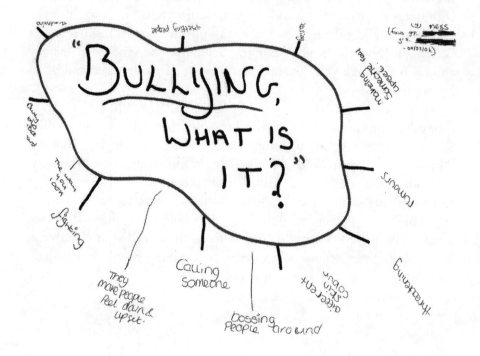

Appendix 2: Spider Diagram, Focus Group, Year 7. Modern Eastern Suburban School

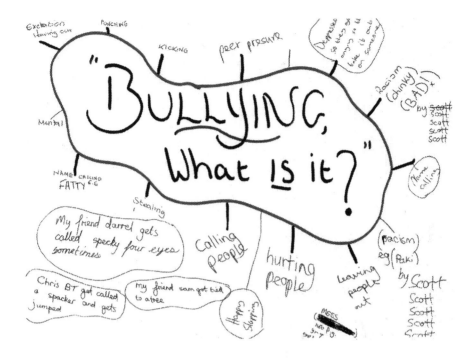

Appendix 3: Spider Diagram, Focus Group, Year 7. Old East End Community College

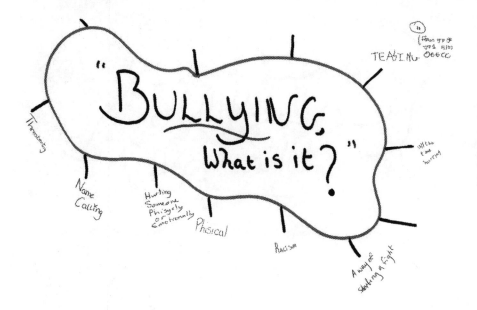

Appendix 4: Spider Diagram, Focus Group, Year 9. Old East End Community College

Appendix 5: Racism Learning Module/Activities.

Using Social and Emotional Learning to Promote Confidence and Pride in Ethnic Difference and Diversity

Overall learning objective/aim

To allow adults and young people to consider and celebrate ethnic differences and diversity and to encourage confidence, pride and tolerance in being different

Overview

This module is intended to support adults (parents; educators; teachers; community workers) and young people (aged 8-17+) to learn, discuss and understand mixed culture and the environment in America through the use of social and emotional teaching and learning. It intends to enable individuals to obtain an understanding of 'others' and general racial stereotyping, what it means to the individual from a minority ethnic group (MEG) as well as to the white community.

The module is developed in two parts. Part one of the module focuses on adult learning and discussion around racial cultural backgrounds, identifying cultural differences and racial stereotyping in and out of the school environment, discuss federal, state and local legislation/policies and identify ways in which these can be deterred. Part two of the module is designed to implement these learning's to pupils during class time and after school hours in social youth groups. This will ensure that adults support young people using a social and emotional approach in order to eliminate racial stereotyping and promote tolerance and pride in ethnic difference and diversity. The module can be delivered by adults over a period of three sessions at approximately an hour per session.

Module Learning Objectives:

1) To explore power and privilege issues from the perspectives of (i) individuals from MEG and (ii) individuals who are of a Caucasian race.

2) To identify cultural differences amongst various communities such as; Spanish/Latino; Asian; South Asian; African American communities and consider the socio-economic and geographical factors.
3) To identify cultural aspects that incites racial stereotypes; racial prejudice; racial violence and harassment in schools and in the community.
4) To identify systems and structures in schools that may impacts dealing with issues of race, class, gender, sexual orientation, age, religion, ethnicity, etc.
5) To discuss ways in which such stereotyping, racial harassment and violence can be eliminated; promoting of mixed race and culture as well as individuals from MEG's embracing their own culture whilst integrating.

Module One: Learning Objectives (and activities)

1. Explore what it means to be of a minority ethnic group

Introduction

Very often members from minority ethnic groups, particularly young people identify themselves as individuals growing up with two cultures, yet feel different to those from a Caucasian race. This includes undergoing daily differences with family life routine to cultural and religious differences. Yet, by and large, young people from minority ethnic groups desire to also blend in with their non-ethnic counterparts. As individuals from minority ethnic groups raised in the US, various issues may arise due to physical and cultural differences.

Module one is aimed for parents, teachers and young people to identify and acknowledge key physical and cultural differences between young people from minority ethnic groups, to those from a Caucasian race with the intention to draw out possible challenges that each may come across.

Key questions to consider during the discussion:

BULLYING AND RACIST BULLYING IN SCHOOLS

- How do individuals from MEG's perceive themselves at home and then at school and in the community?
- What challenges do they face at home and in trying to 'fit in' with their white and ethnic counterparts?
- How do individuals of a Caucasian race feel amongst mixed ethnic groups, particularly in an environment where they are of the minority? Included/excluded? What factors cause this? Social climate of the school
- What challenges do they face and why?

(Activities: Questionnaire—10 mins
Discussion—15 mins,

'The Bag Exercise'—30 mins. To allow participants briefly experience rank and privilege, especially economic class.

Module One—Questionnaire

1) In your home and local community environment, would you agree that there is a fairly vast population made up of minority ethnic groups (MEG's)?

Not at all _____
Somewhat _____
Agree _____
Strongly agree _____
N/A _____

2) Who are they?

American Indian or Alaskan Native (not Hispanic or Latino)
_____
Hispanic or Latino _____
Asian _____
South Asian _____
Italian American _____
Native Hawaiian or other Pacific Islander (not Hispanic or Latino) _____

White (not Hispanic or Latino) _____
Two or more races (not Hispanic or Latino) _____

3) Do you identify more with one aspect of your ethnic identity than others in the home?

   (a) Yes _____ No _____
   (b) In school? Yes _____ No _____

If yes, in what ways?

_____

_____

_____

_____

_____

_____

_____

4) If any, what challenges are met with growing up in a mixed race environment? (answers may range from food, religion, cultural attitude, dress or any other aspects)

_____

_____

_____

_____

Please explain:

_____

_____

_____

_____

_____

_____

_____

_____

5) How do you believe your MEG background is perceived by others?

_____

_____

_____

_____

_____

6) How do you perceive your ethnicity is ranked in order of preference by others?

Quite important? _____
Important? _____
Equal perception? _____
Less important? _____
None at all? _____

7) What do you believe are the positive aspects of living amongst MEG's in your home and community location and at school?

_____

_____

_____

_____

_____

_____

_____

8) As individuals of a Caucasian race, are you in a:

(a) Minority in your home area and local community? Yes _____/No _____

(b) Majority in your school? Yes _____/No _____

9) What, if any challenges do you face at home/at school? Why?

_____

_____

_____

_____

_____

_____

_____

_____

_____

_____

_____

Thank you for your time in completing this questionnaire!

The Bag Exercise

GOAL:

Give participants a quick experience of rank and privilege, especially economic class

TIME: 10 minutes explanation and play. De-brief can take up to an hour, depending on facilitation purposes.

SPECIAL MATERIALS: Brown paper lunch bags, enough for one for each participant. Packages of small multi-coloured candies (Skittles, M&Ms, Smarties, Goodies, JuJubes, Jelly Beans). 4 larger wrapped chocolates, or 4 mini chocolate bars). Mixed variety of prizes, enough for half the participants (big bag of Chips, large chocolate bar, T-Shirt from your drawer that you no longer use, can of dog food, book off your shelf that you no longer need, ugly knickknack that someone gave you years ago. It is important that the prizes should differ in relative value, so that later prize-winners have less choice and get "worse" prizes.

PREPARATION: Mark the outside of the bags. For a group of 20, give 2 bags a yellow star, 3 bags brown squares and the reminder a green triangle. These markings make it easier to fill the bags, and ensure that the facilitator knows who got which type of bag. Fill bags.

BULLYING AND RACIST BULLYING IN SCHOOLS

Brown Bags: Leave one bag empty. Put one small candy in the other bag, making sure that it unlike any other candy in the room.

Green Bags: Put 3 or 4 candies in each bag, varying in colour and type, but ensuring that there are other candies of same colour and type in the room.

Yellow Bags: Put the four chocolates in one bag

Put all the extra candies in the other bag, so that it is large and full.

How to do the exercise

Tell participants that the goal of this exercise is to get four candies of the same color and type (for instance, 4 blue Smarties). They will be able to talk during this exercise. Once they have got the four identical candies, they are to come to the front of the room and choose a prize. Ostentatiously display the prizes and show off each one to the group. Ask if there are questions. Give out the bags, asking people not to look into them. I give out the bags randomly, with one exception: if there is someone who is really marginalized in the room, I ensure that they do not get one of the brown bags—that just increases their sense of victimization and isolation. Say "Go"—and people start to trade/cooperate/steal to get the required 4 identical candies. give out prizes as people come forward, being sure to call out their victory loudly (and so put pressure on others)

Possible de-brief questions:

How are you feeling?

* What happened in the exercise?
* What gave some people more power than others in this game? What gives some people more power than others in life? (De-brief on rank and privilege)
* What links do you see to real life?

Expected trends to expect: people with brown bags often "opt out" of exercise. People with yellow bags get their first, and then may think about charity. People with less in their bags notice the disparity in bags; people with more in their bags don't notice the disparity.

Tool designed by Karen Ridd in Winnipeg, Canada 1999.

Module Two: Learning Objectives (and activities)

2. Identify cultural differences amongst various communities

Introduction

It can be viewed that the United States of America consists of the most minority ethnic groups and hence the most culturally diverse than any other country worldwide. The state of New York alone is known to be one of most ethnic diverse than most states. New York City particularly is multicultural. Approximately 36% of the city's population is foreign-born, one of the highest among US cities. The Ten nations constituting the largest sources of modern immigration to New York City are: *Dominican Republic, China, Jamaica, Guyana, Mexico, Ecuador, Haiti, Trinidad and Tobago, Colombia*, and *Russia*. As of the 2005 consensus, the nine largest ethnic groups in New York City are:

African American, African or Caribbean, Puerto Ricans, Italians, West Indians, Dominicans, Chinese, Irish, Russian, and *German*. The Puerto Rican population of New York City is the *largest outside Puerto Rico* (Wikipedia 2012).

In consideration of the above facts, particularly in New York schools, further consideration must be given to the curriculum that values cultural diversity and that the school responds as effectively as possible to prevent racism. The objective of module two is to enable parents, teachers and children/young people to consider and discuss immediate differences and ways in which they impact upon various neighborhoods.

Key questions to consider during the discussion:

- Consider immediate physical differences and relate these to cultural differences e.g., skin color; dress; language; food; religions
- In the 5 Boroughs of New York, which communities dominate various Boroughs; neighborhoods?
- What are the socio-economic differences?
- How do these impact upon community lifestyle and education?

(Activities: 'My Multicultural Self'—where conflict can be resolved through awareness, understanding and acceptance and 'Walking Across the Room'. To increase awareness of 'others in the group' as well as increasing awareness in individuals of their own issues around difference
30-40 mins, Resource 'www.tolerance.org' and
'Diversity Welcome', 'www.trainingforchange.org')

My Multicultural Self

- Keywords: Disability; Diversity and inclusion; Gender; Race and ethnicity; Religion; Sexual orientation; Stereotypes and bias; Wealth and poverty
- Level: Grades 3 to 5; Grades 6 to 8; Grades 9 to 12

In today's multicultural schools and classrooms, resolving conflict means being culturally aware.

Framework

Before endeavoring to develop cultural knowledge and awareness about others, we must first uncover and examine personal social and cultural identities. Guided self-reflection allows us to better understand how social group memberships inform who we are. This exercise is an important vehicle in any peer conflict mediation program to help students embrace the concept of being culturally responsive and culturally sensitive.

Objectives

- Students will identify at least 5 facets of their multicultural selves
- Students will reflect on how any one identity facet shapes the way they view the world
- Students will understand the many reasons that miscommunication can occur

Materials

- Teacher prepares model of their own identity before presentation
- Copy of student *handout* (PDF) for each student (see below)

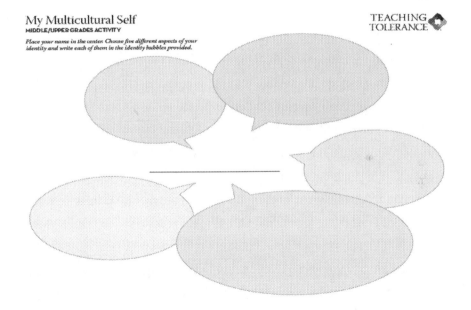

Introduction

What is culture? It is a shared system of meanings, beliefs, values and behaviors through which we interpret our experiences. Culture is learned, collective and changes over time. Culture is generally understood to be "what we know that everyone like us knows."

BULLYING AND RACIST BULLYING IN SCHOOLS

The following exercise explores the roots of cultural learning by naming aspects of identity important to each individual. It highlights the multiple dimensions of our identities and addresses the importance of self-identification.

Step One

The teacher should complete a handout in advance to serve as a model for students. Use an overhead or simply draw your multicultural self-components on the chalkboard. Example:

Mrs. Fattori
Mother—Teacher—Buddhist—Biracial—Marathon Runner

Share how each of your identity bubbles is a lens through which you see the world. Mrs. Fattori might share, for instance, that when she became a mother she became stronger and more sensitive, stronger for having made and given life as well as knowing she would do anything to protect her child. But she also became more sensitive to young life of all kinds around her, whether it be other children, nature or a student just learning to love a certain academic subject.

Step Two

Distribute a handout to each student and give the following directions: "Place your name in the center figure. Use the identity bubbles to name aspects of yourself that are important in defining who you are."

Allow students time to silently reflect on what they have written. Invite them to form pairs and share why the descriptors they chose are important to them. If time permits, invite pairs to introduce one another to the class.

For middle school/high school students:

Form small groups around the same or similar descriptors, i.e. daughters, softball players, band member. Discuss similarities and differences among those of the same "group."

Step Three

Have students reflect on how each individual identity colors and shapes the way they view and interact with the world. The teacher can use her own identity shells to illustrate this concept. Mrs. Fattori, for example, might share how being biracial allows her to be a part of two worlds.

When the teacher is sure that students understand this concept, discuss as a class or in small groups:

- How would you feel if someone ignored one of your multicultural identity bubbles?
- Can you see how ignoring one of your identity bubbles could cause miscommunication? Can anyone give an example?
- Do you have more than these 5 identities?
- If your 5 identity bubbles are communicating with a group of 5 others, how many identities are interacting? (30 minimum)

Set up the next step by sharing with students that we have many identities in our multicultural selves. Not being aware of our own or others' identities causes miscommunication.

Step Four

Our identities are NOT static. We are shaped and reshaped by what goes on around us and our identities constantly change as well. Give examples:

- A parent dies and this reshapes the way we see the world
- We fall in love and this reshapes the way we see the world
- We fall out of love and this reshapes the way we see the world
- We experience an act of violence and this reshapes the way we see the world

So, what we once knew to be true about ourselves and others can change over time. For this reason, we should always try to suspend judgment, ask questions of others and talk with those different from us as much as possible.

Adapted from Ed Change Multicultural Pavilion, *www.tolerance.org*

Diversity Welcome

[*This opening tool is very adaptable to the group. It can be used to name every ethnic group in the room (over 30 groups!). The objective is to name the range of diversity and welcome it—there's power in naming.*

Past experience in using it is that people may feel like "this is hokey" at the beginning of it—but after five or six rotations people tend to relax and begin to accept the welcoming.]

"I'd like to welcome . . .
(and then facilitator names)

- Women, Men, Transgender People & Spirits
- Your bodies
- Specifically name states or provinces represented—pause and invite more input
- Those living with a chronic medical condition, visible or invisible
- Dyslexics
- Your dreams and desires and passions
- Languages spoken by people here (try to know as many as possible ahead of time): Spanish, English, German . . .
- Survivors
- People of Hispanic descent, African descent, Asian descent, European descent
- gay, lesbian, bisexual, heterosexual, queer
- People who identify as activists, and people who don't
- Those in their teens-20s—30s—40s—50s—60s—70s—80s (depending on group)
- Single, married, partnered, dating, celibate, sexually active
- Your emotions: joy & blis, grief, rage, indignation, contentment, disappointment
- Those who support you to be here: Who make it possible
- Your families
- Mystics, seekers, believers of all kinds

- Those dear to us who have died
- Our elders: Those here in this room, in our lives, and those who have passed away
- The Spirits of the Delaware and Arrawak, the natives who lived in this area before the Europeans came (find out beforehand)
- Anyone else who would like to be welcomed?

BY Matt Guynn *www.trainingforchange.org*

Module Three: Learning Objectives (and activities)

3. Identifying cultural aspects that incite racial stereotype, prejudice, violence and harassment in schools and the community

Introduction

Ethnic diversity consists of different cultural and religious practices that often incite stereotype amongst those who have little understanding of minority ethnic backgrounds. How 'others' are perceived by many and how they are treated, depends largely upon the level of exposure, integration followed by an attitude of tolerance and respect. To agree with Gomez, (Quisenberry and McIntyre, 2002; 23), understanding the differences among groups of people will be easier after children and young people have had the opportunity to look at their own families and discuss similarities and differences in everyday routines and then learn about the daily practices of minority ethnic groups. One way that teachers and parents may begin to address this is by identifying everyday practices that all people engage in, while acknowledging that they may do so in different ways. Curriculum activities such as these can help promote intercultural understanding and may well become part of the school curriculum.

Module three is aimed at allowing parents and educators to work with young people to identify all cultural differences, how they can lead to negative perceptions and actions.

Key questions to consider during the discussion:

- Provide examples of cultural issues from various ethnic groups that may incite racial stereotype, prejudice, violence and harassments? Such as, accent, dress, food etc.
- Why would these incite racism?
- What other aspects could incite stereotype and prejudice?

(Activity: 'Checking on Stereotypes' 20 mins. Increasing awareness on how easily people are stereotyped and ways to eliminate stereotypical thinking. 'Defining Multicultural Terminology' 30 mins. Understanding other cultures, Resource, 'www.tolerance.org')

Checking on Stereotypes

- Keywords: *Stereotypes and bias*
- Level: Grades 3 to 5; 6 to 8; 9 to 12

Always guard against the tendency to believe that everyone within a given identity group believes the same way.

Objectives

- Students will identify stereotypes they've experienced or heard
- Students will discuss how these stereotypes are not always true
- Students will identify specific ways to break down stereotypes

Materials

- 3x5 index cards for students

Stereotypes represent a belief or assumed knowledge of an entire group based on an experience with or information about a member or members of that group. It is an easy way of categorizing complex individuals.

Stereotyping often occurs because persistent messages are reinforced by family members, in places of worship, on school campuses and through the media. Stereotyping can be subconscious, where it subtly influences our decisions and actions, even in people who do not want to be biased.

A key component in the development of culturally responsive conflict resolutions models is developing tools to identify and break down stereotyping. Stereotypes can be broken. When we bring people together to open up and honestly share who they are, stereotypes begin to shatter. We discover that other people are not the mental picture created by our stereotype.

Distribute index cards and invite students to write down a stereotype they have heard about themselves or someone close to them.

Shuffle the cards and invite a few students to select one, read it aloud and talk about how they think a person would feel to be stereotyped in that manner.

Close by sharing ways to eliminate stereotypes or by developing class or club pledges where signers commit to ending stereotyping.

Follow-Up Activity

Discussion or writing prompts

1. How did it feel to share a way you have been stereotyped?
2. Did you hear a stereotype shared today that you once bought into? If so, what was it and why did you use it?
3. What are your ideas on eliminating stereotypes?

Defining Multicultural Terminology

- Keywords: Disability; Diversity and inclusion; Gender; History; Race and ethnicity; Religion; Sexual orientation; Stereotypes and bias; Wealth and poverty
- Level: Grades 3 to 5; Grades 6 to 8; Grades 9 to 12

It is important to employ many different lessons to encourage students to seek understanding of other cultures.

To this end, an introductory lesson that focuses on identifying, defining and applying multicultural terms allows students to think they know what a word means, only to discover their application of it might be flawed.

BULLYING AND RACIST BULLYING IN SCHOOLS

To begin, make up a list of multicultural terms. The students are broken into groups of four to six. Each group is given the list of terms and asked to use teamwork to define the words. In groups, share definitions and come to a consensus for each definition. This actively involves everyone in the process.

After agreeing on the definitions, students are given situations that involve one or more of the terms—a situation that illustrates both prejudice and xenophobia, for example, compared with another that illustrates discrimination. These are real-life situations, and students love to "solve" the answer for each one. As a class go over each situation to reach a consensus, this should allow students to begin to feel more confident in their understanding and application of these terms. Students can then go home to search out examples in the newspaper, television or online. The students are required to find at least two articles and defend their choice, in writing, of the terms they applied.

To fully assess the students' understanding of these terms, use the quick quiz in which they must match the terms to the definitions that all agreed upon.

Terms used:

Bias
Discrimination
Stereotype
Prejudice
Ethnocentrism
Nationality
Race
Diversity
Ethnicity
Xenophobia
Culture

By Susan C. Hunt, Hampton Public School District
Hampton, N.J. *www.tolerance.org*

DR. SAIRAH QURESHI

Module Four: Learning Objectives (and activities)

4. Identifying systems and structures in schools that may impacts dealing with issues of race, class, gender, sexual orientation, etc.

Introduction

In order for teachers and parents to identify various support mechanisms that schools employ to combat all forms of prejudice, there is a need to understand government legislation towards bias-based bullying.

The A-832 regulations and Respect for All initiative stipulates that all schools have a mandatory duty to maintain a safe and supportive learning and educational environment that is free from harassment, intimidation, and/or bullying committed by students against other students on account of race, color, creed, ethnicity, national origin, citizenship/immigration status, religion, gender, gender identity, gender expression, sexual orientation, disability or weight. Such bias-based harassment, intimidation and/or bullying is prohibited.

Bias-based harassment, intimidation and/or bullying is any intentional written, verbal, or physical act that a student or group of students directs at another student or students which:

(1) is based on a student's actual or perceived race, color, creed, ethnicity, national origin, citizenship/immigration status, religion, gender, gender identity, gender expression, sexual orientation, disability or weight;
(2) substantially interferes with a student's ability to participate in or benefit from an educational program, school sponsored activity or any other aspect of a student's education;
(3) creates a hostile, offensive, or intimidating school environment;
(4) substantially interferes with a student's mental, emotional or physical well-being;
(5) otherwise adversely affects a student's educational opportunities.

Bias-based harassment, intimidation and/or bullying may take many forms and can be physical, verbal or written. Written harassment, intimidation and/or bullying include electronically transmitted acts, e.g., via Internet, cell phone, personal digital assistant or wireless handheld device.

Such behavior includes, but is not limited, to:
Physical violence;
stalking; threats, taunts, teasing;
aggressive or menacing gestures;
exclusion from peer groups designed to humiliate or isolate;
using derogatory language; furthermore making derogatory jokes or name calling or slurs;

written or graphic material, including graffiti, containing comments or stereotypes that are electronically circulated or are written or printed (NYC Department of Education, A-832 Regulations, pp1-2).

Through a discussion of government legislation on bias-based bullying, Module four allows parents and educators to identify the major problem that occurs in the school. The module should also allow them to reflect upon various ways in which their local school supports victims and young people, identifying any ways in which the system can be improved upon.

Key questions to consider during the discussion:

- Does the school pastoral (emotional wellbeing) curriculum cover all issues on discrimination?
- How often are they taught in class?
- What other support mechanisms are there for pupils?
- Do all pupils know whom to contact if an issue of racist bullying arises?

(Activities: bearing all key questions in mind:

Survey-questionnaire, discuss local, state and federal policies/ legislation and Respect for All initiative. What challenges do schools face? 30 mins)

Module Four—Questionnaire

1) Read the current A-832 Anti-bullying/discriminatory legislation and Respect for All initiative. What is the key mission that schools must abide by for pupils?

_____
_____
_____
_____
_____

2) Understanding the key duty for all schools toward children and young people, does your school include one or more of the following support programs/mechanisms:

Citizenship courses: Yes _____ No _____
Anti-bullying curriculum: Yes _____ No _____
Multicultural education: Yes _____ No _____
School counselors: Yes _____ No _____
Peer mentors: Yes _____ No _____
Pastoral support staff/teachers: Yes _____ No _____

3) How well does the school follow the respected duties so stipulated by the A-832 and Respect for All initiative and guidelines?

Excellent: _____
Very well: _____
Satisfactory: _____
Average: _____
Poor: _____

4) How efficient is the schools own discriminatory policy?

Excellent: _____
Very good: _____
Satisfactory: _____
Average: _____
Poor: _____

5) Do you believe that incidents of bias-based bullying, including racist stereotype may go un-reported in the school? Yes _____ No _____

6) Do you believe in peer mentoring? Yes _____ No _____ Why?

_____

_____

_____

_____

_____

7) In which ways do you believe bias-based bullying could be effectively taught in class?

_____

_____

_____

_____

_____

_____

8) In which ways do you think extra-curricular activities can be used to support victims?

Teaching young people to act as Upstanders and positive role models: Yes _____ No _____
School counselor: Yes _____ No _____
Public Outreach workers: Yes _____ No _____
Any other suggestion:

_____

_____

_____

_____

9) What major problems do you believe the school may encounter(s) in dealing with reported incidents of bias-based bullying as well as raising awareness?

_____

_____

_____

_____

_____

_____

_____

_____

_____

_____

_____

_____

Thank you for your time in completing this questionnaire

Module Five: Learning Objectives (and activities)

5. Discuss ways in which stereotyping, racial harassment and violence can be eliminated; promote mixed race and culture, pride and confidence in MEG's whilst they integrate.

Introduction

Assessing the relationships with peers, as well as with teachers/school staff are key to understanding what, if any, forms of stereotyping, prejudice, harassment and violence may occur. In which ways would teachers consider raising awareness to young people against stereotyping and prejudice?

It could be suggested that implementing a multicultural curriculum would be an effective force to rid of cultural sensitivity. Prior to presenting children and young people with multicultural issues, it is important to be prepared that all activities are safely and responsibly conducted as well as allowing young people to be able to explore their thoughts and perceptions concerning the issues being presented.

Furthermore, the teacher should become culturally synchronized with students in order for the teachers to understand the cultural repertoire of their classroom and work towards expanding their own cultural horizons . . . i.e. learning from each other is beneficial to all. A further suggestion would be that the teacher should ensure that the culture of the classroom is reflective of the students' cultures, relationships, becoming familiar not only with the demography represented by the students, but also with issues that may arise and ways in which young people can support each other. This can be supported by the teacher creating an atmosphere that integrates multicultural issues into the curriculum, rather than presenting isolated cases in which students are exposed to such issues. (Mattai, 2002; 28) These suggestions provide an idea of the complexities that can arise when addressing issues of diversity.

Module five is aimed at teachers' brain storming ideas and perceptions with young people. Through working together on activities, conclude with policies and support mechanisms in order to eliminate racial stereotype and prejudices as well as promote confidence and pride in ethnic difference and diversity.

Key questions to consider during the discussion:

- Is my school doing all it can to effectively deal with race, class, gender, etc?
- What is the parent-pupil, teacher-pupil relationship like in my school?
- Are we as young people effectively taught to become mentors, upstanders and encouraged to report an adult if we witness an incident?
- Can young people confide in adults at our school?
- How much under-reporting really exists?—Little, none, moderate, severe?
- What multicultural activities take place? Would like to see take place?

(Activities: 'Getting Started: Respected Exercise' (20 mins); 'Developing a multicultural curriculum'—'Name Stories' (20 mins) 'Take a Stand for Others' (20-30 mins) Allow students to defend their stance for themselves and others against racism.

Resources:
'www.reachoutfornewfutures.org/tools/resources'
'www.edchange.org/multicultural/quizzes.html'
'www.edchange.org/multicultural/activities/activity.html'
'www.tolerance.org' & 'www.smdp.scoilnet.ie/racism.htm'

Getting Started: Respect Activity (Introductory Level)

Ask everyone to find someone in the room who they do not know. Instruct them to introduce themselves to that person, and spend five to ten minutes talking about respect. What does it mean for you to show respect, and what does it mean for you to be shown respect? After the allotted time, ask the participants to return to their seats, and open the discussion. What ideas did people discuss?

Common responses include the "Golden Rule," looking somebody in the eyes, being honest, and appreciating somebody's ideas even when you do not agree with them. Each of these responses offers interesting points of reflection. They each are informed culturally and hegemonically. So once people have returned to the big group for processing the activity, be sure to inquire where people's notions of "respect" come from and who those notions serve and protect. Does everybody really want to be treated the way you want to be treated? Is it respectful in every culture to make eye contact with whoever is speaking? What if somebody's ideas are oppressive—should we still respect them? And to whose benefit? It is important to mention that respect is a crucial ingredient in any discussion, but especially in a discussion of often-controversial issues such as racism, sexism, and economic injustice. The point is to learn from our differences—to understand each other's understanding. The point is *not* to agree. But the point, as well, is to reflect critically on our assumptions and socializations around the concept of respect.

This activity touches many bases. First, it starts the crucial path toward building a community of respect. This is the first step in maintaining a constructive exchange regarding issues related to equity and social justice. At the most basic level, participants meet someone they did not know and exchange ideas with that person. Second, the community is built through an understanding of how the group perceives respect and how we negotiate its meaning. Third, the similarities and differences in participants' ideas about respect begin to show the first signs of similarities and differences within the group on a larger level, often in ways that reflect power and privilege.

www.edchange.org (approx. 20 mins)

Exchanging Stories—Name Stories

Preparing and Assigning:

Ask participants to write short (one or two page) stories about their names. Leave the assignment open to individual interpretation as much as possible, but if asked for more specific instructions, suggest some or all of the following possibilities for inclusion in their stories:

- Who gave you your name? Why?
- What is the ethnic origin of your name?
- What are your nicknames, if any?
- What do you prefer to be called?

Encourage students to be creative. In the past, some have written poetry, included humor, and listed adjectives that described them etc. Be sure to let them know that they will be sharing their stories with the rest of the class.

Facilitator Notes:

In order to ensure that everybody has an opportunity to share her or his story, break into diverse small groups of five or six if necessary. Give participants the option either to read their stories or to share their stories from memory. Ask for volunteers to share their stories.

Points to remember:

1. Because some individuals will include very personal information in their stories, some may be hesitant to read them, even in the small groups. It is sometimes effective in such situations for facilitators to share their stories first. If you make yourself vulnerable, others will be more comfortable doing the same.
2. Be sure to allow time for everyone to share, whether reading their stories or sharing them from memory.
3. When everyone has shared, ask participants how it felt to share their stories. Why is this activity important? What did you learn?

Sample—My Personal Name Story:

According to my mother, "Paul" means "small". When I say that to other folks, they tell me it doesn't mean "small," though no one seems to know what it means.

My parents wanted to name me "Cameron." "Paul" goes back three or four generations, I'm not sure which. My father and his father and his father are all named "Paul." But my mother liked "Cameron," so "Cameron" it was. But then I was born . . . five weeks prematurely. I was a tiny baby. I was the itsy-bitsiest baby in the new baby room at the hospital. According to my mother, that was a sign. Remember, "Paul" means "small".

So I am Paul Cameron Gorski. My father is Paul Peter Gorski. The exception, of course, is when someone calls my parents' home for one of us. At that point we become Big Paul and Little Paul, the father Paul and the son Paul, or the older one and the younger one (my Dad doesn't appreciate that one too much). Sometimes people call and I'm too exhausted to explain to them the whole idea that there are two Pauls living in one house, so I just pretend to be Paul Peter, and give my Dad the message later. He doesn't seem to mind that, especially when the caller is trying to sell us something. Still, I hope he doesn't do the same thing.

Paul lends itself well to rhyming nicknames. Bill, a good friend of mine, calls me "Tall Paul". He does so sarcastically, usually after blocking one of my shots in a basketball game. I often have to remind him that the whole irony of that nickname is that, according to my mother, "Paul" means "small," which is very nearly the opposite of "tall." In high school, I was often called "Paul Mall" in reference to a brand of cigarettes, because, as they said, my ball handling skills were smokin'. And again, the irony is that generally the small players have better ball handling skills.

The truth of the matter is that I really don't know whether or not "Paul" means "small". Perhaps it means "Jedi warrior" or "sunflower" or "career student". No matter. I've never looked it up, and never will. According to my Mom, "Paul" means "small." That sounds good to me.

Paul C. Gorski, 1995-2012 *www.edchange.org* (approx. 20 mins).

Take a Stand

Level: Grades 6 to 8; Grades 9 to 12

This six-step activity prompts students to defend their stance on a topic

Exploring controversial issues relevant to the curriculum and students' personal lives is a continuing challenge. Use the Take-A-Stand structure to employ a six-step activity to prompt students both to choose and defend their stands on a topic. This will help students to develop a sense of voice and identity, while also engaging in class discussion and the writing process.

Pre-reading
Read the anti-racist poems (see below) and discuss issues related to a given theme.

Pre-writing
Students complete a seven-to-ten minute quick-write in which they express their ideas in response to the main theme of each poem.

Discussion

Students engage in a discussion in which they share their ideas and learn those of others. All points are charted and copied by the class.

Writing

Using the information compiled through the discussion, students write a persuasive short essay (no more than 2 pages) that includes an argument and three supporting ideas chosen from the class chart.

Discussion/Debate

Pose the most essential questions raised in the reading of the poems. Make participation in discussion of controversial topics optional. Encourage students to use details from their own lives as well as synthesized knowledge from the class exercise.

Reflect

Once all students have had a chance to speak, allow them time to reflect on their new ideas regarding the topic through either writing or art. By the end of this activity, students should have a greater understanding of the issues evoked by the poems.

Eric Eisner
University High School
Los Angeles, Calif.

ANTI—RACISM POEMS

RESPECT

Hey, what's the story and what's the crack?
I am white and you are black.
God made me and God made you,
Respect is what we got to do.
We cut our fingers, we bleed the same,
Different colours but different names.
We have things in common,
We like fun and games,
We run, we jump, we hop and skip,
And let no bad words pass our lips.
Because respect is what we got to do,
Repect from me and respect from you.

If you are being slagged because of your
hair colour
or the colour of your skin or your
language, don't try
to slag them back and hurt their feelings.
Just say you're proud, move on and find
new meanings.

By Conor

OUR HEARTS ARE ALL THE SAME

I go to school in Tallaght
And Darragh is my name
My classmates come in different colours,
But our hearts are all the same.

When I'm in the yard and hear
The bullies call children names,
Just because they've different skin,
It shows they have no brains.

Black, yellow white and brown,
We all should take a stand,
Say 'NO' to racism in Erin's Isle,
And the world will be just grand.

By Darragh

Appendix 6: Bullying Classroom Activities on Bystanders as Upstanders (Anti-Bullying Alliance)

The Role of Bystanders as Upstanders in Bullying

This activity is for pupils from Grade 6 upwards and should take about an hour.

Aim:

To highlight strategies and interventions that young people (YP) can use if they witness a bullying situation.

Intended learning outcomes:

- An increased knowledge of the role of bystanders in bullying situations
- An understanding of techniques to enable young people to safely intervene in a bullying situation
- An increased awareness of sources of support available to young people who witness bullying or who are being bullied

Suggested Success Measures:

- Over a period of time more young people are reporting bullying they have witnessed to adults and adults are intervening.
- Young people report that they feel much safer in their school.
- A mapping exercise before the lesson and two months later shows that young people feel there are fewer unsafe areas in school.
- Young people report (either verbally or in a questionnaire) that they are more likely to support someone they see being bullied and know the range of strategies they can take that will be the most effective.

BULLYING AND RACIST BULLYING IN SCHOOLS

You will need:
Post it notes
Pens
Flipchart paper or notice board
Photograph(s) of bullying situations (enclosed)
Intervention cards (enclosed)

How to do it: There are 5 exercises in this session:

1. *What is bullying?*

Ensure young people understand the term 'bullying'. Key features of bullying are the intention to hurt, repetition and imbalance of power. The Anti-Bullying Alliance defines bullying as the:

intentional, repetitive or persistent hurting of one person by another, where the relationship involves an imbalance of power.

Bullying can take different forms, such as:

- **Physical**, e.g. kicking, hitting, taking and damaging belongings
- **Verbal**, e.g. name calling, taunting, threats, making offensive remarks
- **Indirect**, e.g. spreading nasty stories about someone, gossiping, excluding people from social groups
- **Cyber**, e.g. sending nasty or threatening texts or e-mails, phone call bullying via mobile phone, picture/video clip bullying, chat-room bullying, bullying through Instant Messaging (IM) and bullying via websites.

2. *What is a Bystander?*

Ask the group to think of other words to describe a bystander. Examples are witness, onlooker and observer.

3. *Would you support the bullied person?*

This activity asks YP to consider reasons why they would or would not support the person being bullied and in what circumstances. (*Please note: this part of the session is not discussing how you could support the bullied person, as this is considered in part 4).*

Split the YP into small groups. Provide each group with a photograph(s), which illustrates a bullying incident. Ask the YP to consider reasons why they would not support the person being bullied in the photograph and write these on post it notes.

These should be placed on flipchart paper or a notice board under a heading 'No support'. Allow 10 minutes for this activity. Facilitate a discussion on the reasons they have given on why they would not support the bullied person.

Next, ask the YP to consider reasons why they should intervene and ask them to write these on post it notes and put under a heading 'Support'. Allow a further 10 minutes for this activity. Facilitate a further discussion on the reasons they have given in favor of supporting the bullied person.

4. *What could you do?*

This activity is to give YP some ideas of interventions they could use to stop a person being bullied.

In small groups again ask the YP to order the 9 statements provided based on their likely effectiveness. Allow 10 minutes for this activity. Facilitate a discussion on why the group have decided that some strategies may be more effective than others.

5. Hot Spots!

Offer the YP the chance to tell you where the bullying hot spots are at their school, youth club etc. You could provide a box or similar, so they can put their suggestions in anonymously. Make sure you follow up on this activity by informing the school or club of the YP concerns. It may also be useful to have a drawing or plan of the school/club and people mark with coloured stickers for severe, mild etc where the hotspots are.

BULLYING AND RACIST BULLYING IN SCHOOLS

Suggestions to help discussion:

Bystanders play a very important role in bullying situations. Bullying will stop in less than 10 seconds nearly 60% of the time when peers intervene (Pepler). See attached sheet entitled 'Role of Bystanders in Bullying'. Ideas to consider on the intervention strategies are also included.

Issues to consider:

Support sources available, e.g. ChildLine, Kidscape (see Role of Bystanders information sheet)

Final Message to YP: Don't just stand there—do something! It could make a difference. Some young people have come up with the following straplines, which could also be discussed: 'If you are not part of the solution, you are part of the problem'

'Get help, do not look on, do something'

Tell an adult.

Tell an older child.

Encourage the bullied person to tell someone.

Show your disapproval to the bully.

Walk away and ignore the bullying.

Tell the bully to stop, if it is safe to do so.

Use violence against the bully to make them stop.

Go and get a group of mates to help you stop the bullying.

Form a friendship group for the person being bullied to make sure they are not isolated.

As a bystander 'What could you do?'—Ideas to consider

- **Tell an Adult:**

Most adults will want to know about anything that is worrying. You may need to be persistent to ensure that the adult recognizes that something needs to be done. If necessary ask them what they are going to do.

- **Tell an older child:**

It may be a good idea for a young person to talk to someone older to tell them about the bullying. They may be able to support in stopping the bullying or advising what to do next.

- **Encourage the bullied person to tell someone:**

It is important that the bullied person talks to someone that they can trust and tell about the bullying. It is hoped that this person will help the bullied person think of ways of making the bullying stop.

- **Show your disapproval to the bully:**

You can do this by your lack of interest shown in your face or saying something to them. By telling the bully that you do not think what they are doing is right, you can make them think twice about their behaviour. It may make the bullying stop.

- **Walk away and ignore the bullying**

If you see someone being bullied, it may be tempting to ignore it. However, young people should always try and stop it. If they do nothing then they are saying that the bullying is ok. However walking away does deprive the bully of an audience.

- **Tell the bully to stop, if it is safe to do so:**

Be assertive and tell the bully to stop. It may make them think twice about their actions. It is important to make sure that the young person is safe and the bully does not take action against them for speaking out.

- **Use violence against the bully to make them stop:**

It is important to understand that using violence against the bully could get the young person into trouble. This is not the answer to stop bullying!

- **Go and get a group of mates to help you stop the bullying:**

This can be a very effective way of stopping bullies. A young person and a group of mates can tell the bully that what they are doing is wrong. By acting in a group it can be less scary than speaking out alone. This is the power of the bystander.

- **Form a friendship group for the person being bullied to make sure they are not isolated**

This is a very effective way of stopping the bullying because it limits the power of the bully who is more likely to target people who do not have friends. Friends tend to stick up for each other so the group immediately supports the bullied person.

Role of Bystanders as in Bullying—some research.

85% of bullying takes place with bystanders present (Craig and Pepler, 1997, O'Connell and others, 1999)

Research by Pepler should the following reasons why students did not intervene:

- Fear
- It's only a bit of fun
- Ignore it and it will go away
- They deserve it

Bullying will stop in less than 10 seconds nearly 60% of the time when peers intervene.

In playground observations, peers intervened in significantly more episodes than adults did (11% of episodes versus 4%).

A study by Rigby and Johnson (2004) assessed factors, which *incline* or *disincline* bystanders to help a child who is being bullied.

Factors that *incline* students to say they help someone who is being bullied:

- Empathy
- Perception that friends expect them to help
- Some experience of helping a victim in the past
- Age—primary age are more likely to help than secondary.

Factors that *disincline* students to help:

- A belief that people should look after themselves
- Fear of consequences of intervening e.g. embarrassment
- Feeling that one only has responsibility for one's friends
- Enjoyment of conflict
- Sadistic desire to hurt

Research in Finland by Salmivalli (1995, 1999) found that witnesses of bullying incidents can adopt particular roles. The following 'participant roles' were identified:

- **Assistants** who join in and assist the bully
- **Reinforcers** who do not actively attack the victim but give positive feedback to the bully, providing an audience by laughing and making other encouraging gestures
- **Outsiders** who stay away, not taking sides with anyone or becoming actively involved, but allowing the bullying to continue by their 'silent approval'

- **Upstanders** who show anti-bullying behaviour, comforting the victim, taking sides with them and trying to stop the bullying.

Lorna Vyse, Development Officer Young People's Services, Victim Support Norfolk Rita Adair, Anti-Bullying Alliance Eastern Regional Coordinator (2008)

Appendix 7 Anti-bullying class based activities on Upstanders

Bullying Prevention Lesson Plan: The Courage to Be an Upstander

By Naomi Drew, M.A.
Free Spirit Publishing

This lesson helps students build their courage and confidence so they can be upstanders for kids who are bullied.

Students will:

- reflect on why it takes courage to be an upstander for someone who is bullied
- learn specific steps for building their courage and think of other ways to do this as well
- role-play being upstanders for someone who's being bullied

Materials

- chart paper and marker
- handout: "What Real Kids Have to Say About Being an Upstander When Someone Is Bullied" (located at the end of this article)

Preparation

On chart paper, copy the following, leaving blank spaces so students can suggest additional entries:

Build Your Courage to Be an Upstander against Bullying

1. Practice the Dignity Stance. It will help you stand tall to help others.
2. Use deep breathing to keep your cool.
3. Rehearse your words.

4. Picture yourself helping assertively.
5. Partner up. Have a friend join you to confront someone who's bullying.

Introduction

Tell students that today they'll be learning more ways to build their courage "muscles" so they can be upstanders for kids who are bullied.

Ask: *What are you already doing to help when someone is being bullied?* Discuss.

Ask: *Why does it take courage to be an upstander? What stops you from helping someone who's being bullied?* Discuss, emphasizing that each time someone stands up against bullying, this helps put an end to it.

Ask: *What are some things you've learned that can help you gain the courage to be an upstander for kids who are bullied?* Discuss and review strategies that have been introduced.

Discussion

Pass out copies of "What Real Kids Have to Say About Being an Upstander When Someone Is Bullied." Ask for five volunteers to read aloud the quotes from kids who've been upstanders. Ask for students' responses.

Then direct their attention to "Build Your Courage to Be an Upstander Against Bullying" on the handout and chart. Go through steps 1-5 with students, discussing each one and answering questions. For the fifth step, help students recognize how partnering with another person can give them courage by not having to face the situation alone.

Then **ask:** *What else would give you the courage to be an upstander if you see someone who's being bullied?* Write suggestions on the board. Discuss, then ask students which two they find the most helpful. Add these to the chart. If there are more than two, include them as well.

BULLYING AND RACIST BULLYING IN SCHOOLS

Activity

Ask for four volunteers to role-play the following scenario, or another bullying scenario you think students will relate to:

> **Note:** Confronting a bullying situation alone can be daunting. For this reason many experts believe that it's preferable for kids to be upstanders in partner-ship. However, if no one else is around to buddy up with, it's helpful for kids to know how to do it alone. For this reason, you will want to vary the role playing so students can practice being upstanders alone and with others.

Jeffrey sees Tommy being bullied by Stewart on the playground. He decides to be an upstander for Tommy. Jeffrey stands tall, breathes deep, thinks of words to say, and walks over. Then he speaks directly to Stewart about what he's doing. Finally, he asks Tommy to hang out with him on another part of the playground.

After the role play, ask the volunteer who played Jeffrey: *How did it feel to be an upstander for Tommy? Was it easy to do?*

Ask for one new volunteer to join the others and play the part of a student named Claire.

Replay the scene, this time having Jeffrey ask Claire to partner up with him to be an upstander for Tommy.

After the role play, ask the student who played Jeffery: *How did it feel this time to be an upstander?*

Was it easier to do with Claire helping?

Also ask students: *What could have happened if no one had stepped in to help Tommy?*

Discuss, making sure to address students' questions or concerns about being upstanders in bullying situations.

Wrap-Up

Remind students that each time they practice being an upstander for those who are bullied they will strengthen their courage muscle. Say: The more upstanders we have, the closer we get to making ourselves and our school bully-proof.

What Real Kids Have to Say About Being an Upstander When Someone Is Bullied

In a national survey of more than 2,100 students in grades 3-6, kids wrote about finding the courage to be an upstander for someone who is being bullied. Here are some things they wrote:

- "It's hard when you see someone being bullied for something they can't help. If you're scared to help them, do it anyway. You have the right to stand up."
- "I tell the person who is bullying to quit it. Then I take the person who was being bullied to another place, away from the bully."
- "I tell the person who is bullying that what they're doing isn't right and they should stop."
- "I tell the person bullying to stop, and try to comfort the person who was being bullied."
- "I help kids who are bullied by staying with them. I've learned that kids who bully don't go after people if they have at least one friend."

Build Your Courage to Be an Upstander Against Bullying

1. Practice the Dignity Stance. It will help you stand tall to help others.
2. Use deep breathing to keep your cool.
3. Rehearse your words.
4. Picture yourself helping someone by giving an assertive comeback or getting help.
5. Partner up. Have a friend join you to confront someone who's bullying.

6. _____

7. _____

8. _____

Appendix 8: Anti-bullying class based activities, Upstanders

CHRISTINA'S POEM, ANTI BULLYING WEEK (2008)

You don't care!

I sit in my corner,
Dark and isolated,
From the rest of society.
You look and wonder why I don't socialise,
You laugh and walk away.

You don't care!

If you cared you would come,
Come and give me a helping hand.
Talk to me, make people care,
But you leave me to cry.
Alone.
Alone in my corner,
Dark and isolated.

You don't care!

I ask my mum for help,
Asking what's up with me?
Why do I push people away?
Can I not learn to trust, why?

You don't care!

I lie on the cold ground,
Crying.
Looking at the stars, wishing things would be better.
Tears run down my pale frozen cheeks,
I lie alone.

You don't care!

I sit again in my corner,
Dark and isolated.
Waiting . . . Waiting for the bell to go.
You.
A small girl in my year.
I look away; you place your arm around me,
Asking how I am.
I don't respond.
You drag me up by my hand,
You smile and introduce yourself.
You get me to talk,
Then take me with you.

You do care!

You talk to me,
Make me feel happy and human.
No longer an alien.
You introduce me to your other friends and they welcome me.
I am so grateful.

You do care!

I don't sit in my corner hiding,
No longer isolated.
I no longer sit and wait for the bell to go,
I enjoy my break.
My new best friend,
A new start.
I no longer push people away.
I thank you.

You do care!

DR. SAIRAH QURESHI

We shouldn't hide because of a bully.
Embrace life and live everyday different.
Never isolate yourself, it's never your fault.

Love chrisie x

Christina's Poem, Anti-Bullying Alliance, UK 2008.

Note:

Christina's poem is suitable for ages 7 and up. Most ideally, towards the end of a class session on anti-bullying, the teacher should request that each student closes their eyes, reflect upon all they have discussed and learnt in that session and then ask that they imagine themselves as a victim. For about five minutes allow them to be in this mind set as the poem is read aloud, slowly and in character as a victim. This is effective in allowing children and young people to zone in on their social and emotional learning and understanding indeed what it is like to be a victim of bullying.

Appendix 9: Anti-Bullying class based activities/scenario

Is this Bullying or not? What would you do?

The objective of this class based exercise is to demonstrate to young people the power that Upstanders have in preventing a bullying incident from occurring. Taking no more than 20-30 minutes, through enacting the scenario's and discussing the best options with the class, young people are able to decide what they believe would be the best course of action to take and why. From this, the teacher can instruct that empowering young people as a whole to take a positive action, has more effect than by doing nothing (See strategies included at the end).

1). Sally was walking home after school on a cold, winters day and it was snowing. Mark and Steve, in her class came running up to her and began to throw snow balls at her. "Please stop, stop, STOP!" she cried, but they just laughed and continued to throw more snow balls at her. By the time she reached home, she was soaked. The next day when she told her teacher, the boys were severely told off and given a punishment, "But Miss, we were only having fun!"

    Q: Is this bullying or not? How / Why? What would you do?

2). Two boys, Paul and Mike, who were good friends, had a disagreement in class. Paul turned to Mike and said, *"We'll finish this outside".* In the school playground Paul threw the first punch at Mike in the arm. Mike then punched him back. This quickly turned into a fight. A group of pupils rallied around, Mike cried out *"enough, enough, I want this to stop".* All the pupils who where watching this however, yelled out *"fight, fight, fight! Come on, fight!"* Paul continued to hit and kick Mike.

    Q: Is this bullying or not? How / Why? What would you do?

3). Sarah and Jane were the best of friends. During Science class, Jane said to Sarah, *"How was your holiday? You've got a tan and freckles! Freckle face, freckle face!"* Sarah laughed back and said, *"I had a great time, spotty!"* Jane laughed with her.

Q: Is this bullying or not? How / Why? What would you do?

4). Daisy is very ticklish. Maria keeps tickling her, *"Stop! Stop!"* Daisy cries out, but Maria won't stop.

Q: Is this bullying or not? How / Why? What would you do?

5). In the locker room after gym, you hear a lot of shrieking and laughter. Your classmates are spraying Kimberly's open locker with deodorant and perfume, saying *"This girl smells so bad, she must never wash! . . . I thought I would pass out when I had to sit next to her . . . . Yeah, it makes me sick to go anywhere near her . . ."* Kimberly hides in the bathroom; you hear her crying alone in a stall.

Q: What would you do?

There are two appropriate strategies

(i) Say to the whole crowd to stop it, how it's not funny or right and how would you feel if it was happening to you. If it doesn't stop, say you are going to report it. (Objective) ALL PUPILS HAVE THE RIGHT TO BE SAFE, ENCOURAGE PUPILS TO INDENTIFY BULLYING AND REPORT IT WHEN IT HAPPENS.

(ii) Ask a friend to back you up because you are going to 'stand up'. Loudly say, *"Cut it out, this is not a joke. This is bullying and it's wrong".* (Objective) ENLISTING A FRIEND TO BACK YOU UP HELPS IN 2 WAYS.

FIRSTLY, TO GIVE SUPPORT AND ALSO TO REINFORCE THE MESSAGE THAT BULLYING IS WRONG. WHEN PUPILS STAND UP—IT DOES MAKE A DIFFERENCE.

SECONDLY, WHAT OTHER PHRASES COULD THEY USE THAT MAY BE APPROPRIATE?

Anti-Bullying Alliance Resources (2009)

LIST OF REFERENCES

Ambert, A.M. (1994) 'A qualitative study of peer abuse and its effects: Theoretical and empirical implications' *Journal of Marriage and Family* 56 (1), pp. 119-130. [Online] Available at: *http://www.ingentaconnect.com* (Accessed 20 November 2005).

Ahmed, E. (2005). 'Pastoral care to regulate school bullying: shame management among bystanders.' *Pastoral Care*, pp. 23-29. [Online] Available at: *http://www.ingentaconnect.com* (Accessed 18 January 2006).

Ahmed, E. Braithwaite, V. (2006). 'Forgiveness, reconciliation, and shame: Three key variables in reducing school bullying.' *Journal of Social Issues* 62(2), pp. 347-370. [Online] Available at: *http://www.ingentaconnect.com* (Accessed 18 January 2006).

Ahmad, Y and Smith, P.K. (1994) 'Bullying in schools and the issue of sex differences' in Archer, J. (ed) (1994) *Male Violence* London: Routledge, pp. 70-84.

Alderson, P and Morrow, V (2004) *Ethics, social research and consulting with children and young people* Essex: Barnado's

Ananiadou, K and Smith, P, K. (2002). 'Legal requirements and nationally circulated materials against school bullying in European countries'. *Criminal Justice* 2 (4), pp. 471-491. [Online] Available at: *http://www.JSTOR.org* (Accessed 15 March 2005).

Anthias, F. L., Cathie (2002). *Rethinking Anti-racisms.* New York: Routledge.

Anti-Bullying Alliance (2010) *Equalities Act 2010* Anti-Bullying Alliance.

Anti-Bullying Alliance (2011) *Tackling Bullying in Schools: a governors guide* Anti-Bullying Alliance.

Armstrong, D; Hine, J; Hacking, S; Armaos, R; Jones, R; Klessinger, N and France, A; (2005) 'Children, risk and crime; On track youth lifestyle survey' *Home Office Research Study 278*. London: Home Office Research Development and Statistic Directorate, pp. i-108.

Ausdale, D. V. F., Joe. R. (2001). *The first R: how children learn race and racism.* Lanham, Boulder, New York, Oxford: Rowman and Littlefield Publishers, Inc.

Bailey, C. A. (2007). *A guide to qualitative field research—second edition.* California, London, New Delhi: SAGE.

Baldry, A. C. (2005). 'Bystander behaviour among Italian students.' *Pastoral Care*, pp. 30-35. [Online] Available at: *http://www.ingentaconnect.com* (Accessed 18 March 2006)

Barter, C. (1999) 'Protecting children from racism and racial abuse: a research review'. *NSPCC Inform:—Research Findings*, pp. 1-5 [Online] Available at: *http://www.nspcc.org.uk* (Accessed 10 December 2004).

Batsche, GM and Knoff, HM (1994) 'Bullies and their victims: understanding a pervasive problem in the schools' *School Psychology Review* (23), pp. 165-175. [Online] Available at: *http://www.googlescholar.com* (Accessed 18 April 2008).

Bishop, S. (2003) 'The development of peer support in secondary schools.' *Pastoral Care*, pp. 27-34.

Berg, B.L (2007) *Qualitative research methods for the social sciences* Boston, New York, San Francisco: Pearson International Edition, Allyn and Bacon.

Bonilla E-S and Tyrone, AF (2000) "I am not a racist but . . . 'Mapping white college students' racial ideology in the USA' *Discourse and Society* 11(1), pp. 50-85

Bosacki, S. L. Z., A.M and Dane, A.V. (2006). 'Voices from the classroom: pictorial and narrative representations of children's bullying experiences.' *Journal of Moral Education* 35(2), pp. 231-245.

Boxford, Stephen. (2006). *Schools and the Problem of Crime,* Devon: Willan Press

Boulton, MJ and Underwood, K. (1992) 'Bully/Victim problems among middle school children' *British Journal of Educational Psychology* 62, pp. 73-87.

Bowling, B. (1998). *Violent racism: Victimization, policing and social context,* Clarendon Press: Oxford.

Burton, Dawn (2000) *Research training for social scientists.* Reprint, London, California, New Delhi: SAGE *http://www.bullying.co.uk/advice/anti-bullying-advice* (2011) (Accessed: 15th May 2011)

Bradshaw, C, P; Sawyer, A,L and O'Brennan, L, M. (2009) 'A Social disorganization perspective on bullying-related attitudes and behaviours: the influence of school context' *AM J. Community Psychology* (43) pp. 204-220

Braithwaite, J. (1989) *Crime, shame and reintegration.* Wiltshire: Cambridge University Press.

British Sociological Association (2003) 'Code of ethics', pp. 1-8.

Brown, S. (1998). *Understanding youth and crime: Listening to youth?* Buckingham and Philadelphia: Open University Press

Bryman, A. (2004). *Social research methods* Oxford and New York: Oxford Uni Press.

Bulmer, M. S, John (2004). *Researching race and racism* London and New York: Routledge.

Burman, E. P., I (1993). *Discourse analytic research* London and New York: Routledge.

Case, S and Haines, K (2009) *Understanding Youth Offending: risk factor research, policy and practice* Devon

Camodeca, M and Goossens, F. A. (2005) 'Children's opinions on effective strategies to cope with bullying: the importance of the bullying role and perspective' *Educational Research* 47 (1), pp. 93-105. [Online] Available at: *http://ingentaconnect.com* (Accessed 18 September 2005)

Carrington, B. T. B. (1990) *Education, racism and reform.* London and New York: Routledge.

Cary, K., T. (1997) 'Preschool interventions' in Goldstein, J.G. (ed) *School Violence Intervention—A Practical Handbook.* London: The Guilded Press

Chahal, K. J., Louis (1999). 'We can't all be white!' Racist victimisation in the UK. *Joseph Rowntree Foundation*, pp. 1-4.

Chahal, K (2008) 'Empowerment, racist incidents and casework practice' *Housing, care and support* 11, pp. 22-29.

Chaux, E; Molano, A and Podlesky, P (2009) 'Socio-economic, socio-political and socio-emotional variables explaining school bullying: a country-wide multilevel analysis' *Aggressive Behaviour,* 35, pp. 520-529

Christie, G. D., Petrie, S Prof. and Christie, C (1999) 'Reducing and preventing violence in schools' Children and Crime: Victims and Offenders Conference convened by the Australian Institute of Criminology 17-18 June 1999. Brisbane, Australia: National Criminal Justice Ref. Service, pp. 1-34

Coaker, V (2009) 'Bullying incidents to be recorded to help schools clamp down on bullies" [Press Release]. 15 December. Available at: *http://www.dcsf.gov.uk/pns/DisplayPN.cgi?pn_id=2009_0244* (Accessed 23rd March 2010)

Cockburn, T. (2007) "'Performing' racism: engaging young supporters of the far right in England." *British Journal of Sociology of Education* 28(5), pp. 547-560.

Cole, M. S. J., S. (2005) "Do you ride on elephants' and 'never tell them you're German': the experiences of British Asian and black and overseas student teachers in South-east England." *British Educational Research Journal* 31(3), pp. 349-366. [Online] Available at: *http://www.ingentaconnect.com* (Accessed 18 September 2005).

Coloroso, B (2008) *The bully, the bullied and the bystander* Collins Living New York.

Connolly, P. (2005) *Boys and Schooling in the Early Years* New York: Routledge Falmer

Connolly, P. and Keenan, M. (2002). 'Racist Harassment in the White Hinterlands: minority ethnic children and parents' experiences of schooling in Northern Ireland.' *British Journal of Sociology of Education* 23(3), pp. 341-355. [Online] Available at: *http://www. ingentaconnect.com* (Accessed 18 January 2005).

Connolly, P. and Troyna, B (1998). *Researching racism in education:—politics, theory and practice,* Buckingham: Open University Press.

Cowie, H. H.N.; Oztug, O. and Myers, C. (2008). "The impact of peer support schemes on pupils' perceptions of bullying, aggression and safety at school." *Emotional and Behavioural Difficulties* 13(1), pp. 63-71.

Cranham, J. Caroll., A. (2003). 'Dynamics within the bully/victim paradigm: A qualitative analysis.' *Educational Psychology in Practice* 19(2), pp. 113-132. [Online] Available at: *http://www. ingentaconnect.com* (Accessed 18 January 2005).

Craig, Wendy M, Peters, Ray DeV and Konarski, Roman (1998) 'Bullying and victimization among Canadian school children' *Applied Research Branch Strategic Policy, Human Resources Development Canada* W-98-28E, pp. 1-33. [Online] Available at: *http://www.googlescholar.com* (Accessed 20 March 2008)

Crick, NR and Dodge, KA. (1999) "Superiority' is in the eye of the beholder: A comment on Sutton, Smith and Swettenham" *Social Development* 8 (1), pp. 128-131 [Online] Available at: *http://www. informaworld.com* (Accessed 19 November 2009)

Dake, J, A.; Price, J, H. and Telljohann, S, K. (2003) 'The nature and extent of bullying at school' *Journal of School Health* 73 (5), pp. 173-180. [Online] Available at: *http://www.sciencedirect.com* (Accessed 18 October 2008)

David, A, H. (2010) 'The 'collateral impact' of pupil behaviour and geographically concentrated socio-economic disadvantage' *British Journal of Sociology of Education* 31 (3) pp. 261-276

Davies, P; Francis, P and Greer, C. (2007) *Victims, crime and society.* London, California, New Delhi and Singapore: SAGE

Deakin, Jo (2006) 'Dangerous people, dangerous places: the nature and location of young people's victimization and fear'. *Children and Society* 20, pp. 376-390.

Delfabbro, P. W.; Trainor, T.; Dollard, S; Anderson. M; Metzer, S, J and Hammarstrom, A. (2006). 'Peer and teacher bullying/victimization of South Australian secondary school students: prevalences and psychological profiles.' *British Journal of Educational Psychology* 76: 71-90.

Demko, L. (1996) 'Bullying at School: the no-blame approach.' *Health Education* 1, pp. 26-30.

Denscombe, M. (2002). *Ground rules for good research:—a 10 point guide for social researchers*: Open University Press.

Denzin, N. K. L., Yvonna, S. (2008). *Collecting and interpreting qualitative materials.* LA, London, New Delhi and Singapore: Sage.

Dessel, A (2010) 'Prejudice in Schools: promotion of an inclusive culture and climate' *Education and Urban Society* 42 (4) pp. 407-429

Department for Children, Schools and Families (DCSF), (2007) 'Safe to learn—embedding anti-bullying work in schools'. Nottingham.

Department for Children, Schools and Families (DCSF), (2009), 'The children's plan—'Co-operative schools—making a difference' Nottingham.

Department for Children, Schools and Families (DCSF), (2009). 'The characteristics of bullying victims in schools' *National Centre for Social Research*, London.

Department for Education, (DfE) (2011) 'Preventing and tackling bullying: dealing with bullying' London, pp 3-5.

Dixon, Roz. (2008) 'Developing and integrating theory on school bullying' *Journal of School Violence* 7 (1), pp. 83-114.

Donnellan, C. (2001). *Victims of bullying* Cambridge: Independence Educated Publishers Cambridge.

Driel, B. V. (2004). *Confronting Islamophobia in educational practice.* Stoke-on-Trent, Staffordshire: Trentham Books, Ltd.

Dunn, P. (2008) 'Evidence-led or cobbled together? victim policy and victimological research' *Criminal Justice Matters* 72 (1), pp. 28-30

Durrant, JE (2000) 'Trends in youth crime and well-being since the abolition of corporal punishment in Sweden' *Youth and Society* 31 (4), pp. 437-455. [Online] Available at: *http://www.googlescholar. com* (Accessed 15 March 2006)

Ellis, A. A. and Shute, R. (2007). 'Teacher response to bullying in relation to moral orientation and seriousness of bullying' *British Journal of Educational Psychology* (77), pp. 649-663. [Online] Available at: *http://www.ingentaconnect.com* (Accessed 18 May 2007)

Elliott, D, S; Wilson, W, J; Huizinga, D; Sampson, R,J; Ellott, A. and Rankin, B. (1996) 'The effects of neighbourhood disadvantage on adolescent development' *Journal of Research in Crime and Delinquency* 33 (4) pp. 389-426.

Epstein, D. (1993). *Changing Classroom Cultures:—anti-racism, politics and schools.* Stoke-on-Trent: Trentham Books, Ltd.

Espelage, D, L. and Swearer, S, M. 'Contributions of three social theories to understanding bullying perpetration and victimization among school-aged youth' (2009) (Ed. Harris, M.J) *Bullying, Rejection and Peer Victimisation:—A social cognitive neuroscience perspective* New York, NY: Springer Publishing Company, LLC

Farrington, D, P. Ttofi, Maria, M. and Losel, F (2011) 'Editorial school bullying and later criminal offending' *Criminal Behaviour and Mental Health* 21, pp. 77-79

Farrington, D.P, and Ttofi, M.M, (2011) 'Bullying as a predictor of offending violence and later life outcomes' *Criminal Behaviour and Mental Health* 21, pp. 90-98

Feagin, J., R. and Vera, Hernan (1995). *White racism—the basics.* London and New York: Routledge.

Feder, L. (2007). 'Bullying as a public health issue.' *International Journal of Offender Therapy and Comparative Criminology* (51), pp. 491-494. [Online] Available at: *http://www.onlinesagepub.com* (Accessed: 5 March 2008).

Feldman, M. S. (1995). *Strategies for interpreting qualitative data.* London, California, New Delhi: Sage.

Fern, E., A. (2001). *Advanced focus group research.* London, California, New Delhi: Sage.

Ferguson, C, J.; Miguel, C. S; Kilburn, J. J C and Sanchez, P (2009). 'The effectiveness of school-based anti-bullying programs—a meta-analytic review' *Criminal Justice Review* 32 (4), pp. 401-414. [Online] Available at: *http://www.onlinesagepub.com* (Accessed: 18 October 2009)

Fieldhouse, E. A., Kalra, S. Virinder and Alam, S (2002). 'A new deal for young people from minority ethnic communities in the UK' *Journal of Ethnic and Migration Studies* 28(3), pp. 499-513. [Online] Available at: *http://www.onlinesagepub.com* (Accessed 10 October 2008)

Flick, U. (2006). *An introduction to qualitative research*, London: Sage.

Fox, C. L. B., Michael J. (2005). 'The social skills problem of victims of bullying: Self, peer and teacher perceptions.' *British Journal of Educational Psychology* (75), pp. 313-328.

Frey, K., S. (2005). 'Gathering and communicating information about school bullying: Overcoming "secrets and lies"' *Health Education* 105(6), pp. 409-413.

Frisen, A; Jonsson, A and Persson, C (2007). 'Adolescents' perception of bullying: Who is the victim? Who is the bully? What can be done to stop bullying?' *Adolescence* 42 (168), pp. 749-761. [Online] Available at: *http://www.googlescholar.com* (Accessed 17 November 2007).

Furniss, C. (2000). 'Bullying in schools: it's not a crime—is it?' *Education and the Law* 12(1), pp. 9-29.

Gaine, C. (2000). 'Anti-racist education in 'White' areas: the limits and possibilities of change.' *Race Ethnicity and Education* 3(1), pp. 65-81.

Garandeau, C., F. and Cillessen, Antonius, H.N. (2006). 'From indirect aggression to invisible aggression: A conceptual view on bullying and peer group manipulation.' *Aggression and Violent Behaviour* 11, pp. 612-625.

Gelsthorpe, L; Williams, B. And Tarling, R. (2003) 'Code of research ethics—British society of criminology code of ethics for researchers in the field of criminology' *British Society of Criminology*, pp. 1-6. [Online] Available at: *http://www.onlinesagepub.com* (Accessed 4 May 2006)

Gibbs, A. (1997). 'Focus groups.' *Social Research Update* 19, pp. 1-7.

Gill Dawn, B. M. M. B. (1992). *Racism and education:—structures and strategies.* London: SAGE Publications and Open University Press.

Gillborn, D. (1995). *Racism and antiracism in real schools.* Bristol: Open University Press.

Gillborn, D. (1997). 'Racism and Reform: new ethnicities/old inequalities?' British Educational Research Journal 23 (3), pp. 345-360.

Gillborn, David. (2005) 'Education policy as an act of white supremacy: whiteness, critical race theory and education reform' *Journal of Education Policy* 20 (4), pp. 485-505.

Gianluca, G. (2006). 'Bullying as a social process: the role of group membership in students' perception of inter-group aggression at school' *Journal of School Psychology* 44, pp. 51-65. [Online] Available at: *http://informaworld.com* (Accessed 2 June 2006)

Gianluca, G. (2006). 'Social cognition and moral cognition in bullying: what's wrong?' *Aggressive Behaviour* 32, pp. 528-539.

Gianluca, G and Pozzoli, T (2006). 'The role of masculinity in children's bullying' *Sex Roles* 54, pp. 585-588

Gianluca, G; Pozzoli, Ti; Borghi, F and Franzoni, L. (2008) 'The role of bystanders in students' perception of bullying and sense of safety' *Journal of School Psychology* 46, pp. 617-638

Glover, D; Gough, G; Johnson, M. and Cartwright, N. (2000) 'Bullying in 25 secondary schools; incidence, impact and intervention' *Educational Research* 42 (2), pp. 141-156. [Online] Available at: *http://ingentaconnect.com* (Accessed 15 May 2005)

Goodey, J. (1997). 'Boys don't cry.' *British Journal of Criminology* 37(3), pp. 401-418.

Goodey, J. (2005) 'Counting victimisation: who are the victims?' (Ed) Goody, J *Victims and victimology: research, policy and practice* Essex: Pearson Ed. Ltd.

Gordon, P (1993) *Citizenship for some? Race and government policy 1993-1989* London: Runnymede Trust

Graham, J. B., Ben (1995). *Young People and Crime.* London: Home Office Research Study 145.

Graham, P, (1996). 'Violence in children: the scope for prevention'. (Archives of disease in childhood) *Journal of the British Paediatric Association* 74, pp. 185-187. [Online] Available at: *http://ingentaconnect.com* (Accessed 15 May 2005)

Green, R; Collingwood, A; Ross, A (2010) 'Characteristics of bullying victims in schools' Department for Education (DfE) *National Centre for Social Research* pp. 1-5

Greene, M. B. (2006). 'Bullying in schools: a plea for measure of human rights.' *Journal of Social Issues* 62(1), pp. 63-79.

Greenberg, D.F. (1999) 'The weak strength of social control theory' *Crime and Delinquency* 45(1), pp. 66-81.

Griffin, R. S. and Gross, A M. (2004) 'Childhood bullying: current empirical findings and future directions for research' *Aggression and Violent Behaviour* 9, pp. 379-400.

Hall, N. (2009) *Hate Crime* Devon: Willan Publishing.

Hamarus P and Kaikkonen P, (2008). 'School bullying as a creator of pupil peer pressure' *Educational Research* 50 (4), pp. 333-345.

Harber, C (2008). 'Perpetrating disaffection: schooling as an international problem' *Educational Studies* 34 (5), pp. 457-467

Hart, A. (2009) 'The myth of racist kids: summary and recommendations to government' *The Manifesto Club*, pp. 1-4

Hawkins, A. (2007). *Bullying in schools: an exploration of significant adults' perceptions of UK school based bullying.* Unpublished BA thesis: Northumbria University.

Heller, F. (1986). 'Use and abuse of science' in Heller, F (ed) *The use and abuse of social science*, London: Sage, pp. 123-141

Hewitt, R (2005) *White Backlash and the Politics of Multiculturalism* UK: Cambridge University Press.

Hudson, R. (1997) 'Restructuring region and state: the case of North East England' *Tijdschrift voor Economische en Sociale Geografie* 89(1), pp. 15-30.

Hunter, S. C., Boyle, J.M.E and Warden, D (2007). 'Perceptions and correlates of peer-victimization and bullying.' *The British Psychological Society* (77), pp. 797-810. [Online] Available at: *http://www.sciencedirect.com* (Accessed 15 March 2008)

Hunter, S.C; Boyle, J.M.E. and Warden, D (2004). 'Help seeking amongst child adolescent victims of peer-aggression and bullying: the influence of school stage, gender, victimisation, appraisal and emotion.' *British Journal of Educational Psychology* (74), pp. 375-390.

Hunt, C, (2007) 'The effect of an education program on attitudes and beliefs about bullying and bullying behaviour in junior secondary school students' *Child and Adolescent Mental Health* 12 (1), pp. 21-26. [Online] Available at: *http://www.sciencedirect.com* (Accessed 15 March 2008)

Hurst, T. (2001). 'An evaluation of an anti-bullying peer support programme in a (British) secondary school.' *Pastoral Care,* pp. 10-14.

Joscelyne, T. Holttum, S. (2006). 'Children's explanations of aggressive incidents at school within an attribution framework.' *Child and Adolescent Mental Health* 11(2), pp. 104-110.

Jupp, V. (2006). *The SAGE dictionary of social research methods.* London, California, New Delhi: SAGE.

Kailin, J. (1999). 'How white teachers perceive the problem of racism in their school: A case study in 'Liberal' Lakeview.' *Teachers College Record* 100(4), pp. 724-750. [Online] Available at: *http://www. ingentaconnect.com* and *http://www.googlescholar.com* (Accessed 10 January 2005)

Kelly. T. and Cohen, E. (1988). *Racism in schools—new research evidence.* Chester: Trentham Books.

Kehoe, J, W. (1993). 'The limitations of multicultural education and anti-racist education' *Anti-Racist Education,* pp. 3-8

Kidscape.org. (2001). Preventing racist bullying; what schools can do.' Available at: http://*www.kidscape.org.uk.* (Accessed 18th March 2005)

Kitzinger, J. (1990) 'Audience understanding of AIDS media messages: A discussion of methods' *Sociology of Health and Illness,* 12(3) 319-55

Knight, C and Chouhan, K (2002) 'Supporting Victims of Racist Abuse and Violence' *Williams, B., Reparation and Victim-Focused Social* Work, pp. 105-130.

Knights, L. (1998). 'A student and staff-developed anti-bullying initiative.' *Pastoral Care,* pp. 33-34. [Online] Available at: *http:// www.ingentaconnect.com* (Accessed 10 January 2005)

Kristensen, S. M. and Smith, P, K. (2003). 'The use of coping strategies by Danish children classed as bullies, victims, bully/victims, and not involved, in response to different (hypothetical) types of bullying' *Scandinavian Journal of Psychology* (44), pp. 479-488.

Kshirsagar, V.Y; Agarwal, Rajiv and Bavdekar, Sandeep, B (2007). 'Bullying in schools: prevalence and short-term impact' *Indian Paediatrics* 44, pp. 25-28

Lane, J. (2008). *Young children and racial justice:—Taking action for racial equality in the early years—understanding the past, thinking about the present, planning for the future.* London: National Children's Bureau.

Langford, J. and. Deana, M (2003). *Focus groups—supporting effective product development.* London and New York: Taylor and Francis.

Lewis J. (2006) 'The school's role in encouraging behaviour for learning outside the classroom that supports learning within. A response to the 'Every Child Matters' and extended school initiatives' *Support for Learning* 21 (4), pp. 175-181. [Online] Available at: *http://www.sciencedirect.com* (Accessed 15 March 2008)

Lewis, R; Romi, S; Qui, X and Katz, YJ (2005) 'Teachers' classroom discipline and student misbehaviour in Australia, China and Israel' *Teaching and Teacher Education* 21, pp. 729-741. [Online] Available at: *http://www.sciencedirect.com* (Accessed 15 March 2008)

Lines, D. (2005). 'A peer counselling service in a secondary school to combat bullying: Issues in planning and ongoing management' *Pastoral Care,* pp. 19-27. [Online] Available at: *http://www.sciencedirect.com* (Accessed 15 April 2006)

Lines, D. (2008). *The Bullies—understanding bullies and bullying.* London and Philadelphia: Jessica Kingsley Publishers.

Li, Q (2007) 'New bottle but old wine: A research of cyberbullying in schools. *Science Direct* 23, pp. 1777-1791.

Littlechild, B. (2009) 'Conflict resolution, restorative justice approaches and bullying in young people's residential units' *Children and Society* pp. 1-12

Ma, X; Stewin L.L. and Mah.D. L, (2001). 'Bullying in school: nature, effects and remedies.' *Research Papers in Education* 16(3), pp. 247-270. [Online] Available at: *http://www.ingentaconnect.com* (Accessed 20 May 2005)

Macnaghten, P. Myers. G. (2004). 'Focus Groups'. in Seale, C; G Giampeitro; Gubrium, J.F and Silverman, D (eds) *Qualitative Research Practice* London, California and New Delhi: Sage, pp. v-620.

Marina C, Fritz A. G; Mark M. T and Carlo S, (2002). 'Bullying and victimization amongst school-age children:—Stability and links to proactive and reactive aggression.' *Social Development* 3 (11), pp. 1-14.

Martyn, B. D. H. (1996). 'Analysis of Unstructured Data'. in Sapsford, V. R. J. (ed) *Data Collection and Analysis.* London, California, New Delhi: Sage, pp. v-360.

Mason, D. (2000). *Race and ethnicity in modern Britain.* Oxford and New York: Oxford University Press.

Maung, N.A. and Mirrlees-Black, C (1994) 'Racially motivated crime: British Crime Survey analysis' HORS154 in Fitzgerald, M. and

Hale, C. (ed) (1996) *Ethnic Minorities: Victimisation and Racial Harassment. Findings from the 1988 and 1992 British Crime Surveys* (Home Office Research Study 154)

McDougall, L. (1999). 'A study of bullying in further education.' *Pastoral Care, pp.* 31-37.

McGhee, D. (2005). *Intolerant Britain? Hate, citizenship and difference.* Berkshire and New York: Open University Press and Two Penn Plaza.

McLaughlin C, Arnold R and Boyd E, (2005). 'Bystanders in schools: what do they do and what do they think? Factors influencing the behaviour of English students as bystanders.' *Pastoral Care,* pp. 17-22. [Online] Available at: *http://www.informaworld.com* (Accessed 10 June 2006)

McNeill, P. and Steve C, (2005) *Research Methods* London and New York: Routledge.

Menard, S. (2000) 'The 'normality' of repeat victimization from adolescence through early adulthood' *Justice Quarterly* 17 (3) pp. 543-574

Melde, C (2010) 'The victim-offender overlap and fear of in-school victimization: a longitudinal examination of risk assessment models' *Crime and Delinquency* 55 (4) pp. 499-525

Miles, R., and Brown, M, (2003). *Racism.* London, Canada and USA: Routledge.

Miles, B, (2009) 'Prevention and the role of education: reporting and challenging racism—an opportunity won or lost?' *Race Equality Teaching* (68), pp. 1-6.

Miles, B, (2011) 'Support from the Top v top-down prescription: tension over prevention and responding to prejudice-related bullying' *Race Equality Teaching* 29 (2), pp. 41-44

Mills, M. (2001). 'Challenging violence in schools:—An issue of masculinities' in Epstein, D and Mac an Ghaill, M (eds) *Educating Boys Learning Gender* Philadelphia: Open University Press, pp. 1-169

Miller, J. (2004) 'Population and Housing Background Paper' *Newcastle Local Development Framework Key Issues Consultation* Newcastle-upon-Tyne: Newcastle City Council

Mishna, F., Beverley J. and Antle, C. R (2004) 'Tapping the perspectives of children—emerging ethical issues in qualitative research.' *Qualitative Social Work* 3(4), pp. 449-468.

Modern Eastern Suburban School (2007) 'Ofsted inspection report' pp. 1-12. Available at: http://*www.ofsted.gov.uk* (Accessed 10 June 2008)

Modern Eastern Suburban School (2009) 'Anti-bullying policy', pp. 1-4

Modern Eastern Suburban School (2002) 'Equal opportunities—race equality report', pp. 1-8

Modern Eastern Suburban School (2009) 'School prospectus 2009/10', pp. 1-109

Moore, K., Mason, P and Lewis, J, (2008). "Images of Islam in the UK'—the representation of British Muslims in the national print news media 2000-2008'. *Cardiff School of Journalism, Media and Cultural Studies*, pp. 1-40. Available at: *http://www.sciencedirect.com* (Accessed 15 September 2008)

Morgan, D. L. (1997). *Focus groups as qualitative research.* California/ London / New Delhi: Sage.

Morrison, B. (2002). 'Bullying and victimization in schools: A restorative justice approach.' *Australian Institute of Criminology* (219), pp. 1-6.

Morrison, B. (2007). 'Schools and restorative justice'. in Johnstone, G. V. N. Daniel W *Handbook of Restorative Justice.* Devon: Willan Publishing: 325-350.

Monks, C.P. and Smith, P, K. (2006) 'Definitions of bullying: Age differences in understanding of the term, and the role of experience'. *British Journal of Developmental Psychology* 24, pp. 801-821 [Online] Available at: *http://www.ingentaconnect.com* (Accessed 23 January 2009)

Moon, B; Hwang, H.W and McClusky, J. D. (2008) 'Causes of school bullying—empirical test of a general theory of crime, differential association theory and general strain theory' *Crime Delinquency Online First* 20 (10), pp. 1-28 [Online] Available at: *http://www. onlinesagepub.com* (Accessed: 24 April 2009)

Muncie, J. (2004). *Youth and crime.* London, California, New Delhi: SAGE.

Nayak, A. (2003). *Race, place and globalization: youth cultures in a changing world.* Oxford/ New York: Berg-Oxford International Publishers.

Naylor, P. and Cowie, H, (1999) 'The effectiveness of peer support systems in challenging school bullying: the perspectives and experiences of teachers and pupils.' *Journal of Adolescence* (22), pp. 467-479. [Online] Available at: *http://www.sciencedirect.com* (Accessed 22 November 2004)

Naylor, P; Cowie, H and Rosario, D.R, (2001) 'Coping strategies of secondary school children in response to being bullied.' *Child Psychology and Psychiatry Review* 6(3), pp. 114-120. *http://www.ncb. org.uk* (2011) (Accessed May 15th 2011)

Newcastle City Council (2002) 'School provision in the outer west of Newcastle-upon-Tyne:—A review of the Three-Tier System' *Newcastle City Council,* pp. 2-26.

Newcastle City Council (2003) 'The future of schools in the outer west area of the city:—consultation with parents, staff, governors and community' *Newcastle City Council,* pp. 2-48.

Newcastle City Council (2006) 'Newcastle plan for children and young people April 2006-April 2009' *Newcastle City Council,* pp. 1-78.

Newcastle-upon-Tyne Local Authority Children's Services Inclusion (2007) 'Anti-bullying good practice guidance and award scheme' *Newcastle City Council,* pp. 1-32. [Online] Available at: *http://www.pct.com*

Newcastle City Council (2008) 'Behaviour strategy; 2005-2008' *Newcastle City Council; Every Child Matters* pp. 1-69

Newcastle City Council (2009) 'Newcastle plan for children and young people 2009-2010' *Newcastle City Council,* pp. 1-96.

Newcastle City Council (2010) [Online] Available at: *http://www. newcastle.gov.uk/core.nsf/a/school_general_info?opendocument* (accessed February 18th 2010).

Noaks, J. and Noaks, L. (2000). 'Violence in school: risk, safety and fear of crime.' *Educational Psychology in Practice* 16(1), pp. 69-73. [Online] Available at: *http://www.informaworld.com* (Accessed 23 November 2004)

Northumbria University Ethics Committee (2003) 'Ethics in research and consultancy—policy statement', *Research Strategy and Support, Northumbria University,* pp. 1-7.

Oates, C. I. and Dawn, B (2000). 'The use of focus groups in social science research' in Burton, D. (ed) (2000) *Research Training for Social Scientists.* London, CA and New Delhi: Sage publications, pp. vi-503.

O'Brien, C. (2007). 'Peer devaluation in British secondary schools: young people's comparisons of group-based and individual-based bullying.' *Educational Research* 49(3), pp. 297-324. Online]

Available at: *http://www.informaworld.com* (Accessed 22 February 2008)

O'Connell, P. Pepler, D. and Craig, W (1999). 'Peer involvement in bullying: insights and challenges for intervention.' *Journal of Adolescence* (22) pp. 437-452. [Online] Available at: *http://www.sciencedirect.com* (Accessed 23 November 2004)

Ojala, K. Nesdale, D. (2004). 'Bullying and social identity: The effects of group norms and distinctiveness threat on attitudes towards bullying.' *British Journal of Developmental Psychology* (22), pp. 19-35. [Online] Available at: *http://www.ingentaconnect.com* (Accessed 22 November 2004)

Oka, K.U (2005) 'Racism "Renewed" national practices, citizenship and fantasy Post-9/11' in Karumanchery, L. (ed.) (2005). *Engaging equity—New perspectives on anti-racist education* pp: 27-40. Calgary, Canada: Detselig Enterprises, Ltd.

Old East End Community College, (2007) 'Ofsted inspection report', pp. 1-11. Available at: *http://www.ofsted.gov.uk* (Accessed 10 June 2008).

Old East End Community College, (2009) 'School Prospectus 2009/10', pp. 1-31.

Old East End Community College, (2005) 'Bullying policy statement', pp. 1-5.

Old East End Community College, (2002) 'Equal opportunities policy incorporating racial equality policy', pp. 1-17.

Oliver, C. and Candappa, M (2007). 'Bullying and the politics of 'telling'.' *Oxford Review of Education* 33(1), pp. 71-86. [Online] Available at: *http://www.informaworld.com* (Accessed 22 February 2008)

Oliver, C and Candappa, M (2003) 'Tackling bullying: listening to the views of children and young people' *Institute of Education*, pp. 5-95. [Online] Available at: *http://www.dcsf.gov.uk/research/data/uploadfiles/RR400.pdf* (Accessed 1 July 2008)

Olweus, D (2000). *Bullying at school—What we know and what we can do* Oxford: Blackwell Publishers, Ltd.

Pellegrini, AD (1998) 'Bullies and victims in school: A review and call for research' *Journal of Applied Developmental Psychology* 19 (2), pp. 165-176

Pepler, D, J. and Craig, W, M. (1995) 'A peek behind the fence: Naturalistic observations of aggressive children with remote audiovisual recording' *Developmental Psychology* 31 (4), pp. 548-553

Perry, D.G, Kusel, S.J, and Perry, L.C (1988) 'Victims of peer aggression' *Developmental Psychology* 24 (6), pp. 807-814. [Online] Available at: *http://www.googlescholar.com* (Accessed 23 March 2010)

Phillips, C. and Bowling B, (2003). 'Racism, ethnicity and criminology:—Developing minority perspectives.' *British Journal of Criminology* (43), pp. 269-290.

Phillips, C. (2003). 'Who's who in the pecking order?' *British Journal of Criminology* 43 (4), pp. 710-728

Phillips, A; Powell, H; Anderson, F and Popiel, A (2009) 'Youth survey 2008; young people in mainstream education' *Youth Justice Board for England and Wales* London, pp. 1-75.

Pilkington, A. (1999). 'Racism in school and ethnic differentials in educational achievement: a brief comment on a recent debate.' *British Journal of Sociology of Education* 20 (3): 411-417. [Online] Available at: *http://www.informaworld.com* (Accessed 20 March 2006).

Pilkington, A. (2003). *Racial disadvantage and ethnic diversity in Britain.* London: Palgrave, Macmillan.

Pitts, J. and Smith, P (1999). 'Preventing school bullying'. *Crime Detection and Prevention Series paper 63.* P. R. Group. London, Home Office Police Department, pp. iii-74.

Punch, K. F. (2005). *Introduction to social research—quantitative and qualitative approaches—second edition.* London, California, New Delhi: SAGE.

Raby, R. (2004). "There's no racism at my school, it's just joking around': Ramifications for anti-racist education.' *Race, Ethnicity and Education* 7(4), pp. 367-383.

Rai and Hesse (2008) 'Racial victimization: an experiential analysis' in Spalek, B (ed) (2008). *Ethnicity and Crime: A Reader*, Berkshire and New York: Mcgraw Hill, Open University Press, pp. 204-237.

Ratcliffe, P. (1994). *Race, ethnicity and nation.* London and Pennsylvania: UCL Press Ltd.

Ratcliffe, P. (2001). *The politics of social science research.* New York: Palgrave.

Ratcliffe, P. (2004). *'Race', ethnicity and difference.* Berkshire and New York: Open University Press.

Ray, L. and Smith, D. (2001) 'Racist offenders and the politics of 'Hate Crime" *Law and Critique* 12, pp. 203-221

Ray, L. and Smith, D. (2002) 'Racist violence as hate crime' *Criminal Justice Matters* 48, pp. 6-7

Ray, L; Smith, D and Wastell, L (2004) 'Shame, rage and racist violence' *British Journal of Criminology* 44 (3), pp. 350-368.

Ray, L; Smith, D and Wastell, L (2003a) in Stanko, E, A. Ed (2003) *The meaning of violence* London and New York: Routledge, pp. 112-129,

Ray, L and Reed, K. (2005) 'Community, mobility and racism in a semi-rural area: comparing minority experience in East Kent' *Ethnic and Racial Studies* 28 (2), pp. 212-234.

Reid, P. Hansen J and Rivers, I, (2004) 'Pyschology's contribution to understanding and managing bullying within schools' *Educational Psychology in Practice* 20(3), pp. 241-258. [Online] Available at: *http://www.ingentaconnect.com* (Accessed 23 November 2004)

Reid, J. A and Sullivan, C, J. (2009) 'A latent class typology of juvenile victims and exploration of risk factors and outcomes of victimization' *Criminal Justice and Behavior 36*(10) pp. 1001-1024

Response Anti-Bullying News (2008) 'Response Newcastle action against bullying' *Newcastle Response Newsletter* pp: 1-2

Runnymede Research Report. (1989). 'Racism, anti-racism and schools:—a summary of the Burnage report'. London: Runnymede Research, pp. 1-48.

Richards, L. (2005). *Handling qualitative data—a practical guide.* London, California and New Delhi: SAGE.

Richardson, R. (2003). 'Inclusion, inclusion, inclusion—mental maps and great expectations! in Richardson, R. and Miles, B. (ed) (2003) *Equality stories: recognition, respect and raising achievement.* London: Trentham Books, pp. 1-8.

Richardson, R. (2007). 'Bullying around racism, culture and religion? Resources, advice and prevention/classroom and corridors—DfES advice on racist bullying in schools.' *Race Equality Teaching* (Summer 2007), pp 1-6.

Richardson, R. (2007). "How dare they?'—Islamophobia, the media and an educational resource." *Race Equality Teaching* 25(2), pp. 1-11.

Richardson, R. (2009) '*The myth of racist kids' Notes towards a reply, 2nd November 2009*. Available at: *http://www.insted.co.uk/mrk-reply.pdf* (Accessed November 8th 2009)

Richardson, R. and Miles, B. (2008) *Racist incidents and bullying in schools: how to prevent then and how to respond when they happen.* Stoke on Trent UK and Sterling, USA: Trentham Books.

Richardson, R. and Woods, A, (2000). *Inclusive schools, inclusive society:—race and identity on the agenda.* Staffordshire, Stoke on Trent: Trentham Books.

Rigby, K.P. (2002) *New perspectives on bullying,* London: Jessica Kingsley Publishers Ltd.

Rigby, K. P. (2003). 'In review: consequences of bullying in schools.' *Can J Psychiatry* 48(9), pp. 583-590.

Rigby, K. P. (2006). 'Expressed readiness of Australian schoolchildren to act as bystanders in support of children who are being bullied. *Educational Psychology in Practice* 26(3), pp. 425-440. [Online] Available at: *http://www.informaworld.com* (Accessed 10 January 2006)

Rigby, K. (2003). 'Addressing bullying in schools: theory and practice' *Australian Institute of Criminology* 259, pp. 1-6. [Online] Available at: *http://www.informaworld.com* (22 January 2009)

Rigby, K. (2002) 'What it takes to stop bullying in schools: an examination of the rationale and effectiveness of school-based interventions' in Furlong, M.J. (ed) (2004) *Appraisal and prediction of school violence: methods, issues and contents* New York: Nova Science Publishers, Inc., pp. 165-192

Ritchie, J.and Lane, J (2003). *Qualitative research practice:—A guide for social science students and researchers,* London: Sage Publication Ltd.

Rolider, A. and Maytall, O (2005). 'Bystander behaviours among Israeli children witnessing bullying behaviour in school settings.' *Pastoral Care*, pp. 36-39. [Online] Available at: *http://www.informaworld. com* (Accessed 10 January 2006)

Roffey, S. (2008) 'Emotional literacy and the ecology of school wellbeing' *Educational and Child Psychology* 25(2), pp. 29-39.

Rowntree, M. (2010) 'Socio-economic profiling for Newcastle-upon-Tyne' *Newcastle City Council*, pp. 1-3

Salmivalli, C. (1999). 'Participant role approach to school bullying: implications for interventions.' *Journal of Adolescence* (22), pp. 453-459.

Salmivalli, C. (2002). 'Is there an age decline in victimization by peers at school?' *Educational Research* 44(3), pp. 269-277.

Salmivalli, C. A., Kaukiainen and Voeten, M (2005). 'Anti-bullying intervention: implementation and outcome.' *British Journal of Educational Psychology* (75), pp. 465-487.

Samara, M. and Smith, S, (2008) 'How schools tackle bullying, and the use of whole school policies: changes over the last decade.' *Educational Psychology* 28(6), pp. 663-676. [Online] Available at: *http://www.informaworld.com* (Accessed 29 September 2008)

Samara M. and Smith, P. K (2003). 'Evaluation of the DfES anti-bullying pack: research brief. London, Goldsmiths College, University of London: Department for Education and Skills, 2003, pp. 1-5

Salmon, G.J.A and Smith, DM (1998) 'Bullying in schools: self-reported anxiety, depression, and self-esteem in secondary school children' *British Medical Journal* 317, pp. 924-925 [Online] Available at: *http://www.googlescholar.com* (Accessed 22 January 2010).

Schafer, M. K.S.; Smith, P.K.; Hunter, S C.; Mora-Merchan, J.A.; Singer, M. M and Meulen, K. V D. (2004). 'Lonely in the crowd: recollections of bullying.' *British Journal of Developmental Psychology* 22, pp. 379-394. [Online] Available at: *http://www.ingentaconnect. com* (Accessed 23 November 2004)

Sharp, P. K. (2000) 'Promoting emotional literacy: emotional literacy improves and increases your life chances' *Pastoral Care,* pp. 8-10. [Online] Available at: *http://www.informaworld.com* (Accessed 17 November 2009)

Schrock, A and Boyd, D (2008) 'Enhancing child safety and online technologies: final report of the internet safety technical task force' *Berkman Center for Internet and Society. Harvard University,* Boston, pp. 1-82. [Online] Available at *http://www.googlescholar. com* (Accessed 2 June 2009)

School for the Socially Excluded (2008) 'Ofsted inspection report' 1-11. Available at: *http://www.ofsted.gov.uk* (Accessed 10 June 2008).

School for the Socially Excluded, (2004) 'Bullying policy', pp. 1-6.

School for the Socially Excluded (2007) 'Anti-racist policy', pp. 1-4.

Sibbitt, R. (1997). Home Office Research Study 176 'The perpetrators of racial harassment and racial violence.' *Home Office Research and Statistics Directorate,* pp. 1-126.

Silverman, D. (2000). *Doing qualitative research: a practical handbook.* London, CA, New Delhi: Sage Publications.

Slee, P., T. and Mohyla, J (June 2007). 'The PEACE pack: an evaluation of interventions to reduce bullying in four Australian primary schools.' *Educational Research* 49(2), pp.103-114.

Smith, P; Carvalho, M and Tippett, N. (2006). 'An investigation into cyberbullying, its forms, awareness and impact, and the relationship between age and gender in cyberbullying. A report to the Anti-bullying Alliance' *Unit for School and Family Studies,* London: Goldsmith College, University of London, pp. 1-69

Smith, P. K. and Sharp. S. (1994). *School bullying—insights and perspectives.* London and New York: Routledge.

Smith, K. P. Cowie, H, Ragnar, F. O and Liefooghe, P.D. A (2002). 'Definitions of bullying: a comparison of terms used and age and gender differences, in a fourteen-country international comparison' Child *Development* 73, pp. 1119-1133.

Smith, P., K; Cowie, H and Blades, M (2003). *Understanding children's development,* London: Blackwell Publication

Smith, P., K; Talamelli, L; Cowie, H; Naylor, P and Chauhan, P. (2004). Profiles of non-victims, escaped victims, continuing victims and new victims of school bullying.' *British Journal of Educational Psychology* (74), pp. 565-581.

Smith, P. K., Pepler, D and Rigby, K (2004). *Bullying in schools: how successful can interventions be?* Cambridge: Cambridge University Press.

Smith, P. K. (2004). 'Bullying: recent developments.' *Child and Adolescent Mental Health* 9(3), pp. 98-103.

Smith. S. and Tomlinson, D. J. (1989) *'The school effect:—a study of multi-racial comprehensives.* London: Policy Studies Institute.

Smith, P. K; Smith, C; Osborn, R and Samara, M. (2008) 'A content analysis of school anti-bullying policies: progress and limitations' *Educational Psychology in Practice* 24 (1) pp. 1-12

Stephens, R., D (1997). 'National trends in school violence: statistics and prevention strategies.' in Goldstein, J.G. (ed) (1997) *School violence intervention—a practical handbook.* London: The Guilded Press, pp. 72-84.

Stewart, E. A (2003) 'School social bonds, school climate and school misbehaviour' *Justice Quarterly* 20(3), pp. 575-604

Sullivan, K. C., Mark and Sullivan, G. (2004). *Bullying in secondary schools: what it looks like and how to manage it.* London and California: SAGE, Paul Chapman Publishing and Corwin Press, Inc.

Sutton, J. Smith P. K and Swettenham, J (1999). 'Bullying and 'theory of mind': a critique of the 'social skills deficit' view of anti-social behaviour.' *Social Development* 8(1), pp. 117-127.

Sweeting, H and West, P (2001). 'Being different: correlates of the experience of teasing and bullying at age 11' *Research Papers in Education* 16 (3), pp. 225-246. [Online] Available at: *http://www.informaworld.com* (Accessed 22 November 2004)

Stephens, R.D and Carey, K.T. (1997). ch. 5 'National trends in school violence: statistics and prevention strategies' and ch. 6 'Preschool interventions' in A. P. G. J. F. Conoley (ed) *School violence intervention: a practical handbook* London, The Guildford Press, ch 5: pp 72-84 and ch 6: pp 93-105.

Stephenson, M. (2007) *Young People and Offending: education, youth justice and social inclusion* Devon: Willan Publishing

Tattum, D. P. (1989). *Bullying in Schools.* Stoke-on-Trent: Trentham Books.

Tomlinson, S. (2005). 'Race, ethnicity and education under new labour.' *Oxford Review of Education* 31(1), pp. 153-171.

Tomaney, J. 'North East England: a brief economic history' *Centre for Urban and Regional Development Studies* Newcastle-upon-Tyne: University of Newcastle-upon-Tyne

Train, A. (1995). *The bullying problem—how to deal with difficult children.* London: Souvenir Press.

Troyna, B and Hatcher, R. (1992). *Racism in children's lives: a study of mainly-white primary schools.* London: Routledge.

Troyna, B. And Williams, J. (1986) *Racism, education and the state* London:Croom Helm

Ttofi, M. M; Farrington, D.P; Losel, F and Loeber, R. (2011) 'The predictive efficiency of school bullying versus later offending: A systematic/meta-analytic review of longitudinal studies' *Criminal Behaviour and Mental Health* 21, pp. 80-89

Uwe F; Kardorff, E. and Ines, S, (2005). *A companion to qualitative research.* California, New Delhi and London: SAGE.

Verkuyten, M. and Thijs., J. (2002). 'Racist victimization among children in the Netherlands: the effect of ethnic group and school.'

Ethnic and Racial Studies 25(2), pp. 310-331. [Online] Available at: *http://www.informaworld.com* (Accessed 15 April 2005)

Verma, G. (1994). *The ethnic crucible:—harmony and hostility in multi-ethnic schools.* London and Pennslyvania: The Falmer Press.

Veland, J; Midthassel, U, V and Idsoe, T. (2009) 'Perceived socio-economic status and social inclusion in school: interactions of disadvantages' *Scandinavian Journal of Educational Research* 53 (6), pp. 515-531

Virdee, S. (1995). *Racial violence and harassment.* London: PSI—Policy Studies Institute.

Vogt, S. D; King, Daniel W and King, A.L. (2004). 'Focus groups in psychological assessment: enhancing content validity by consulting members of the target population' *Psychological Assessment* 16 (3), pp. 231-243 [Online] Available at: *http://www.psycnet.apa.org* (Accessed 13 October 2009)

Webster, C. (1994). *Youth crime, victimisation and racial harassment:—the Keighley crime survey.* Bradford: Bradford and Ilkley Community College Corporation.

Webster, C; Simpson, D; MacDonald, R; Abbas, A, Cieslik, M; Shildrick T and Simpson, M (2004) 'Poor transitions: social exclusion and young adults' *Policy Press* 1, pp. iii-49.

Webster, C (2007) *Understanding race and crime* Berkshire and New York: Mcgraw Hill and Open University Press.

Wengraf, T. (2002). *Qualitative research interviewing: biographic narrative and semi-structured methods.* London, California, New Delhi: Sage Publications.

Wessler, S. L. and Leila D.A.L, (2006) 'Slurs, stereotypes and student interventions: examining the dynamics, impact and prevention of harassment in middle and high school.' *Journal of Social Issues* 62(3), pp. 511-532. [Online] Available at: *http://www. ingentaconnect.com* (Accessed 2 March 2007)

Whitney, I and Smith, P. K, (1993) 'A survey of the nature and extent of bullying in junior/middle and secondary schools' *Educational Research* 35 (1), pp. 3-25

Willis, J. W. (2007). *Foundations of qualitative research—interpretive and critical approaches.* California, London, New Delhi: SAGE.

Wilkinson, S. (2004) 'Focus Groups' ch 14 (Ed. Breakwell, G.M) *Doing Social Psychology Research* Oxford: The British Psychological Society and Blackwell Publishing, Ltd.

Winant, H. (2006). 'Race and racism—towards a global future.' *Ethnic and Racial Studies* 29(5), pp. 986-1003. [Online] Available at: *http://www.informaworld.com* (Accessed 29 September 2008)

Wood, M. (2005) 'The victimization of young people: findings from the crime and justice survey 2003' *Home Office Report 246*, pp. 1-6

Woods, R, (2007) 'Children defining and experiencing racism in 21st century Britain' *Paper presented at CRONEM conference on Nationalism and National Identities, Multidisciplinary Perspectives* Canterbury Christ Church University, pp. 1-28 [Online] Available at: *http://www.informaworld.com* (Accessed 1 February 2010)

Woods, R (2009) 'The use of aggression in primary school boys' decisions about inclusion in and exclusion from playground football games' *British Journal of Educational Psychology* 79, pp. 223-238. [Online] Available at: *http://www.bpsjournals.co.uk* (Accessed 19 June 2009)

Woodhead, M (2005) 'Early childhood development: a question of rights, 1' *International Journal of Early Childhood,* pp. 1-19. [Online] Available at: *http://www.springerlink.com* (Accessed 12 February 2010)

Worrall, A. (1997). *Punishment in the community: the future of criminal justice* New York: Addison Wesley Longman Ltd.

Woolfson, R. C., Harker, M.E. and Lowe, D. A. (2004). 'Racism in schools—no room for complacency.' *Educational and Child Psychology* 21(4), pp. 16-30.

Wolke, D; Woods, S and Samara, M (2009) 'Who escapes or remains a victim of bullying in primary school?' *British Journal of Developmental Psychology* 27 pp. 835-851

Yoneyama, S and Naito, A. (2003) 'Problems with the paradigm: the school as a factor in understanding bullying' *British Journal of Sociology of Education* 24 (3), pp. 315-330. [Online] Available at: *http://www.jstor.org* (Accessed 1 August 2009)

Further Recommended Reading

Isal S. 2005 'Preventing Racist Violence Work with Actual and Potential Perpetrators—Learning from Practice to Policy Change' London: Runnymede Trust, pp.1-60.

Stone, R. DR. 2004 *Islamophobia: issues, challenges and action—a report by the Commission on British Muslims and Islamophobia* Stoke-on-Trent, London, pp. iii-92

Werbner, P. (2005). "Islamophobia—Incitement to religious hatred—legislating for a new fear?" Anthropology Today **21**(1): 5-9. [Online] Available at: *http://www.googlescholar.com* (Accessed 20 November 2006)